Past and Present Publications

Puritanism and Theatre

Past and Present Publications

General Editor: T. H. ASTON, *Corpus Christi College, Oxford*

Past and Present Publications will comprise books similar in character to the articles in the journal *Past and Present*. Whether the volumes in the series are collections of essays – some previously published, others new studies – or monographs, they will encompass a wide variety of scholarly and original works primarily concerned with social, economic and cultural changes, and their causes and consequences. They will appeal to both specialists and non-specialists and will endeavour to communicate the results of historical and allied research in readable and lively form. This new series continues and expands in its aims the volumes previously published elsewhere.

Volumes published by the Cambridge University Press are:
Family and Inheritance: Rural Society in Western Europe 1200–1800, edited by Jack Goody, Joan Thirsk and E. P. Thompson
French Society and the Revolution, edited by Douglas Johnson
Peasants, Knights and Heretics: Studies in Medieval English Social History, edited by R. H. Hilton
Towns in Societies: Essays in Economic History and Historical Sociology, edited by Philip Abrams and E. A. Wrigley
Desolation of a City: Coventry and the Urban Crisis of the Late Middle Ages, by Charles Phythian-Adams
Puritanism and Theatre: Thomas Middleton and Opposition Drama under the Early Stuarts, by Margot Heinemann

Volumes previously published with Routledge & Kegan Paul are:
Crisis in Europe 1560–1660, edited by Trevor Aston
Studies in Ancient Society, edited by M. I. Finley
The Intellectual Revolution of the Seventeenth Century, edited by Charles Webster

Puritanism and Theatre

Thomas Middleton and Opposition Drama under the Early Stuarts

MARGOT HEINEMANN
Fellow of New Hall, Cambridge

CAMBRIDGE UNIVERSITY PRESS

Cambridge
London New York New Rochelle
Melbourne Sydney

Published by the Press Syndicate of the University of Cambridge
The Pitt Building, Trumpington Street, Cambridge CB2 1RP
32 East 57th Street, New York, NY 10022, U.S.A.
296 Beaconsfield Parade, Middle Park, Melbourne 3206, Australia

First published 1980

Printed in Great Britain by
Western Printing Services Ltd, Bristol

Library of Congress Cataloguing in Publication Data
Heinemann, Margot.

Puritanism and theatre.

(Past and present publications)

Includes index.

1. Middleton, Thomas, d. 1627 – Criticism and inter-
pretation. 2. Puritans – England. 3. English drama –
17th century – History and criticism. 4. Theater –
England – History. 5. Great Britain – History – Early
Stuarts, 1603–1649. I. Title.
PR2718.P87H44 822'.3 79–14991
ISBN 0 521 22602 3

Contents

Contents

Introductory note

This book sets out to look at Thomas Middleton's work in relation to the society and social movements of his time, and, in particular, to trace what connections it may have had with radical, Parliamentarian or Puritan movements and groupings. The more we come to know of these complex opposition movements through the recent work of seventeenth-century historians, the less satisfactory it seems to treat Parliamentary Puritanism simply as anti-theatre, anti-dramatist. I hope this study may both suggest fresh meanings and implications in Middleton's own writings, and perhaps contribute something towards rethinking the place of drama in that confused and changing society.

The range and time-span of Middleton's work indeed make it central for such a study. He wrote his earliest poems as a boy of seventeen or eighteen in the last years of Queen Elizabeth, at the time when *Henry IV* and *Henry V* were first being acted in the popular playhouses. He was already a rising dramatist when James I came to the throne in 1603, and wrote consistently for the stage throughout the reign. By the time of his death in 1627 not only had fashions in plays changed many times – like fashions in clothes, as he said himself – but the whole social context of the theatre and its audience had been transformed. To understand Middleton's development we need to be conscious of the movement not only of theatrical taste and technique but of history.

He was a productive dramatist even by Jacobean standards – author or part-author of some twenty plays, as well as the masques and City pageants which occupied much of his time from 1613 onwards. His work took many forms: first, city comedy and farce for the boys' companies and popular theatres; then tragi-comedy and moral comedy after he went to work for the King's Men; finally the boldest dramatic satire of the time, *A Game at Chess*, and two remarkable tragedies, *The Changeling* and *Women Beware Women*. It is part of Middleton's fascination for us that he was able to write what are generally considered his most compelling and confident plays when the conditions for serious drama were becoming more difficult, when what Coleridge called 'the wonderful philosophic impartiality in Shakespeare's politics' was no longer possible, and when so much dramatic talent was being diverted into the unreal or trivial. He could do so, I believe, partly because in terms of sympathy and ways of seeing, as well as patronage, he was closer than most dramatists to the growing trends of Parliamentary Puritan criticism and opposition inside and outside the court.

To see clearly the nature and importance of 'opposition' trends in early Stuart drama one needs to look beyond Middleton's lifetime; this is what I have tried to do in the last two chapters of the book. Chapter 12 shows how, despite tightening censorship on the one hand and anti-theatre bias on the other, subversive ideas and feelings still worked their way into plays in the twenty years before the Civil War. The final chapter traces the thread of continuity which I believe exists between early Stuart theatre and the upsurge of popular pamphleteering and radical journalism in the 1640s.

In considering the relation between what I have tentatively called 'opposition drama' and its social context, it has been necessary to examine at some length the religious and cultural attitudes and social position of Middleton's patrons and the circles in which they moved. It is with some regret that I have decided to present the results of this work as an appendix (Appendix A), but I could find no way of incorporating so much factual and historical detail in the main text without either cutting essential evidence or holding up the argument. I hope therefore that readers interested in cultural history will be tolerant about this arrangement.

Anyone who works on the frontiers between literature and history, as I have tried to do, must be very heavily indebted to the learning and kindness of other scholars. An investigation such as this could never have been attempted without the monumental labours of G. E. Bentley and his collaborators on *The Jacobean and Caroline Stage*, and the many scholarly editions of Middleton's plays that have appeared in recent years. I have tried to acknowledge in the references how much I owe to these and other printed sources.

The interest of *Past and Present* in the book has been of the greatest value, both in sponsoring its publication and in providing telling criticism of earlier drafts, which has helped me to correct many errors and misinterpretations. In particular I have to thank Trevor Aston for his ready assistance in this respect.

Among the many friends who have helped me with information

and suggestions, I would like to mention particularly those who gave their time to read and comment on the typescript: Leo Salingar, Elsie Duncan-Jones, Valerie Pearl, Jean Pace, Peter Clark, Vera Gottlieb, and Lisa Jardine. I am especially grateful to Simon Adams and Marie Gimmelfarb, who cleared up several important problems and generously allowed me to make use of their unpublished research material. I am also indebted for suggestions and practical help of various kinds to Jeremy Goring, Peter Thomas, Samuel Schoenbaum, Kenneth Muir, Arthur Kinney, M. Fuidge, and Lt Col. R. H. Myddleton. My greatest debt is to Christopher Hill, without whose generous help and encouragement throughout the book would never have got written. None of those I have named is responsible for the errors and imperfections still remaining; these are entirely my own.

I am grateful to Goldsmith's College for allowing me a term's sabbatical leave during which much of the initial research was done; and to New Hall, Cambridge, where I have had the opportunity as a Fellow to complete it.

MARGOT HEINEMANN

1. Time and Place

The energy of Middleton's plays is above all theatrical; the poetry works as part of the drama. If his tragedies are much more widely appreciated now than they were a generation ago, this is largely because a greater openness about sexual themes allows them to be freely staged in the theatre, viewed as Plays of the Month, or read aloud in the Sixth Form.[1] Students are surprised to find them so accessible, even psychologically modern, though the harsh social standards and conflicts assumed are strikingly different from our own. And television audiences coming fresh to *The Changeling* have responded without difficulty to its totally human terror and despair.

Yet though it is pretty generally agreed that Middleton is at times, and in some plays, a great dramatist, we are still none too sure how to take him. Different minds seem indeed to read him very differently. His comedies have been variously seen as cynical, amoral, heartlessly making fun of the citizen milieu he came from, disgusting or boring;[2] or (less frequently) as profoundly serious moral fables, in which even the bawdy is edifying.[3] In Middleton's tragedies, T. S. Eliot thought he had no point of view, was merely a great recorder.[4] Some later critics, however, have sensed a strong Calvinist bias, foredooming the protagonists from the beginning;[5] others have felt that the 'overtly religious' moral and the grotesquely

[1] *The Changeling* has recently been set as an A-level text, which would scarcely have been possible even twenty years ago.
[2] See e.g. L. C. Knights, *Drama and Society in the Age of Jonson* (1935; repr. Harmondsworth, 1962), pp. 215–24; A. L. Harbage, *Shakespeare and the Rival Traditions* (New York, 1952; repr. London, 1970), pp. 100, 190, 196 and *passim*; L. B. Wright, *Middle-Class Culture in Elizabethan England* (Chapel Hill, 1935; repr. Oxford, 1970), p. 653.
[3] See David Holmes, *The Art of Thomas Middleton* (Oxford, 1970).
[4] T. S. Eliot, *Selected Essays* (London, 1932), p. 169.
[5] I. Ribner, *Jacobean Tragedy* (London, 1962), p. 125; J. Roussell Sargent, 'Theme and Structure in the Plays of Thomas Middleton' (Univ. of London Ph.D. thesis, 1965–6); R. Chatterji, 'A Critical Study of Thomas Middleton as a Dramatist' (Univ. of Cambridge Ph.D. thesis, 1972–3).

ingenious punishment visited on sinners strike a false and in-congruous note in what is otherwise a realistically conceived human drama, and alienate all sympathy in the audience.[6] This uncertainty about intention and interpretation may be one reason why pro-fessional productions are still comparatively rare – and for the comedies, very rare indeed.

I have tried here not to write another general study of Middleton, but rather to suggest answers to some specific problems which the considerable amount of valuable recent criticism still seems to leave unresolved, and thence to throw some new light on the work as a whole. Why, to begin with, are Middleton's great tragedies so different in tone from other late Jacobean tragedy (and in general, so much more consistent and powerful dramatically)? Why and how did his work change so much, from the early satirical comedy and journalism through the sensational tragi-comedy of his mid-career to those late plays, perhaps the finest of the whole period outside Shakespeare – and indeed reaching to certain *kinds* of tragic effect which are not in Shakespeare's line?

Most puzzling – and the part of the study which in one sense gave rise to the rest – is the strange case of *A Game at Chess*, the greatest box-office success of the whole Jacobean period, staged in 1624. How could this sharp satire on royal policy, embodying the line of attack of the Parliamentary Puritan opposition and popular anti-Popish feeling, have been staged in the public theatre at a time of political crisis? And why was the punishment for it so light? If all Puritans were, as we are told, against the theatre, who backed such a risky venture? And where did the audience come from? Was it just a matter of one court faction against another? If so, why were some courtiers willing to rouse the political passions of the 'many-headed multitude', people normally considered by Stuart governing circles as only 'to be ruled'? The attempt to answer these latter questions (which has had a detective as well as a critical interest) has thrown new and sometimes unexpected light on the relationships between the drama, its patrons and the audience for which it was produced.

The subtitle 'Opposition Drama under the Early Stuarts' is meant to emphasise a continuity which the boundaries of literary periods and genres sometimes tend to obscure. We have learned,

---

[6] G. R. Hibbard, 'The Tragedies of Thomas Middleton and the Decadence of the Drama', *Renaissance and Modern Studies*, i (1957), p. 53.

looking back, to see the Elizabethan and Jacobean drama as the end of a great tradition of popular culture going back to the Catholic Middle Ages, rooted in the rural communities.[7] Looking forward, we can recognise that Middleton and his contemporaries were writing only a generation away from the upheavals of the 1640s. A young London theatre-goer when *The Changeling* or *The City Madam* were new would be a man in his thirties at the start of the Civil War. Apprentices and law students who stood in the yard of the Globe to watch *A Game at Chess* would still have been youngish men when the barricades went up to bar the City to the troops of Charles I, and may well have stood on opposite sides of them. Their ideas were formed not only by the preachers but also by plays and players.

The Jacobean drama, then, was not only the end of a tradition. Some of it fed into another kind of popular tradition, intellectual as well as political, centred in the towns and especially in London, that came to the surface in the 1640s with the relaxation of censorship (as I attempt to show in my final chapter, 'From Popular Drama to Leveller Style'). And this is relevant to our understanding of the plays themselves.

To put it another way: this was a time of unusually rapid change and tension, involving most social groupings in one way or another. Many of the recurrent themes and situations developed in tragedy and especially in comedy were suggested or given audience appeal by real conflicts in society and its standards of value, which were new enough to be newsworthy. England was in process of change from a society based on rank and status to one based more directly on wealth and property; and this meant a shake-up of social and moral codes. There was an exceptional degree of social mobility, and contemporaries were very conscious of this shifting and changing – above all in London, the melting-pot for the whole kingdom.

II

What, then, was the nature of these deep social changes, and how did they touch the dramatist and his audience?

In this rough (and necessarily oversimplified) summing-up I have

---

[7] This idea has been most fully developed by Glynne Wickham in his monumental *Early English Stages, 1300 to 1600*, 3 vols. (London, 1959–   ).

drawn heavily on the work of recent historians, whose writings the student of Jacobean drama will do well to consult for himself.[8] I have avoided using here directly literary evidence: that will come later.

Firstly, the immense and rapid growth of London gave the opportunity for and became the main centre of the commercial theatre. Of all the social changes of the time, this growth must have been the most obvious and striking to those who lived through it. The population increased by four times from around 50,000 in Henry VIII's reign to 160–180,000 by 1600, with a further sharp rise by 1640 – much faster than the increase in the country as a whole.[9] No other town had more than 20–30,000 people – this huge amorphous city was something quite new. A high proportion of London's people had been there for a generation or less, or lived there only part of the year. The settled stratification and relationships of the medieval city were eroded and partly dissolved in the new expansion.

This headlong growth was based in the first place on London's importance as a trading port and industrial centre, the main channel for the growing cloth trade with Europe and the new and highly profitable trade with the Indies. As capital city and administrative focus, housing a magnificent court, Parliament and law-courts, London was also becoming a place to spend money, a centre for the conspicuous consumption of wealth produced elsewhere (mainly, of course, on the land). Shopkeeping flourished, as did pubs, ordinaries and the entertainment industries.

In this commercial environment merchants (who were now normally different people from producers) grew very rich. The richest merchants, by the early seventeenth century, were wealthier than most peers. Out of their profits they lent massively to the Crown as well as the nobility, and gained privilege, power and sometimes land thereby. Degree was put up to auction,[10] and

---

[8] In particular, those of Christopher Hill, Charles Wilson, Valerie Pearl, Lawrence Stone and Perez Zagorin. Much of the historical ground was covered by Knights in *Drama and Society in the Age of Jonson*, and later by Brian Gibbons in *Jacobean City Comedy* (London, 1968), and it would be pointless to try to repeat it here.

[9] The figure of 250,000 in 1600, often cited in textbooks, has been shown by recent research to be too high. For the estimate quoted here I am indebted to Valerie Pearl.

[10] The phrase is C. Wilson's (*England's Apprenticeship* (London, 1965), p. 18).

became less sacred in the process. Abbeys with their estates, confiscated at the Reformation, passed from monarch to courtier or officer of state, from him to merchant or moneylender. Merchants of City descent, or younger sons of the gentry who had been apprenticed to City trades, often bought their way back into county society as purchasers of feudal castles or builders of manor-houses.[11]

Within the London trades and companies, merchants were becoming all-powerful, while smaller craftsmen were increasingly dependent on them for materials and sales outlets, and often in their debt. Many journeymen, having served their time, could never hope to become masters themselves, lacking the money to make a start. The City government (by mayor and court of aldermen) and the regulation of trade was by now largely in the hands of the big men, the smaller ones having little voice in the government of the livery companies. Thus the rich merchant was often regarded with hostility as an upstart and exploiter, not only by hard-up gentry, but by artisans and craftsmen as well.[12]

Court and Parliament drew great numbers of the aristocracy and gentry to London – a movement pushed forward by social changes in the countryside. With villeinage virtually at an end by 1600, feudal obligations and loyalties there had given way to the cash relationship between landlord and tenant; and landowners, faced with the steady rise in prices, needed more cash to pay their way and maintain customary standards, especially if they hoped to secure lucrative office at court.

Aristocracy and gentry found the money by raising rents and shortening leases; improving yields on their own estates through enclosure, land drainage or mining; and often by turning out old tenants and letting to the man who could bid most. In the endless lawsuits attending this process the advantage went to the man with the longest purse. Many lawyers made their fortunes (Sir Edward Coke was said to have made £100,000 in one year as attorney-general),[13] and it became customary for the gentry to send their sons

[11] For relations between moneylenders and noble borrowers, see L. Stone, *The Crisis of the Aristocracy* (Oxford, 1967), ch. IX.
[12] For a detailed account of the City government in this period, see Valerie Pearl, *London and the Outbreak of the Puritan Revolution* (Oxford, 1961), pp. 45–62. On the relations between merchants and craftsmen, see Wilson, *England's Apprenticeship*, pp. 49–50.
[13] Wilson, *England's Apprenticeship*, p. 10.

to the Inns of Court for a while as a necessary part of a landowner's education.

Other possibilities for the hard-up gentry were investment in foreign trade or the more speculative business of privateering (both organised mainly through London). Those who still failed to make ends meet had to borrow from the big merchants, marry a City heiress or sell land. The cost of maintaining a feudal standard of dignity – the great country house with its patronage and charity – in a world where retainers and hospitality had to be paid for, was indeed formidable.[14] Many gentlemen now saw it as more economical, as well as enjoyable, to cut down on 'housekeeping' and live at least part of the year in a house or rooms in London with only a few personal servants.

As the other side of these changes, farmers who had regarded their state as being 'as good as inheritance', working the same land from father to son, were being converted into 'free' and evictable tenants, and thence often into landless labourers or unemployed. With population expanding much faster than industry was providing jobs, there was a terrifying increase in the numbers and poverty of the poor, and a widening of the gulf between them and the rest of society; this was happening at a time when the traditional way of providing for the poor, through the charity of the monasteries, had disappeared. Though many big merchants gave generously to alms-houses and hospitals in their wills, charitable bequests and poor rates were nothing like enough to meet the need.

Real wages were falling throughout the period, to reach perhaps the lowest level ever recorded in the 1620s; and many were without any work at all. Despite the savage penalties imposed on vagabonds, beggars and runaway servants, the poor flocked to the towns, and especially to London, in search of the casual work or charity which was more easily available there (apprenticeship and skilled work being usually reserved for sons of skilled workers or younger sons of the gentry). The City authorities tried to keep them out, with limited success. They provided a reservoir both for what industry there was, and for the underworld of con-men, tricksters and thieves. In the streets in and around London whipping-posts, stocks and gibbets were a constant reminder of their existence.[15]

[14] Stone, *Crisis of the Aristocracy, passim*, but esp. ch. X, 'Conspicuous Expenditure', pp. 249–68.
[15] Christopher Hill, *Reformation to Industrial Revolution* (London, 1967), pp. 40–4; Wilson, *England's Apprenticeship*, pp. 16–17; W. K. Jordan,

Thus London became a magnet for both rich and poor. As well as citizens proper, merchants and craftsmen and shopkeepers, it attracted increasing numbers of gentry and aristocracy, engaged in lawsuits, business or education, attending Parliament or following the court. The richer gentry came to spend their wealth, the poorer to retrieve it. Wives and daughters often wanted to accompany their men, and there were the beginnings of a fashionable London season and of smart society[16] – then, as now, useful for those with surplus wealth to display, and even more for those trying to meet and marry wealthy heiresses and get rid of their debts.[17] Hence both the need and the opportunity for extravagance and showing off, for the imported silks and wines, the fashionable clothes and coaches and elaborately mounted weapons, the lessons in dancing and sword-play, the lavish banquets and compulsive gambling of which we see so much in the comedy of the time.[18]

The opportunities for private citizens to invest cash and get rich quickly were also something quite new. There was only the beginning of an organised land and money market, and the whole thing was highly speculative. The profits pious merchants made by investing in Drake's or Raleigh's voyages might reach 500 per cent, or again they might lose it all (like that privateering Earl of Cumberland who was said to have thrown all his land into the sea). To distinguish a genuine prospect from a confidence trick must have been extraordinarily difficult; investment was a 'venture' or gamble. So hard-up gallants expert in the ways of 'the town', and willing to introduce country gentry into sophisticated society, could often

Philanthropy in England (London, 1959), and Jordan, *The Charities of London* (London, 1960). See also Christopher Hill, *The World Turned Upside Down* (London, 1972), pp. 33–4.

[16] See F. J. Fisher, 'The Development of London as a Centre of Conspicuous Consumption in the Sixteenth and Seventeenth Centuries', *Transactions of the Royal Historical Society*, 4th ser., xxx (1948), pp. 37–50.

[17] That this was common practice and not merely stylised dramatic presentation can be seen from contemporary records such as John Chamberlain's letters, or those collected in T. Birch, *The Court and Times of James I*, 2 vols. (London, 1848–9).

[18] Hence too the angry outburst of James I, who intensely disliked the city, against 'those swarms of gentry who, through the instigation of their wives, and to new-model and fashion their daughters (who, if they were unmarried, marred their reputations, or if married, lost them) did neglect their country hospitality, and cumber the city, a general nuisance to the Kingdom', *Calendar of State Papers Venetian* [*CSP Venetian*], 1632–6, p. 38, cited in Fisher, 'Development of London as a Centre of Conspicuous Consumption', p. 45.

hope to live well if precariously by their wits, even without court or legal office, or regular employment of any kind.[19]

The physical layout of London too was changing. Within the City itself and its closer suburbs rich and poor still lived close together. But, as the records show, the rapid growth of population not only overcrowded the centre with insanitary slums, but spilled over far beyond the traditional built-up areas, creating new suburbs and outparishes. Town houses for the gentry were built westward from Drury Lane and the Strand, the beginnings of a West End as we know it. Meanwhile industries and crafts expanded in the suburbs, where there was more space, and where small masters and casual workers were free from the strict control of the City and its companies. Clothworkers and brickmakers were centred in the north-east; shipwrights and ropemakers, dockers and sailors, glass-works and sugar refineries eastward along the Thames in Stepney and Wapping; and innumerable smaller crafts across the river in Southwark. It was in the outparishes that immigrants, unemployed and beggars were most likely to find a refuge; they held a large part of London's population and probably most of its wage-earners.

Alongside these social changes, political attitudes and allegiances were shifting too. The monarchy on the whole was losing in popularity and confidence. James inherited Elizabeth's debts and financial problems without her charisma and prestige to hold conflicting interests together, especially after peace with Spain in 1604 had taken away the sense of national unity against the foreigner. The Crown's financial burdens were made heavier by the cost of a consort and children, the rise in prices and the diminishing supply of saleable Crown lands, as well as the wealth lavished by the new King on his favourites. Sale of titles became a notorious scandal and depreciated their value. Compared with that of Elizabeth, James' court was seen as extravagant, Scottish and permanently hard-up. Hostility was felt especially by men of property who had to vote and pay taxes; merchants and craftsmen whose trade was restricted by the 'monopolies' granted to courtiers and their friends or to City oligarchs; and rich men who were forced to lend to the King and found the Crown defaulting on the loans. The poor had their own resentments against rich clerics, court parasites and taxes on food, as well as harsh masters and magistrates.

[19] L. G. Salingar has noted an early example of the type – it became much more common after the Restoration – in Fletcher's play *Wit Without Money*.

As the reign advanced, conflict sharpened between court and country – that is, between the divine-right monarchy and its aristo-cratic and city-oligarch supporters on the one hand, and what later began to be called the Country Party: the alliance of up-and-coming City merchants and craftsmen, successful yeomen, sections of the prosperous gentry and common lawyers, which came to dominate the House of Commons and had some influential sup-porters among the peers.

The divisions were partly economic, partly religious. Rising businessmen and improving landlords wanted low taxes, cheap administration, freedom from government restrictions and feudal tenures, protection and help for foreign trade (especially against the great rival, Spain). An influential section wanted further reformation in religion, less ceremony, more preaching, more control of the Church by its members, a firmer stand against anything savouring of Catholicism. And the strength of both Parliamentarian support and militant Protestantism – what opponents called Puritanism – had always been in the towns, ports and industrial areas, especially in London and the south-east, and among the 'industrious sort of people'. It was not sharply distinguished from the lower-class anti-clericalism, reaching back to the Lollards, which had likewise been strong in these centres.

These trends were marked in London, especially in the out-parishes and liberties such as Clerkenwell, Blackfriars and South-wark, which were also the sites of the principal theatres. This was not a coincidence; the theatres were built by choice in areas outside the direct control of the City government.[20] Discontent, turbulence and rioting were especially common there. These districts were also the centres for the lower-class separatist sects, the carriers of radical ideas – Anabaptist, libertarian or levelling.

[20] See Valerie Pearl, *London and the Outbreak of the Puritan Revolution*, pp. 40–1: 'The suburbs and some of the liberties very quickly earned a reputation for Puritanism and, after 1640, for radicalism. Puritanism was, perhaps, particularly strong there because the magistrates of these areas were much less well organised than the City aldermen and less likely to report seditious preaching to the Privy Council…Even the theatre reflected this radicalism, although its dramatists were often extremely anti-Puritan in sentiment and were themselves under constant attack by the Puritans. Situated in the liberties and outparishes, the playhouses were close enough to the people who flocked to them to express this opposition to authority and good order.'

III

One aspect of the changing social structure was, of course, the change in the position of the theatre and the dramatist. Without the growth of London, a full-time, professional, commercial and popular theatre could scarcely have come into existence; and the altered social relations within it were a microcosm of those in the wider society.

First, it was a secular theatre, unlike the religious and Church-controlled popular theatre from which it inherited much of its tone and technique. Indeed, one might call it compulsorily secular, since it was debarred by state control from treating controversial religious themes, and religious drama of any kind risked being associated with Popery.

Secondly, it was a commercial theatre run for profit, not commissioned art. Although the theatrical companies had to have noble, and in Stuart times royal, patrons, they were no longer in practice the private household servants of some great lord or the amateurs of school and college drama or village festival plays.[21] The companies depended financially not so much on the occasional lucrative court or great-house performance (vital though these were for their status and survival) as on the money the audiences put in the box, audiences which in Jacobean times still included courtiers and gentry at one end of the spectrum and penny standing customers, 'groundlings', at the other. An evening in the cheapest part of the theatre at a penny was cheaper than an evening in the pub, where a quart of ale cost fourpence.[22] Apprentices and even labourers could sometimes afford a play. The audience was never to be so wide again till the coming of film and television. In that way, it was a popular theatre.

The dramatist was thus in a sense working for the equivalent of the mass media. Despite insecurity and commercial pressures, this gave him a degree of freedom that earlier writers had not had. A dramatist in regular work might earn as much as other minor intellectuals – curates or schoolmasters – though some, like Dekker and Daborne, were continually in debt to their manager for plays overdue. All in all, playwriting probably provided as good a living

---

[21] See Wickham, *Early English Stages*, ii, pt 1, chs. II–III, esp. pp. 15–19.
[22] See A. L. Harbage, *Shakespeare's Audience* (1941; repr. New York, 1964), pp. 58–60.

as most for the university graduate without influence in high places.[23] A few dramatists, like Shakespeare, who were also actors, were sharers in the company's profits and became men of some property (though none as rich as the great actor Alleyne). Most of them, however, experienced enough insecurity and penury to identify with the poorer as well as the richer part of the audience, and to long at times for the older pattern of dependence and noble patronage. Yet to understand the limitations that pattern imposed on a writer we need only consider the contrasted experience of Donne, originally a courtier and state official who wrote as an amateur and not for publication. When he lost his post because of what Walton calls the 'remarkable error' of a secret love-marriage with a girl of higher social status, he spent a dozen precarious years in commissioned controversy and complimentary verses for rich patrons, until the King's refusal to give him state office and his need for money and employment finally drove him into the Church career he had so long refused. Although there are wonderful things in the poems written for patrons like Sir Robert Drury and the Countess of Bedford, it is hard to feel that the poet in these middle years was free to write as he wished. And outside the theatre, it was still very hard to make a living as a professional writer for the book market.[24]

A great deal of scholarly work has been done on the audiences for whom the Jacobean drama was written, more than enough to show that a wide variety of people and social groups went to the theatre.[25] We do not know, and probably never will, exactly what proportion of the 'groundlings' at the Globe were craftsmen or

[23] See G. E. Bentley, *The Profession of Dramatist in Shakespeare's Time* (Princeton, 1971), pp. 88–110.

[24] See e.g. E. H. Miller, *The Professional Writer in Elizabethan England* (Cambridge, Mass., 1959), pp. 1–26, 203–32.

[25] See e.g. Harbage, *Shakespeare's Audience*, pp. 150–7, which first tellingly refuted the traditional view of the 'groundlings' as an ignorant and dissolute mob; the same author's *Shakespeare and the Rival Traditions*, which tries to establish what seems to me an excessively sharp distinction between indoor and outdoor theatre audiences; J. Jacquot (ed.), *Dramaturgie et Société* (Paris 1968), esp. the essays by Salingar *et al.*, J. Jacquot and W. Gair; W. A. Armstrong, 'The Audience of the Elizabethan Private Theatres', *Review of English Studies*, n.s., x (1959), pp. 240–2; and A. J. Cook, 'The Audience of Shakespeare's Plays: A Reconsideration', *Shakespeare Studies*, vii (1974), pp. 283–305, which disputes Harbage's view of the audience as predominantly 'working-class', in the sense of craftsmen, and suggests that shopkeepers, servants, students and soldiers on leave took up much of the cheaper theatre space. Shopkeepers would normally, however, be craftsmen too, so this may be a distinction without much difference.

prentices, law students or shopkeepers, labourers or soldiers on leave, men-about-town or petty thieves; but for our purposes this may not greatly matter. The broad social basis of the drama seems sufficiently clear.

In the 1590s, the dramatists were working in the main for a single national public, a rough cross-section of London's people, with Queen and court seeing many of the same plays that ran in the public theatres. In Jacobean times, with the growth of a West End and of the more plebeian areas to the east and south, there was a growing division of the audience. At court the fashion was for spectacular and enormously expensive masques and shows, with elaborate scenery, in which the courtiers themselves took part.[26] Indoor theatres like the Blackfriars, Cockpit or Phoenix, charging higher prices, were established in the more fashionable districts, catering largely for courtiers, lawyers and gentry up in London, and for the new groups of men-about-town. Meanwhile it seems likely that ordinary citizens, craftsmen and apprentices and wage-earners went in greater numbers to the cheaper outdoor theatres in the suburbs, such as the Globe on the Bankside and the Red Bull at Clerkenwell.[27] The publics were not indeed sharply distinct.[28] There were some shop-foremen and mechanics at the Blackfriars – even if a minority in the house – and some gentry at the Globe. Several companies played in both indoor and outdoor houses, notably the King's Men, who used the Blackfriars in the fashionable winter months and the Globe in the summer when court and lawyers were out of town. Audiences and repertories overlapped a good deal; but the two kinds of theatre probably did tend to concentrate on rather different types of play. Satirical court allusions and comedy of manners seem to have gone better in the private theatres, jigs, domestic tragedy, militant patriotism and anti-Popery with the lower orders at the Globe or Red Bull. These differences in taste

[26] It was particularly these performances that were denounced by later Puritan writers like Lucy Hutchinson and Richard Baxter. They were also the primary target of William Prynne in *Histriomastix*, though Prynne of course included the whole professional and public stage in his attack.
[27] See A. Gurr, *The Shakespearean Stage* (Cambridge, 1970), pp. 142–4.
[28] Harbage, in *Shakespeare and the Rival Traditions*, certainly overstates the difference. There is plenty of violence and bawdy in plays written for the popular theatres as well as in 'coterie' productions. But his discussion of differences in taste had its value after so much confident writing about what 'the Jacobeans' (all Jacobeans?) liked, even if one strongly disagrees with his dismissal of Middleton's comedies as anti-citizen, 'coterie' work.

must have corresponded at least in part to the different codes and interests of differing social groups.

As well as audiences, the royal persons and great men who patronised and lent their name to the dramatic companies seem to have exercised at least a negative influence on what they produced, and often more than that. In Elizabethan times, indeed, great courtiers like Leicester, Walsingham and Hunsdon gave their livery and protection to players mainly so as to be able to entertain the Queen; but they may also have had an eye to influencing public opinion. A dangerous or indiscreet performance might lead to the withdrawal of the patron's support, a serious matter since liberty to tour and exemption from City interference depended on it. After James' accession, when officially only royalty could act as patrons, the Lord Chamberlain and his officers were in closer contact with the players and took on part of the patron's role.

Another aspect of patronage was the dedication of printed books, including playbooks, to great men. The motive here was sometimes direct financial reward, sometimes pure advertising, sometimes other kinds of favour or protection. Authors of risky works might try to safeguard them against suppression by a well-selected dedication – for instance George Wither's dedication of his satires and Jonson's of his *Catiline* to the Earl of Pembroke. Sometimes, again, the patron had a more active role in commissioning or suggesting a book – as Archbishop Bancroft with Nashe's anti-Marprelate tracts, or Sidney with Spenser's poems.[29]

A great many Jacobean plays were printed with dedications, usually to the nobility, the Earls of Pembroke, Montgomery, Dorset, Caernarvon, members of the Howard and Walsingham families being among those most often named. Others were dedicated to minor officials about the court, and a few to leading City magnates. The difference between, for example, Howard and Herbert taste may have had its own importance for the content of the plays.

IV

The influence of society on plays and dramatists is still often treated in terms of a general intellectual 'climate of the age', ruling ideas

[29] On the custom of dedications and their significance, see Miller, *Professional Writer in Elizabethan England*, H. S. Bennett, *English Books and Readers, 1558–1603* (Cambridge, 1965), and Bennett, *English Books and Readers, 1603–1640* (Cambridge, 1970), pp. 23–39.

and conceptions assumed to prevail over society as a whole. E. M. W. Tillyard's *Elizabethan World Picture*[30] is a classic (and valuable) example of this method: 'The conception of world order was for the Elizabethans a principal matter' (p. 29). 'The Elizabethans pictured the universal order under three main forms: a chain, a series of corresponding planes, and a dance' (p. 37). 'Hooker...speaks for the educated nucleus that dictated the current beliefs of the Elizabethan Age' (p. 22). The homilies read on Sundays from the pulpit by order of the Queen thus become *the* Elizabethan view. 'The Puritans and the courtiers were more united by a common theological bond than they were divided by ethical disagreements' (p. 12). And yet the disagreements were enough to make a minority risk imprisonment and even execution – unimportant as Marprelatists, Barrowists and Brownists may seem in the universal scheme.

Certainly it is important to be aware of common assumptions in the early seventeenth century, especially where they are different from our own. All the same, we should not be too confident that these represent what 'the Jacobeans' felt and thought. There were at the least (as Kenneth Muir has pointed out) several world pictures to choose from; and it is from the conflicts and discrepancies between them that the greatest drama often arises. *Doctor Faustus* could not have been written in an age where no one much questioned man's free will or the omniscience of the Church – any church. Neither could *Richard II* or *King Lear*, if everyone had been agreed on the King's status as God's irremoveable deputy, right or wrong, never to be called to account. *Troilus and Cressida* or *Coriolanus* hardly suggest that total subordination of the commons' grievances to the will of the nobility was universally felt as natural and right, though most people may have thought it inevitable. And *Romeo and Juliet* and *The Duchess of Malfi* could scarcely have been popular if there had been no new ethic challenging the traditional right of a noble family to dispose of its women in marriage.

The social environment, then, affects the dramatist's handling of his subject partly through the moral, social and political framework he acquires in the course of his personal and family life, his education, and his mastery of language itself – assumptions and ways of seeing which may remain half-conscious and unchallenged. But

[30] First published 1945; repr. Harmondsworth, 1963.

it impinges also in a more conscious and tangible form, in the course of writing and producing for a particular theatre and audience, gaining the favour of particular patrons, and keeping out of trouble with the law. Within these limitations the playwright can render his own version of life and express his own sense of values, of what constitutes a fate worse than death or a happy ending; and the limitations may sometimes themselves become a source of strength. They may force an author to break out of the assumptions of a small circle and consider how a story can convincingly be presented to engage the sympathy of a wider audience. (This has been one effect, admittedly not the only one, of television on our contemporary drama.) Or his position may compel him to embody unorthodox moral or religious convictions so completely in character and situation that they cannot be separated out as 'message', and yet work more effectively than if he were free to be as didactic as he chose. (This is perhaps partly true if we compare the early works of Brecht, written as demonstrations of accepted truth to a largely converted audience, with later plays like *Mother Courage* or *Galileo*, written and presented originally in exile, and having to penetrate their audience by an alternation of warm sympathy and intellectual shock.) Sometimes the external conditions may be much more obviously frustrating and restrictive for the writer.[31] The playwright has to give the audience something it likes, but dare not give it what it would like best. In either case there is an interaction of influences between the writer, the audience and the medium in which he works.

It seems that in the early seventeenth century audience feeling often pulled one way (or two or three ways, since there were several audiences), patronage and censorship another. As tension grew between court and country in Parliament, and even within the Privy Council, the influences of great patrons and royal censorship might also conflict (*A Game at Chess* may well be an example of this). We cannot directly know what the dramatists thought – they did not keep personal diaries or write autobiographies, like Sir Simonds D'Ewes or Lucy Hutchinson. But we can perhaps see how, under all these pressures, the changes and conflicts are embodied in their plays, and how the plays in turn help to form the mental habits and ways of seeing of their audience.

---

[31] For example, the high price of seats in the modern live commercial theatre, which effectively determines the social composition of its audience.

V

I have come to think that *A Game at Chess* was not an isolated freak, either in Middleton's career or in the theatrical history of the time. Throughout James' reign, especially in the latter half of it, and under Charles I, there is a clearly discernible line of dramatic production (albeit a minority one) which appeals to and encourages 'anti-establishment', generally Parliamentary Puritan sympathies – and this despite a censorship which severely limited the expression of this kind of feeling. Some treatment of this element in the work of other dramatists in the 1620s and 1630s is given in the last chapters of this book.

More important, however, than the directly partisan plays themselves is the evidence they provide that people with some kind of Parliamentarian, Puritan and even radical sympathies were inside as well as outside the theatre world. They must have been in the audience, and occasionally among the highly placed sponsors and connoisseurs of the drama. This might make us see not only *A Game at Chess* or *The Duchess of Suffolk*, but the recognised major drama of the time – Shakespeare as well as Middleton – in a slightly different perspective. We should, perhaps, be less confident that all the greater dramatists identified themselves with the 'traditional' values currently being defended by the Court party than L. C. Knights was when he wrote, in his brilliant pioneering study forty years ago:

> The interests represented by most of the dramatists were not the same as those represented by most members of the House of Commons: the latter tended more and more to express the new commercial opinion, whilst the enlightened conservatism of the better playwrights drew upon traditional opinions and attitudes that were more potent in the Privy Council than in Parliament.[32]

For anyone who wants to get a vivid sense of the plays as happening in a real world of human suffering, unemployment and greed, *Drama and Society in the Age of Jonson* remains the best book to read. (It is no accident that it dates from the nineteen thirties, when these things were much in people's minds.) And certainly discontent and social protest were most often expressed, in life as in the drama, in a 'socially conservative' demand to restore the *traditional* rights of Englishmen as they had existed at

[32] *Drama and Society in the Age of Jonson*, p. 147.

some earlier time – before the last rent rise, under Queen Elizabeth, before the Conquest – rather than calling for or even imagining a *new* social order. It is much less clear that the 'better' dramatists (or their audiences) necessarily felt that these traditional rights and values were being defended by the Crown and its advisers. It was after all the court that gave scandalous 'monopolies' to 'new men' like Mompesson and Cokayne: it was Parliament that pulled them down. It was the court that leagued with Spain and imprisoned godly preachers. A few years later the demand to restore 'traditional' liberties – those that Englishmen had allegedly lost under the Stuarts and the Norman yoke – became an important ideological support of Cromwell and, in a more radical sense, of the Levellers.[33] 'Enlightened social conservatism' proved to be potentially revolutionary.

Meanwhile the assumption, in which many later critics have concurred, that all the 'better' Jacobean dramatists were naturally aligned with the Crown against Parliament will not really stand examination, and may lead us to misread the plays.[34] A close factual study of Middleton's work and associations does, I think, confirm this. The conflicts of ideas and values embodied in the greater Jacobean plays are, in their context, irreconcileable. To see them merely as aberrations from generally accepted order, religion and morality – essentially Royalist, absolutist order, Laudian religion and aristocratic morality – is to oversimplify and diminish the plays themselves.[35]

[33] Christopher Hill, 'The Norman Yoke', in Hill, *Puritanism and Revolution* (London, 1958; repr. 1962), pp. 50–122.
[34] L. C. Knights in *Drama and Society* seems to agree with this judgment; at least he considers that Middleton, until his last two plays, was *not* one of the 'better' dramatists.
[35] This point is admirably argued with reference to Tourneur, Webster, Greville and Chapman by J. W. Lever in *The Tragedy of State* (London, 1971).

2. *Puritanism, Censorship and Opposition to the Theatre*

That Parliament in 1642 ordered the theatres to be closed is probably the best-known fact in English theatrical history. And since the Parliamentary Puritans were then in power, all critics of the theatre are commonly assumed in literary history to be Puritans, and all Puritans hostile to the theatre, as if the two things were synonymous.

The identification of Puritans and Parliament with total hostility to art, culture and beauty has become almost axiomatic. It is, indeed, so integrated into the language that to speak of Puritans who were not 'puritanical' sounds like splitting hairs (though it is what contemporaries often did). The popular notion of Puritans in literary history (as distinct from modern historical studies) still remains in essentials not unlike the memorable image of the 'rigid sect' in the early seventeenth century presented by Macaulay (and derived through him from Dryden and the Royalist pamphleteers):

> It was a sin to hang garlands on a maypole, to drink a friend's health, to hawk, to hunt a stag, to play at chess, to wear lovelocks, to put starch in a ruff, to touch the virginals, to read the Fairy Queen...Some precisians had scruples about teaching the Latin grammar, because the names of Mars, Bacchus and Apollo occurred in it. The fine arts were all but proscribed. The light music of Ben Jonson's masques was dissolute. Half the fine paintings in England were idolatrous, and the other half indecent.[1]

It is easy to show that this stereotype does not fit many of those we most readily think of as seventeenth-century Puritans – Milton or Marvell, Cromwell or Colonel Hutchinson. Yet, despite the reservations and qualifications made by many literary historians since,[2] the conception of Puritanism satirically sketched here has

---

[1] *History of England* (London, 1907), p. 21.
[2] See e.g. C. V. Wedgwood, *Seventeenth-Century English Literature* (Oxford, 1956), p. 140. 'The theatre habit was too strong among the English to be lightly killed, nor were the Puritans by any means unanimously opposed to it.' For discussion of the relationship of literature in general to later Puritan movements, see *ibid.* pp. 170–5, and the same author's *Poetry and Politics under the Stuarts* (Ann Arbor, 1964).

remained important in literary criticism.[3] The assumptions had indeed scarcely changed a hundred years later, when Henri Fluchère wrote in *Shakespeare and the Elizabethans* (1947), a book which T. S. Eliot strongly recommended to English readers for its unusual insight into the ideas and philosophy of the period:[4]

Refusing to compromise with Sin, with anyone who might welcome, encourage or tolerate it, Puritanism had a horror of beauty, sensuousness and sensuality. . .The stage appeared to them a school of corruption and lies, a vast industry of debauchery, an ever-increasingly degenerate activity.   (p. 70)

It must be remembered that the first victims of the Roundheads were the unruly playwrights. It is not enough to say that their entertainments were a danger to morality: they were especially so to the mind. . .Beauty. . .was the *bête noire* of the Puritans and remained dangerous.   (p. 63)

Again, Patrick Cruttwell wrote in his lively and provocative study *The Shakespearean Moment*:[5]

The Puritan, then, for our purposes, is a man whose rejection of the sensuous seems natural, a part of his very being, rather than simply a conviction.

And again:

[The Puritan mind] was a mind which divided and excluded – in direct opposition to that society previously described,[6] which aimed at uniting and including. It would be unjustifiably ecclesiastical, and absurdly narrowing, to describe the metaphysical and mature Shakespearean manner as an Anglo-Catholic style *tout court*; but it is true that Anglo-Catholicism agreed with it, while Puritanism did not and could not, and that the difference between an including and an excluding mentality is at the root of this difference. For the more you exclude, the farther

[3] To trace the notions of Puritanism in later critical writing would require a separate study, and cannot be attempted here, though it might prove interesting and fruitful.

[4] Foreword to *Shakespeare and the Elizabethans* (English trans. 1947; repr. New York, 1960).

[5] New York, 1960, p. 141.

[6] 'The Society of the Shakespearean Moment', as Cruttwell calls it. In more recent writings Cruttwell has himself criticised his original formulation as 'over-simplification', perhaps containing 'a whiff of nostalgia for a golden past' ('The Love Poetry of John Donne', in D. J. Palmer and M. Bradbury (eds.), *Metaphysical Poetry* (London, 1970), p. 16). The view remains one which is still widely held.

you go from the rich variety and complexity of material which drama requires.   (p. 143)

The argument is, of course, a circular one. If one defines Puritan in this way there ceases to be any point in discussing traces of Parliamentary Puritan ideas or sympathies in the drama, which are by definition excluded. Few literary critics, however, make so explicit the sense in which they intend to use the word: they rather assume agreement about it.

Thus in a recent standard literary history Brian Morris refers to 'perpetual war' by 'the Puritans' upon the stage from the opening of the public theatres in 1576 to their closing in 1642. He cites a famous passage from Stubbes' *Anatomy of Abuses* (1583) against contemporary plays:

Do they not maintain bawdry, insinuate foolery, and renew the remembrance of heathen idolatry? Do they not induce whoredom and uncleanness? Nay, are they not rather plain devourers of maidenly virginity and chastity? For proof whereof mark but the flocking and running to Theaters and Curtains, daily and hourly, night and day, time and tide, to see plays and interludes, where such wanton gestures, such bawdy speeches, such laughing and fleering, such clipping and culling, such winking and glancing of wanton eyes, and the like is used, as is wonderful to behold.[7]

The Puritan fear, Morris thinks, arises from a sensitive instinct. 'The key word in the passage from Stubbes is "idolatry". He realised that the attention which the plays commanded is not unlike the involvement of worship.' Morris believes there are analogies between dramatic and religious expression in the ritual participation of actor and audience, in the use of heightened language and dressing up, which make Stubbes see the drama as a particularly dangerous temptation to wickedness.[8]

This intensely felt dichotomy between the Church and the playhouse, between the world of the spirit and the world of the flesh, is close to the heart of English Puritanism in the sixteenth and seventeenth century. The inclusive, mediaeval sense of the whole-

[7] Cited in Christopher Ricks (ed.), *Sphere History of Literature in the English Language* (London, 1971), iii, p. 65.
[8] Stubbes was indeed in Church matters a moderate reformer, who considered the rule of bishops as necessary. He did not object to surplice and corner-cap, and thought a clergyman who resigned his living rather than wear them was neglecting his flock. But it is going rather far to suggest that he saw 'dressing up' as an important aspect of religious expression.

ness of all creation had been sharply and effectively challenged by the theology emanating from Wittenberg and Geneva, which stressed the fallen nature of Man, the unredeemed quality of created Nature, and the deadly sinfulness of sin.[9]

One sees what these writers mean. It seems convincing if we think of many Puritan opponents of the stage, of William Prynne for example,[10] or of William Perkins. Yet there is, on the face of it, something oversimplified about an argument which has to ignore so many obvious cases. Milton was a passionate theatre-goer in his youth, profoundly sensuous in *Paradise Lost*, yet surely in some sense a Puritan. Leicester and Walsingham were noted patrons both of Puritans and players. The 3rd Earl of Pembroke, Shakespeare's patron, was considered leader of the Puritan group in James I's government,[11] and his brother the 4th Earl, joint dedicatee of the First Folio, was a Parliamentarian in the Civil War. Bulstrode Whitelocke was a *habitué* of the Blackfriars, and as a Cromwellian official persuaded the Protector to allow operas. The Puritan Sir Thomas Barrington's library included Shakespeare's First Folio. Among the outstanding Parliamentarian leaders in 1640, the Earls of Essex and Warwick patronised and employed the playwright Arthur Wilson. Peter Sterry, Cromwell's chaplain, quoted from Shakespeare and admired his work. One could extend the list. Perhaps it should be added that Hamlet, who came from the Protestant University of Wittenberg and would have liked to return there, was also a patron of players.

It seems to me that these are something more than isolated exceptions, that they indicate a different and more complex relationship between the drama and people's religious and political attitudes which deserves more detailed investigation. Certainly the growing hold of the court over the theatre, both in terms of censorship and patronage, must have tended to alienate many Parliamentary Puritans from playgoing in the years immediately before the Civil War. To see all Puritans as automatically hostile in principle to the theatre and the arts generally is, however, to misunderstand the

[9] Morris, in *Sphere History*, p. 66.
[10] J. Dover Wilson, in the *Cambridge History of English Literature* (1932 edn), wrote: 'If it be ever possible for one man to sum up a movement in his own person, Prynne summed up Puritanism' (vi, p. 404). This again is in line with Macaulay.
[11] The Venetian Secretary, in a dispatch of 1 July 1616, explicitly refers to him as 'head of the Puritans' (*CSP Venetian*, xiv, p. 245).

depth and complexity of the intellectual and social movements that led to the upheavals of the 1640s.

Parliamentary Puritanism as a broad movement

What is important for our purposes about the Parliamentary Puritan movement is its great breadth and variety – a variety which was the cause both of its strength and of its later disunity.[12]

Originally, separatists seem to have been called Puritans, rather than those who wished to reform the Church from within. If we narrow the term to separatism and Presbyterianism, it represents a relatively small minority until after 1640. But most modern historians have used the term more widely, to describe something which was already important in Elizabethan times and increasingly so up to the Civil War. If we define Puritanism broadly, with Trevelyan, as 'the religion of all those who wished either to purify the usage of the established Church from the taint of Popery, or to worship separately by forms so purified', we are no longer speaking of a small minority, but of a broad movement or convergence of movements – varied and even contradictory in social basis as well as in religious outlook and strategy, yet capable in a crisis of sufficient unity to defeat royal absolutism.

The word Puritan was already used in the seventeenth century, however, to define a political as well as a religious alignment. James I described Puritans to his first Parliament in 1604 as 'a sect rather than a religion – ever discontented with the present government and impatient to suffer any superiority, which maketh their sect unable to be suffered in any well-governed commonwealth'. Men are called Puritans, said Henry Parker in 1641, 'if they ascribe anything to the laws and liberties of this realm, or hold the prerogative royal to be limitable by any law whatsoever...If they hold not against Parliament and with ship-money, they are ever injurious to Kings...If all reformers are Puritan, then Parliament is Puritan.'[13]

Among the points considered by contemporaries to be typical of religious Puritanism were Sabbatarianism, opposition to Popery and hostility to oaths, a high valuation of preaching, and a dislike

[12] In this section I am especially indebted to Christopher Hill's chapter, 'The Definition of a Puritan', in *Society and Puritanism in Pre-Revolutionary England* (London, 1966), pp. 13–29.

[13] *A Discourse Concerning Puritans.* Cited in Christopher Hill, *Society and Puritanism in Pre-Revolutionary England*, p. 23.

of ceremony and vestments. The right to choose a minister who would preach and not merely read the officially prepared homilies, and some right for the congregation to hear the preachers they preferred, were among the forms in which freedom of speech and discussion became a central issue in the period.

Socially, the movements of discontent and opposition to absolute royal power in London at this period cannot usefully be thought of simply as 'City Puritan' in contrast to 'Anglo-Catholic court'. The main basis was the alliance of the 'industrious sort of people' – the clothiers, craftsmen, manufacturers, merchants outside the privileged oligarchies, yeomen and the more prosperous tenant farmers – with a large section of the 'natural rulers', the Puritan gentry, JPs and a sprinkling of Puritan lords.

The basis of the division which produced 'Puritan gentry' and 'Puritan aristocracy' has been much debated, some historians seeing the motivation as primarily direct economic self-interest, and others giving more weight to religious and political beliefs. Many of the families most consistent in their support and patronage of Puritan preachers and writers were certainly among those enriched with monastic lands at the Reformation, the 'new' aristocracy of the mid Tudor period, who had thus a particular fear of a Catholic restoration which might severely deprive them. (Examples were the Herberts, Russells, Dudleys and Sidneys.) Again, those especially interested in trade and colonisation in the West Indies, and in privateering at Spain's expense while the war lasted, were faced with economic difficulties when peace broke out in 1604. There is some evidence too that 'improving' landlords and entrepreneurs, such as the Earls of Pembroke, Bedford and Warwick, tended to identify their interests with those of the clothiers and merchant adventurers with whom they had close business associations. Later, rivalry between those who held high office at court and those who did not was another major factor: Buckingham's monopoly of patronage itself produced an opposition.

However, the reforming religious tradition, the passionate concern that England should actively support the Protestant cause in Europe, the patronage of Puritanism even as a semi-legal movement are also realities which cannot everywhere and always be equated with immediate economic interest. Sir Philip Sidney, for example, first made himself unpopular with Queen Elizabeth by writing against her possible marriage to the Catholic Alençon and then insisted on enlisting under Leicester for the war in the Low Countries where he was killed in action, which events must be related to a set of ideas rather than a direct eye to the main chance. His influence, even after his death, was intellectual, religious and political.

Within this broad movement there was also a more plebeian trend – the separatists, the sects, those who were called Brownists and Anabaptists. These were most prevalent among the lower classes, and when Jacobean dramatists satirise Puritans they usually aim at these sects, with their lay preachers, their claims to congregational independence and democracy, and their rejection of control by a single national church. Fear of social disorder and upheaval – like the Anabaptist revolt at Munster which had established a form of communist rule – made these trends feared not only by monarchs and bishops, but also by other Puritans. Even Martin Marprelate, the most bitter and scathing opponent of bishops, 'accounted no Brownist to be a Puritan',[14] and John Field, organiser of the semi-legal Presbyterian classis movement in Elizabethan times, thought them 'heretics'.

The Parliamentary Puritan forces included, at the outset, a section of gentry and aristocrats as well as merchants and apprentices; they included both the Presbyterian preachers who were for a strict and single discipline, and the sectaries who recognised no authority wider than the individual congregation or even the individual conscience. There were narrow Bibliolaters, scientists, poets and historians.[15] And among the masses who helped to throw up the barricades that barred London to the King, there must have been many who over the previous five years had stood in the audience for seditious anti-Laudian plays at the Red Bull and Fortune.

As Valerie Pearl expresses it in her masterly study of Puritan London:

A sprinkling of Puritan lords and sons of the nobility, sometimes expressing a predilection for aristocratic government, headed the

---

[14] *Marprelate Tracts*, ed. W. Pierce (London, 1911), p. 252.
[15] See Christopher Hill, *Intellectual Origins of the English Revolution* (Oxford and London, 1965), and his *Puritanism and Revolution* for a full treatment of the ideas that helped to form these revolutionary trends. See also W. Haller, *The Rise of Puritanism* (New York, 1938), M. M. Knappen, *Tudor Puritanism* (Chicago, 1965), and Conrad Russell, *The Crisis of Parliaments* (Oxford, 1971), pp. 162–72.

movement and rubbed shoulders with substantial middle-rank merchants of the trading companies, often the victims of oligarchic privilege and financial extortion. Joining them came humbler shopkeepers and traders with their apprentices: of inferior social position, the butt of Royalist writers, many of them would soon display their talents as soldiers, organisers and business men in the upheavals of the Civil War. Below the respectable classes, the anonymous labouring poor, swayed violently, as among the seamen, by religious, political or economic pressures, were ready to lend a hand in their own fashion. In a position apart were the many divines and preachers, inspiring the alliance with a fervent faith and yet, in the many-sided nature of their Puritanism, reflecting the different tendencies within their congregations. In other less exalted ways, a common activity helped to unite the movement. The Artillery Garden with its 'manly' and martial exercises, and, perhaps not far off in kind, the crowded Tavern Clubs, loud with the din of drinking and debate, were favourite haunts of the more proselytising of the parliamentary puritans. Ardent propagandist and pleasure-seeking citizen alike – few had the kill-joy qualities given to all the Puritans by later legend.[16]

Contemporaries seem to have thought that one might be a Puritan in religion without being 'puritanical', and were conscious that the word was used in several senses. The poet George Wither argued that one ought not to be afraid of the name:

> And do we not perceive that many a man,
> Fearing to be entitled Puritan,
> Simply neglects the means of his salvation?[17]

And again,

> Who are so much termed Puritans as they
> That fear God most? (p. 276)

To be called Puritan by an atheist he considered an honour. True, 'the hollow crew, the counterfeit elect', sometimes called Puritans, who contemn charity and denounce May-games, are often greedy hypocrites in his opinion. But so are those anti-Puritans who pride themselves on affording the poor 'some slender cheer' at Whitsun

---

[16] *London and the Outbreak of the Puritan Revolution* (Oxford, 1961), p. 279.
[17] George Wither, *Abuses Stript and Whipt* (1613; repr. in *Juvenilia*, 1622; *S.T.C.* 25911), p. 247.

ales or hocktide feasts, and complain of too much preaching. As for the theatre, it is 'malicious ignorance' to say it corrupts and teaches vice, bad though some plays are. Did not the 'divine Sidney' defend it as a way of teaching men to be better? And have not writers like Jonson and Chapman provided good examples?[18] Wither himself was imprisoned several times as an opposition satirist, became an officer in the Parliamentary Army, and was again imprisoned at the Restoration.

The nature of Puritan opposition to the theatre

It is generally agreed that the Reformers were at first not at all, and never completely, hostile to the stage,[19] and indeed used it as a valuable means of influence. In England Thomas Cromwell apparently commissioned Protestant propagandist interlude-writers, notably John Bale, Bishop of Ossory, author of the famous anti-Catholic *King Johan* (first performed in Archbishop Cranmer's house). Simon Fishe and Skelton were involved in stage satire against Wolsey. John Foxe, himself the author of sacred plays such as *Christus Triumphans*, declared in his *Book of Martyrs* that it was no marvel that Bishop Gardiner attempted to thwart the players, printers and preachers, 'for he seeth these three things to be set up of God, as a triple bulwark against the triple crown of the Pope, to bring him down, as, God be praised, they have done meetly well already'.[20]

All these media, it was plain, could appeal to popular support over the head of Church and state. Hence successive monarchs suppressed those plays they saw as dangerous to their régime and religion – Mary Tudor, as it happens, on a rather wider scale than Elizabeth.[21]

At the beginning of Elizabeth's reign, while miracle plays were put down as Popish, Cecil made use of interludes as a political weapon against Philip of Spain and the Catholics. Both Philip and

[18] *Ibid.* p. 264.

[19] Melanchthon advocated its use for controversy, and many Reformers, such as Beza, Bucer and Kirchmayer, themselves wrote plays on sacred subjects. Even Calvin, though stricter, allowed the production of a Biblical play at Geneva (Dover Wilson, *Cambridge History of English Literature* [*C.H.E.L.*], vi, ch. 14). See Knappen, *Tudor Puritanism*, p. 489.

[20] Cited by E. K. Chambers, *The Elizabethan Stage*, 4 vols. (Oxford, 1923), i, p. 242n.

[21] See Russell Fraser, *The War Against Poetry* (Princeton, 1970), p. 129.

James VI of Scotland at various times complained about the free use of their names by the London players. 'Similarly, when it was desired that Puritanism should be unpopular, the players were not debarred from satirising Puritans.'[22] David Bevington, in *Tudor Drama and Politics*,[23] has shown how far-ranging were the social and political concerns in Tudor plays, long before the rise of the commercial London theatre.

The later campaign by some Puritan preachers against the public stage was not always directed at drama in principle (the wickedness of disguise or impersonation). Most would concede that college or Inns of Court plays might be allowable, especially on sacred subjects. It was primarily though not exclusively an attack on the common players as idlers and vagabonds, on the danger to law and order, and on the social atmosphere in the commercial theatres, as well as the content of the plays themselves.

This hostility to plays was not, however, exclusively Puritan. We find it in Catholic Europe as well as in England – Montaigne, for instance, classing interlude players with harlots and courtesans, and Cardinal Borromeo and the Jesuit publicist Mariana denouncing the evils of the theatre and recommending its strict regulation.[24] Pope Pius IV, in the austere anti-humanist climate of Counter-Reformation Rome, was so offended by the naked figures in Michelangelo's 'Last Judgment' fresco in the Sistine Chapel that he ordered loin-cloths to be painted on to them.[25] In Spain many of the clergy repeatedly expressed hostility to the popular theatres. Archbishop Grindal, who inclined towards Puritanism, in 1568 demanded that the actors be inhibited from playing in London for one year,

---

22 *Dramatic Records of Sir Henry Herbert*, ed. J. Quincy Adams (New Haven, 1917), Introduction.
23 Cambridge, Mass., 1968.
24 Cited in E. N. S. Thompson, *The Controversy Between the Puritans and the Stage* (1902; repr. New York, 1966). See also Richard S. Dunn, *The Age of Religious Wars, 1559–1689* (London, 1971). Borromeo managed to get many plays suppressed in Milan, and ordered the preachers to 'detest and unremittingly curse' them. His secretary suggested one might usefully bankrupt acting companies by seizing the playbook for censorship purposes and failing to return it till after the advertised time for the play (C. Dejob, *De L'Influence du Conseil de Trente sur la littérature et les beaux-arts* (Paris, 1884)). I am indebted to Leo Salingar for this reference. Much additional evidence and analysis are given in Peter Burke, *Popular Culture in Modern Europe* (London, 1978), pp. 207–43, which appeared too recently for me to make full use of it.
25 See Dunn, *Age of Religious Wars*, p. 192.

'and if it were for ever, it would not be amiss'.[26] But in later times High Anglicans like Giles Fletcher and Nicholas Ferrar (in his last years) condemned playhouses and players in terms no different from the Puritans.[27] And Bishop Lancelot Andrewes, despite the practice of the court, in his *Exposition of the Ten Commandments* (p. 284), numbered playgoers on the Sabbath among those ill employed.[28] Moreover he attacked plays as a temptation quite apart from Sunday playing. 'From without our lust is watered, either by corrupt company, or by reading lascivious books wantonly; or by beholding wanton pictures, or plays, and spectacles of love.'[29] Denouncing bad company and art, books and pictures that 'stir up wicked and lustful thoughts', as tending to breach of the Commandment, he condemned 'by analogy thereunto, all wanton dancings, Mark 6.22, or stage plays, or things pertaining to them; because... a man cannot touch pitch but he shall be defiled, nor see wanton actions, but his affections will be moved'.[30] Archbishop Laud himself would go no further than arguing against Prynne that plays were not necessarily evil: in 1637 he was concerned, against the Lord Chamberlain, with preventing the theatres from reopening.

The best-known Elizabethan writers against the stage were not, in most cases, Puritans in a theological or doctrinal sense (though they are usually described as such in the textbooks, apparently on the assumption that hostility to the theatre is in itself a certificate of Puritan religious views).[31] Philip Stubbes, the most eloquent and

---

[26] Cited by Dover Wilson, *C.H.E.L.*, vi, ch. 14.

[27] See L. A. Sasek, *The Literary Temper of the English Puritans* (Baton Rouge, La., 1961), p. 93. Ferrar at the end of his life made a bonfire of his playbooks (A. L. Maycock, *Nicholas Ferrar of Little Gidding* (London, 1938), p. 298).

[28] Cited by Thompson, *Controversy Between the Puritans and the Stage*, p. 152. Andrewes might have expressed himself still more strongly but for his deference to the King.

[29] *A Pattern of Catechistical Doctrine, and the Whole Succinctly and Judiciously Expounded* (London, 1630), p. 379.

[30] *Ibid.* p. 401. Perhaps owing to Andrewes' personal inclinations, presentments for playing games on the Sabbath continued to be common in the diocese of Winchester after the Book of Sports (P. A. Welsby, *Lancelot Andrewes* (London, 1958), p. 118).

[31] See John Carey, 'Elizabethan Prose', in *English Poetry and Prose, 1540–1674*, ed. C. Ricks (London, 1970), p. 367, for a similar view. See also Sasek, *Literary Temper of the English Puritans*: 'A "puritan" opponent of the stage may be an orthodox Anglican who fought the puritans and, conversely, an active Puritan opponent of the established Church can, in literary history, turn out quite unpuritanical. For instance George Herbert, the loyal

readable of them, in the second part of his *Anatomy of Abuses* (1583) defends episcopacy in a qualified way.[32] He dedicated the first edition of his book to Philip Earl of Arundel, who was under house arrest as a suspected Catholic in 1583 and who announced his conversion in 1584,[33] and can hardly therefore be regarded as a likely Puritan patron in 1582. Nor does Stubbes denounce *all* plays, only such as profane the Sabbath and maintain idle professional players: only six of his two hundred and eight pages deal with plays. In his preface he specifically exempts edifying drama:

> All abuses cut away, who seeth not that some kind of plays, tragedies and interludes, in their own nature are not only of great ancientie, but also very honest and very commendable exercises, being used and practised in most Christian common weals, as which contain matter (such they may be) both of doctrine, erudition, good example, and wholesome instruction; conducible to example of life and reformation of manners. For such is our gross and dull nature, that what thing we see opposite before our eyes, do pierce further, and print deeper in our hearts and minds, than that thing which is heard only with the ears.

Stephen Gosson, himself a not unsuccessful dramatist, was almost certainly hired by the City fathers (as W. A. Ringler has shown) to attack the stage in his *School of Abuse*: and he was not a Puritan either.[34] His attack is full of vivid descriptions of actual scenes in

---

Anglican, was more "puritan" in literary temper than Andrew Marvell, the civil servant of the puritan government' (p. 15).

[32] 'To doubt whether there ought to be bishops in the Churches of Christians is to doubt of the truth itself' (*Anatomy of Abuses*, pt 2, 'Containing the Display of Corruptions', ed. Furnivall (London, 1877–82), p. 101).

[33] *Dictionary of National Biography* [*D.N.B.*].

[34] His sermon, *The Trumpet of War* (1598; *S.T.C.* 12099), is bitterly anti-Puritan, denouncing 'the presbytery', defending the altar, and mocking at predestination. It is dedicated, appropriately, to Richard Bancroft. See also W. A. Ringler, Stephen Gosson (Princeton, 1942). Gosson is so often cited as the typical *Puritan* opponent of plays that it is startling to find how bitterly he attacks 'the new presbytery, couching down at the gates of great persons, with her belly full of barking libels to disgrace the persons of the best men, and the labours of the best learned in the Church of England'. He denounces 'heretics and schismatics' as 'vermin'. It is wrong to try to deal with Presbyterians by conference, toleration, argument in books and sermons – 'one dram of Elleborus would have purged this humour'. Opposition to altars and bishops and the belief in predestination come in for special attack: 'If the preacher come to you with a painted fire, and tell you that all is well, because you be predestinate you shall go to Heaven sleeping, as men carried in a coach without any action or motion of your own, we shall never be gainsaid. But come to you with a true fire, and tell you you must work out

the London theatres, bringing Ovid up to date ('such heaving and shoving, such itching and shouldering to sit by women');[35] but the underlying motive which gave rise to the work is not simply a theological conviction, but includes the practical concern of the City authorities with the Sabbath, absenteeism, law and order, public decency, infection and the danger of sedition.

Gosson found by experience that not all leaders of the militant Protestant cause were hostile to players when without authority he dedicated his book to Sir Philip Sidney, and was 'for his labour scorned, if it be in the goodness of that nature to scorn' (as Spenser put it), and later dazzlingly rebutted in the *Apology for Poetry*. It is not without significance that the two best-known Elizabethan–Jacobean defences of the stage, Sidney's *Apology* and Thomas Heywood's *Apology for Actors*, are both by authors known to have had some Puritan sympathies.

Many of the Puritan preachers who attacked the stage seem to have been concerned primarily with Sunday playing. Thus John Northbrooke (1577) groups plays with dicing and dancing as forbidden on the Sabbath, but would allow them in schools, as long as the profit motive, 'gawdy apparel' and 'wanton toys of love' are excluded. John Stockwood and Nicholas Bound also deal mainly with Sabbath playing, and Bound, in sanctioning lawful recreation on weekdays, does not exclude stage plays.[36] William Perkins' objection was more fundamental, however. He objected to the use of Bible stories on the stage, to making amusement out of the sins of men, and to boys dressed up as girls, and denounced 'lascivious representations of love matters in plays and comedies'.[37] Few would go so far as to stop all school and university plays. In a debate at Oxford William Gager argued that they were allowable, John Rainolds that they were not. Gervase Babington, once tutor to the 2nd Earl of Pembroke's family at Wilton, and later a bishop, thought *all* plays, public and private, should be banned.

On the other hand, the Marprelate pamphlets, the most effective popular Puritan propaganda against bishops, continually use theatre

your salvation with fear and trembling, you begin to murmur' (*The Trumpet of War*, pp. 66, 72, 75, 86).
[35] *School of Abuse*, ed. E. Arber (London, 1868), p. 35.
[36] See Thompson, *Controversy Between the Puritans and the Stage*, pp. 56–80, 106–7.
[37] 'A Golden Chain', in W. Perkins, *Works* (Cambridge, 1603; *S.T.C.* 19647), p. 60.

jokes and allusions, and obviously assume an audience which, like the writer, enjoys a play. Indeed one episcopalian counter-propagandist, in *Martin's Month's Mind*, complained of them that 'the stage is brought into the church, and vices make play of church matters'. 'I think Simony be the bishops' lackey', jeers Martin. 'Tarleton took him not long since in Don John [Aylmer] of London's cellar.'[38] There are several references to Tarleton, to characters in *Ralph Roister Doister* and *Gammer Gurton's Needle*, which would hardly be understood except by readers who went to the plays. There is nothing of the kill-joy about Martin, though he does disapprove of Parson Glibbery of Halstead, who was diverted from his sermon by the arrival of 'the Summer Lord with his May-game, or Robin Hood with his Morris dance'. It is true, however, that some of those Puritans whom Martin calls 'our precise brethren', such as Thomas Cartwright, disapproved of Martin and his 'disordered proceeding'.[39] The popular, plebeian, anti-clerical support for Puritanism certainly existed, but the Puritan gentry and City fathers were uneasy about appealing to it. And a similar feeling must have made many of them distrustful of the popular theatres.

The fear of disorder

The City fathers' main objections to the theatre were, indeed, as much practical as doctrinal. Probably it was not, for most of them, a matter of believing, with Gosson and Rabbi Busy, that disguise is sinful and imitation a form of lying. The Aldermen themselves freely staged shows, plays and masques privately in their own houses. They lavished thousands of pounds on Lord Mayors' pageants to impress Londoners with the wealth and glory of their city, and to preach, through allegorical tableaux, the virtues of industry and thrift. Their objections to the theatre, as set out for example in letters from the Lord Mayor and Aldermen to the Privy Council in 1597, were all related to the ill effects of plays on discipline and order, so necessary and so difficult to maintain in the rapidly and chaotically growing city, with its mass of new-comers, uprooted people and unemployed.

Plays on Sunday were the greatest cause of complaint, since they

[38] *Martin Marprelate* (Menston, 1967), p. 19.
[39] *Marprelate Tracts*, ed. Pierce, pp. 226, 238.

drew people away from sermons. During the week, they encouraged apprentices to absent themselves from work – again, an objection of the most practical kind. They caused traffic jams and spread infection in time of plague: and they gave an opportunity for the unemployed and idle to meet in riotous assemblies. Indeed, unruly apprentices and servants had admitted that they foregathered at stage plays to organise their 'mutinous attempts', 'being also the ordinary places for masterless men to come together'. There were probably more of these 'masterless men' in London than anywhere else – their number was guessed at 30,000 in 1602, and the City authorities were continuously worried about the threat represented by this vast mass of poor and near-poor. As Christopher Hill puts it:

> London was for the sixteenth century vagabond what the green-wood had been for the medieval outlaw – an anonymous refuge. There was more casual labour in London than anywhere else, there was more charity, and there were better prospects for earning a dishonest living...What matters for our purposes is the existence of a large population, mostly living very near if not below the poverty-line, little influenced by religious or political ideology, but readymade material for what began in the later seventeenth century to be called 'the mob'.[40]

The ruling sections, whether in court or city, were always nervous about a form of entertainment which could so easily get out of hand. Their fear of the 'many-headed multitude' reflected itself in the demand to control, to limit and to censor what appeared in the popular theatres. College and Inns of Court plays did not involve the same dangers and animosities – or not to the same degree.[41]

The content of at least some of the popular plays was in any case felt to be demoralising, especially for the young, who when they saw stories of 'unchaste matters, lascivious dances and shifts of cozenage' enacted on the stage were more likely to imitate than to avoid these vices in real life. The argument is still current in relation to television, especially for children: does crime, sex and

---

[40] *The World Turned Upside Down*, p. 33.
[41] When John Preston at Cambridge in 1615 objected to his pupil's appearing in a play presented before King James, it was not necessarily because of a principled objection to all academic drama. The particular play concerned was *Ignoramus*, a bawdy satire on the common lawyers (with whom Preston was closely connected), and on Brakyn, the Recorder of Cambridge, in particular. (See *D.N.B.* on George Ruggle, author of *Ignoramus*, and *Chamberlain Letters*, ed. E. McClure Thompson (London, 1966), p. 132.)

violence on the box act as a substitute outlet for aggression, or a stimulus to do likewise? Any art so popular as theatre in Jacobean times or television today is likely to worry the responsible authorities in a way that *avant-garde* or coterie art does not.

The Sabbatarian City fathers in London seem to have effectively carried their point when in May 1603 the new King issued a proclamation forbidding common plays and similar entertainments on Sunday:

> And for that we are informed there hath been heretofore great neglect in this kingdom of keeping the Sabbath-day. For better observing the same, and avoiding all impious profanation, we do straightly charge and command that no Bear-baiting, Bull-baiting, Interludes, Common Plays, or other like disordered or unlawful Exercises or Pastimes be frequented, kept or used at any time hereafter upon the Sabbath day.

It seems that this prohibition was effective, since there are no statements to the contrary by the Sabbatarian Puritans who had attacked Sunday performances in Elizabeth's time, and who sharply denounced Sabbath-breaking at court under Charles I. The anti-theatre *Refutation* (1615) of Heywood's *Apology for Actors* confirms this when it asks: 'If plays do so much good, why are they not suffered on the Sabbath, a day select wherein to do good?'[42] This is no doubt one reason why the City fathers' attacks on the stage virtually ceased after 1603, since they continued to be fierce upholders of the Sabbath. It was not that the plays got morally better (indeed the amount of bawdy, violence and perversion probably increased), but that the maintenance of the godly Sabbath had always been the City's major concern. With the taking over of the patronage of the companies exclusively by the court and the royal family, further resistance and criticism was no doubt more difficult. But the City fathers had not been afraid to challenge royal support for Sunday playing; and if they were passive now it was probably because their major demand had been met.

Outside London, the opposition of the city authorities in the main towns to performances by touring companies was demonstrably more marked in times of economic crisis. This led to a very rapid decline of the provincial theatre with the growth of economic

[42] G. E. Bentley, 'Sunday Performances in the London Theatres', in Bentley, *The Jacobean and Caroline Stage*, 7 vols. (Oxford, 1968), vii, Appendix B, p. 10.

distress and unemployment in the 1620s, which made the corporations, Puritan or not, very nervous about large assemblies of poor
and hungry people, especially in towns affected by the crisis in the
cloth trade.[43] For example, in Norwich in 1623 the council refused
permission to two troupes of players on the grounds of economic
crisis and fear of disorder ('as well for the cause of the poor whose
work cannot be wanted as for some contagion feared to be begun
as also for fear of tumults of the people').[44] And the Privy Council
endorsed their view, adding that 'the purses of poor servants and
apprentices and of the meaner sort of people are drained and
emptied. . .which pinches so much the more in these times of scarcity
and dearth'.[45]

The authors of the most detailed statistical study of the provincial theatre in these years conclude that the fear of disorder and
the need to maintain production, rather than Puritan ideology,
were the main considerations in the minds of the city corporations.
It was, they believe, the same fear of disorder and possible rioting
that underlay the closing of the theatres by Parliament during the
Civil War. Certainly this was the view taken at the time by Royalist
pamphleteers.

Nor was the worry about the *content* of plays at this time confined to Puritans. Thus Robert Anton in *The Philosopher's Satires*
(1616) attacks Puritans and sectaries as scornfully as Marston or
Jonson, and the 'lustful theatres' as bitterly as Prynne – sometimes
both on the same page.[46] While Puritans are presented as hypocrites,
secret lechers, kill-joys 'spiced with austerest schism', the 'hellish
confluence of the stage' is a great incitement to wickedness, and
women who crowd to see 'Cleopatra's crimes' in the theatre are
encouraged to do likewise.

> Why do our lustful theatres entice
> And personate in lively action vice
>   . . .
> Draw to the City's shame, with gilded clothes
> Such swarms of wives to break their nuptial oaths?

---

[43] Between 1615 and 1619 fewer than 16 per cent of the visits of touring
companies to provincial towns were met with refusal of permission to play.
In 1620–4 the figure rose to 36 per cent, the rise being especially marked in
clothing towns and ports hit by the crisis (L. Salingar *et al.*, *Les Comédiens
et leur Publique en Angleterre, 1520–1640*, in Jacquot (ed.), *Dramaturgie et
Société*, pp. 570–1).
[44] *Ibid.* p. 571.   [45] *Ibid.* p. 572.   [46] See p. 46 of the 1616 edn (*S.T.C.* 686).

Again, Richard Brathwaite, known as an anti-Puritan satirist,[47] and reputed to have fought as a Royalist in the Civil War, declares in *The English Gentleman* (1630), dedicated to Thomas Viscount Wentworth, that players who become involved in matters of state or cast 'aspersions on men of eminent rank and quality...deserve no better censure than as they whipped, so to be whipped themselves for their labour; for they must know that some things are privileged from jest'; namely 'religion, matters of state, and great persons'.[48] Moreover, while moderate playgoing does no harm, excess in it may leave 'not a minute's space for devotion'; witness the sad case of the young woman so corrupted by daily playgoing that on her death-bed she called not on God but on Hieronymo.[49]

It has been customary to regard Puritan doctrinal objections as the primary reason for opposition, and the authorities' practical worries about plague, riots and traffic jams as mere excuses. In fact, it appears often to have worked the other way round. It was the City, with strong practical reasons for restricting playing, which paid Stephen Gosson and Anthony Munday to think of the theoretical arguments and find authority for them in the Bible and the Ancients. Later, as the court, the exclusive patron of theatrical companies, became increasingly remote in its standards and attitudes from the majority of citizens, the conflict of codes (expressed among other things in customary Sunday plays at court) hardened into the familiar clash of principle around Prynne's *Histriomastix*. But that did not end the tradition of radical criticism in the popular theatres.

Neither did it end the use of drama by opposition elements in ruling circles to express social criticism. The Inns of Court replied to *Histriomastix* by presenting a masque of their own, arranged by a committee of members including Noy, Selden, Edward Herbert and Bulstrode Whitelocke, the last of whom left an account of the show. The procession passed through the City on its way to

---

[47] Author, *inter alia*, of the doggerel satire *Barnabee's Journal* (1638, *S.T.C.* 3556), which includes the well-known anti-Sabbatarian jeer:

> To Bambury came I, O profane one!
> There I saw a puritane one,
> Hanging of his cat on Monday
> For killing of a mouse on Sunday.

[48] *The English Gentleman* (1630; *S.T.C.* 3563), p. 192. A similar combination of bitter anti-Puritanism and hostility to the theatre is found in Anton, *The Philosopher's Satires*, pp. 46, 47.

[49] *English Gentleman*, p. 195.

Whitehall headed by a hundred gentlemen nobly attired; these were followed by civic Puritans, comic antimasquers, including 'most popular of all with the groups of civic Puritans who lined the streets, a masque satirising those projectors who begged the illegal and unpopular patents from the king', and then the rest of the masque proper.[50] Although the main object of this masque was to demonstrate (to the tune of £21,000) the loyalty of the lawyers to the Crown and its dramatic entertainments, Edward Herbert and Whitelocke, among its leading spirits, were later identified with the Parliamentary opposition.[51]

Censorship

I

Whatever the City may have thought about plays, the actual censorship after 1603 was carried out on behalf of the court by the Master of the Revels (who held office under the Lord Chamberlain), and had undoubtedly a great influence on what was staged. For every prosecution that we know about, for every manuscript examined that has been cut or altered by the censor or under his direction, there must be many similar cases of which no record survives. But more important, this strict control and supervision must have been in the minds of players and writers, who would usually accept it as one of the limitations under which they had to work, and avoid writing or producing what they knew would get them into trouble.

Control and censorship on behalf of the Crown in Jacobean times was much tighter than it had been under Elizabeth.[52] Within three or four years of his coronation James had virtually taken into royal hands the control of players, plays, dramatists and theatres. Those few great nobles (barons and above) who had formerly been allowed to license players to travel were now deprived of that right, and all the companies that remained came under direct royal patronage: the Chamberlain's Men became the King's; the Admirals' and the Earl of Worcester's, Prince Henry's and Queen Anne's; the

[50] See Thompson, *Controversy Between the Puritans and the Stage*, pp. 179–80.
[51] I am indebted to Ruth Spalding for this reference.
[52] Though in the later 1590s there was already trouble over *Richard II* and *The Isle of Dogs*.

Chapel Children, the Children of the Queen's Revels; and the Children of St Pauls, the Children of the King's Revels. Glynne Wickham has emphasised the effects of this change on the quality of the drama:

> The actors and their playmakers, as royal servants, could scarcely avoid aligning the subject-matter of their plays in future to suit the tastes of their patrons and protectors in preference to that of humbler citizens.[53]

It was not merely a matter of patronage, but also of the direct censorship of kinds of material which would have been acceptable in the 1590s. Investigating the censorship in the stricter sense, G. E. Bentley shows that while only a small number of the 2,000 or more plays produced in the fifty years before the Civil War directly offended, the effects were much more far-reaching. Few were punished as severely as William Beeston, manager of the company at the Phoenix in 1640, who was imprisoned and dismissed from his post, but all managers and dramatists knew that such punishments were within the censor's power:

> The inhibitions which such knowledge provided are not difficult to imagine. They affected what the professional dramatist wrote for the companies; they affected what the managers and the sharing members were willing to accept; and they affected what the book-keeper did to the MS. as he worked on the prompt copy and the players' sides.[54]

It was, of course, almost exclusively a *political* censorship. Except for the specific ban on oaths and profane language introduced in 1606, the censor was scarcely concerned with questions of morality or good taste. At incest, adultery, rape, sexual invective and innuendo, or Rabelaisian sex-and-lavatory clowning he seems not to have turned a hair.

The *power* to censor in this way had of course existed under Elizabeth: but as long as there was a degree of harmony between Crown, aristocracy, gentry and City, it was seldom used. Towards the end of Elizabeth's reign divisions were opening, and they became much sharper under James, who never commanded the loyalty and respect Elizabeth had, and who seems to have found the freedom of the drama as puzzling and offensive as he did the

---

[53] Wickham, *Early English Stages*, ii, pt 1, p. 94.
[54] Bentley, Regulation and Censorship, in *Profession of Dramatist in Shakespeare's Time*, p. 196.

curious institution of Parliament in his new kingdom. Wickham, indeed, attributes decadence in the drama mainly to the operation of the censorship, which prevented (though perhaps less completely than he suggests) the serious treatment of political, moral and religious issues:

> The most topical of all subject matter, the relation between Church, State and individual human being – the topic which had kept English drama so vividly in touch with life in the Tudor era – was the very material which the whole machinery of censorship and control had been devised to suppress. And suppressed it most surely was. The decadence in Jacobean and Caroline dramatic writing. . .is thus, in my view, due in far greater measure to the censorship (in the widest sense of that word) as exercised by early Stuart governments than to any particular failing in the writers themselves.[55]

The group of prosecutions in the early years of James' reign affected, as it happens, largely though not exclusively the private, indoor theatres. *Sejanus* was a Globe play, but *Philotas, Eastward Ho!, Isle of Gulls, Bussy d'Ambois, Charles Duke of Byron* were first put on by the Children's companies in the private theatres. Thus if the later drama no longer treats deeply or satirically the moral responsibilities of kings and subjects, this cannot have been simply because of a narrowing of the audience by the exclusion of many of its poorer members; for it seems from these plays that the Black-friars audience, with its greater proportion of lawyers, courtiers and gentlemen up from the country (including MPs), was also interested in these matters. It must, in fact, be much more a question of what the censor could be expected to allow: and that in turn was narrowed by the growing lack of confidence by City and country in the integrity and dignity of monarch and court. In the 1620s, and especially in the 1630s, we shall find these conflicts with censor and state power becoming more serious, the challenge in the popular theatres much more direct.

II

The dramatists and companies did not, however, immediately or completely acquiesce in the status of 'royal slaves'. They tried to go on dealing with 'the most topical of all subject matter, the relation

[55] *Early English Stages*, ii, pt 1, p. 94.

between Church, State and individual human being', so far as they could. But very early in the new reign it became obvious that anything in the nature of the relatively free comment we find in the history plays of Shakespeare in the 1590s would be impossible in the future – at least in normal conditions.[56]

The guiding principles on which Jacobean and Caroline censors worked have been crystallised by G. E. Bentley from a careful analysis of the available deletions in manuscripts and early texts, and of prosecutions of authors and companies. They were to forbid:
1. Critical comments on the policies or conduct of the court.
2. Unfavourable presentation of friendly foreign powers or their sovereigns, great nobles, or subjects.
3. Comment on religious controversy.
4. Profanity and oaths (from 1606 onwards).
5. Personal satire on influential people.

To these may be added a ban on the representation of any ruling sovereign, even a favourable one.

To get into trouble for criticising court conduct and policies it was not necessary to criticise directly, or even intentionally. If the action of the play suggested to the censor an analogy with contemporary politics he would intervene, even though the dramatist might protest that the parallel had never occurred to him.[57] It was for analogies of this kind that Jonson was called before the Privy Council over *Sejanus* – and this although the play keeps very close to the Latin sources it is dramatising in Tacitus and Suetonius.[58] Some of the passages which gave particular offence were cut out in the first printed text, the Quarto; but one of them at least was left, no doubt by accident, and altered by Jonson only in the Folio. The Quarto makes Silius complain of the ingratitude of the Emperor in terms which reflect on 'princes' in general. The original reads:

[56] The conditions at the time when Middleton's *A Game at Chess* was performed in 1624 were, of course, anything but normal. See below, pp. 151–5.
[57] This happened over Shakespeare's *Richard II*, a performance of which was actually commissioned by Essex's friends for the night before he rode through London to rouse citizen support for his cause: the analogy must have been felt as compelling by the conspirators, if not by the audience. The play, however, was an old one, so the company were able to convince the authorities that they had intended no topical reference, and to avoid punishment. But Queen Elizabeth had been seriously offended by what she certainly regarded as subversive. 'I am Richard II, know ye not that?' she said to Lambarde.
[58] See Jonson, *Works*, ed. C. H. Herford and P. and E. Simpson, 11 vols. (Oxford, 1925–52), ix, pp. 587–91; ii, pp. 4–5.

> So soon all best turns
> With princes, do convert to injuries
> In estimation, when they greater rise
> Than can be answered. Benefits, with you,
> Are of no longer pleasure, than you can
> With ease restore them; that transcended once,
> Your studies are not how to thank, but kill.
> It is your nature to have all men slaves
> To you, but you acknowledging to none.   (III.302–10)

In the Folio the opening lines read:

> So soon, all best turns
> With doubtful princes, turn deep injuries. . .

which is clearly specific and not applicable to *all* princes.

Jonson complained that he had been 'accused to the Lords. . .by great ones' on the basis of lines taken out of their context, 'which read entire, would appear most free'. There are certainly plenty of lines in *Sejanus* which informers could seize on.

> *Cordus.* Rarely dissembled.
> *Arruntius.* Prince-like, to the life.   (I.395)

> The prince, who shames a tyrant's name to bear,
> Shall never dare do anything but fear.
> All the command of sceptres quite doth perish
> If it begin religious thoughts to cherish.   (II.178)

> Excused
> Are wiser sovereigns then, that raise one ill
> Against another, and both safely kill.   (III.656)

However, the context in this case was about as dangerous as the particular lines. The central characters – Tiberius, the indolent, self-indulgent, deceptively shrewd emperor, and Sejanus, his homosexual lover and unscrupulous favourite – were an offence in themselves. The representation of a decadent Rome under the emperors, declined from her former republican and warlike virtues, burning the historian's books, riddled with spies and yes-men, could all too readily be made into a parallel.[59]

In 1605 Samuel Daniel was summoned before the Privy Council over the publication of *Philotas* (which had been staged by the Queen's Revels' boys the year before), to explain the resemblance

---

[59] It is noteworthy that the initiative for the prosecution, according to Jonson, seems to have come from the Earl of Northampton, a leading member of the Howard family and a Spanish pensioner.

between his tragedy of the general who conspired against Alexander and the trial and execution of the Earl of Essex. Cecil, who had led the prosecution of Essex, and Mountjoy, who had been on friendly terms with the Essex group, both resented the analogy they saw in the play. Daniel defended himself by arguing that he had written the first three acts before Essex's rebellion and never meant to refer to that event; he wished Essex's faults might now be forgotten and his virtues remembered. But as well as the parallel between Essex and Philotas, the play also contains (especially in the last two acts, to which Daniel's excuse could hardly apply) very sharp denunciations of the arbitrary power of monarchs, who tyrannise openly in despotisms, but covertly even in 'free' countries like Greece – or England. Thus in the chorus which introduces the final act a Greek and a Persian comment acidly on the condemnation (after torture) of the noble Philotas. The Persian wonders why Alexander should trouble to go through the formality of a trial, since it is obvious that the man is to be condemned anyway:

> *Grecian.* Ah, but it satisfies the world, and we
> Think that well done which done by law we see.
>
> *Persian.* And yet your law serves but your private ends.[60]

The Grecian defends Alexander for joining in the trial himself, rather than staying above it like a god, as Persian monarchs do:

> *Grecian.* Where Kings are so like gods, there subjects are not men.
>
> (p. 148)

But he too condemns the execution of Philotas:

> The wrath of Kings doth seldom measure keep.
> Seeking to cure bad parts they lance too deep. . .
> Great elephants and lions murder least:
> Th'ignoble beast is the most cruel beast. (p. 155)

Daniel seems bitterly to have resented the way he was treated over *Philotas*. That he was a conscious political critic (or the mouthpiece of critics), and not simply a naïve innocent man of letters who did not understand the ins and outs of politics, is pretty clear from the remarkable dedication to Prince Henry which he wrote for the 1605 edition of *Philotas*, the year he lost his job as licenser to the Queen's Children after the trouble over *Eastward Ho!* In this he hopes to see glorious actions from Henry's reign:

> Though I the remnant of another time
> Am never like to see that happiness.

[60] *Philotas*, ed. L. Michel (New Haven, Conn., 1949), p. 147.

He laments the decline of poets since the time of Elizabeth, which
gave birth to more

> Than all the Kings of England did before.

It may be that poetry will never reach the high standard it did in
her 'peaceful reign':

> For since that time our songs could never thrive
> But lain as if forlorn: though in the prime
> Of this new rising season, we did strive
> To bring the best we could unto the time.

He himself, an Elizabethan poet, has never been a scurrilous or
slanderous writer, even against bad men.

> yet naught prevails
> And all our labours are without success
> For either favour or our virtue fails.
> And therefore since I have outlived the date
> Of former grace, acceptance, and delight,
> I would my lines late borne beyond the fate
> Of her spent line, had never come to light.
> So had I not been taxed for wishing well,
> Nor now mistaken by the censuring stage,
> Nor in my fame and reputation fell
> Which I esteem more than what all the age
> Or th'earth can give. But years hath done this wrong,
> To make me write too much, and live too long.

He affirms his zeal

> To kings, and unto right, to quietness
> And to the union of the Commonweal.

And the conclusion is bitter but dignified:

> But this may now seem a superfluous vow:
> We have this peace; and thou hast sung enow,
> And more than will be heard, and then as good
> As not to write, as not be understood.[61]

Prince Henry was well known for his warlike valour, and hopefully looked to by those who objected to the peace with Spain,
whether for religious or economic reasons. This dedication seems
boldly and publicly to assume Henry's sympathy for the poet's
views, to which the court has been hostile – an attempt to exploit
known divisions between the King and the heir to the throne, not
unlike that of the King's Men in 1624.

[61] Dedicatory epistle quoted from 1605 edition (no pagination).

The case of Daniel is particularly interesting, because he was very much under the patronage and influence of Lady Pembroke and her circle at Wilton. He had been tutor there in the 1590s to William Herbert, who became 3rd Earl of Pembroke in 1601, and to whom he had dedicated his *Defence of Rhyme* in 1602. Daniel may well have got his introduction to Queen Anne (and his exceptional post as manager and licenser to her boys' company) through Herbert's influence. Certainly the concern of *Philotas* with the powers and duties of kings, as well as its neo-classical style, is common to plays of the Pembroke circle, notably those of Fulke Greville, *Mustapha* and *Alaham*, both of which, like *Philotas*, can be read as anti-tyrant plays.

From the time of Sidney this Wilton group had had associations with advanced Huguenot political thinkers like Du Plessis Mornay, who had argued (in *Vindiciae Contra Tyrannos*) that in some circumstances a rebellion against an unjust king might be morally right, as long as it was led by the nobility and not by mere commoners.[62] Greville's plays are commonly described as closet drama, not intended for the stage, though their quality of verse and political thinking is admitted to be very fine; but if *Philotas* was staged, so could Greville's work have been. It was not wholly absurd for the Council to see this literary trend as subversive, and perhaps Greville, who was not a hero, was wise to burn his play *Cleopatra* for fear lest another kind of Elizabeth–Essex analogy might be seen in that.

III

Some of the plays which got their authors into trouble were frankly poking fun at individuals and topical goings-on at court. James' indiscriminate dubbing of knights, his fondness for his Scottish favourites and his personal manners were particularly sensitive points. Thus in 1605 Jonson, Marston and Chapman were in prison, threatened with losing their ears and having their noses slit, for publishing *Eastward Ho!*, in which a hard-up fortune-hunting gentleman, setting out on a voyage after treasure in the New World,

---

[62] See I. Ribner, *The English History Play in the Age of Shakespeare* (London, 1957), for relevant extracts from this work. On Sidney's association with Du Plessis Mornay, see J. Buxton, *Sir Philip Sidney and the English Renaissance* (London, 1964), pp. 93, 172, 178.

is untimely wrecked on the Isle of Dogs in the Thames, whereupon
a character on the bank comments in broad Scots,

> *1st Gent.* I ken the man weel, he's ane of my thirty-pound
> knights.   (IV.i.178)[63]

The attractions of the New World have earlier been set out by
Captain Seagull:

> And then you shall live freely there, without sergeants, or cour-
> tiers, or lawyers, or intelligencers, only a few industrious Scots
> perhaps, who indeed are dispersed over the face of the whole
> earth. But as for them, there are no greater friends to English-
> men and England, when they are out on't, in the world, than they
> are. And for my part, I would a hundred thousand of 'em were
> there, for we are all one countrymen now, ye know; and we
> should find ten times more comfort of them there than we do
> here.   (III.iii.40)

These passages were deleted in later editions, and indeed are not
central to the play; they are merely worked in to get a laugh. In
contrast, the topical reference provides the main theme in Day's
scurrilous *Isle of Gulls*, staged by the Children of the Revels around
1605–6. This was at once interpreted as a satire on the King's
Scottish favourites, and some of the actors were apparently committed to Bridewell,[64] though Day defended himself in Star Chamber by arguing that his story was taken from Sidney's *Arcadia* – as
indeed in outline it was. How obvious the allusions to Scotland,
and to the Earls of Dunbar and/or Somerset, were made in performance cannot be judged from the printed text;[65] but even that
seems decidedly risky. Basileus, the Duke, is shown as a passionate
huntsman, fond, like King James, of bathing his hands in the blood
of the deer, and preferring the sound of hounds to that of cannon.
His chief favourite is Dametas, called by the princesses 'the court
surfeit, he that dwells in your eye like a disease in your blood', and
described by a captain as 'a little hillock made great with others'
ruins'. More insultingly still:

> *Basileus.* We know Dametas loves us.

[63] Text of *Eastward Ho!* in Jonson, *Works,* ed. Herford and Simpson, v.
[64] Letter from Sir Edward Hoby, March 1605–6, cited in Introduction to
John Day, *Works,* ed. A. H. Bullen, 2 vols. (London, 1881; repr. with intro.
by R. Jeffs, London, 1963).
[65] Indeed another commentator thinks the allusions are to *Cecil*. For my
purposes, this is not so important as the general aim.

Violetta [his daughter]. As captains and courtiers do old widows,
    for profit and preferment.[66]

Like the homosexual favourite Gaveston in Marlowe's *Edward II*,
Dametas exhibits his evil influence (quite apart from his villainies in
the main melodramatic plot) by going out of his way to prevent
scholars and soldiers (briefly introduced for this purpose) from
gaining preferment:

> I'll have more officers, and one shall be to keep scholars and
> soldiers out of the Court: for they dare not come in the Great
> Chamber for want of good clothes.   (p. 224)

Like James' favourites, Dametas has cornered the court patronage,
and makes a good thing out of his 'patent' to confer titles and
liquidate enemies:

> I could hang thee by my patent if it were granted once. . .It allows
> me 24 knaves, 6 Knights, 10 fools, 13 felons and 14 traitors by
> the year, taken how, when and where I please.   (p. 224)

And his hubristical boast of his own power is much in the manner
of Sejanus':

> Why so, this 'tis to be in authority. Inferior persons, aye, and the
> princes themselves fly from my presence like the chirping birds
> from the sight of the falcon; my very breath, like a mighty wind,
> blows away inferior officers (the Court rubbish) out of my way,
> and gives me a smooth passage: I am the morning star, I am
> seldom seen but about the rising of the sun.   (p. 262)

It is hardly surprising that this time the company and not only
the dramatist were in trouble: they lost Queen Anne's patronage
and had to drop her name from their title. A little later (1608) the
same company, reconstituted under a new manager, were again in
trouble over a play, probably by Marston, in which they reportedly
showed the King out hunting with his favourites, having a gentleman beaten for hurting his dogs, and getting drunk at least once a
day: 'whereupon the King vowed they should never play more, but
should first beg their bread'. This seems to have been the last straw,
and after it the company was disbanded.

   In another notable case of censorship, Chapman's two plays on
Byron (played 1605, published 1608), the French ambassador
complained that the King of France was portrayed on the stage,
and it may be that James was too – once again as a more enthusiastic huntsman than statesman. The printed text of the second part of

66 Day, *Works*, p. 218.

the play, *The Tragedy of Byron*, is heavily cut (the second act is missing) and we do not know what scandalous matter was excised before printing. However, it is certain that this play deliberately reminded the audience of a parallel between Byron's conspiracy and the Essex rebellion; for in the first part, the *Conspiracy of Byron*, the Duke's embassy to Elizabeth is narrated, and much is made of her good advice to him not to be over-ambitious:

> But for a subject to affect a kingdom
> Is like the camel that of Jove begged horns
> For, to aspire to competence with your King,
> What subject is so gross and giantly?   (IV.i.138)

No doubt Daniel and the Queen's Revels' management thought their patronage in high places would be enough to protect them if their more risky plays got them into serious trouble; and here they seem to have miscalculated.

The prosecutions of *Sejanus* and *Philotas* in particular must have made it clear that serious political-historical drama was becoming impracticable. This is the situation that leads eventually to the Beaumont and Fletcher type of court play, in which kings have wives, daughters and mistresses, favourites and rivals in love, but no subjects below the degree of nobility. They make love or war. The one thing we never see them do is govern a country, in the sense that Shakespeare's kings and Roman leaders are seen to do so. The commons may rebel in a cardboard sort of way, as they do in *Philaster*, for example, in favour of a prince victimised by tyranny: but they no longer voice their own point of view as lower orders, their own grievances against their rulers, with the vigour and realism of Jack Cade and his mates in *Henry VI*, or the soldiers in *Henry V*, or the citizens in *Coriolanus*; nor do we find consistent republican opponents of tyranny as we do in *Sejanus*.

A later illustration of the kind of political inhibition under which the dramatists worked is in the manuscript of the *Second Maiden's Tragedy*,[67] licensed by Sir George Buck in 1611 subject to the 'reformations' he made in the text. We do not know exactly how many of the cuts are by Buck himself, but where they are not, 'somebody took the hint and made a pretty thorough expurgation of the text'.[68] In this play a tyrant-usurper attempts by force to

---

[67] Some scholars have attributed this to Middleton.
[68] W. W. Greg, Introduction to edn of *Second Maiden's Tragedy*, Malone Society Reprints (Oxford, 1964), p. xi.

seize a lady betrothed to the rightful ruler, Govianus. She commits suicide, and Govianus returns in disguise to take vengeance on the king. The 'reformations' delete references to the absolute power claimed by the monarch; corruption at court; exploitation of the poor to finance court luxury; and praying in Latin. Thus in one deleted speech the lady's old father tries to persuade her to submit to the king's lust.

> What should a husband do with all this goodness?
>
> . . .
>
> Nor is it fit a subject should be master
> Of such a jewel: 'tis in the King's power
> To take it for the forfeit – but I come
> To bear thee gently to his bed of honours,
> All force forgotten. (p. 24)

Again, marked for deletion is Govianus' speech to a foolish young lord at court:

> You scorn to be a scholar, you were born better,
> You have good lands, that's the best grounds of learning.
> If you can conster but your doctor's bill,
> Pierce your wife's waiting women, and decline your tenants
> Till they're all beggars, with new fines and rackings,
> You are scholar good enough, for a lady's son
> That's born to living. (pp. 3–4)

It is not surprising to find that as kings, in the later drama, commonly lack subjects, so lords normally lack tenants. The spirit of the alterations is seen with almost absurd clarity in the single line of Govianus, returning in disguise as revenger:

> I would not trust at Court and [if] I could choose.

Buck, probably in his own hand, makes the tactful change:

> I would not trust *but few* and I could choose. (p.73)

The reformations here are very like those that someone, whether censor or book-keeper, appears to have made in the original text of Middleton's *Hengist, King of Kent* (see below, Chapter 9).

Like most censorships, the Jacobean one was probably inconsistent, letting allusions slip in one play of a type which was ruthlessly censored in another. But its general direction – court against country – is sufficiently clear.

3. *Middleton as Satirical Journalist*

Unlike Shakespeare or Marlowe, Thomas Middleton began his career as a writer when the moment of national unity between court and middle class, at its strongest around the time of the Armada, was already passing.[1] Militant Protestantism and Puritanism, so influential on Elizabeth's Privy Council in the days of Leicester and Walsingham, had been increasingly excluded from the political establishment since the mid 1590s. The war with Spain, which had made anti-Catholic satire and polemics acceptable in the drama, ended in 1604. By 1604 James I had disappointed the hopes of the Puritans (and the Commons) by rejecting Puritan demands for Church reform and appointing the anti-Puritan Bancroft as his archbishop.

At the same time royal control and censorship of the drama was being tightened up, as we have seen, and the division of the theatres into fashionable indoor houses and plebeian popular outdoor ones was well under way. All this tended to make the expression of militant anti-Catholic, radical or sceptical viewpoints less easy and less direct than it had been when Marlowe wrote *The Massacre at Paris* or the anti-Papal clowning in *Doctor Faustus*. On another side, the festive social harmony which frames Shakespeare's romantic comedies of the 1590s – love and folly at different social levels, clearly separated though in counterpoint, celebrated under the confident leadership of humanist aristocracy and ruler – could no longer be the dominant mode in comic writing in the early years of the seventeenth century.[2]

Thomas Middleton was himself of City origin.[3] His father,

[1] See L. Salingar, 'The Social Setting', in Boris Ford (ed.), *The Age of Shakespeare* (Harmondsworth, 1977), esp. pp. 35–42; R. Weimann, 'The Soul of the Age', in A. Kettle (ed.), *Shakespeare in a Changing World* (London, 1964); A. L. Morton, 'Shakespeare's Historical Outlook', in Morton, *The Matter of Britain* (London, 1966), pp. 36–52.

[2] This harmonising of social levels which are kept sharply distinct is characteristic in plays like *Midsummer Night's Dream*, *Love's Labour's Lost*, *Much Ado*, and *As You Like It*, as it is in other Elizabethan romantic comedies like Greene's *Friar Bacon and Friar Bungay*. Even in Shakespearean comedy this begins to change with *All's Well* and *Measure for Measure*, which create rather than simply follow a fashion.

[3] The best concise source for Middleton's life is still R. H. Barker, *Thomas Middleton* (New York, 1958). Articles of importance citing primary sources

William Middleton, was a Londoner, a bricklayer and builder, though he had a coat of arms and Thomas usually signed himself 'T.M., gent.'[4] William married Anne, daughter of another Londoner, William Snow, in 1574 in the church of St Lawrence Jewry, apparently one of the more Puritan parishes;[5] and Thomas was baptised in the same church in 1580.

William Middleton appears to have been in a fair way of business, for he died in 1586 leaving a total estate of £335; he owned or leased two substantial pieces of property, one in Limehouse with a tenement and a wharf on it, the other adjoining the Curtain Theatre with several tenements built by the owner. One-third of the estate was to be divided between Thomas and his sister Avice. However, Mrs Middleton's remarriage within a year to a grocer and sea-captain, Thomas Harvey, who seems to have been a spendthrift after her money, resulted in a series of disputes and lawsuits about the property. There were further disputes later with Roger Waterer, a clothworker and reputedly a Brownist (whose brother Allan had married Avice and later died of plague).

Thomas went to Queen's College, Oxford, and used part of his inheritance for his education there. He apparently left without taking a degree, possibly returning to London to help his mother in her lawsuits against Waterer.[6] At all events, by 1601 (when he was

include M. Eccles, 'Thomas Middleton, a Poet', *Studies in Philology*, liv (1957), pp. 516–36, and Eccles, 'Thomas Middleton's Birth and Education', *Publications of the Modern Language Association*, 1931, pp. 431–41.

[4] It was, of course, common for the younger sons of the gentry to be apprenticed to City crafts.

[5] John Davenport was later a lecturer there, financed by the vestry. The next-door parish, All-Hallows-in-the-Wall, was likewise Puritan in tendency, its minister Andrew Janeway belonging to a noted family of nonconformist divines. This church was attended by William Hammond, the merchant to whom Middleton later dedicated *A Game at Chess*.

[6] The dramatist's stepfather, Thomas Harvey, is said in one legal document to have obtained a fellowship for him at Oxford, which he lost on returning to London. Middleton's biographer, R. H. Barker, thinks it unlikely that Harvey, 'an ex-grocer living abroad', would have had enough influence; but it is not impossible. Harvey had been on the Roanoke colonising expedition organised by Raleigh and led by Sir Richard Grenville, and had apparently lost whatever he invested in that unsuccessful venture. But he may have had connections with richer and more successful members of the Grocers' Company, for instance with Sir Thomas Myddleton, who acted as treasurer for several of Raleigh's expeditions and was a large investor in them. It is not improbable that Thomas Middleton's City patronage was aided by some such early connection.

twenty-one) he was reported as 'remaining in London accompanying the players' – as so many university-trained men without fortune
or patronage were now doing.

About this time he married Mary Marbecke, who came from a
family of rather more distinction than his own. His new wife had a
strongly Puritan grandfather, John Marbecke, a distinguished
musician who narrowly escaped martyrdom for his faith under
Mary; he was pardoned, possibly because his services as organist
and choirmaster at St George's Chapel, Windsor, made him too
valuable to burn – or perhaps because he had powerful friends.
Later he retired from music to devote himself to theological controversy and propaganda for the Puritan cause. He published the
first English Concordance to the Bible, and other commentaries on
the liturgy and lives of the saints. One of his sons, Dr Roger
Marbecke, was Provost of Oriel College, Oxford, and became the
university's first public orator for life and later chief physician to
the Queen. He sailed with Howard to Cadiz in 1596, and wrote an
account of the expedition which was later printed in Hakluyt's
Voyages. He was presumably on friendly terms with his niece,
Mary Middleton, since he left her a legacy. Another son, Edward
Marbecke, Mrs Middleton's father, was one of the Six Clerks in
Chancery.[7]

John Marbecke's decided Puritan views are most evident in his
A Book of Notes and Commonplaces with their Expositions,[8] a kind
of encyclopedia for the godly, dedicated to the Puritan Earl of
Huntingdon with gratitude for help received. Here he favours
election of bishops, and prefers the title of elder to that of priest.
He is fiercely opposed to altars and the notion of the priest as sacred
mediator between God and man:

> Wheresoever altars be used…they be an occasion of great
> idolatry…Our altars did teach us that He was offered up there
> anew every day for our redemption by a priest, which is most
> false and untrue. And to the end to pluck this opinion out of
> simple people's heads, it ought to be judged of all the King's
> people, as good a deed of the King and his Council to beat down
> and destroy the altars in England, as that King Ezekias did,
> when he brake and bent the brazen serpent.   (p. 33)

---

[7] A co-worker in this office was the father of the Puritan squire Sir Simonds
D'Ewes.
[8] London, 1581; *S.T.C.* 17299.

Predictably, he argues strongly for predestination and for election by divine grace alone, stressing however that 'none living wickedly can have the assurance that he is predestinate to life everlasting' (p. 858). Ministers must be preachers – 'no priest, no more than a dead man is a man, which doth not preach'. His social teaching is likewise on familiar Puritan lines. Alms should be generously given, 'not among such as respect only the belly and make a living or trade throughout their lifetime of begging, but among such as are ashamed to beg'. Mixed dancing is frowned upon, and he especially attacks the sect called 'Nicholaites' who wrongly and 'perversely supposed that the wives among Christians ought to be common' (p. 769).[9] Moreover he includes a special denunciation of the Anabaptists at Munster and of all sects advocating similar subversive communist doctrines.

There is no evidence as to whether later generations of his family held John Marbecke's doctrinal views. We know, for instance, that one of his grandsons, brother to Mary Middleton, was for a time an actor with the Admiral's Men, and it may have been through him that Mary met her husband. (A similar transition occurred in the family of the Elizabethan Presbyterian leader John Field, whose son Nathan became a leading Jacobean player, and author of a well-known defence of the theatre.) Nevertheless, the old Puritan's combination of stern Calvinist predestination, opposition to ceremonial and church hierarchy, and repudiation of the lower-class sects is not so unlike the pattern we find in Middleton's work, both in youthful satires like *Father Hubbard's Tales* and *The Family of Love* and in the later plays. And Middleton also showed that he knew how to work in the Marbecke tradition of Biblical exegesis in his *Marriage of the Old and New Testament*. The chances are that Marbecke and his family would have been known to many of Middleton's Puritan patrons of the older generation, such as Sir Thomas Myddleton, Richard Fishbourne and John Browne (see Appendix A); and respect at least for the Marian Protestant resistance may well have remained in his descendants.

Middleton's early work strongly suggests that he came from a moderate Puritan background.[10] Indeed his first published poem,

---

[9] This appears to be the same sect as the Family of Love, founded by Henry Niclaes, and satirised by Middleton in his play *The Family of Love*, though Marbecke gives a different derivation for the name.
[10] See Appendix A for a summary of his Puritan connections.

The Wisdom of Solomon Paraphrased, is a pious religious exercise, hopefully dedicated (in 1597, when the author was only seventeen) to the Earl of Essex, at that time widely expected to carry on Leicester's role as a noble patron of Puritan writers.[11]

Much more interesting, though still imitative, are the early prose satires, *The Black Book* (a kind of pastiche-sequel to Nashe's *Pierce Penniless*) and *Father Hubbard's Tales* (both published in 1604). The style here has much of Nashe's own grotesque inventiveness and colloquial vigour, and rivals him in its caricature sketches of the underworld of sordid lodging-houses, counting-houses and brothels. Middleton is frank and generous in acknowledging his debt to Nashe and admiration for his work.[12] Yet his tone and social attitudes are quite distinct from Nashe's (and the very similarity of the traditional subject matter of the Seven Deadly Sins makes the differences more striking). Nashe, for all the irreverent ebullience of his manner, is a consistent upholder of the Elizabethan establishment.[13] His main social targets throughout are upstarts, merchants and craftsmen who set up to be as good as lords, city wives who dress above their station and ape the aristocracy, Puritan preachers and seditious sectaries. Middleton's pamphlets place the stress differently, even when handling similar traditional materials. They express rather a radical city contempt for the rich and idle – for courtiers and lawyers and parasitic gentry at least as much as dishonest merchants and moneylenders – and an unforced sympathy for the hardships of small tenant-farmers and the working poor.

[11] Leicester's role as patron and protector of Puritan preachers and writers has been fully discussed by Eleanor Rosenberg in *Leicester, Patron of Letters* (New York, 1955).

[12] In the *Ant and the Nightingale* Middleton criticises Nashe for railing in bitterness, and then begs that 'honest soul' to forgive him for the criticism, since the 'railing' was merely the product of Nashe's pamphlet-war with Gabriel Harvey and his brothers, and they the original aggressors:

> Thou wast indeed too slothful to thyself,
> Hiding thy better talent in thy spleen. . .
> Thy name they bury, having buried thee.
> Drones eat thy honey – thou wert the true bee.
> Peace keep thy soul.

The picture of Nashe's death-bed in *The Black Book* is of squalid poverty, described, despite the grotesque humour, not without pathos. (Extract from Middleton, *Works*, ed. A. H. Bullen, 8 vols. (London, 1885–6), viii, p. 63. All succeeding references to Middleton's works, unless otherwise noted, are from this Bullen edition.)

[13] See J. B. Steane, Introduction to Nashe, *The Unfortunate Traveller and Other Works* (Harmondsworth, 1972).

Puritans and sectaries do not, at this stage, rate a mention at all.

A difference in *emphasis* such as this is naturally difficult to show by selected quotations. All the same, it is worth making the comparison more closely, since it shows the starting point and first example for Middleton's satirical art, and the importance in it of social codes and prejudices which he came to reject.

Nashe was, as his latest editor has put it, a 'social conservative', patronised probably by Whitgift and Bancroft to write against Marprelate and the Puritans. In his famous quarrel with Gabriel Harvey the basic conflict was 'that ancient opposition between the old and the new, between servility and independence, between prejudice and the right of a man to that consideration which his abilities and achievements deserved. And it was the Harveys who stood for the future and Nashe for the past.'[14] Nashe, as a clergyman's son, was a gentleman, and never tired of taunting the Cambridge don Harvey with being the son of a ropemaker and yet not content to remain lowly.

In *Pierce Penniless* (1592) the scholar's special anger at social upstarts is already a dominant theme. Pierce (Nashe himself) is furious that 'base men that wanted those parts that I had', 'carterly upstarts', prosper better than the learned man. 'I called to mind a cobbler, that was worth £500; an hostler that had built a goodly inn, and might dispend forty pound yearly by his land; a car-man in a leather pilch, that had whipped out a thousand pound out of his horse-tail.'[15] And all these mere tradesmen do better than the scholar, now that discriminating noble patrons like Sidney are dead.

Among writers, Nashe's gibes are aimed at those of low origin who presume to criticise the running of affairs. 'All malcontent sits the queasy son of a clothier, and complains, like a decayed earl, of the ruin of ancient houses' (p. 64).[16] And again:

> Is it not a pitiful thing that a fellow that eats not a good meal's
> meat in a week, but beggareth his belly quite and clean to make
> his back a certain kind of brokerly gentleman, and now and then,
> once or twice in a turn, comes to the eighteenpence ordinary,
> because he would be seen amongst cavaliers and brave courtiers,
> living otherwise all the year long with salt butter and Holland

[14] R. McKerrow, in his edn of *Thomas Nashe, Works*, 5 vols. (London, 1904–10), v, p. 67.
[15] *Unfortunate Traveller and Other Works*, ed. Steane, p. 53.
[16] This may refer to Anthony Munday.

cheese in his chamber, should take up a scornful melancholy in his gait and countenance, and talk as though our commonwealth were but a mockery of government, and our magistrates fools, who wronged him in not looking into his deserts, not employing him in state matters.   (pp. 65–6)

The satire here touches more than an individual – it hits at the presumption of all those who are born, in Sir Thomas Smith's phrase, 'to be ruled' (as were the majority in Elizabethan society), and yet claim to have a say in high matters and criticise the bishops and the court.

Thence *Pierce Penniless* passes easily into a searing attack on the devil's 'predestinate children', the Puritans who 'because they will get a name to their vainglory, they will set their self-love to study new sects of singularity, by having their sects called after their names'. Such 'new faith-founders' have filled England with confusion of religion, so that many learned in classical philosophy 'take occasion to deride our ecclesiastical state and all ceremonies of divine worship as bugbears and scarecrows'. All this leads to the rise of sects, like the Anabaptists, the adulterous Familists, 'to conclude some like the Barrowists and Greenwoodians, a garment full of the plague, which is not to be worn before it be new washed' (p. 68).[17] No bishop could inveigh better against the freethinkers and philosophers of the time:

Hence atheists triumph and rejoice...I hear say that there be mathematicians abroad that will prove men before Adam; and they are harboured in high places, who will maintain it to the death that there are no devils.[18]

The anti-Puritan satire, however, is not here central but incidental.[19] What is most striking is Nashe's continual insistence on maintaining social gradation, on 'degree' as the guarantee of honesty and stability:

Beware you that be great men's favourites: let not a servile, insinuating slave creep betwixt your legs into credit with your lords: for peasants that come out of the cold of poverty, once cherished in the bosom of prosperity, will straight forget that

[17] This tract was published in 1592, when Barrow and Greenwood were in jail for heresy, for which they were hanged the next year.
[18] P. 68; the opinions are those attributed by rumour to Raleigh, Marlowe and Hariot, among others.
[19] In *An Almond for a Parrot*, published in 1590 as an answer to Marprelate, and probably by Nashe, it is of course central.

ever there was a winter of want, or who gave them room to warm them. The son of a churl cannot but prove ungrateful, like his father. Trust not a villain that hath been miserable, and is suddenly grown happy. Virtue ascendeth by degrees of desert unto dignity. (p. 72)

In the traditional censure of pride and gluttony, Nashe's poison darts are aimed principally at 'whelps of the first litter of gentility'; at the pride of 'Mistress Minx a merchant's wife' with ideas of dress and coaches above her station; at the over-eating of merchants ('there is no mast [pig-food] like a merchant's table'). Even sloth is emblematised 'like a stationer that I know, with his thumb under his girdle', rather than like a courtier; and the idle young heir is half-jokingly excused, compared with the idle glutton at home, farmer or tradesman:

If my youth might not be thought partial, the fine qualified gentleman, though unstaid, should carry it clean away from the lazy clownish drone. (p. 110)

Of course, the whole tract is based on semi-serious special pleading for Nashe and young men like him – as in the defence of plays against citizen objections, which is its most famous passage. Even here the line of argument chosen is characteristic – the players would be glad not to have among their audience the city youth and apprentices they are accused of corrupting, who behave like hooligans anyway. And as for the hindrance of other trades by plays, 'that is an article foisted in by the vintners, alewives and victuallers, who surmise, if there were no plays, they should have all the company...lie boozing and beer-bathing in their houses every afternoon'.

Middleton's characteristic tone, in contrast to Nashe – it will be found over and over again in his city comedies – is a rough irreverence towards arrogance, hypocrisy and greed, in whatever rank it is found, and often a humane sympathy with the lower sort of people who are its direct victims. The note is struck at once by Lucifer himself in the fine verse prologue to *The Black Book*, where having 'vaulted up so high above the stage-rails of this earthen globe', he explains how he comes up to London every term-time to stir up lawsuits between country men:

So comes it oft to pass dear years befall,
When ploughmen leave the field to till the Hall;
Thus famine and black Death do greet the land,

When the plough's held between a lawyer's hand.
I fat with joy to see how the poor swains
Do box their country thighs, carrying their packets
Of writings, yet can neither read nor write. (p. 8)

Middleton had already had his own harsh experience of the law as the small client sees it.[20] And it is compassion, rather than contempt, that is evoked for the poor farmer-litigants with their 'hard naily soles' wearing out the brass in the aisle of St Paul's. The Devil's catalogue of his heirs, for whom he combs the slums and bawdy-houses of London, has a kind of social impartiality which is very different from Nashe's – smoky gallants, riotous heirs, strumpets, gilded-nosed usurers, panders, brothel-keepers and catchpolls.[21] The tract has plenty of jeers at greedy city characters, at the miserly usurer and the mercer whose thumb is so small that he measures the stuff too short, and at city luxury, 'that smooth glittering devil, satin, and that old reveller, velvet, in the time of Monsieur, both which have devoured many an honest field of wheat and barley, that hath been metamorphosed and changed into white money'. But it is the luxury itself, rather than the presumption of the low-born who indulge in it, that is mocked. The villains of the piece are the greedy rich – whether lawyers, landlords, brokers, merchants or highwaymen.

Wherefore was vice ordained but to be rich, shining and wealthy, seeing virtue, her opponent, is poor, ragged and needy? Those that are poor are timorous-honest and foolish-harmless; as your carolling shepherds, whistling ploughmen, and such of the same innocent rank. (p. 19)

Even in the denunciation of highwaymen there is a side-swipe at the gentry:

These [the thieves] are your great head-landlords indeed, which call the word *robbing* the gathering in of their rents, and name all passengers their tenants-at-will. (p. 20)

There is, moreover, a distinction made between the genuine merchant, who takes risks, and the mere usurer, who gets money for nothing:

I met...an hoary money-master, that had been off and on some six-and-fifty years damned in his counting-house, for his only

---

[20] See P. G. Phialas, 'Middleton's Early Contact with the Law', *Studies in Philology*, lii (1955), pp. 186–94.
[21] Sergeants of the law, who arrested wanted men.

recreation was but to hop about the Burse before twelve, to hear what news from the Bank, and how many merchants were banqrout the last change of the moon.   (p. 29)

And there is as much scorn as pity in the picture of the catchpoll dragging a thriftless gentleman through Fleet Street to Newgate, 'to the utter confusion of his white feather, and the lamentable spattering of his pearl-colour silk stockings' (p. 40).

Father Hubbard's Tales is more independent of Nashe than is *The Black Book*, and in itself a more amusing and better-con-structed piece of satire. The decline of courtly patronage, lamented by Nashe, is here epitomised in the mock-dedication of the tract by one Oliver Hubbard to the 'true general patron...Sir Christopher Clutchfist, knighted at a very hard pennyworth, neither for eating musk-melons, anchovies or caviare, but for a costlier exploit and a hundred-pound feat of arms' (p. 51).[22] It is the meanness of would-be courtly patrons, rather than the corruption of 'upstart' writers, that is pilloried.

A separate preface to the reader (signed 'T.M.') explains that the book is entitled *Father Hubbard's Tales* to avoid the danger of having it 'called in again as the *Tale of Mother Hubbard*'. The reference here is to Spenser's *Mother Hubbard's Tale* (published 1591, but written about 1580), which lampooned the Elizabethan Church and its dumb-dog priests, and especially Burghley and his project to marry Elizabeth to the Catholic d'Alençon. This Puritan satire had been very offensive to Burghley a generation before, and attempts may well have been made at the time to suppress it. Certainly the deliberate reference here suggests that the young Middleton saw himself as continuing this tradition of Elizabethan Puritan satire, patronised by Leicester and Raleigh, against the court and Church establishment – and thus on the opposite side from Nashe.[23] However, neither of these early satires handles

---

[22] The year before, James had knighted more than three hundred persons on his way to London (D. H. Willson, *King James VI and I* (London, 1971), p. 161). By the end of his first year he had created 838 new knights at a fee of £30 a time, and announced that anyone owning land worth £40 a year or more must be knighted or pay a fine.

[23] Middleton in his preface explains that *his* beast-fable ought not to be censored, since he deals neither with ragged bears nor apes (*Works*, ed. Bullen, viii, p. 54). The bear with the ragged staff was the emblem of Leicester, while the ape in Spenser's *Mother Hubbard's Tale* stood for d'Alençon, and the fox for Burghley. Middleton refers again in *The Black Book* to Mother Hubbard, 'she that was called in for selling her working

Church matters, as Spenser had done – perhaps because Middleton took no interest in the subject, or because the vicious repression of the Marprelate writers in the 1590s and the declared hostility of King James to Puritanism made it too dangerous.

There can be no doubt, at any rate, about the tone of radical protest in the tales themselves. *The Ant and the Nightingale* (the alternative title of *Father Hubbard*), like its Spenserian original, has the framework of a beast-fable, and the verse prologue sets its scene in the bad new times. The tales are told by an industrious ant to the nightingale, who has graciously refrained from eating the ant as a spy. The nightingale herself is a distressed princess in disguise, and her mercy proves her royal virtue:

> She did not, as a many silken men,
> Call'd by much wealth, small wit, to judgment's seat,
> Condemn at random; but she pitied then
> When she might spoil: would great ones would do so,
> Who often kill before the cause they know.   (p. 57)

The nightingale confides to the ant how she, who once had palaces and pleasures, is now neglected:

> They that forget a queen soothe with a King;
> Flattery's still barren, yet still bringeth forth.   (p. 60)

The general lines on which the allegory was likely to be read are clear enough. Elizabeth is dead, and her courtiers fawn on the new monarch:

> But regal wisdom knows it is not strange
> For curs to fawn: base things are ever low;
> The vulgar eye feeds only on the show.
>   . . .
> Else would not soothing glosers oil the son
> Who, while his father liv'd, his acts did hate:
> They know all earthly day with man is done
> When he is circled in the night of fate.
> So the deceasèd they think on no more,
> But whom they injur'd late, they now adore.

(pp. 60–1)

For the main part of the pamphlet, the beast-fable is forgotten, as the ant narrates his adventures and worldly disasters in his

bottle-ale to bookbinders and spurting the froth upon courtiers' noses'. In his mind, the anti-court satire seems to have been more important at this stage than the anti-church aspects.

successive changes of shape as ploughman, soldier and scholar – all alike industrious, all put down and exploited by the rich and idle. The story of the ant as ploughman is particularly revealing of Middleton's social attitudes at this time. In its directness and power it is more like Latimer and the Puritan preachers than like Nashe. The ploughman (or copyholder tenant-farmer) tells how once upon a time, though poor enough, he 'had a plough and land to employ it...and for tillage I was never held a truant'. Moreover, for many generations tenants in his district had had 'fair commons for the comfort of the poor, liberty of fishing, help of fuel by brush and underwood never denied', until the death of their old landlord; 'and as soon as he was laid in his grave, the bell might well have tolled for hospitality and good housekeeping'. The young landlord immediately turns away all his old father's servants, and, attended only by a French page and a footman, goes back to enjoy 'wild and unfruitful company about the court of London (whither he was sent by his sober father to practise civility and manners)'.

Soon the tenants are called to London to end their old tenures by custom, and sign new leases for a term of years, for which they must pay fines ('no fine word to please poor labouring husband-men, that can scarce sweat out so much in a twelvemonth as he would demand in a twinkling'). The prodigal heir himself appears in all the finery for which he is mortgaging his inheritance and exploiting his tenants:

His head was dressed up in white feathers like a shuttlecock, which agreed so well with his brain, being nothing but cork, that two of the biggest of the guard might very easily have tossed him with battledores...

His breeches, a wonder to see, were so large and wide withal, that I think within a twelve-month he might very well put all his lands in them; and then you may imagine they were big enough, when they would outreach a thousand acres...All this while his French monkey bore his cloak of three pounds a-yard lined through with purple velvet, which did so dazzle our coarse eyes, that we thought we should have been purblind ever after, what with the glorious aspect of that and his glorious rapier and hangers all bost with pillars of gold, fairer in show than the pillars in Pauls or the tombs at Westminster; besides, it drunk up the price of all my ploughland in very pearl, which stuck as thick upon those hangers as the white measles in hog's flesh.   (p. 69)

The ploughman is asked to make his mark to a legal document transferring the lease to the heir's City creditors, merchant and mercer.

I took the pen first of the lawyer, and turning it arsy-versy, like no instrument for a ploughman, our youngster and the rest of the faction burst into laughter at the simplicity of my fingering: but I, not so simple as they laughed me for, drew the picture of a knavish emblem, which was a plough with the heels upward, signifying thereby that the world was turned upside down since the decease of my old landlord, all hospitality and good house-keeping kicked out of doors, all thriftiness and good husbandry tossed into the air, ploughs turned into trunks, and corn into apparel.   (p. 74)

Another tenant makes his mark by drawing a wild colt, as a comment on the irresponsible young heir. But the joke is lost on the lawyers and mortgagers, 'for they little dreamed that we plough-men could have so much satire in us to bite our young landlord by the elbow'. And so the poor farmers plod home to their wives, to a sad Christmas without carols, wassail or dancing, 'for that one word *fines* robbed us of all our fine pastimes'.

In the next tale the ant is turned into a soldier and fights abroad, where he loses an arm and a leg. The commanders say all their money is 'thumped out in powder', so he returns home with only one month's pay for ten months' service, and, as a special favour, 'a passport to beg in all countries'. But on reaching his home town, 'I was not only unpitied, succourless and rejected, but threatened with the public stocks, loathsome jails, and common whipping-posts, there to receive my pay', and finally with prison – which he escapes by turning back into an ant.

In the third and last tale the ant is transformed into a scholar, a young man much like Middleton himself, setting off to the univer-sity with all his possessions in 'less than a little hood-box, my books not above four in number, and those four were very needful ones too, or else they had never been bought; and yet I was the valiant captain of a grammar-school before I went'. At the univer-sity he becomes 'a poor scholar and servitor to some Londoner's son, a pure Cockney that must hear twice a-week from his mother, or else he will be sick of a University mulligrub'. The rich student spends his time playing tennis, while the poor one reads philosophy and hopes to gain money and fame as a professional writer, if he can but find a patron. He therefore presents a special copy of his poem, beautifully bound, to that same Sir Christopher Clutchfist, with a flattering dedication:

> The book he entertained but, I think, for the cover's sake, because it made such a goodly show on the backside; and some two day after, returning for my remuneration I might espy. . .my book dismembered very tragically; the cover ript off, I know not for what purpose, and the carnation silk strings pulled out and placed in his Spanish-leather shoes; At which rueful prospect I fell down and swounded; and when I came to myself again I was an ant, and so ever since I have kept me.   (p. 108)

The gay self-mockery and exaggeration of this expresses a real bitterness which seems to derive from Middleton's own experience. The poor scholar feels a natural sympathy with other hardworking and exploited people, the 'ants', the bottom of the heap. Middleton's own early attempts to find a steady patron (for example Lord Compton) were apparently unsuccessful. Patrons of unknown writers were not as generous as in Spenser's time, and no doubt he had good reason to leave the university and take to 'following the players', the one field where literary talent could make a living without noble patronage.[24]

Thus in this satire Middleton makes his own first diagram of the Human Comedy. Like Balzac more than two centuries later, he shows feelingly what the growth of the new society meant for those who belong neither to the old nor to the new privileged classes. He is on the side neither of the idle gentry nor of what he sees as parasitic lawyers, moneylenders and merchants. His is, at least in part, the popular view of the industrious labouring people, for whom the greatest period in English dramatic history was also a time of exceptional insecurity, poverty and stress, to be overcome, if at all, only by hard work and thrift. His analysis, then and later, is made within the bounds of that society. We must always be afraid, says the nightingale in the verse epilogue, that our complaints may be 'blabbed' by traitors. On this note of keeping quiet for fear of punishment the work ends:

---

[24] The immediate cause of his leaving was probably to help his mother in a series of lawsuits over her property with his stepfather and brother-in-law. But he may also have felt that a degree would have little value to him without patronage.

Away she flew,
Crying Tereu!
And all the industrious ants in throngs
Fell to their work and held their tongues.   (p. 109)

Compared with Thomas Dekker, with whom he was on friendly terms and with whom he collaborated, Middleton in his satire is drier and more clear cut. One gets the impression that while he too uses traditional material, he understands very well the economic process at work – there is no mystification about money and its workings. Neither is there the censorious attitude to the poor and unfortunate which certain divines like William Perkins enjoined as the right Puritan view.

4. *Early Satirical Comedies*

Middleton found his right medium early. He was writing his first plays not later than 1602, when he was twenty-two, the earliest being two for Henslowe, now lost – *Caesar's Fall, or Two Shapes* and *The Chester Tragedy, or Randal Earl of Chester*. But his success began with the plays, mainly London comedies, that he wrote for the private theatres over the next eight years or so, and it is these that have mainly been quoted as evidence of his anti-citizen and anti-Puritan attitudes.

In his first years as a dramatist Middleton worked mainly for the boys' companies, particularly for the Children of Paul's (for whom he did six plays). This was the only period of his life when he was so closely linked with one company,[1] and perhaps the only time when he may have been dependent entirely, or almost entirely, on his earnings from the commercial theatre for a living.

These early 'city comedies' both followed and helped to create a fashion for unromantic, realistic prose satire, though this does not imply that Middleton was simply imitating what Jonson or Marston had begun, against his own inclinations (in fact his satirical line is clearly though subtly distinguishable from theirs). An irreverent and cynical view of the acquisitive London of his time, where the weak and naive go to the wall and the greedy and ruthless lawyer, merchant and courtier take the profit, is what Middleton was also showing in *The Black Book* and *Father Hubbard's Tales*, where he was not directly tied by a Paul's or Blackfriars audience. There was, indeed, a theatrical tradition of thriftless young heirs, cunning courtesans and ruthless money-men all the way back to Roman comedy; there was a medieval tradition of 'complaint' against usury and luxury and the decay of housekeeping; but there was also a great deal in the dramatist's own experience to make satire on the greed and trickery of the world a congenial form.

[1] Even in these years his plays for Paul's were interspersed with a play or two for the Queen's Revels and one for Prince Henry's Company (Bentley, *Profession of Dramatist in Shakespeare's Time*, p. 35).

It has been suggested that the private theatres tended to an 'anti-citizen' repertory because of their socially superior 'coterie' audience. The boys' audience at the private theatres was indeed to some extent 'select', mainly because the prices were higher than in the open-air public theatres, where penny and twopenny customers formed a large proportion of the spectators.[2] A character describes them in Marston's *Jack Drum's Entertainment* (I.i):

> Ifaith, I like the audience that frequenteth there
> With much applause. A man shall not be choked
> With the stench of garlic: nor be pasted
> To the barmy jacket of a beer-brewer.

To call this a coterie or court audience at this period may, however, be misleading. The typical private-theatre audience included, besides aristocracy and court gentry, lawyers and law students, soldiers on leave and country gentlemen up on business, as well as gamblers, con-men and courtesans (citizens and artisans are less frequently mentioned in the plays and other records).[3] Among them must have been many of the groups most knowledgeably critical of the new court and its ways. Select prices would not keep away the kind of informed people who, as MPs or lawyers, were just beginning to form an alternative focus of power – as the inclusion in the repertory of such allusive pieces as Daniel's *Philotas* and Day's *Isle of Gulls* suggests.[4]

While Middleton's plays for this 'good gentle audience' do not spare greedy or corrupt citizens or merchants, the satire is usually directed not against citizens as such, but rather at the whole acquisitive society of contemporary London and all its social

[2] According to one recent study, the Paul's audience was distinguished at the outset less by wealth than by sophisticated tastes. The minimum entry price there around 1600 was 2d., the same as the gallery at the public theatres, whereas the Blackfriars was charging 6d. in 1604. In some cases the audience may have been invited, and asked to contribute to a collection for expenses (W. Gair, 'La Compagnie des Enfants de St Paul, Londres, 1599–1606', in Jacquot (ed.), *Dramaturgie et Société*, pp. 655–74).

[3] In the 1630s regular habitués of the private theatres included future Parliamentarians like Bulstrode Whitelocke and the Mildmay brothers, Anthony and Humphrey, grandsons of the Puritan founder of Emmanuel College and brothers of Sir Henry, judge at the trial of Charles I.

[4] For example, the Paul's children in 1599 had presented the seizure of Turnholt from the Spaniards by Prince Maurice of Nassau, in a play by an unknown author. Rowland Whyte reported to Sir Robert Sidney that the play used 'all your names that were at it, especially Sir Francis Vere's and he that played that part hath got a beard resembling his' (Gair, 'La Compagnie des Enfants de St Paul', p. 88).

groupings, including courtiers and gentry. Everyone is on the make, everyone out for himself: the atmosphere is more like that of *The Jew of Malta* than the Cheapside of *The Shoemaker's Holiday*.

To see this as 'anti-citizen' is too simple. But it is, of course, true that there is none of the straightforward glorification of merchant heroes and patriotic citizen ideals that, say, Heywood was putting into a 'popular' play like *If You Know Not Me You Know Nobody* about the same time. There the great merchant Gresham is as much the hero as Queen Elizabeth is the heroine. The sheer scale of his wealth is held up for admiration, when he pays the King of Barbary £60,000 for the sugar crop, loses the lot when the next king breaks the contract, and drinks off the pearl sent him as a consolation prize in a health to the Queen.

> I do not this as prodigal of my wealth,
> Rather to show how I esteem that loss
> Which cannot be regained, a London merchant
> Thus tread on a King's present.[5]

Gresham is no less admirable in using his wealth for the public good, building Gresham's College and the Royal Exchange (compared with which St Mark's Square at Venice is 'but a bauble'). His friend Hobson, another model merchant, who prides himself on being plainspoken, insists on lending the Queen four times the money she asks without security.

> Aye, by this hand, Queen Bess, I am old Hobson,
> An haberdasher, and dwelling by the stocks.
> When thou see'st money with thy grace is scant,
> For twice two hundred pound thou shall not want.
> *Queen Elizabeth.* Upon my bond.
> *Hobson.*   No no my sovereign,
> I'll take thy own word without scrip or scroll.   (1. 2086)

Following which Hobson makes a poor honest debtor master of his hospital, Parry's plot to assassinate the Queen fails, Sir Francis Drake beats the Armada, and everyone including the Earl of Leicester lives happily ever after.

There is here a sizeable element of nostalgia for a golden past, only partly mythical, in which relations between Crown and City were based on deep mutual respect and trust, and Elizabeth's

---

[5] *If You Know Not Me*, ed. M. Doran (Malone Society Reprints, Oxford, 1935), 1.1559.

ngland was the terror of Spain. By 1605, when the play was per-
ormed, Queen Elizabeth's debts had descended to James, whose
extravagant court was rapidly increasing them, and the problem of
royal finances was less easily solved.[6] Although Elizabeth's reign
is idealised by Heywood, there had been a real change of relations
between monarch and merchant, monarch and citizens, compared
with 1588. The play dramatises a pattern of feeling which is passing,
if not past; Middleton is not just more satirical and cynical, but
more up to date.

II

Middleton's city comedies, like much of the major drama of the
period, present a society changing from one regulated by inherited
status to one ruled increasingly by the power of money and capital,
with much greater social mobility, and hence with an increasing
sense of opportunity and insecurity. Conflicts between merchant
and gentry, City and courtier, lawyer and client, had their roots in
the social reality of the time, and the plays are full of them.

It is true that Middleton's purpose is not documentary, in a
naturalistic sense. A play is not a photograph but a highly selective,
constructed picture which attempts to make sense and pattern of
the confusion of life. His plots and characters are conceived as
typifying the deeper forces at work in Jacobean London, rather
than photographically recording.[7] The merchant's greed, the heir's
extravagance and gullibility, are singled out and exaggerated to
bring out the moral point – just as Gobseck's greed or Hulot's
gullibility are in Balzac. This is not only because the characters
derive partly from earlier morality or interlude plays (which, after
all, had originally derived *their* embodiments of the sins of lechery
or avarice from real people), but because the drama, especially
where it makes a social comment, and handles a large cast of

---

[6] The 1604 session of Parliament had refused to vote James a subsidy, and
the customs had been leased out to three businessmen for a rent of £112,000
a year. The remaining deficit of the Crown had to be financed by loans at
10 per cent, but the amount required was far beyond the resources of the
London money market. Only a few very rich merchants (including the
customs farmers) were able to lend on this scale, and the debt continued to
increase (Russell, *Crisis of Parliaments*, pp. 271–3).
[7] Brian Gibbons, *Jacobean City Comedy* (London, 1968), ably develops this
point in relation to Marston, Jonson and Chapman as well as Middleton.

characters, has to operate with clear-cut simplifications for comic impact. This makes a kind of working model of a social and economic world, fast-moving and entertaining as actuality is not, yet disclosing like a diagram what makes the wheels go round.

Nevertheless, the element of medieval type-casting in terms of the seven deadly sins can easily be overstated. Quomodo in *Michaelmas Term* may owe something dramatically to the comic vice in the morality play, but he is probably directly modelled on a particular contemporary swindler. Anyone who reads the contemporary newsletters collected in Birch's *The Court and Times of James I* or the letters of John Chamberlain will find Middleton's world of rich widows and needy fortune-hunters, 'crazy' old men and impatient heirs, familiar enough.

The realism here is purposeful and critical, rather than a passive reflection of the world. Middleton's moral realism is slightly unusual, however, in presenting *all* social groups and their codes of behaviour with irreverent scepticism. The 'traditional morality' of social subordination to hereditary aristocracy and gentry gets little more respect from him than the 'New Men's' morality of doing as one likes with one's own and making wealth the means to rise in the social scale. While usury is a form of avarice, so is the gentry's resource of rack-renting.

As the automatic assumptions about 'degree' are weakened, and there is no longer felt to be a noble traditional order to reassert, Middleton moves away from the kind of endings in which praise and blame are justly awarded by some kind of impartial court or Providence (*Phoenix, Michaelmas Term, Your Five Gallants*) to those where the cleverest rogues triumph over the rest, with no nonsense about merit (*A Trick to Catch the Old One, A Mad World, My Masters, A Chaste Maid in Cheapside*). In unsettled times it is difficult for the dramatist to organise his comedy round a single standard or norm of acceptable civilised behaviour. The 'man of sense' as we find him in Molière, for example, by whom the deviations of silly or vicious characters can be measured, is not typical of Jacobean comedy – and certainly not of Middleton's mature work.

III

The Phoenix (perhaps written 1603–4) is one of the few of Middleton's plays that does suggest a possible bid for court interest, and it was apparently performed before King James.[8] As a play it is experimental, a mixture of conventional and autobiographical episodes, but with impeccable political framework and moral. All the same, the didactic form of 'advice to the ruler' hardly seems to suit Middleton; all the vigour is in the criticism of everyday life.

The design of the play assumes good and bad factions at court contesting for mastery. The virtuous young prince, Phoenix, sent by his old father the Duke to travel for the good of his education, suspects a sinister design in this. The Duke may die at any time, and the plan has not been made by his wise counsellors, but by 'wild' favourites who want to get the rightful heir out of the way. Phoenix decides, therefore, to travel in disguise through his own territories, with one faithful friend, and thus educate himself in what really goes on. Through this traditional device the vices of the age can be shown like those of a morality play, with Phoenix acting as presenter and commentator.[9] As in *Measure for Measure*, the presence of the prince in disguise reassures the audience that nothing too dreadful will happen to the good characters, and frees it to enjoy the scheming and duping of rogues and gulls (who in this play are social types, rather than 'humours', embodiments of single qualities).

One of the points, however, in which Middleton (like Jonson and other Jacobean dramatists) most obviously differs from Shakespeare is his greater emphasis on money and its importance in the state.[10] When the Duke disguises himself in *Measure for Measure*, it is to check on the misuse of power by lust:

> Then shall we see,
> If power change purpose, what our seemers be.

---

[8] The title-page of the Quarto says it was. E. K. Chambers thought 'the only available date' for it at court was February 1604 (*Elizabethan Stage*, iii, p. 439).

[9] The idea is a very old one: we find Harun al-Rashid so disguised in the *Arabian Nights*. This kind of story has been especially popular with the poor of pre-industrial cities, whose political helplessness made them look to a good king (if he could but be separated from evil counsellors) against the rapacity of the new city rich. (See E. J. Hobsbawm, *Primitive Rebels* (Manchester, 1971), ch. VII.)

[10] Shakespeare relies, by and large, rather little on money as a motivating force: the main instances to the contrary being *The Merchant* and *Timon* (the evolution of attitude between the two is significant). Still, Iago, though aiming at rank, needs Roderigo's money: and Richard II's financial troubles prophetically foreshadow those of Charles I.

But though there are two memorable confrontations with a judge, comic with Escalus, tragic with Angelo, bribery in terms of money never comes into the matter. Middleton's Prince Phoenix from the outset expects to find the social fabric rotted by money, and indeed he does:

> *Phoenix.* So much have the complaints and suits of men, seven, nay, seventeen years neglected, still interposed by coin and great enemies, prevailed with my pity, that I cannot otherwise think but there are infectious dealings in most offices, and foul mysteries throughout all professions.
>
> For oft between King's eyes and subjects' crimes
> Stands there a bar of bribes. The under office
> Flatters him next above it, he the next. . .   (I.i.105)

The first piece of corruption the Prince uncovers has, as it happens, a direct analogue in Middleton's personal life.[11] The mother of Phoenix's faithful friend Fidelio has recently married a sea-captain, and Fidelio wants to find out how she is being treated. The mother has not disgraced herself by this match, says the Prince:

> If he be good, and will abide the touch;
> A captain may marry a lady, if he can sail
> Into her good will.   (I.i.163)

But the captain turns out a brute who would make any woman's life a misery. Having squandered his virtuous wife's money and got into debt, he resents being tied down by marriage; he arranges to sell her to the vicious courtier Proditor, invest the proceeds in a plundering expedition, and go back to sea. In a splendidly satirical scene Fidelio, disguised as a scrivener, reads out the legally itemised deed of sale of his mother, while the captain counts his gains – of which the two young men soon relieve him, and pack him off to sea again.

The whole thing reads like a parody of the behaviour of Middleton's own seaman stepfather Thomas Harvey, who seems to have been just about as mercenary as the captain in the play, and involved Mrs Harvey and her children in endless lawsuits as he tried to get control of her property, though the dramatist's mother, less passive and more ruthless than Fidelio's, did manage to keep hold of some of it and force him out of the country. At all events, this is Middleton's first and most brutal treatment of widow-hunting and property marriage, a subject which he had emotional as well as satirical

[11] See Phialas, 'Middleton's Early Contact with the Law', pp. 186–94.

reasons to return to many times in both comedy and tragedy.[12]

Courtiers and city wives are shown, with even-handed justice, as using and corrupting one another. The jeweller's wife, whose husband is rich and elderly, keeps a hard-up knight as her lover – both for sexual enjoyment and social advancement. Their mode of greeting in the play sums up their relationship:

Knight. My sweet Revenue.

Jeweller's wife. My Pleasure, welcome.

The laughter is (as usual in Middleton even at this early period) nicely balanced between the two social groups. The knight is introduced to the lady's father, the corrupt Justice of the Peace Falso:

Falso. Daughter, what gentleman might this be?

Jeweller's wife. No gentleman, sir; he's a Knight.

Falso. Is he but a Knight? troth, I would a' sworn had been a gentleman. (I.vi.148)

And Falso makes the same mistake again later:

I cry your mercy, sir; I call you gentleman still; I forget you're but a knight; you must pardon me, sir.

Knight. For your worship's kindness – worship! I cry your mercy, sir; I call you worshipful still; I forget you're but a justice.

(II.iii.3)

The ladder of degree is shaken indeed, and the jokes about James' indiscriminate handing-out and sale of titles are only one symptom of it. Increasingly the traditional labels of rank and status are losing their reality. The most outrageous case is Falso himself, a true Watergate justice of the peace, much too peaceful to arrest a criminal if he gets his bribe. He is too old to be a highwayman in person now, but looks back nostalgically to his career in that line:

I have been a youth myself. I ha' seen the day I could have told money out of other men's purses. . .I remember now betimes in a morning, I would have peeped through the green boughs, and have had the party presently, and then to ride away finely in fear; 'twas e'en venery to me, i' faith, the pleasantest course of life! one would think every woodcock a constable, and every owl an officer. But those days are past with me; and, a' my troth, I think I am a greater thief now, and in no danger. I can take my ease,

---

[12] Wife-selling was not, however, all that uncommon. 'Many actual transactions of this kind seem to have taken place', says K. V. Thomas in 'The Double Standard', *Journal of the History of Ideas*, xx (1959), no. 2, citing evidence from H. W. V. Temperley and others.

sit in my chair, look in your faces now, and rob you; make you
bring your money for authority, put off your hat, and thank me
for robbing of you.   (III.i.59)

Now, when his own men are brought before him for taking purses,
he first tries to get them acquitted, and then, to be 'as cruel as you
can wish', locks them up in his own house in the charge of their
fellow gangsters so that they can escape at leisure. It is the same
Falso who, as guardian to his niece, refuses to approve her marriage,
so that he can keep her dowry and sleep with her himself.

Is not a husband a stranger at first? and will you lie with
a stranger before you lie with your own uncle?   (IIi.iii.65)

This is farce and not heavy moralising – the disreputable Falso
has something of the good humour and ready answers that we relish
in Falstaff. But the satire on the law in the play is sharp-edged
none the less, especially in the character of Tangle, a kind of
envenomed version of Scott's Peter Peebles, who has been to law so
much himself that he knows all the terminology, and can offer bad
advice to country clients for money, which he then ploughs back
into lawsuits.

A time of social mobility and rapid land turnover was necessarily
a time of much litigation, and a degree of prosperity for lawyers
which mystified their gentry and citizen clients. Middleton was
never a law student or law-writer, like Scott or Dickens, but as a
boy he had seen only too much of the law, and since his wife's
father was one of the Six Clerks in Chancery he may have had
access to expert advice when he needed it; at all events, Tangle's
ravings are boringly technical.

A more serious and melodramatic note is struck at the climax,
when the wicked courtier Proditor bribes the disguised Prince to
kill the Duke his father.

Proditor. Does not the sky look piteously black?
Phoenix. As if 'twere hung with rich men's consciences.   (V.i.9)

The plot and its failure are, however, roughed in rather than
dramatically developed.[13] In the final unmasking, royal wisdom is
vindicated as the Prince exposes all the sinners. Proditor, the traitor,
is banished. The rest lose their ill-gotten gains, and, one hopes,

---

[13] This may indicate merely that the dramatist wished to keep the play a
comedy, and saw this episode as a logical rounding-off. But it may be also
that any fuller treatment of conspiracy ran the risk of offending some great
man by an imagined allusion (as Jonson did in *Sejanus*).

repent, while the wise young Prince takes over from his ageing father the responsibilities of the state. It may even have added to the point, for some of the original audience, that King James, like the Duke in the play, had a promising young son, Prince Henry, who was reputed to be more discerning in his choice of friends, and a better hope for the future of the realm.[14]

[14] W. Power ('Thomas Middleton vs King James I', *Notes and Queries*, ccii (Dec. 1957), pp. 526–34) suggests that the ageing Duke is meant to be identified with Elizabeth, Phoenix with King James, and Proditor, the villain, with Raleigh, recently found guilty of treason. This seems to me not only not proven (as most such identifications must be) but unlikely: (1) It would be difficult for the audience to guess at sight that a live duke was meant to represent a dead queen and a young prince a middle-aged king. If we are going in for identifications, Phoenix would be much more readily identified with Prince Henry, who, as it happens, was a supporter of Raleigh's – 'who but my father would keep such a bird in a cage?' In fact the customary ban on staging living sovereigns prevents such ready assumptions either way. The point was probably intended to be much more general. (2) Proditor as Raleigh does not fit at all well with what we know of Middleton's political sympathies at this time. He was moderately Puritan or reform-party in his origins and sympathies, as we know from (*a*) his family connections, (*b*) the dedications of his early poems and prose satires to Essex and Lord Compton, (*c*) above all, by his deliberately making himself the heir to Spenser's satire against abuses in court and Church in *Mother Hubbard's Tale* (see above, p. 57). To a young man with this attitude, Raleigh would more likely appear as a victim of intrigues by his enemies (as of course *A Game at Chess* assumes later). One might offer Cecil or Northampton as Proditor if one were determined to find a model. But the whole method of trying to establish detailed correspondences seems to me questionable.

5. How Anti-Puritan are Middleton's City Comedies?

I

Middleton has often been assumed to be fundamentally anti-Puritan on the evidence of his city comedies. But the ridicule of Puritans so common in the Jacobean drama may perhaps exaggerate how unpopular they were with the audience (or the dramatists, for that matter). Religious hypocrisy and pompousness has always been a rich source of humour, from Chaucer's Monk and Friar to Wilde's Canon Chasuble and Trollope's Mr Slope.[1] But the Church of England in Jacobean times was protected from mockery by a very tight political censorship. Martin Marprelate had been highly successful in making fun of the bishops; but fun like that could be a hanging matter.[2] So although we know that there was a strong element of anti-clericalism and scepticism about the established Church among Londoners, satire against pious hypocrisy and godly greed was possible on the stage only against Puritans, or (if one did not mind shifting the scene to Italy or Spain) against friars and cardinals, so that it chimed with a widespread and traditional anti-Popery among craftsmen and lower orders.

A roll-call of Jacobean dramatis personae, at least in plays with a contemporary rather than a historical setting, shows clergymen of the Church of England almost entirely absent. There are Anglican bishops in the militant Protestant chronicle-romances dramatising the Reformation and the glorious reign of Elizabeth, in plays like *When You See Me You Know Me* and *If You Know Not Me You Know Nobody*. But there are scarcely any parsons or vicars in the city comedies,[3] no dumb dogs like Sir Oliver Martext, no pedants

---

[1] It has also been a favourite theme of satirists in times of pre-revolutionary feeling, as in Voltaire's *Candide* or Brecht's *Galileo*. Marlowe satirised friars and popes; it is possible that, in a free situation, he might have chosen to hit at other 'religious caterpillars' as well.

[2] Literally so for John Penry, one of those concerned in the publishing of Marprelate, executed for treason in 1593.

[3] Excluding purely functional ones, like the parson who marries the lovers at the end of *Chaste Maid*.

like Holofernes. Marston has none, Middleton none, Dekker none.[4]
Jonson, whose great themes were hypocrisy and self-deception,
created marvellous *exempla* of these in his Puritan pastor Tribulation Wholesome, deacon Ananias and lay preacher Zeal-of-the-
Land Busy; and undoubtedly he was strongly anti-Puritan himself
(no one who was not would have had the idea of naming the holy
usurer's dogs Block and Lollard). But even Jonson had other kinds
of venality and simony in mind too, and in his 'dotage', in *The
Magnetic Lady*, he presents a rare example of the smooth submissive parson, who does well for himself by obeying the squire and
enjoying food, drink and other perquisites out of his plural Church
emoluments:

> He is the prelate of the parish here,
> And governs all the dames, appoints the cheer,
> Writes down the bills of fare, pricks all the guests,
> Makes all the matches and the marriage feasts
> Within the ward; draws all the parish wills,
> Designs the legacies, and strokes the gills
> Of the chief mourners; and whoever lacks
> Of all the kindred, he hath first his blacks. . .
> Comforts the widows, and the fatherless
> In funeral sack. . .   (I.ii)

For money and his own advantage he will do anything: marry anyone to anyone.

> Can you think, sir,
> I would deny you anything, not to loss
> Of both my livings?   (IV.vi)

It is significant that this play got the actors and the censor into
trouble with Laud and the Court of High Commission, though in
the end Sir Henry Herbert was able to satisfy the Archbishop that
only the actors, not himself and the dramatist, were to blame because
they had added words to the original text. The complaint *may* only
have been about the use of oaths,[5] but it seems likely that the satire
on Parson Palate irritated Laud too. Perhaps Jonson, who was old

---

[4] Fletcher, in *The Spanish Curate* (acted 1622), safeguards himself in
presenting a caricature of a greedy dumb-dog vicar by (a) making him
Spanish, hence presumably Catholic, and (b) giving him a few Puritan
catch-phrases ('edifying' and so on) as double insurance. Killigrew's *Parson's
Wedding*, written abroad possibly in the 1640s, was acted only after the
Restoration.

[5] Herford and Simpson assume this was the main point at issue.

and paralysed at the time, had forgotten how little of that kind of criticism it was possible to get away with:[6] conceivably he no longer cared.

Once, and only once, does Middleton satirise a bishop of the established Church – in *A Game at Chess*; and there he could plead that it was allowable, since De Dominis had only pretended to be an Anglican bishop and soon reverted to his Romish allegiance.

Anti-Puritan satire was, of course, particularly likely to go down well with the private-theatre audience (though one can overstate this point: Middleton's *Chaste Maid in Cheapside* was first performed at a 'popular' house, the Swan). Both Marston and Jonson have a great deal more of it than Middleton. In so far as this satire hit at those who wished for further reform within the Church of England and not only at sectaries and 'Anabaptists', it must have reinforced the hostility of moderate Puritan preachers to the theatre. William Crashaw's well-known Paul's Cross sermon of 1607 denouncing stage plays was directly occasioned by *The Puritan*,[7] in which two of the unco guid are ridiculed under the names of Nicholas St Antlings and Simon St Maryoveries. They are called after City churches well known for their Puritan preachers, and it was this that particularly incensed Crashaw:

> The ungodly plays and interludes so rife in this nation, what are they but a bastard of Babylon. . .a hellish device (the devil's own recreation to mock at holy things)? Nay, they grow worse and worse, for now they bring religion and holy things upon the stage. . .Two hypocrites must be brought forth, and how shall they be described but by these names, Nicholas St Antlings, Simon St Maryoveries? Thus hypocrisy and a child of hell must bear the names of two churches of God, and two wherein God's name is called on publicly every day in the year, and in one of them his blessed word preached every day (an example scarce matchable in the world). Yet these two shall be by these

[6] It may, of course, have become more difficult under Laud than it had been in Archbishop Abbot's time to get away with anything at all.

[7] Some scholars have attributed this play to Middleton, but it seems most unlikely to be his. The title-page of the quarto assigns it to 'W.S.' – possibly Wentworth Smith. Middleton is known to have written a play called *The Puritan Maid, The Modest Wife and The Wanton Widow*, but this title does not at all fit *The Puritan*, which has no modest wife or wanton widow but only a widow and her two daughters. See Appendix B, 'Notes on Authorship'.

miscreants thus dishonoured, and that not on the stage only, but even in print. Oh, what times are we cast into that such wickedness should pass unpunished![8]

II

Middleton has often been considered as strongly anti-Puritan, at least in his comedies, mainly on the strength of the early *Family of Love* (variously dated 1602 or 1605) and the hilarious christening-scene in *A Chaste Maid in Cheapside* (*c.*1611). This has led to the suggestion that if his later plays, and especially *A Game at Chess*, made him the Puritans' favourite dramatist, he must have changed sides for what one critic describes as 'blatantly commercial' reasons. There is indeed a change in emphasis and tone after 1613, when we first know him to have worked for City Puritan patrons. But a good deal else was changing at that time; and even in the early comedies the satire is in no sense pro-establishment. It is aimed primarily at religious hypocrisy and cant, and while its tone is highly irreverent and secular, it is not hard to see how a young man with a moderate Puritan background might have come to write it. It may be noted that the author of the Martin Marprelate tracts, who showed the possibilities of the cynical popular style in Puritan reforming polemic, was also opposed to the sects and accounted 'no Brownist to be a Puritan'. No one would suggest that Middleton's comedies are 'Puritan' polemic, whatever meaning one attaches to the word. But a jeering, sceptical manner does not necessarily imply a frivolous attitude to basic issues at this period.

Part of the problem lies in the definition of the term 'Puritan'. Originally separatists seem to have been called Puritans, rather than those who wished to reform the church from within: and it is in this sense that Middleton uses the word. In the seventeenth century, however, it came to be used much more widely, as we have seen, in relation to both religious and political opposition.[9]

If we take Puritanism in a broader sense to be 'the religion of all those who wished either to purify the usage of the established Church from the taint of Popery, or to worship separately by forms

---

[8] *Sermon at Paul's Cross*, 14 Feb. 1607 (London, 1608; *S.T.C.* 6027), pp. 170–1.
[9] See Christopher Hill, 'The Definition of a Puritan', in *Society and Puritanism in Pre-Revolutionary England*, and above, pp. 22–6.

so purified',[10] it seems that a great part of the London popular audience, and a number even among the 'select' audience and great court patrons of the drama, could be included within the Puritan spectrum.[11] But Middleton never uses the word 'Puritan' in a favourable sense, even though from 1613 onwards he had a number of City patrons who were what we should call active Puritans. For him, a Puritan always means a sectary, and what he is satirising is not the broad main stream of reforming opposition, or the opinions of most of the 'middling sort' in the early years of the seventeenth century, but rather 'ultra-holiness' and hypocrisy. It is possible, nevertheless, that some moderate Puritans would be offended, and their committed opponents delighted, by such scenes as the christening party in *A Chaste Maid in Cheapside*. In fact Middleton's satire may not always have meant to his audience exactly what it meant to him.

III

The only play of Middleton's where religious unorthodoxy is at all central is *The Family of Love*, and that is a very special case, worth examining in more detail. The Familists satirised here were a lower-class separatist sect, who far from being typical Puritans had been denounced by the great Elizabethan Puritan leader John Field as heretics (along with Arians, Anabaptists and libertines). They held their property in common, and believed that all things come by nature and that only the spirit of God within the believer can understand Scripture. Theirs was 'an anti-clerical, layman's creed',[12] and they might well seem fair game even for a dramatist with moderate Puritan sympathies. There is no need to suppose that in laughing at them Middleton was particularly trying to gain favour with James I,[13]

---

[10] Quoted in A. G. Dickens, *The English Reformation* (London, 1967), p. 426. See moreover Russell, *Crisis of Parliaments*, p. 167, which defines Puritans as 'including all those who wanted to reform the church in a Protestant direction, and those who wanted to presbyterianise it from within, but excluding separatists and sectaries'.

[11] Among court patrons, the 3rd and 4th Earls of Pembroke, the 1st Earl of Holland, and possibly Lucy, Countess of Bedford. The audience at the 'select' theatres included common lawyers, MPs and law students, many of whom must have been Parliamentary Puritan in sympathy.

[12] Christopher Hill, *The World Turned Upside Down*, p. 23.

[13] W. Power has argued this view in 'Thomas Middleton vs King James I', *Notes and Queries*, ccii (Dec. 1957).

who, having attacked Puritans indiscriminately in his *Basilikon Doron*, had to explain in his 1603 preface that

> the name of Puritan doth properly belong only to that vile sect amongst the Anabaptists, called the Family of Love; because they think themselves only pure...Of this special sect I principally mean when I speak of Puritans...and partly, indeed, I give this style to such brainsick and heady preachers their disciples and followers, as refusing to be called of that sect, yet participate too much with their humours.[14]

As we know, James' hostility to Puritans turned out to be a good deal wider than that passage suggests: but there is no evidence that the same is true of Middleton. What James' reference did indicate was that to mock at holiness in the shape of these particular groups was unlikely to get anyone into trouble with the censorship.

The reputation of the Family for free-love practices (which was probably all that most of the audience would know about them) lent itself well to bawdy farce anyway, much as nudist camps and health cults do nowadays. Middleton makes only glancing reference to their other radical ideas, for instance common ownership or the doubt whether heaven or hell exist apart from this life. Yet the way his Familists speak suggests that he knew enough about them at least to mimic the turn of phrase – in particular the insistence on 'feeling', on the direct experience of the spirit of God as the only true guide to believers. (It is interesting that Roger Waterer, with whom Middleton's mother had several legal disputes, is known to have been a separatist and Brownist.)

Even on this tempting subject, Middleton did not write a play merely jeering at citizens and their sects to flatter a 'good gentle' audience. Indeed the conceited court gallants, hoping to seduce citizens' wives, are even more severely ridiculed than the Familists themselves, though it is certainly assumed that the Family engage in free love and religious love-feasts as part of their ritual, and see no sin in it (which may sometimes have been true).

There are two plots in *The Family of Love* – romantic or burlesque-romantic in verse, bawdy-comic in prose – linked by a common theme of the sex drive and its fulfilment. Maria, betrothed to Gerardine, a landed gentleman with a somewhat encumbered estate, is forbidden to marry him by her citizen uncle and guardian

[14] *Basilikon Doron*, ed. J. Craigie (Edinburgh, 1944), p. 15.

Dr Glister, who locks her up to wait for a better match. The lovers, however, resist this as unnatural:

Maria. O silly men, which seek to keep in awe
  Nature's affections, which can know no law.   (I.i.60)

Gerardine, pretending to travel abroad, gets himself smuggled into the house in a trunk, and the lovers bed together. Their plan is, when Maria in due course proves pregnant, to accuse Glister of fathering the child, and blackmail him into allowing them to marry. This stratagem is evidently meant to have the audience's sympathy, since they, like the lovers, will accept public betrothal followed by consummation as a valid marriage,[15] and one based on love rather than on Glister's property calculations.

In the second plot, which provides the title and most of the fun, two marriages are involved. Dr Glister, whose wife is waspish and fanatically house-proud, picks up sex on the side among his women patients. Purge the apothecary regards *his* wife as merely a means of increasing his profits, and is quite ready to be cuckolded by gallants if it will bring him business:

> He that tends well his shop, and hath an alluring wife with a graceful what d'ye lack? shall be sure to have good doings...I smile to myself to hear our knights and gallants say how they gull us, when indeed we gull them, or rather they gull themselves. Here they come in term-time, hire chambers, and perhaps kiss our wives: well, what lose I by that?...Tut, jealousy is a hell; and they that will thrive must utter their wares as they can, and wink at small faults.   (II.i.3)

His wife, Mistress Rebecca Purge, a sexy and quick-witted woman, reacts by having affairs (with the doctor for one) and by going to 'exercises' and 'lectures' at the Family of Love, where she finds better company, notably the jolly merchant Dryfat, who is or pretends to be a Familist. (Significantly, he has tried to persuade Maria's uncle to let the lovers marry, and becomes Gerardine's confederate in the plot to bring their marriage about.) The suggestion is that city wives with narrow-minded and sexually inadequate husbands find satisfaction and independence at such exercises, and this gives plenty of scope for mockery and 'blue' humour – as when

---

[15] As in *Measure for Measure* and *Duchess of Malfi*, betrothal followed by consummation is regarded as equivalent to a legal marriage, though the church ceremony ought to complete it according to canon law. The indignation of some modern critics at Gerardine's and Maria's behaviour is perhaps excessive in the light of this.

the brethren say their exercises are held by candlelight because 'we fructify best in the dark'.

> *Dryfat*. Indeed I think we perform those functions best when we are not thrall to the fetters of the body...the organs of the body, as some term them.
>
> *Mistress Purge*. Organs? fie, fie, they have a most abominable squeaking sound in mine ears; they edify not a whit; I detest 'em; I hope my body has no organs.   (III.iii.25)

The foolish court gallants, Lipsalve and Gudgeon, would like to seduce Mistress Purge too, but their attempts all end in disaster. Instead they are first fooled by the doctor-astrologer into whipping one another naked, and then reduced to helpless humiliation and diarrhoea by his medicine. 'They were infamous in the Court, and are now grown as notorious in the City.'

When Purge discovers his wife's intrigue with Dryfat, he is roused to jealous fury after all. He is not presented 'straight', however, as a decent outraged husband with whom we are to sympathise, but as a weakling and bully, threatened with losing his domination and the property value his wife represents.[16] He follows her to the Family in disguise, has intercourse with her in the dark, and gets her wedding ring, with which he intends to confront her as proof of her adulterous behaviour.[17]

In arranging the finale Middleton evens the balance. Having mocked the nonconformist sects, he now has Gerardine and Dryfat disguised as officers of the established (and unpopular) ecclesiastical court, summoning the moral offenders of the play before them and pocketing bribes right and left before giving judgment.[18] Dryfat, when a Familist, has given his credentials:

> I live in charity, and give small alms to such as be not of the right

---

[16] See his comment when he overhears his wife with Dryfat: 'What, so close at it? I thought this was one end of your exercise: byr lady, I think there is small profit in this' (III.3).

[17] He incidentally cuts out Lipsalve and Gudgeon, who have likewise dressed up as Familists in the hope of getting their innings with the lady. As Lipsalve comments:

> Sure there's some providence
> Which countermands libidinous appetites,
> For what we most intend is counterchecked
> By strange and unexpected accidents.   (IV.iv.1)

The diagnosis of 'providence' may not be altogether burlesque.

[18] Proctors and apparitors seem to have been rather safer targets than parsons.

sect: I take under twenty in the hundred, nor no forfeiture of
bonds unless the law tell my conscience I may do't.   (III.iii.68)
Now Gerardine, disguised as Placket the apparitor (or summoner)
of the ecclesiastical court, gives *his* credentials: he is

> of the devil's trade, for I live, as he does, by the sins of the people.
>   (IV.v.109)

Dryfat mock-prosecutes Mistress Purge on the grounds that as a
Familist she is infringing property rights and property marriage:

> If they be not punished and suppressed by our club-law, each
> man's copyhold will become freehold, specialities will turn to
> generalities, and so from unity to parity, from parity to plurality,
> and from plurality to universality; their wives, the only ornament
> of their houses, and of all their wares, goods and chattels the chief
> moveables, will be made common.[19]   (V.iii.194)

The ending is consistent with the rather cheerful view taken of
sex and sexual irregularities in the play. Gerardine as judge hands
out to each their deserts. Glister must allow Gerardine and Maria to
marry, and add to her dowry. The courtiers are to 'learn the ABC
of better manners: go back and tell how you have been used in the
City. . .keep yourselves clean and the bed undefiled'. Meanwhile
the Glister and Purge marriages are to be mended. Purge, trying to
expose his wife's wickedness, can produce no evidence but the
wedding ring she gave him, and she has a ready explanation for that,
like Falstaff's after Gadshill:

> Husband, I see you are hoodwinked in the right use of feeling
> and knowledge – as if I knew you not then as well as the child
> knows his own father!. . .Now as true as I live, Master doctor, I
> had a secret operation, and I knew him to be my husband e'en
> by very instinct.   (V.iii.288)

Purge makes a last attempt to assert his male domination – he
will forgive her if she will 'promise to come no more at the Family'.
But Rebecca has the final word:

> Truly, husband, my love must be free still to God's creatures:
> yea, nevertheless, preserving you still as the head of my body, I
> will do as the spirit shall move me.   (V.iii.425)

Rebecca is a caricature, of course, but a caricature of something
real – the independent, strong-minded women who really did play

---

[19] The same legal phrase, describing a wife as a 'moveable', occurs in
the satire on wife-selling in *The Phoenix*, where the seller is obviously a
villain.

an active part as leaders and even preachers in the nonconformist sects, based as these were on family-organised religion.

Middleton, then, makes fun of his sectaries in quite a different tone from Jonson's in *The Alchemist*. There is none of the real bitterness and sarcasm attached to Ananias and Tribulation selling the orphan's goods to get power and money, or Rabbi Busy, 'fast by the teeth in the cold turkey pie', sermonising against the pleasures of the flesh. Middleton's Familists are randy laymen who are mocked for setting up their own ceremonies and making religious nonconformity a cover for promiscuous sex. But in the contrast with the conventional morality of property-marriage they come out, in terms of drama, rather well. Gerardine, adjudicating on the others, is the character whose point of view the audience tend to adopt, and he, as a successful and potent lover, can scarcely be too hard on Mistress Purge: it is her mercenary husband who is made to look a fool. Sympathy here seems directed to the less virtuous, who are only doing what comes naturally (this is, after all, true of Gerardine and Maria too).[20]

All this makes one doubt whether the play was written directly to please King James. As an attack on 'that vile sect' it is perhaps not slashing enough for his taste.

It is instructive to set Middleton against Marston here. In Marston's *Dutch Courtesan* there is a physical, sexual disgust and contempt, and Puritans are swindlers or diseased brothel-keepers. He thinks it funny to make his 'worshipful, rotten, rough-bellied bawd', Mary Faugh, call herself one of the Family of Love, and 'none of the wicked that eat fish o' Fridays'; and his vintner Mulligrub say: 'Nay, if heaven forget to prosper knaves, I'll go no more to the synagogue.' Meanwhile Mistress Mulligrub, who abhors 'ungodly tobacco' because it's not used in the Familist congregation, can hardly wait to see her husband hanged so that she can get into bed with the clown Cocledemoy. Marston does not distinguish between ordinary citizen morality and that of the Family, whereas Middleton makes it quite clear that the Family is a particular sect whose practices would seem outrageous to their pious neighbours.

[20] This point is, perhaps, more easily taken by a modern reader than by nineteenth-century critics, who whether conventionally moral or romantically immoral usually found the whole thing too shocking to be funny. See Swinburne's view of it as 'unquestionably the worst of Middleton's plays: very coarse, very dull, altogether distasteful and ineffectual' (Introduction to Mermaid edn (London, 1887), i, p. xiv).

Both in realism and in moral tone (if one can call it that) Middleton is much closer to what he is describing. His sectaries are caricatures, but they are not, like Marston's, monsters.[21]

IV

Middleton's device of alternating gibes at nonconformists and at other denominations is found again in *A Mad World, My Masters.* Here the courtesan, acting as a bawd between Penitent Brothel and the citizen's frivolous wife, Mistress Harebrain, pretends to be a Puritan, 'a good wholesome sister of the Family' converting the wife, in order to disarm the suspicious husband. But the satire is carefully aimed at religious hypocrisy in general, rather than at sects alone. Thus the courtesan is set to read to the lady for her edification out of a *Jesuit* tract; and the wife is reproved by her husband for believing that 'every sin is damned' in terms which ridicule Church and court as well as sects and city:

> *Harebrain.* Fie, wife, be converted. There's a diabolical opinion indeed! then you may think that usury were damned; you're a fine merchant, i' faith! or bribery; you know the law well! or sloth; would some of the clergy heard you, i' faith! or pride; you come at court! or gluttony; you're not worthy to dine at an alderman's table! (I.ii.130)

The best-known and the funniest of Middleton's Puritan scenes is that in *A Chaste Maid in Cheapside* (III.ii) where the Puritan gossips get drunk at the christening party for Mrs Allwit's dubiously fathered baby. There is plenty of unconscious irony in the pious congratulations offered by the sisters, who believe the baby's father to be the thrifty husband Allwit, whereas the audience know that the real father is the extravagant Sir Walter Whorehound, who is acting as godfather and paying for the lying-in, christening, silver apostle-spoons and all.

> *Third Gossip.*
> O, she had great speed;
> We were afraid once, but she made us all

---

[21] Admittedly the coarseness of *The Dutch Courtesan* is not confined to the presentation of the Puritans. What its latest editor calls the 'witty banter' of Crispinella, who is supposed to be one of the heroines, is apt to nauseate the reader. (See *The Dutch Courtesan*, ed. M. Wine (London, 1965), pp. 50, 73.)

Have joyful hearts again: 'tis a good soul, i' faith
The midwife found her a most cheerful daughter.
First Puritan.
'Tis the spirit: the sisters are all like her.   (III.ii.20)
They admire the godfather's handsome appearance:
Second Gossip. Methinks her husband shows like a clown to him.
Third Gossip. I would not care what clown my husband were too,
So I had such fine children.

. . .

First Puritan. Children are blessings
      If they be got with zeal by the brethren
      As I have five at home.   (III.ii.29)
But the strongest condemnation of Puritan forms is put into the
mouth of the profiteer-cuckold Allwit, which rather takes the edge
off it as moral comment:
      First Puritan. Verily, thanks, sir.   (*Exit*)
      Allwit. Verily, you're an ass, forsooth.   (II.iii.19)
And again as the sisters leave:
      Go take a nap with some of the brethren, do,
      And rise up a well-edified, boldified sister.   (III.ii.178)
The Puritans are hypocrites, no doubt, but not a patch on their
anti-Puritan host. This particular play was performed, as it happens,
not at a 'select' but at a public theatre, and the nice balance of the
satire,[22] religious and social, would no doubt appeal to a variety of
opinions in the audience, radical as well as courtly.

Middleton seems, as a rule, to avoid making his usurers and
financial swindlers Puritans, as Jonson and others commonly do.[23]
(Quomodo occasionally swears 'a' my religion' to convince a
wavering customer, but that is hardly anti-Puritan satire, since
Puritans refused to take an oath.) In contrast, in Jonson's *Eastward
Ho!*, old Security explains at some length why his moneylenders'
business ('with moderate profit, thirty or forty in the hundred') is
not only safer but more godly than that of the merchant, who is
always blaming heaven for bad weather. He recommends his whore
Syndefie (a good godly name) as maid to a city lady, on the grounds

[22] Thus the new and stricter laws about the observance of Lent are guyed
in the episode of the promoters searching for flesh, and turning a blind eye
when bribed. The Allwit baby, on the other hand, was christened according
to the rite of Amsterdam.
[23] With city dramatists like Dekker and Heywood, usurers are more commonly atheists.

that she needs saving from her honest humours, 'for she had a great desire to be a nun'. Pennyboy Richer, the miser-usurer in Jonson's *The Staple of News*, complains that the legal restriction of interest to 8 per cent has robbed the poor of their inheritance, because he could only spare them alms when he took 10 per cent; he has named his dogs Block and Lollard. Sir Moth Interest in Jonson's *Magnetic Lady* is proud of his 'calling'. Sir Tyrant Thrift, in Davenant's *The Wits*, is too mean to pay for meat and drink at a funeral:

> I do not like this drinking of healths to the memory
> Of the dead: it is profane.[24]

The old she-miser in the same play is 'more devout than a weaver of Banbury, that hopes/T'entice heaven by singing to make him Lord/Of twenty looms'. But Middleton's Frippery, Quomodo, Hoard, Lucre, Dampit, are not so characterised: the absence of the routine godly catch-phrases is very striking in *A Trick to Catch the Old One*, where usury and the rivalries of usurers are a central theme.

Neither does Middleton particularly dramatise Puritans as kill-joys and enemies to cakes and ale, though the controversy over the Book of Sports and Sabbatarianism would give support to this as *one* meaning of the word in the seventeenth century. Malvolio is 'a kind of Puritan', and Angelo may be intended as such: Busy fixes the type for ever. But we never see Middleton's Puritans interfering with anyone else's pleasures; indeed the Puritan master-merchant or City father as a figure of authority never appears at all.

There is little ridicule even of the Puritan sects in Middleton's work after *A Chaste Maid* (c.1611) – that is, after he began to work for the City. He does, however, revert to one aspect of it in *The World Tost at Tennis* (1620), an amusing masque in which soldier and scholar commiserate with one another on their poverty, and the scholar attributes his unemployment to the rise of 'mechanic Rabbis' or lay preachers:

> There's Rabbi Job a venerable silk-weaver,
> Jehu a throwster dwelling in the Spitalfields,
> There's Rabbi Abimelech a learned cobbler,
> Rabbi Lazarus a superstitious tailor;
> These shall hold up their shuttles, needles, awls
> Against the gravest Levite of the land,
> And give no ground neither.   (p. 156)

[24] *Six Caroline Plays*, ed. A. Knowland (Oxford, 1962), p. 407.

And again:

> The devout weaver sits within his loom,
> And thus he makes a learned syllogism,
> His woof the major and his warp the minor,
> His shuttle then the brain and firm conclusion,
> Makes him a piece of stuff that Aristotle,
> Ramus, nor all the logicians can take a'pieces.   (p. 158)

At the end, generosity by the masque king provides the scholar with a benefice.

Evidently here Middleton is in line with the social prejudices of a court audience. But it is also true that most Puritan opinion at this date was for reforming the Church by the appointment of properly educated and properly paid preaching ministers to livings and lectureships, and certainly not by lay preaching. The Feoffees for Impropriations themselves about this time set out to increase Puritan influence in the Church by the appointment of 'godly and learned' preaching ministers with the right paper qualifications, instead of pluralists or ill-educated 'dumb dogs'.[25] Once again the satire is anti-sectary, rather than anti-Puritan; Middleton is not just ridiculing his City patrons because his audience here happens to be an aristocratic one.

It is perhaps inevitable that reading early-seventeenth-century writers now, with our knowledge of the greater conflicts to come, we should tend to expect all those who are not Puritans to be Anglo-Catholics.[26] But most people in the era of the city comedies obviously did not think of it quite like this; the undistributed middle of the spectrum was very large. There was, besides, a long tradition of secular scepticism and iconoclasm in religious matters, the expression of which (as K. V. Thomas has pointed out) is usually described as Lollard, which some of it certainly is, because we cannot imagine real scepticism as possible at that time.[27] It is already very evident in Chaucer's treatment of the clergy, to which anti-episcopal writers like Milton and Wither so often refer; and it was more freely voiced

---

[25] Spenser had made the same point in *Mother Hubbard's Tale*, imitated by Middleton in his early satire *Father Hubbard's Tales*.

[26] The term 'Anglo-Catholic' is anachronistic in the seventeenth century anyway; I owe this point to Elsie Duncan-Jones. But it is hard to find a more satisfactory one, and that we tend to see it unhistorically is of course the point.

[27] K. V. Thomas, *Religion and the Decline of Magic* (Harmondsworth, 1973), p. 168.

by soldiers and lower orders after 1642.²⁸ Something of this feeling exists in Middleton's city comedies, alongside the more convention- ally religious morality expressed in the Penitent Brothel scenes of *A Mad World* and the terrifying downfall of Sir Walter Whore- hound.

²⁸ See Christopher Hill, *The World Turned Upside Down.*

6. *Money and Morals in Middleton's City Comedies*

I

To see Middleton as merely 'anti-citizen' is an oversimplification. Villain-citizens in Middleton's plays, as in most Jacobean comedy, are more often moneylenders than mere merchants: for it was in this capacity that the powerful citizen most menacingly confronted the easygoing gentleman at the end of his resources. The mechanism which enabled a rich man to become richer purely by lending money, without obvious risk or industry on his part, was still regarded as something of a mystery at this early stage of capitalist development. Although medieval canon law had frowned on it, lending at interest had long been essential in the commercial economy, and had been accepted in practice for many years; and in the big merchant moneylenders, especially the goldsmiths, London had already the rudiments of a banking system.

Contemporary thought, however, still distinguished between *necessary* usury – to finance government or normal commerce, with interest to cover the risk – and what was known as *biting* usury, where the creditor charged excessive interest rates and was quick to foreclose on mortgaged land and property. This was considered to be exploiting the necessities of the poor craftsman or farmer, who could not survive a bad year without a loan, but had no hope of paying back much more than he had borrowed: or else as a deliberate attempt to twist gullible gentry out of their lands. It is significant that while Calvinist religious teaching had first legitimised interest, it was the popular Puritan preachers who inveighed most strongly against 'biting' usury – no doubt because their congregations consisted largely of the small men who were most likely to fall into debt-slavery.[1]

Of all Middleton's comedies, *Michaelmas Term* (1604–6) is the most easily seen (mistakenly I think) as proof of his 'positive

---

[1] I am greatly indebted here to Christopher Hill for allowing me to consult an unpublished paper by him on contemporary attitudes to usury, on which the above paragraphs are largely based.

animus' against citizens, the kind of drama that is supposed to have alienated City opinion from the theatres.[2] Indeed the play centres on a wonderfully vivid portrayal of the rascally woollen-draper merchant Quomodo, and his skilful plot to swindle the young heir Easy out of his land in Essex, which Quomodo has picked out as the ideal estate on which to set himself up as a county gentleman. From the outset of his scheming, Quomodo does use language suggesting war of citizens as a class against the gentry, lusting after their land as lecherous gallants after city wives:

Shortyard [his confederate]. What is the mark you shoot at?
Quomodo.
> Why, the fairest to cleave the heir in twain,
> I mean his title: to murder his estate,
> Stifle his right in some detested prison.
> There are ways and means enow to hook in gentry,
> Besides our deadly enmity, which thus stands:
> They're busy 'bout our wives, we 'bout their lands.

(I.i.106)

He dreams of his future estate as a passport to enjoy culture and beauty, something which, it is implied, his sort of people have no right to:

> O, that sweet, neat, comely, proper, delicate parcel of land, like a fine gentlewoman i' th' waist, not so great as pretty, pretty; the trees in summer whistling, the silver waters by the banks harmoniously gliding. I should have been a scholar; an excellent place for a student, fit for my son that lately commenc'd at Cambridge, whom now I have placed at Inns of Court. Thus we that seldom get lands honestly, must leave our heirs to inherit our knavery. (II.iii.91)

Easy, a naive young heir new to the city, is persuaded to stand surety for a drinking-companion (really Quomodo's apprentice in disguise) and mortgage his estate against a loan given in cloth, which turns out to be unsaleable at any reasonable price. The loan cannot be repaid, the crook for whom he has stood surety cannot be

---

[2] See e.g. Hibbard, 'Tragedies of Thomas Middleton', in *Renaissance and Modern Studies*, i (1957), p. 39: 'It is difficult to see any good reason why a respectable London tradesman and his family should wish to attend a performance of *Michaelmas Term*, *A Trick to Catch the Old One* or *A Chaste Maid in Cheapside*...The solid middle class went to the theatre less and less in the decade 1610–1620, and the playwrights of the time were partly to blame for their absence.'

found, and Quomodo is able to foreclose. He exults not only in the
wealth he has got but in the status the land will bring him; and it is
the snobbish belief that as a landed proprietor he will automatically
be superior to the mere industrious sort that is mocked:

> The land's mine; that's sure enough, boy.
>
> . . .
>
> Now shall I be divulged a landed man
> Throughout the Livery; one points, another whispers,
> A third frets inwardly, let him fret and hang.
>
> . . .
>
> Now come my golden days in.
>
> – Whither is the worshipful Master Quomodo and his fair bed
> fellow rid forth? To his land in Essex! Whence comes that goodly
> load of logs? From his land in Essex! – Where grows this pleasant
> fruit? says one citizen's wife in the Row – At Master Quomodo's
> orchard in Essex – Oh, oh, does it so? I thank you for that good
> news, i' faith.   (III.iv.13)

Nevertheless, to take Quomodo at his own valuation, as a typical
respected London citizen, is to oversimplify the view the play offers.
For he is not, in fact, an honoured member of his company engag-
ing in normal merchant business or even normal moneylending,
but a confidence trickster recognised as such by his own order.
Such tricks are common in the coney-catching pamphlets of Greene
and Dekker. Middleton seems to have derived the plot and the name
of his rogue from the real-life case of a merchant named Howe,
sentenced in 1596 to imprisonment, pillory, whipping and fines for
swindling young heirs in much the same way as Quomodo swindles
Easy.[3]

The point is underlined at the end of the play, when Quomodo
(like Volpone) pretends to be dead for the fun of seeing how people
will take it. His mock-funeral is staged, very expensively he is
pleased to see, with the choirboys from Christ's Hospital and the
worshipful Liverymen in the cortège. But the only Liveryman who
speaks shows in his one-line comment (it is the whole of his part)
that decent members of the company have nothing but contempt for
their departed brother.

---

[3] *Michaelmas Term*, ed. R. Levin (London, 1967), Introduction, p. xii. After
the trial in Star Chamber, the Lord Treasurer 'would have those that make
the plays to make a comedie hereof, and to act it with these names' –
which may even have suggested the idea to Middleton.

First Liveryman. Who, Quomodo? Merely enriched by shifts
And cozenages, believe it.   (IV.iv.18)

In the end the biter is bit; Quomodo is double-crossed by his
wife, who has fallen in love with Easy, and the land reverts to its
original owner – an ending which, though improbable, is felt to be
morally satisfying, since the young heir was an innocent abroad
rather than a prodigal, and the whole crime somewhat like taking
sweets from a baby (as indeed the victim's name Easy implies).
The villain has been foiled in his attempt to con his way into the
landed class, and order is restored – though without the heavy
moralising on the virtues of degree that orchestrates this kind of
finale in *Eastward Ho!* or *A New Way to Pay Old Debts*.

In this play, then, the dramatist may seem to be clearly upholding the 'traditional order', siding with the generous, unsuspicious
young gentry against the rapacious city sharks. But even here, as we
have seen, there are reservations. Easy is presented as foolish
rather than charming. And Middleton seems to go out of his way to
emphasise that Quomodo is *not* typical of the worshipful company
of Drapers. Neither are merchants the only ones turning a dishonest
penny. Andrew Lethe, a courtier adventurer anxious to forget his
humble origins as Andrew Gruel in the land of oats, offers to sell
titles to casual pub acquaintances:

Gruel. Are you not knights yet, gentlemen?
Rearage, Salewood. Not yet.
Gruel. No? That must be looked into – 'tis your own fault.

(I.i.191)

He hopes to get favour with Quomodo and marry his rich daughter by claiming to have influence at court, and be able to 'make us
rich in customs, strong in friends, happy in suits, bring us into all
the [court] rooms on Sundays, from the leads to the cellar, pop us
in with venison till we crack again, and send home the rest in an
honourable napkin'. The waste and corruption in the royal household were a notorious grievance with taxpayers, and it is like
Middleton to take a side-swipe at court abuses and Scots favourites
too.

It seems unlikely that the play would in fact cause resentment
among citizens not already on principle opposed to the theatre. A
rich merchant in what was now a recognised moneylending and
banking business was unlikely to identify himself with a small-time
swindler like Quomodo. Great customs farmers like Sir Baptist

Hickes and Sir Thomas Myddleton,[4] who had the King and many of the most reputable courtiers on their books as debtors, and held mortgages on a good proportion of the castles and prodigy houses of the peerage, would scarcely recognise a parallel in a disreputable trickster conning a young innocent.[5] Many of the middling sort, on the other hand, small craftsmen resentful of the big merchants who were now coming to dominate the livery companies, would probably identify with the debtor rather than the lender – just as the dramatists themselves would[6] – and would therefore rejoice when he got his estates back.

Far from being anti-Puritan satire, the play is exactly the kind of moral *exemplum* we find in the popular Puritan sermons – so exactly that it is hard to say whether the dramatist or the preacher originated it. Thus for example Thomas Adams, a personal friend of the Earl of Pembroke and a minister victimised by Laud, denouncing usurers who charge 40 per cent, mentions the identical trick:

> A landed gentleman wants money, he shall have it; but in commodities; which some compacted Broker buys of him, for half the rate they cost him, in ready money. Are these Christians?[7]

Again, precisely the routine techniques of dishonest shopkeeping practised by Quomodo and his assistants are held up to obloquy in the same sermon:

> The avarous Citizens, whom the glad Devil can never find without a false measure in one hand and a cozening weight in the other. . .care not for repentance.   (p. 134)

So too in a sermon by Thomas Scot:

> And. . .what one can cheat or cozen his neighbour of, either by sophisticated wares, or false weights and measures, or by any other close device or conveyance, he thinks it tolerable, nay laud-

---

[4] Myddleton did, as it happens, use some of the profits of his moneylending business to buy an estate at Stansted Mountfichet in Essex. It was bequeathed to his second son Timothy, a Parliamentarian in the Civil War.

[5] Foreclosure was not, of course, the way to make the most out of such influential clients. The favours and business privileges they were in a position to put in the lender's way were probably a more important gain from their unpaid debts.

[6] Many of his writers seem to have been permanently in debt to Henslowe: and Dekker's long imprisonment for debt is notorious. Their situation here was analogous to that of the poor peasant or craftsman becoming a debt-slave.

[7] *A Divine Herball* (London, 1616; *S.T.C.* 111), dedicated to the Earl of Pembroke, p. 130.

able, a part of his trade, a mistery (as he calls it) of his profession.[8]

These were not anti-citizen preachers, but Puritan preachers suiting their moral instruction to the everyday lives of their hearers. If they sometimes drew examples from plays, that too may be significant.

To see these plays as consistently upholding gentry against citizens is, perhaps, to take too literal and documentary a view, ignoring the element of fantasy. In folk-tale the hero dear to the hearts of the people, who wears coarse clothes and suffers hardship and heavy work like them, often turns out to be a prince in disguise, or marries a princess: if he were a real 'average' peasant, it would limit the possibilities of a brilliantly happy ending. So in city comedy, hard-up citizens and masterless men can enjoy the sufferings of the disinherited heir because he has the chance (as they scarcely have) of winning through to wealth and ease. In Hollywood films of the 1930s, the beautiful poor girl often marries her boss, but it would be risky to deduce from this a high degree of social mobility into the millionaire class in the depression years.

In his earliest verses, the 'snarling satires' of *Microcynicon*, published in 1599 when Middleton was nineteen (and burned by order of the ecclesiastical censors in that year, along with books by Hall and Marston), he had already shown the same direction of attack and sympathy within the classical satirical form. He makes a distinction and yet a connection, for instance, between the honest merchants and Cron, the usurer:

> Th' Exchange for goodly merchants is appointed;
> Why not for me, says Cron, and mine anointed?
> Can merchants thrive, and not the usurer nigh?
> Can merchants live without my company?   (viii, p. 120)

When 'young Prodigal' rides past in his finery, the man in the street who fails to take his hat off is sent to prison. The vice of pride (Superbia) is depicted as 'fine Madam Tiptoes in her velvet gown', taking it out of her servants, and our sympathy is directed to the poor bullied little maid:

> Where is this baggage, where's this girl?
>   . . .
> Then in comes Nan – Sooth, mistress, did you call?
> Out on thee, quean! – now by the living God –

[8] *The Highways of God and the King* (London, 1623; *S.T.C.* 22102), p. 66.

And then she strikes, and on the wench lays load.
Poor silly maid, with finger in the eye,
Sighing and sobbing, takes all patiently.   (p. 126)

The image of the fine lady and her servants is in Middleton's mind
twenty years before he creates Beatrice and Diaphanta in *The
Changeling*. Indeed it may have been because of real or fancied
portrayal of actual people that the book was censored.

II

The satire on citizens, merchants and usurers in Middleton's
comedies is usually balanced by equally irreverent treatment of
decadent, extravagant or idle aristocrats and gentlemen. Thus in
Your Five Gallants (c.1607) the satire is principally at the expense
of aristocratic and court vices like lechery, dandyism, duelling and
gambling, and needy gallants prey on society by highway robbery.
So the young prodigal Follywit in *A Mad World, My Masters*, who
cannot wait to inherit his grandfather's landed estate, leads a gang
of thieves to steal some of it in advance. In the jolly lecherous old
grandfather, Sir Bounteous Progress, the comic 'humour' is the
good old gentry virtue of indiscriminate hospitality; he keeps open
house for these titled strangers, who play on his credulity and his
love of a lord to rob him. But he gets his own back when Follywit is
conned into marriage with his grandfather's mistress – Sir Bounteous
being willing to back the bawdy joke with a handsome cash hand-
out:

The best is, sirrah, you pledge none but me;
And since I drink the top, take her; and hark,
I spice the bottom with a thousand mark.   (V.ii.289)

In *A Chaste Maid in Cheapside* (c.1611) Allwit the goldsmith is
a willing cuckold, because his wife's aristocratic lover Sir Walter
Whorehound pays all the family expenses, fondly believing that his
liaison is secret. The laughter goes both ways – against the shameless Allwit and the foolish lecher Whorehound, who indeed comes
off worst at the end. In the sub-plot, impotent old Sir Oliver Kix,
the used-up aristocrat, is kindly provided with heirs by hard-up
Touchwood, who administers the necessary medical treatment to
Lady Kix in her coach. Lady Kix has been a court lady, and says
she was never barren till she was married. It is for financial reasons,
to prevent Sir Walter inheriting, that she needs children ('Think

but upon the goodly lands and livings/That's kept back through want on't' (II.i)). If all this is uncomplimentary to the citizens, it cannot be said to show birth and breeding in a very flattering light either.

III

Satire on usurers – the general term for all sharp financial dealers – was indeed not seen necessarily as satire on a new social class: anyone who could accumulate capital might use it unscrupulously to get power over others. Of the three usurers discomfited in *A Trick to Catch the Old One* (1605), one has made his money as a merchant, one as a lawyer, the third comes from a gentry family – the uncle, as the play stresses, of the young heir Witgood he has got into his clutches.[9] And the young heir himself is no innocent: his situation, as he says himself in the opening soliloquy, is entirely his own fault:

> All's gone. Still thou'rt a gentleman, that's all, but a poor one, that's nothing. What milk brings thy meadows forth now? where are thy goodly uplands and thy Downlands, all sunk into that little pit, Lechery?...But where's Longacre? in my uncle's conscience, which is three years' voyage about.   (I.i.1)

His uncle's conscience, he says, will allow him to foreclose, because it is Witgood's indulgence in brothels, drink and gambling that has led him into debt.

Ten years earlier Shakespeare in the *Merchant of Venice* had softened the issue. Bassanio too has been a prodigal, but the vices on which he spent his 'faint means' are neither specified nor shown; and only the Jew is mean enough to charge interest on a loan, whereas the Christian merchant Antonio lends for love. Middleton's portrayal is less reassuring, and more realistic. Society has ceased to be based on inherited status; it is now a trading, venturing society based on exchange and credit, which needs the moneylender though

---

[9] *A Trick to Catch the Old One*, ed. C. L. Barber (Edinburgh, 1968), p. 2. Their religious position is not dwelt on, but seems likewise varied: Witgood's creditors say 'Call us devils, you shall find us puritans', whereas Dampit is an *atheistical* usurer (I.iv). It was, of course, quite common for the younger sons of the gentry to be apprenticed, to become great merchants and moneylenders, and buy their way into estates and gentry again. Cranfield, Hugh Myddleton, Heathcote, Duncombe were examples (Wilson, *England's Apprenticeship*, p. 10).

it may still dislike him. Squandering generosity, on the old feudal pattern, will not get you the hand of the fairy princess – it is more likely to get you into debt and Newgate, as indeed Shakespeare himself suggests in *Timon of Athens*, written about the same period as *A Trick*. That sharp dealing was no monopoly of *Jewish* traders was a frequent theme of the Puritan preachers.[10]

From the outset there is no presentation of Witgood in *A Trick* as having a *moral* right to get back his estate, either because of his own innate goodness or because he is the representative of a better 'traditional order' in the countryside. He first confronts us as a mercenary lover, concerned to get out of debt by winning 'a virgin's love, her portion and her virtues', a project which makes his courtesan an embarrassment; and as a landlord he is assumed from the beginning to be an exploiter of poor farmers, as he has been of women. This comes out in the opening scene between him and his courtesan, who is presented throughout with an unexpected degree of sympathy. Witgood denounces her with the conventional abuse, as the 'consumption of his purse', 'round-webbed tarantula', to which she replies with spirit:

> I've been true unto your pleasure; and all your lands
> Thrice racked was never worth the jewel which
> I prodigally gave you, my virginity:
> Lands mortgaged may return, and more esteemed,
> But honesty once pawned is ne'er redeemed. (I.i.36)

Witgood generously admits the charge (they are on excellent terms for the rest of the play):

> Forgive: I do thee wrong
> To make thee sin, and then to chide thee for't. (I.i.41)

Whereupon they become confederates again, and the courtesan, passed off as a rich widow about to marry Witgood, becomes the means to re-establish his credit and get the mortgage back from his uncle. The reference to 'your lands thrice racked' is interesting because, brief as it is, it helps to establish the audience's angle of vision, and indicates that in Middleton's mind rent (raised to meet the heir's expenses) is not much more sacred than interest as a

---

[10] Thus Thomas Scot, author of *Vox Populi*, Middleton's main source for *A Game At Chess* (1624), denouncing the hypocritical Puritan merchant: 'He will not break the Sabbath, no not to eat, no not to feed others, not to do good, he is a strict Sabbatarian, a Jew in opinion; but that day or any other he will not stick to cozen his credulous brother, and as well may you trust a Jew as trust him' (*Highways of God and the King*, p. 67).

means of unearned income. (He was, as we have seen in *Father Hubbard's Tales*, perfectly clear about the relationship between them.) There is no overt moral condemnation of Witgood, either here or later: but he succeeds (like Face in *The Alchemist*) by using his wits more skilfully than the moneylenders, not by the superior moral right of gentry as against citizens, or wastrels as against usurers.

The mystery of credit itself is brilliantly dramatised in *A Trick*, and provides indeed its central theme. In the country, where everyone knows everyone else, Witgood is known to be ruined, greeted as 'Bully Hadland'. But in the anonymity of the city his standing depends on what people *think* he is, Witgood of Witgood Hall, finely dressed and about to marry a rich widow. His moneylending uncle, Lucre, is deceived first into lending him more money, and finally – to prevent the match with the 'rich widow' being called off – into restoring his mortgage; while the second usurer, Hoard, cunningly abducts the 'rich widow', with all his troop of hangers-on claiming the credit for bringing them together.

The theme is universalised as the minor lenders copy the greater. Witgood's three creditors, hearing of the marriage, compete with each other to lend him money free of interest, each hoping for a monopoly of his future borrowing, and warning him against the others ('I would not have you beholden to those bloodsuckers for any money'). When he is reported to have lost the widow again, they instantly have him arrested for debt ('We must have either money or carcass'). But he still has the fake 'pre-contract' with the widow, in exchange for which he induces Hoard to pay off the creditors at ten shillings in the pound, legally renouncing with mock-grief all the lady's

> manors, manor-houses, parks, groves, meadow-grounds, arable lands, barns, stacks, stables, doveholes and coney-burrows; together with all her cattle, money, plate, jewels, borders, chains, bracelets, furnitures, hangings, moveables or immoveables.

(IV.iv.262)

All are rogues, but Witgood is the most intelligent, the quickest to understand and exploit the vices of others, and in that sense only 'deserves' to win and to marry the usurer's rich niece – whose fortune has presumably no nobler origin than her uncle's. Hoard has dreamt of being a landed gentleman with a beautiful wife, a place in the country to entertain his city friends, and ten men in livery (though he insists they must all be skilled men; he will not waste money on idlers). At the end he comes down to earth to find himself married to Witgood's courtesan.

It is noteworthy that the courtesan here comes in for none of the whipping and carting imposed on the deserted prostitute Franceschina in Marston's *The Dutch Courtesan*, after desertion and jealousy have led her to try to murder her former lover. The hero, Freevill, in that play expresses the conventional wisdom of the upper class when he defends brothels to his foolishly idealistic friend Malheureux as most necessary buildings.

> Ever since my intention of marriage I do pray for their continuance. . .lest my house should be made one. I would have married men love the stews as Englishmen lov'd the Low Countries: wish war should be maintain'd there lest it should come home to their own doors.[11]

And the cynicism is the more brutal because Freevill recognises that women become prostitutes mainly through poverty:

> A poor, decayed, mechanical man's wife, her husband is laid up; may not she lawfully be laid down when her husband's only rising is by his wife's falling? A captain's wife wants means, her commander lies in open field abroad; may not she lie in civil arms at home? Why is charity grown a sin? or relieving the poor and impotent an offence?   (I.i.95)

Those who regard brothels and whores as necessary to safeguard sound upper-class marriages have no hesitation in punishing the woman if she claims any rights of fidelity in a man; so Freevill does here. But Middleton rejects this double standard. Hoard's behaviour deserves worse than he has got, as the courtesan tells him, and a woman who has sinned can yet repent and make a good wife.[12]

It is, perhaps, a matter of personal taste whether one finds Marston's moral tone here preferable to Middleton's (I don't myself). But those who think that Middleton is immoral or amoral, while Marston upholds the traditional decencies, need to explain Shakespeare's bad taste in having Lucio, at the end of *Measure for Measure*, compelled to marry the prostitute whose child he has

[11] *The Dutch Courtesan*, ed. M. Wine (London, 1965); I.i.65.
[12] See Thomas, 'The Double Standard', *Journal of the History of Ideas*, xx (1959), no. 2, which cites *inter alia* the tracts of William Gouge, *Of Domestical Duties*, and Daniel Rogers, *Matrimonial Honour*, in support of this view.

fathered. While the 'double standard' was traditional, and indeed has not yet wholly died out, many Puritan preachers in the six-teenth and seventeenth centuries were trying to establish that the duty of chastity was equally binding on man and women, and the lack of it equally sinful in either.[13] In treating prostitution as no better and no worse than property marriage entered into with-out love for material ends, Middleton boldly anticipates Gay and Brecht.

The same angle of vision dominates *The Roaring Girl*, whose picaresque heroine Moll Cutpurse (based on a real-life model) wears men's clothes and weapons and mixes in taverns with thieves, yet stands out as the champion of decent non-commercialised human and sexual values. Determined never to marry, because she resists the roles given to women in her society, she uses her quick wit and skill with the sword to shame lechers and help forward honest love-marriages. On behalf of all women she rejects the 'double standard' and exposes the sexual conceit and selfishness of her would-be seducer:

> Th'art one of those
> That thinks each woman thy fond flexible whore.
> If she but cast a liberal eye upon thee,
> Turn back her head, she's thine.
>
> . . .
>
> How many of our sex, by such as thou,
> Have their good thoughts paid with a blasted name
> That never deserved loosely or did trip
> In path of whoredom beyond cup and lip?   (III.i.72)

Women who do fall into prostitution and whoredom are often driven to it by poverty and hard times, she says:

> In thee I defy all men, their worst hates
> And their best flatteries, all their golden witchcrafts,
> With which they entangle the poor spirits of fools.
> Distressed needlewomen and trade-fallen wives,
> Fish that must needs bite or themselves be bitten,
> Such hungry things as these may soon be took

---

13 The same point – that a prostitute can reform, and that to argue 'Once a whore, always a whore' is cruel and unjust – is central in *The Honest Whore*, Pt 1, attributed to Middleton and Dekker. Pt 2, however, prob-ably by Dekker alone, has much more brutality against convicted prosti-tutes.

With a worm fastened on a golden hook:

Those are the lecher's food.   (III.i.93)

By clever scheming she entraps not only this debauched gallant,
but also the greedy knight who forbids his son to marry the girl he
loves because her dowry is too small. Pretending to be betrothed to
the son herself, Moll makes the horrified father glad to settle for the
lesser evil of the love-match and the happy ending.

In the controversy then raging over women's role and rights, their
wearing men's hats or masculine dress was supposed to be one of
the signs of moral degeneration (King James himself had pronounced against it).[14] By presenting a bold, coarse-spoken, aggressive woman in breeches as the liberator and defender of her sisters,
Middleton takes what might be called a popular feminist stance,
not unlike that widely reported among Ranters and sectaries after
1640. The unassailable virtue of Moll within the play, despite her
bawdy conversation, may owe something to Dekker's more romantic and sometimes sentimentalising style: but the searing attack on
male chauvinism is unarguably Middleton's.[15]

IV

The attempts of semi-bankrupt gentry to marry money by making a
parade of their own feudal grandeur are delightfully parodied in
the banquet given for the rich usurer's widow Lady Goldenfleece by
her gentry suitor Weatherwise in *No Wit, No Help Like a Woman's*
(1610). The stage-direction reads:

*The Banquet is brought in, six of Weatherwise's Tenants carrying
the Twelve Signs* [of the Zodiac] *made of banqueting stuff.*

(II.i.97)

The tenants are invited by the lady to join the feast:

Lady Goldenfleece. There be your tenants, sir: we are not proud,
   you may bid them sit down.

Weatherwise. By the mass, it's true too! – Then sit down, tenants,

---

[14] Wright, *Middle-Class Culture in Elizabethan England*, pp. 481, 483,
492ff.
[15] The scene quoted here has always been accepted as Middleton's, and so
almost certainly is the general design of the action. Where Dekker was
working on his own or with other collaborators, as in *Honest Whore*, Pt 2,
the attitude to prostitutes and fallen women is totally different and much
harsher. Heywood's privateering Bess Bridges in *The Fair Maid of the
West* is as virtuous as Moll and as handy with a sword, but without her
aggression or her liberating mission.

once with your hats on; but spare the meat, I charge you, as
you hope for new leases. . .Sit round, sit round, and do not
speak, sweet tenants; you may be bold enough, so you eat
little. [*Tenants sit.*] How like you this now, widow?

Lady Goldenfleece. It shows well, sir,
   And like the good old hospitable fashion.   (II.i.132)

The tenants who must curb their appetites 'as they hope for new
leases' remind us who paid for the 'conspicuous waste' of the
courtiers which made such a strong impression on London citizens.
Later in the same play the fool Pickadill underlines the point when
he refuses to help the other servants tidying up:

First Servant. You can prate and domineer well, because you
   have a privileged place: but I'd fain see you set your hand
   to't.

Pickadill. Oh base bone-pickers, I set my hand to't! When did
   you e'er see a gentleman set his hand to anything, unless it
   were to a sheepskin, and receive a hundred pounds for his
   pains?

Second Servant. And afterwards lie in the Counter for his pleasure.
                                                     (IV.ii.6)

In this play, the economic conflict between City and gentry is
resolved (as so often in life) by a cross-class marriage. Lady
Goldenfleece restores to the impoverished gentlewoman Mistress
Low-Water the estate which her usurer first husband Goldenfleece
has got by foreclosure; and since Lady Goldenfleece cannot marry
the second husband with whom she went to the altar (because he
turns out to be Mistress Low-Water in disguise), she gets his brother
Beverill instead. Everyone is to live happily ever after. There
appears to be no feeling whatever that Beverill, as a gentleman, is
demeaning himself by marrying a merchant's widow, whereas the
idea of a marriage between Lord Lovell and Overreach's virtuous
daughter is dismissed with horror by Massinger in *A New Way to
Pay Old Debts* (1621–5), and *Eastward Ho!* ridicules the unnatural
presumption of a merchant's daughter aspiring to match with the
gentry.

Just this kind of impartiality between social classes seems to be
responsible for some critics calling Middleton detached, cynical
and amoral. To uphold the sacred rights of the gentry, however
dissolute, to their estates, as Massinger seems to do in *A New Way*,
endorses the morality of what is sometimes called 'popular tradi-

tion' – in fact of feudalism. But this simple insistence on order and degree and keeping us in our proper stations was already becoming old-fashioned and decadent in Jacobean times, and a shrewd Cockney wit like Middleton can no longer present it as a self-evident standard of values.

The difference between Massinger and Middleton here is especially revealing, because Massinger too can be seen in some respects as an 'opposition' writer. Patronised by the Pembroke family, in whose household his father had been steward, he often embodies in his plays the Puritan aristocracy's criticism of Crown policy, especially of over-mighty favourites, patents to greedy monopolists, and foreign affairs (see pp. 215–21). Socially, however, especially in his comedies, Massinger assumes the stable, hierarchic order as the natural and desirable one, the old titled families as the natural rulers. Monopolists, usurers and upstarts are dangerous because they threaten this established scheme of things.

Thus in *A New Way to Pay Old Debts* the desire of Sir Giles Overreach,[16] usurer and financial shark, to engross Wellborn's ancestral lands and to marry his daughter to Lord Lovell is deliberately presented as a class war. Overreach, a mere citizen, longs to triumph sadistically over 'true gentry'.

> And 'tis my glory, though I come from the city,
> To have their issue whom I have undone
> To kneel to mine as bondslaves.
>   . . .
>
> And therefore I'll not have a chambermaid
> That ties her shoes, or any meaner office,
> But such whose fathers were right worshipful.
> 'Tis a rich man's pride! there having ever been
> More than a feud, a strange antipathy
> Between us and true gentry.   (II.i.81)[17]

The 'popular Lord Lovell', however, has far too high a regard for his own rank to entertain such an alliance for a moment. The choice of a wife, he says, demands equality of birth and fortune. And all the good characters in the play endorse this view, including the virtuous Margaret herself:

[16] Usually considered to have been modelled on the monopolist Sir Giles Mompesson – who operated largely in Wiltshire, the Herberts' own district. See R. H. Ball, *The Amazing Career of Sir Giles Overreach* (Princeton, 1939). He, however, was a courtier and client of Buckingham's.
[17] Mermaid edn (London, 1887), p. 129.

> You are noble,
> I of a low descent, however rich,
> And tissues matched with scarlet suit but ill.
>
> (III.ii.197)

In the happy ending, status and degree are exactly preserved. Lord Lovell marries the rich Lady Allworth, 'descended nobly, and allied so'. Margaret marries Tom Allworth, who attends on Lord Lovell, but has been treated by his master with the respect proper to his rank as minor gentry, not as a servant.[18]

Lord Lovell.

> I can make
> A fitting difference between my footboy
> And a gentleman by want compelled to serve me.   (III.i.26)

Finally, the prodigal Wellborn[19] has his ancestral estates restored to him as a result of the joint plotting of all the virtuous characters, and he redeems his reputation by becoming an army officer, my Lord graciously agreeing to 'confer a company' upon him. Sir Giles, the villainous upstart, goes mad. Amid the growing conflicts of the 1620s, the older hierarchic scheme is nostalgically reimposed on a mercenary world.

The City Madam shows the same pattern in a London setting. The merchant's wife Lady Frugal and her daughters are entitled to a modest degree of finery – satin on feast-days, a velvet hood, a gold chain or a pearl pin,

> It being for the city's honour that
> There should be a distinction between
> The wife of a patrician and plebeian.   (IV.iv)[20]

But when they start to copy court fashions, with powdered hair and diamond and pearl necklaces, embroidered petticoats and lying-in like 'an absolute princess', they deserve to be humiliated, and so they are. Sir John Frugal, the virtuous merchant, draws the general moral, addressing his womenfolk at the end of the play:

> Make you good
> Your promised reformation, and instruct

---

[18] There is an implication here that the true aristocracy (such as the Herberts) treat their serving gentlemen (as Arthur Massinger was) with proper dignity, whereas 'some great men' use them 'without distinction of their birth, like slaves'.

[19] The very names express a contrast in approach; Middleton's Witgood, Massinger's Wellborn.

[20] New Mermaid edn, T. W. Craik (London, 1964).

> Our city dames, whom wealth makes proud, to move
> In their own spheres, and willingly to confess,
> In their habits, manners, and their highest port,
> A distance 'twixt the city and the court.   (V.iii.150)

It is not luxury as such that is condemned here, but city women aspiring to luxuries beyond their rank. The morality is that of the sumptuary laws, rather than an attack on luxury in the name of the poor and oppressed, as we find it in Dekker's *If This Be Not a Good Play the Devil is In It* (1611–12) or *The Wonder of a Kingdom*.

The relationship between money and morals is powerfully dramatised in a more sinister tone in *The Revenger's Tragedy* (1607), which some modern scholars confidently assign to Middleton, though others (with whom I am inclined to agree) still regard this attribution as highly doubtful.

Ideologically it is tempting to see Middleton as the author. The corruption of courts, central in this play, is of course an obsessive leading theme in a great deal of Jacobean drama – in much of Shakespeare, Marston, Webster, Chapman, Ford, even Jonson, as well as later Middleton. What is unusual about it in *Revenger's Tragedy* is that the luxury and hypocrisy of the court, its expensive clothes and more expensive masques, its idleness and sexual anarchy, are so explicitly and insistently related to the break-up of the traditional social and economic organisation in the countryside, while a rootless court aristocracy throng the palace. Vindice, tragic satirist as well as revenger, continually dwells on these relationships, which are so often the mainsprings of the plot in city comedy, though they have no direct role in this particular story. Repeatedly he refers to young heirs mortgaging their land to usurers, and eventually forced to sell; usurers' sons who become gentlemen; meadows sold and trees felled to pay the tailor's bills – very much as Middleton had described all this in *Microcynicon* or *The Black Book*. Tempting his mother to prostitute her daughter, Vindice concentrates the social and moral tensions of the hard-up gentry into a bitter speech:

> Who'd sit at home in a neglected room,
> Dealing her short-lived beauty to the pictures
> That are as useless as old men, when those
> Poorer in face and fortune than herself
> Walk with an hundred acres on their backs,
> Fair meadows cut into green foreparts? Oh,
> It was the greatest blessing ever happened to women

When farmers' sons agreed and met again
To wash their hands and come up gentlemen.

. . .

Lands that were mete by the rod – that labour's spared:
Tailors ride down and measure 'em by the yard.
Fair trees, those comely foretops of the field,
Are cut to maintain head-tires.   (II.i.212)[21]

However, while the social attitudes underlying this are compar-
able with Middleton's, when one considers dramaturgy, poetic style
and playhouse evidence the case for his authorship is far less convincing.[22] The verse does not sound like that of the Tourneur who
wrote *The Atheist's Tragedy* either. Whoever wrote it – perhaps
neither of these – the play does seem to embody, in a hyperbolic
form, patterns of thought and ways of seeing that later became
characteristic of the 'country' against the court, and indeed must be
seen as the kind of art that helped to form those patterns.

v

Middleton in these earlier plays has affinities with Brecht, not only
in his detached stylised presentation of roles to make the audience
think, the almost circus-like style of his comic turns, but also in the
all-embracing quality of his irony. Plays like *The Threepenny
Opera*, or even *The Good Person of Szechuan*, dramatise the dis-
tortion and division of human personality in a divided society, as
distinct from the quality and nature of the human effort required to
change it. The main characters are parasites. Even Brecht's later
plays are usually revolutionary by implication rather than by direct
presentation of alternatives in the form of 'positive heroes'.
Middleton here is less consciously committed, however: and if he is
cynical about both contending groups – citizen merchants and old
landed aristocracy and gentry – this may be not only because he is
writing within a society which distorts the humanity of both, but
because neither code offers much of a way of life for the property-
less part of the population, with which the dramatist, lacking secure
patronage and landed or City wealth, has a degree of sympathy.

One cannot be dogmatic about a line of development in Middleton's work, especially as we cannot be sure in exactly what order

---

[21] *Mermaid Dramabook* (New York, 1969), p. 329.
[22] See Appendix B, 'Notes on Authorship'.

the plays were written, or, in many cases, what part of them Middleton himself wrote, or planned, and what must be assigned to Dekker or Rowley. All the same, it seems fairly clear that the city comedies up to *A Chaste Maid* have much in common both technically and in their meanings. They are fast-moving, witty, irreverent, scornful of greed and hypocrisy, and emotionally detached. They satirise abuses among both citizens and courtiers; they contain comic Puritan sectaries, but little animus against Puritanism as such; and virtuous characters are thin on the ground. Finally, they treat sex satirically, not only in bawdy episodes, but especially in a consistent and increasingly powerful vein of satire on property marriage. This kind of interest is much more central than in Jonson, but there is little of the sexual disgust and horror one finds in Marston. The treatment is more consistently cool and comic.

No one, probably, would deny that after *A Chaste Maid* something changes in the whole tone and approach of the work; and for a time the plays seem, to us at any rate, less satisfying. Partly this is because tragi-comedy, the fashion for which had been set by Beaumont and Fletcher, tends to look to us a contrived and superficial form. Even Shakespeare seems to have found it a difficult fashion to fit in with: students need a good deal of convincing to accept *Cymbeline* for what it is, in a way that has not been found necessary with *King Lear* or *Much Ado*. For Middleton, whose strength had been in ruthless consistency of character and plot, and brilliance of realistic urban detail, the demands of court tragicomedy or romantic tragedy may have been particularly uncongenial. But there are also signs of a conflict of pressures and feelings.

7. *Middle Years: Tragi-comedy and Moral Comedy*

We do not know exactly how and when Middleton began to write extensively (though never exclusively) for the King's Men, the best dramatic company of the time and the most favoured royal entertainers: but it seems likely that it was after his connection with the City was established, perhaps around 1615 (see below, Chapter 8). In this employment he would be working partly for the public theatres, since the King's Company, while playing in winter at the indoor Blackfriars, used the Globe as their summer theatre from about May onwards. Moreover he seems to have worked on adapting their repertory, including Shakespeare, an experience which may well have influenced his own later work. He would also, inevitably, be closer now to court and political affairs. The ultimate responsibility for the King's Men was the Lord Chamberlain's. Technically, they were members of the King's household and wore his livery on state occasions; practically, they performed at court much more often than any of the other companies, and some at any rate of the leading members of the company were personally acquainted with the Lord Chamberlain himself.[1]

Although the chronology of the plays is uncertain, it seems likely that *The Witch* dates from about 1616.[2] There are strong grounds

[1] See the well-known letter of the Earl of Pembroke, then Lord Chamberlain, to Viscount Doncaster in Germany, more than two months after Burbage's death in 1619: 'Now you have all that I know that past since your departure, but that my Lord of Lennox made a great supper to the French Ambassador this night here, and even now all the company are at the play, which I being tender-hearted could not endure to see so soon after the loss of my old acquaintance Burbage' (Egerton MS. 2592, fo. 81; cited in Bentley, *Jacobean and Caroline Stage*, i, p. 6).
[2] R. C. Bald (in *Mod. Lang. Rev.*, xxxii (1937), pp. 33–43) favoured a date of about 1616 for the play, because he found allusions in it to the activities of Simon Forman and Mrs Turner in preventing the consummation of the Essex marriage by witchcraft, which did not become known till 1615. Some other scholars (e.g. F. Sullivan and J. Dover Wilson) have dated it earlier, around 1610, mainly because of a supposed attempt to re-use for the popular stage the material for the witches' antimasque in Jonson's *Masque of Queens*. But, as G. E. Bentley points out (*Jacobean and Caroline Stage*, iv,

for believing that it was designed to appeal not only to the general interest in witchcraft,[3] but to the particular excitement about the subject aroused by the unedifying divorce proceedings between the Earl and Countess of Essex, which had been the talk of the town in 1613, and the even more sensational and highly publicised trial in 1616 of the Earl of Somerset, King James' favourite, and his wife, the former Countess of Essex, for the murder of Sir Thomas Overbury in the Tower.

There was much to give Middleton and his patrons a particularly close interest in the Somerset affair. The Earl of Pembroke (who became Lord Chamberlain in 1615 on the fall of the favourite) as a Privy Councillor had been involved in the whole business from the time of the Essex nullity proceedings. It was his close political associate, Archbishop Abbot, who had stood out against the divorce on grounds of conscience, and been overruled by the King's intervention; and Pembroke himself had been made use of as an intermediary to get Overbury (Somerset's follower and an opponent of the marriage) consigned to the Tower, where he was more easily done to death. Moreover, the Howard family, in particular Lady Frances' uncle and close adviser the Earl of Northampton, were not only the main contenders with the Herberts for court office and patronage, but also the main supporters of the pro-Spanish policy at court, while Pembroke was the leader of the strongly Protestant opposing group. Although (or perhaps because) the Puritans had taken their stand against the Carr–Howard marriage, James insisted that the Puritan Lord Mayor, Sir Thomas Myddleton, and the City fathers should feast the favoured couple: and when he asked to be excused on the grounds that his house was too small, James insisted that the mayor could command any hall in London. The City's banquet was duly held at Merchant Taylors' Hall, and Middleton

p. 905), this is long before Middleton's known series of plays for the King's Men, and before he is known to have been writing tragi-comedy. The evidence for the earlier date seems speculative.

[3] There was no necessary contradiction in the seventeenth century between religious faith and belief in magic and alchemy: indeed it was widely believed among adepts that only the pure could achieve results. 'The influence of this presumed connection between magic and holiness...underlay the conduct of a Puritan like Sir Thomas Myddleton, who could commission (from Richard Napier) the manufacture of astrologically-based magic sigils, but felt it necessary to pronounce a special prayer before putting them on' (Thomas, *Religion and the Decline of Magic*, p. 323). Myddleton's son took the astrologer's niece as his second wife.

the dramatist was hired to present *The Masque of Cupid*[4] and other shows for the occasion.

When, two years later, suspicion fell on the Somersets and they were found guilty of having Overbury poisoned (the Countess actually confessing it, though Somerset continued to deny that he was a party to the crime), the shock spread far beyond the immediate court circle. Ordinary citizens saw the accomplices Mrs Turner and Weston executed, while the principals were pardoned, and after being confined together in the Tower were released and allowed to live comfortably on £4,000 a year on their country estates. All this must have confirmed a sense that there were indeed two laws, one for the great and another for the commoner. The King's credit was directly involved, since Somerset had been his favourite, the divorce had only been made possible by his direct and public intervention, and it was owing to him that the couple never paid the full penalty for the murder.[5]

In *The Witch*, corrupt courtiers and duchess consult Hecate and her familiars (presented with much lurid detail) for charms to prevent a marriage from being consummated, to induce passionate love or wasting sickness. The witches oblige with hideous recipes and ritual blasphemies, taken mainly from Reginald Scot's *Discovery of Witchcraft*[6] – knotted snakeskins to cause impotence, a magic ribbon as a love-charm, and wax images melted before a fire 'kindled with dead men's eyes' to kill by slow degrees. The witch scenes are longer and more elaborate than those in *Macbeth* (which Middleton had probably been revising for the King's Men), and the stage horror is effective in a deliberately grotesque way – though, since this is tragi-comedy, the direst results are averted, and those who consulted the witches survive to repent.

These spells and magical practices *need* not, of course, have been suggested by those cited in the Essex divorce case. The material was readily available in Reginald Scot's book and in popular

---

[4] Now lost. The payment to the dramatist is noted in the City records. (See Barker, *Thomas Middleton*, p. 19.)

[5] S. R. Gardiner comments: 'It may be doubted whether [James'] rupture with the House of Commons contributed so much to widen the breach between himself and his subjects as his conduct on this occasion' (*History of England, 1603–1642* (London, 1883), ii, p. 174).

[6] See Thomas, *Religion and the Decline of Magic*, pp. 684–5. Scot was himself a sceptic about witchcraft, and it is not improbable that Middleton was so too, though in view of King James' well-known belief in witches, one would hardly expect the play to show it directly.

witch-lore. They do, however, fit the topical context admirably. Essex had claimed to be impotent with his wife but fully potent with other women, like the bewitched husband in the play; and images and spells as well as poison were reported to have been used by the Countess's accomplices.

Another suggestion of a link with the Somerset business is that the most striking and fully realised character in the play (she has no direct connection with the witch-plot) is a delinquent sixteen-year-old girl named Francisca,[7] who indignantly finds herself pregnant by her 'friend' Aberzanes, as a result of a casual liaison entered into without deep feeling on either side:

> *Fran.*
> I have the hardest fortune, I think, of a hundred gentlewomen.
> Some can make merry with a friend seven year
> And nothing seen; as perfect a maid still,
> To the world's knowledge, as she came from rocking.
> But 'twas my luck, at the first hour, forsooth,
> To prove too fruitful.   (I.i.34)

She must at all costs 'save her credit'. Her plots to conceal the birth of her child, and dishonour her virtuous sister-in-law before she can reveal it, create powerful episodes of oddly real-life immorality among the fantastic witch scenes and Fletcher-type melodramatic disguisings. Francisca's secret lying-in is suggested with a wealth of homely detail about childbed linen, putting on weight and losing it again, sugar and spice for caudles, and exhaustion after labour. Then we see the callous lover hand over the baby to an old woman to be left as a foundling on the doorstep of a tailor, who has just turned his maidservant out for being with child:

> Away with him! I love to get 'em
> But not to keep 'em. . .It's well for the boy too,
> He'll get an excellent trade by't.   (II.iii.1)

Illegitimate babies are no longer treated as comic, as they were in *A Chaste Maid*.[8] Francisca and Aberzanes are shown with contempt and anger, and when he is forced at the sword's point to

[7] Lady Frances was only thirteen when, through James' influence and for political reasons, she was married to Essex; and fifteen when they began to live together after Essex's travels abroad.

[8] There the Country Maid disposes of her baby by putting it in a basket with a leg-of-mutton, and making the meat searchers swear to mind it till she comes back – a piece of broad traditional parody, without any of the realism or edge of the *Witch* scene.

marry her, there is no sentimentalised repentance or reconciliation.

Francisca, indeed, seems like a first sketch for Beatrice-Joanna in *The Changeling*. In her irresponsibility, her terror of exposure, and the utter ruthlessness she shows in trying to avoid it, she may well have been suggested to the dramatist's imagination by Frances Countess of Somerset herself. The tone in this part of the play is wholly serious, and the morality affirmed is humane. It is not sex and pregnancy outside marriage that horrifies (in plays where this happens between young lovers, as in the early *Family of Love*, or in *A Fair Quarrel* about the same period as *The Witch*, Middleton treats it with a sympathy that is anything but 'puritanical'). What repels here is cold-hearted sex, and concern for one's 'credit' at the expense of a living child. One may compare the treatment of Jane Russell, courageous heroine of *A Fair Quarrel*, who is securely delivered of a 'much beloved' child by the man she loves, but has her physician's threat to expose her unless she will sleep with him:

> I care not,
> I shall have then a clean sheet. I'll wear twenty,
> Rather than one defiled with thee.

She successfully defies her father's attempt to marry her to a rich but coarse country squire, and gets her own man in the end.

The Witch is not, as a whole, a satisfactory play. The melodramatic devices are too elaborate for the human motivation and passions to work consistently and freely. Yet it does, in a strange way, suggest an atmosphere of court corruption, of sexual intrigue and fashionable witchcraft, that is both more realistic and more disturbing than has commonly been allowed. Middleton's witches, as has often been pointed out, are creatures of a lesser order than Shakespeare's – they afflict the body, not the mind; they do not evoke the fatal force of cosmic evil that terrifies us in the weird sisters. They are probably much more like Simon Forman and Mrs Turner, who were real enough.

If Middleton did write here with the interest of anti-Somerset patrons in mind, he was not the only author to do so. John Davies of Hereford in 1616 published a curious and rather unpleasant series of poems on the Overbury murder,[9] with a punning verse

---

[9] *A Select Second Husband for Sir Thomas Overbury's wife, now a matchless widow* (London, 1616; *S.T.C.* 6342).

dedication to his former pupil, William Earl of Pembroke. In *Mirum in Modum* in this volume he denounces the great people who are guilty of the murder, and whose accomplices have been executed for their crimes:

> Say, Greatness, what account wilt make to heaven
> For making those that tend thee, to attend
> On nought but mischief not to be forgiven?
> Stand'st thou not charged with both their crime and end?

He dwells at length on Overbury's tortured death:

> And (Oh!) suppose you hear your captive's calls,
> Deep groans, and outcries while in's bowels rag'd
> An hell of heat, yet moaned but by the walls
> Resounding but his grief's cries unassuaged.
> In whom the force of Nature (being young)
> Wrestled with pain, his torments to prolong.

Examining the role of witchcraft in the case, he wonders why the devil should be willing

> on mere frailty's spells
> For mankind's plague to leave the nether hells.
> . . .
> Thou art a Spirit: and therefore canst thou look
> Into the breast of Nature, and thence take
> Her chiefest secrets from the darkest Nook
> Or Love, or Lust, t' enflame, enrage, or slake.
> Thou can'st by such make puppets, though of lead,
> To strike desire, in liveliest bodies, dead.

He discusses the nature and the limits of the power of witchcraft to corrupt men:

> Can witchcraft in the abstract so bewitch
> The minds of those of Mind and Means, to be
> So base for Lucre, so to touch Shame's pitch
> As still will cleave to their posterity?
> But charms can make no souls to sin so sore
> But such as grace had left, for sin, before.

The poet concludes with deferential praise of King James, who, though grieved, has done his duty in bringing his former favourites to justice and tempering it with mercy.

> Now (prostrate) let me, dear Liege, turn my speech
> To thee, who in thy justice look'st like God:
> No such Crime spar'st thou: yet, stand'st in the breach

Thy justice makes, to stay Heaven's justest rod.
So thou (like God) dost grieve, when thou hast cause
To cut off those, whom thou hast made, by laws.

The poem may, despite this eulogy, have been less pleasing to
King James than to Pembroke, who took over Somerset's offices
and could see in his fall the weakening of the rival Howard and
Catholic grouping. Middleton's play, acted at the Blackfriars,
would doubtless also have been acceptable to the new Lord
Chamberlain, now the supreme patron of the King's Men. *The
Witch*, it seems from the dedication to Thomas Holmes, was not a
great success at the Blackfriars. It is probable that, if we could
consult the stage annals of Elsinore, we should find that *The Murder
of Gonzago* was not a great success at court either.

Another lampoon on the nullity proceedings is in *Philomythie or
Philomythologie, wherein Outlandish Birds, Beasts and Fishes are
taught to speak true English plainly.*[10] This odd series of fable-
poems, printed in 1616, is by Thomas Scot, gent.: it is uncertain
whether he was the same Thomas Scot who later wrote the famous
anti-Gondomar pamphlet *Vox Populi* (see below, Chapter 10),
though Locke the news-writer thought he was. Each poem is named
for a fabulous bird or beast, and *The Phoenix* is quite clearly about
the Essex divorce, though the author has prudently explained in a
postscript that the *Phoenix* represents Unity in Religion, the *Vulture*
Rome and the *Cynosure* self-will. This fable is dedicated to Sir
Robert Rich, Essex's cousin, and the references to Phoenix and his
wife the Bird of Paradise are quite unmistakable.

> She [the Bird of Paradise] now did hate and loathe the
>   sweet she had,
> And linger after something that was bad.
> Her tail was too too large for him to tread,
> He too too little her to overspread.
> . . .
> And now she gins to hate, and wish in heart
> A fit occasion offered were to part.
> But wanting such, she frames one: doth traduce
> And wound his honour for her own excuse,
> And still pretending modestly a cause
> Immodestly the trial claims by laws.
> Although the Phoenix her with tears did woo,

[10] *S.T.C.* 21869.

She separation sought, and gets it too.
The sentence passed, she Cynosure doth wed,
An unknown fowl, by th'air begot and bred.

The outcome of this second wedding is addled eggs. No direct reference is made to murder, and perhaps the poem was written before the Somersets were convicted. It sold well enough for a second edition to be printed in 1622, with a curious Premonition to the reader added:

> Yet pardon them, and judge aright.
> A free-man (not a slave) did write.
>
> . . .
>
> The intelligent within may pry
> But bar th' intelligencer's eye.

II

Middleton's best comedies of this period differ from his earlier city comedies not so much in their plots (which remain highly ingenious and stageable) as in their angle of vision. Instead of the quick-witted bawdy-satirical approach, with all the characters and social groups impartially mocked, there is here a concern to arouse sympathy for the domestic virtues as well as contempt for the wicked.

Thus *A Fair Quarrel*, by Middleton and Rowley (1615–17), turns on the folly of duelling, and of the aristocratic code whereby a gentleman must revenge an insult with his sword or be dishonoured for ever. A heroic mother, Lady Ager, tries to save her son, Captain Ager, from fighting a fellow-officer, who has called him 'son of a whore', by telling him that she really *has* broken her marriage vows – a desperate lie which shows up the absurdity of this ethic. The whole nature of honour – is it a civic virtue like chastity, or a badge of rank and status? – is brought into question[11] in a play which would have appealed particularly to the King, before whom it was acted: for James had been earnestly trying, though with limited success, to stamp out the increasing number of savage

---

[11] On the change in the predominant meaning of the word 'honour' during the sixteenth and seventeenth centuries, from a feudal military sense to a private upper-class one, see the valuable study by C. L. Barber, *The Idea of Honour in the English Drama, 1591–1700* (Gothenburg, 1957). See also R. Levin, *Multiple Plot in English Renaissance Drama* (Chicago, 1971), pp. 66–75.

duels among the gentry.[12] It would appeal also to law-abiding citizens, for whom aristocratic duelling and brawling were part of the old feudal disorder the City authorities were out to suppress. Captain Ager himself has, indeed, a scrupulous conscience, and his soliloquy on whether he is right to fight the Colonel is very much in the style of Puritan self-examination.

> I am too full of conscience,
> Knowledge, and patience, to give justice to't.
> So careful of my eternity, which consists
> Of upright actions, that unless I knew
> It were a truth I stood for, any coward
> Might make my breast his foot-pace: and who lives
> That can assure the truth of his conception
> More than a mother's courage makes it hopeful?
> . . .
> Oh, there's the cruelty of my foes advantage!
> Could but my soul resolve my cause were just,
> Earth's mountain nor sea's surge should hide him from me!
> Even to hell's threshold would I follow him,
> And see the slanderer in before I left him!
> But as it is, it fears me. (II.i.9)

In *The Old Law* (possibly written 1617–18) the framework is satirical-fantastic. The Duke of Epirus has enacted a law that men at eighty and women at sixty should be executed, so that their children can inherit their wealth while they are young enough to enjoy it. The comic possibilities of this situation are fully exploited, and much of the fooling is near the bone even today. The selfish young heirs hustle their parents to the scaffold, and the comics fake the birth dates in the parish register so that they can get old wives killed off and marry young ones:

> *Simonides.*
>
> > O lad, here's a spring for young plants to flourish.
> > The old trees must down kept the sun from us. (I.i.72)

---

12 The pamphlet *The Peacemaker or Great Britain's Blessing*, entered to Middleton in the Stationer's Register, is now thought to have been written in part by James himself, in the main by Lancelot Andrewes; it deals extensively with the duelling issue (Willson, *King James VI and I*, p. 271). But see also Rhodes Dunlap, 'James I, Bacon, Middleton and the Making of The Peacemaker', in J. W. Bennett (ed.), *Studies in the English Renaissance Drama* (New York, 1959), pp. 82–94, where it is attributed mainly to Middleton.

The main social targets of the satire are court luxury and venal lawyers:

1st Courtier.

'Tis as a Court should be,
Gloss and good clothes, my lord, no matter for merit.

(II.i.36)

The good old counsellor Creon, doomed to die, speaks his mind to the Duke in words that have the true ring of religious resistance to tyranny:

Creon. 'Tis just
I die indeed, my lord. . .I've a' late
Employed myself quite from the world, and he
That once begins to serve his Maker faithfully
Can never serve a worldly prince well after:
'Tis clean another way.   (II.i.86)

Over against the heartless, however, are set the virtuous pair Cleanthes and Hippolita, who refuse to accept the law, and risk their lives by staging a mock-funeral for their old parents and hiding them in a wood. They are betrayed by a shameless court lady with an ageing husband, and the noble couple face death. But much to their relief, and the audience's, it turns out that the Duke was only pretending so as to test his people, and no one really has been or will be executed at all. The greedy are shamed, and those who have been speculating on future wives lose their 'ventures'. In the last resort piety and loyalty, seriously and emotionally treated, are presented as triumphant, just as they are in *A Fair Quarrel*. The good characters are those who follow conscience and natural law, defying the unjust and unnatural law laid down by the state.[13]

In what is probably the last of Middleton's comedies, *Anything for a Quiet Life* (1621), the social balance of the satire has shifted remarkably from Jonson's or Marston's, or even that in *Michaelmas Term*. Here honest and generous citizens are swindled by idle young heirs; the city wife resists prostitution to a lecherous lord; and the old-fashioned virtues of 'housekeeping' and generosity are halted at the eleventh hour to prevent the ruin of an old gentry family. The reversal of the traditional treatment is so marked that it almost suggests a deliberate intention to defeat expectations; and this

---

[13] This point is developed by Carolyn Asp in *A Study of Thomas Middleton's Tragi-Comedies* (Salzburg, 1974).

becomes even more striking if one compares the play with Massinger's comedies of roughly the same period, *A New Way to Pay Old Debts* and *The City Madam*, where the older social attitudes are powerfully and nostalgically reaffirmed. The whole action in Middleton's comedy is seen essentially from the moral point of view of the 'middling sort of people'.

Sir Francis Cressingham, an elderly widower, good-natured but over-credulous and easy about money, has just taken as second wife a young court-bred lady who insists on having every luxury money can buy. Up to now he has given hospitality freely, lavished his wealth on Jonsonian projects like alchemy and fen drainage, and kept open house for 'a farcel of silenced ministers'. Now the new wife demands it all:

> One gown of hers
> When 'tis paid for, will eat you out the keeping
> Of a bountiful Christmas. (I.i.13)

The wedding itself has cost £1,500 in silks, velvets and cloth of gold alone. But Lady Cressingham orders still more expensive custom-woven materials for her own dresses, while refusing any new clothes for her husband or her two younger stepchildren, whom she has unkindly sent to be boarded out (and finally apprenticed) with the good mercer Water-Camlet. She gets her husband to withhold the jewels left to the stepchildren by their dead mother, reduces Sir Francis to a shabby pauper in his own house, and puts pressure on him to disinherit his eldest son. Finally she demands that he sell the family estate, with its unfashionable old manor house, to buy bog-lands in Ireland, which with a little drainage she swears will be very profitable – an obviously fraudulent deal.

> *Knavesby* [the lawyer, showing map]. Look you, sir, here is
> Clangibbon, a fruitful country, and well wooded.
> *Sir Francis.* What's this? marsh ground?
> *Knavesby.* No, these are bogs, but a little cost will drain them,
> this upper part, that runs by the blackwater. . .yields excellent
> profit by the salmon and fishing for herring.
> (IV.ii.179)

Englishmen being forced to buy lands they had never seen in Ireland was a wry joke in 1612; the City had burned its fingers badly over the Irish lands it had been compelled by the Crown to take over and colonise.

In the two secondary plots the satire tends even more definitely to criticise fashionable fop-ethics as against those of the industrious middle sort. The young heir George Cressingham and his friend Franklin, who has just come back from the disastrous Guiana voyage and cannot get another ship, decide they cannot live on their parental allowances in the style they think necessary ('scarlet and gold lace, play at the ordinary/And bevers at the tavern'), and therefore decide, rather than serve in the Low Countries, to live by their wits at home. They begin by swindling honest Water-Camlet (whom we have already seen befriending the younger Cressingham children). Pretending to be a tailor and his titled customer, they convince the merchant that he is dealing with a rich courtier, and so walk out of his shop with hundreds of pounds' worth of the most expensive material on credit. Traditionally in city comedy this kind of prank has been treated as excusable gentlemanly high spirits – like Prince Hal's youthful purse-taking, as George Cressingham himself suggests. Indeed not to pay one's tailor seems to have been considered the most gentlemanly of offences right up to the later nineteenth century.[14] But Franklin's father takes a much more severe view:

> Yes, I have heard of that too; your defeat
> Made upon a mercer; I style't modestly,
> The law intends it plain cozenage. (V.i.16)

And he insists on paying off his son's creditors at a fair rate, so that the young man can repent and make a fresh and honest start:

> By my blessing rooted, growing by his tears.

(V.ii.378)

Water-Camlet the mercer is not sentimentally presented, in the style of Heywood or Dekker; he, like Sir Francis, is comically hen-pecked. But the jokes about Mrs Water-Camlet's bad temper and meanness are not class jokes against citizens. They are rather the kind that would appeal to a craftsman and apprentice audience, as when the loyal apprentice explains how she persuaded his master 'to buy spectacles for all his servants, that they might have worn 'em dinner and supper...to have made our victuals seem bigger than 'twas'.

---

[14] This depended, of course, on one's point of view. One of Dekker's principal complaints against the devil-influenced King and Court in *If This Be Not a Good Play, the Devil is In It* (1611) is that they refuse to pay their bills, and thereby bankrupt poor tailors and mercers. It is obviously a small-tradesman-craftsman element in the audience that will most strongly identify with this presentation.

In the third plot, the most striking case of all, the rascally lawyer Knavesby agrees to prostitute his wife to the lecherous Lord Beaufort for money and preferment. 'Methinks', he tells her, 'thou art a rare monopoly, and great pity one man should enjoy thee.' The wife is horrified, but manages to get the better of the pair of them by pretending to be in love with the lord's page, and asking for his lordship's good offices. She then has the satisfaction of telling my lord what she thinks of him:

> Why, you've done worse without a sense of ill,
> With a full, free conscience of a libertine:
> Judge your own sin:
> Was it not worse, with a damn'd broking fee
> To corrupt a husband, 'state him a pander
> To his own wife, by virtue of a lease
> Made to him and your bastard issue, could you get 'em?
> What a degree of baseness call you this?   (III.ii.152)

From a citizen's wife to a peer of the realm, the language is decidedly sharp.

As in so many late-Jacobean and Caroline plays, what seems like a strong central satirical situation suddenly collapses into nothing at the very end. Halfway through the last scene (V.ii), without any attempt to let the audience know in advance, it is suddenly revealed that Lady Cressingham has been converted, or (according to her own account) has only been *pretending* to be wasteful and wicked, in order to cure Sir Francis of his extravagance and excessive hospitality. His land is restored, his children reinstated, and all ends well. But this disclosure comes so late in the play, and is so unrelated to what has gone before, that although it may have satisfied the censor, and the management, that no dangerous attack on court luxury was involved, it cannot prevent the play as a whole from working as a contrast of honest citizen thrift and industry against new-fangled court vices. Dramatically the belated volte-face is of course a weakness, and makes the neglect of the play in later times less surprising.[15]

It is interesting to compare Lord Beaufort with the noble and incorruptible Lord Lovell who sets matters to rights in Massinger's

---

[15] The surprise ending of *The Old Law* does not have the same effect, since it is consistent and prepared for by the earlier scenes, and the duke has a clear motive for his actions, which is familiar from the behaviour of stage rulers in *Measure for Measure* and *The Phoenix*.

A New Way, or the anonymous Lord who suddenly steps in at the end of *The Puritan* (probably by Wentworth Smith) to sort out the intrigue, and assign the rich city women to husbands in an appropriate station of life. The difference of handling between Middleton and Massinger cannot, of course, be explained simply by Middleton's Puritan patronage. His lack of respect for mere rank was deeper and more long-standing. At no period would he have made a character intended to be sympathetic, as Lord Lovell is, reject marriage with a citizen in these terms:

> Were Overreach's states thrice centupled, his daughter
> Millions of degrees much fairer than she is,
> Howe'er I might urge precedents to excuse me,
> I would not so adulterate my blood
> By marrying Margaret, and so leave my issue
> Made up of several pieces, one part scarlet
> And the other London blue. In my own tomb
> I will inter my name first.   (IV.i.219)

It would be strange, however, when Middleton was spending so much of his time working for the City and had so much contact with Parliamentary Puritan circles, if this had not affected at all the way in which court and city, court and country are presented in the plays.

8. *City Employments*

I

During the last half of his career as a playwright Middleton also worked often and profitably for the Lord Mayor and the livery companies of London. Between 1613, when he was first employed to write and design a Lord Mayor's pageant, and his death in 1627, he was responsible for seven Lord Mayor's shows, as well as a number of other City entertainments, such as the shows at the opening of the New River waterworks, the Mayor's welcome to the annual shooting by the trained bands at Bunhill, and the City entertainment for the Somerset wedding celebrations. Moreover from 1620 onwards he held the post of City Chronologer, with the duty of recording important events and transactions in London – an office he seems to have discharged efficiently, though the records he wrote have been destroyed. A considerable part of his income, perhaps the greater part of it, came from these City employments.

The Lord Mayor's show, presented at the annual inauguration of the Lord Mayor of London,[1] dated back to the mid sixteenth century, supplanting the 'Midsummer Shows' of the trade guilds which were a survival of medieval pageantry. Essentially it was a popular holiday, and the pageants in the streets and water-shows on the Thames were designed to impress and entertain not only the Lord Mayor and his eminent guests on their journey from the City to Whitehall and back, but also the crowds out for the day. The City company to which the incoming Lord Mayor belonged paid for the pageant, which thus served to advertise the wealth and grandeur of that company, and of the City as a whole.

It was usual by Jacobean and Caroline times for leading dramatists to be appointed to design the elaborate symbolic pageantry, write the speeches and songs, and produce and rehearse the actors. Dramatists and artificers were invited to submit their designs to the livery company concerned, and tendered for the work on a

[1] Held on Simon and Jude's day, 28 October. The Lord Mayor's Shows were inaugurated in 1535 by the Mercers' Company (Wickham, *Early English Stages*, ii, pt 1, p. 46).

competitive basis. Among the other dramatists responsible for shows in Jacobean and Caroline times were Anthony Munday (fifteen of them), Thomas Dekker (seven), John Webster (one) and Thomas Heywood (seven), all dramatists previously associated with the popular public theatres.[2] Once he had taken to this line of work Middleton was by far the most successful competitor, partly it seems because of his close working partnership with the carver and artificer Garret (or Gerard) Christmas, regular decorator and wood-carver to the Navy.[3] From 1617 onwards Middleton and Christmas enjoyed a near-monopoly.

The cost of these shows was enormous by the standards of the time. Thus the Grocers in 1613 spent £1,800 on their pageant (the first designed by Middleton and the most expensive mayoral pageant of the whole period).[4] The Grocers' pageant of 1617 cost £882, and the Drapers' of 1623, £707. This lavish expenditure on shows, entertainment and dressing-up should in itself qualify some of our simpler conventional notions about the City fathers as a set of kill-joys who objected on principle to 'fictions', disguisings or spending money on enjoyment. One wonders, for instance, what actively Puritan Lord Mayors of Jacobean times like Sir Thomas Myddleton or Sir George Bowles, at whose pageants almonds, ginger, dates and nutmegs were scattered broadcast in the streets, would have made of Patrick Cruttwell's definition of the Puritan as 'a man whose rejection of the sensuous seems natural, a part of his very being, rather than simply a conviction'.[5]

Indeed the Haberdashers, with the Mercers the only City company who consistently appointed Puritans to the livings and lectureships in their gift, seem to have applied the same principles to the Lord Mayor's show. In 1620 they gave the devising of their pageant

[2] Webster may perhaps be considered partly a private-theatre dramatist. *The Duchess of Malfi*, however, was a Globe (public theatre) play. Webster was not one of the regular show-writers, and may have been brought in in 1624 because Middleton was in hiding after *A Game at Chess*.

[3] Christmas had been appointed to the post by Lord Admiral Nottingham, the original patron of the Admiral's Men, the company for whom Middleton first wrote. Christmas seems to have had Puritan connections, and was given the contract for the monument to the Calvinist Archbishop Abbot at Guildford (on his death it was completed by his sons). The name Garret (or Gerard) suggests that, like many carvers and painters of the time, he was from the Netherlands, possibly a political refugee, like his fellow-artists Gheeraerts and Colt.

[4] David Bergeron, *English Civic Pageantry* (London, 1971), p. 179.

[5] *The Shakespearean Moment* (New York, 1960), p. 141.

to John Squire, vicar at St Leonard's Shoreditch, who also preached the inaugural sermon for the Lord Mayor, Sir Francis Jones. In a sermon of 1618, also addressed to a congregation largely of Aldermen and dedicated to Sir Francis Jones, Squire concentrates on strict enforcement of the Sabbath and the necessity for active preachers to replace hireling 'dumb dogs' – two of the most popular controversial issues with the City Puritans.[6] His show, *The Triumph of Peace*, gives suitable prominence to Mount Parnassus, with Apollo and the Muses, a very appropriate device for a scholar, and concludes with submissive War standing with fire and sword to defend the Lord Mayor's gates.

Undoubtedly, however, the pageant served for more than mere enjoyment and allegorical instruction. The Lord Mayor's show, like the court masques from which many of its scenic devices were directly imitated, was also a conscious demonstration of the wealth and power of the great merchants of London.

In Elizabethan times the sovereign had been involved in a great deal of civic pageantry, royal entries, royal welcomes and so on. Elizabeth brought to these occasions a love of display and a keen sense of the style and popular image that would please the crowds. James I and Charles I, on the contrary, disliked mixing with social inferiors and exhibiting themselves to the vulgar, and greatly preferred the even more expensive court masques devised by Jonson and Campion with the scenic genius of Inigo Jones, and held in their own private court circle. Indeed at his accession in 1626 Charles refused to make a royal entry into London at all, and gave instructions that the pageants which had been prepared should be

---

[6] Bentley, in *Jacobean and Caroline Stage* (v, p. 1185), suggests that the Short Title Catalogue must be in error in ascribing this pageant and several sermons printed 1618–37 to the authorship of the same John Squire, on the grounds that 'it does not seem likely that a Lord Mayor's pageant would have been written by a clergyman'. This particular clergyman, however, in dedicating a sermon printed in 1621 to this same Lord Mayor, Sir Francis Jones, thanks him for his 'many favours', and is also on record as having preached Jones' inaugural sermon – so it seems very likely that he was the author of the pageant too. Indeed it is only a rooted belief that preachers and pagcantry must be opposites which makes it 'unlikely'.

John Squire was lecturer on behalf of the Haberdashers to the congregation of St Bartholomew's Exchange, which included Middleton's patrons Fishbourne and Browne. He was a grandson of Bishop Aylmer, was appointed to his living by Archdeacon Aylmer, and seems to have given up any Puritan views in later years. In 1641 he was denounced by his parishioners to Parliament for ceremonialism and Papist tendencies, and sequestered.

taken down. The two forms of display proceeded as it were in competition, with increasing separation and rivalry between the court dramatists who worked on the masques, and the popular theatre writers who worked for the City shows. Glynne Wickham has tellingly commented:

> Indeed it is by no means far-fetched to regard the swelling splendour of the Lord Mayor's shows in Jacobean and Caroline times as deliberately rivalling the opulent masks of the Court at Westminster; for in the underlying basis of flattery and inflated self-esteem, in the extravagance of the expenditure, and in the spectacular quality of both types of entertainment, there is a similarity so remarkable as to be more than coincidence. As great powers among nations in our own times use military parades to impress the strength of their resources upon their rivals as tension mounts between them, so it is possible to sense in the ostentatious Masks of Twelfth Night and Shrovetide on the one hand and the elaborate land and water triumphs of St Simon and Jude's Day a similarly dangerous and aggressive spirit beneath the theatrical cloak of these festivities at Court and in the City.[7]

In this respect the lineal descendants of the pageant-cars and ships of Stuart times are the decorated floats of twentieth-century May Day processions, with tableaux of trade unionists, students or cooperators' children representing the triumph of labour or the abolition of the atom bomb, and trade union banners with semi-allegorical devices.

II

Middleton had first taken a hand in civic pageantry as a young man, when he contributed a speech for Zeal to Dekker's entertainment on the entry of James I into London in 1603. But he became seriously involved only from 1613, when he wrote the Lord Mayor's pageant for Sir Thomas Myddleton, of the Grocers' Company.[8]

Sir Thomas was an extremely rich merchant trading with

---

[7] *Early English Stages*, ii, pt 1, p. 237.
[8] He also wrote a speech in honour of Myddleton's opening of the New River in the same year. This, which gave London a fresh water supply, was the work of Sir Hugh Myddleton, brother of Sir Thomas, a goldsmith and banker, and lessee of lead and silver mines in South Wales.

Holland and the Indies, and a devout Puritan.[9] His rise to fortune owed much to his intimacy with Walsingham, leader of the Puritan group on Elizabeth's Privy Council, who in 1587 gave him the right of customs collection. Myddleton used part of the proceeds to finance a share for himself and his brothers in voyages to the West Indies, often in effect privateering expeditions against Spain. In these enterprises he was associated with Sir John Hawkins, Sir Walter Raleigh and his son, Sir Francis Drake, and his own partner, Nicholas Ferrar the elder. The profit on some of these voyages reached 400–500 per cent. Especially profitable was that financed partly by Raleigh in 1592, to which Myddleton acted as treasurer: this expedition captured the carrack *Madre de Dios*, the richest prize of the whole war, whose cargo Myddleton continued to sell off for the next four or five years. As his wealth accumulated he became a large-scale moneylender, with important clients among the gentry and aristocracy,[10] and seems to have been a reasonable and fair creditor. He owned land in Montgomery and Merioneth as well as his native Denbigh, to which he was steadily adding.

Myddleton was in many ways the typical Puritan businessman. His Elizabethan account books record payments to the 'Dutch preacher' and the 'parson's wages'. With Alderman Rowland Heylyn (who was chairman of the Feoffees for Impropriations) he sponsored publication of a Welsh translation of the Bible (1630). It seems likely, though his accounts for the Stuart period are lost, that he may later have contributed to lectureships and other means of increasing Puritan influence in the Church. From his mayoralty in 1613 he represented the very Puritan ward of Coleman Street, and in 1624 was MP for the City of London.

Probably it was through Sir Thomas Myddleton that his namesake the dramatist acquired his favoured position with the City. The quality of his work on the 1613 Lord Mayor's show seems to have been exceptionally high, and he wrote two more shows for

9 Unless otherwise stated, information here on Sir Thomas Myddleton's career is derived from A. H. Dodd, 'Mr Myddleton, The Merchant of Tower Street', in S. Bindoff, J. Hurstfield and C. H. Williams (eds.), *Elizabethan Government and Society* (London, 1961); from A. H. Dodd, *Studies in Stuart Wales* (Cardiff, 1952); and from *Dictionary of National Biography*.
10 They included Job Throckmorton, who may have been the author of the illegal Puritan Marprelate tracts; Lady Bacon and her son Francis; Sir John Fortescue, Lord Keeper Egerton, Sir Thomas Gorges, the Earl of Shrewsbury, Lord Chief Justice Popham, Sir John Norris, and Walsingham's stepson Christopher Carleill.

the Grocers in 1617 and 1622. He seems also to have had several patrons among the livery of the Haberdashers, who, with the Grocers, are known to have been more strongly influenced by the Parliamentary Puritans than most of the other livery companies in this period.

That Middleton had Parliamentarian and Puritan patrons, as well as Puritan and Calvinist views, can also be seen from the pious pamphlet he published in 1620, *The Marriage of the Old and New Testament, or God's Parliament House*, dedicated to Richard Fishbourne (a Mercer) and John Browne (a Merchant Tailor), merchants of Puritan sympathies. This compilation consists of prophetic texts from the Old Testament, printed opposite passages deemed to show their fulfilment in the New Testament. The preface, signed by T.M., Chronologer to the City, uses Parliament as a metaphor for the world.

> He kept his day and sent a Saviour: in him the obligation of the Ritual Law was cancelled; in him all Jewish Ceremony ended. . .
> It is he that hath married the Old and New Testament together, five thousand years and more hath a Parliament been held about his birthright, and both the Upper-house and the Lower-house (Heaven and Earth) are now agreed upon it.

A later edition (1627) has on the title-page: '*God's Parliament House, or the Marriage of the Old and New Testament*'; presumably the printer thought the reference to Parliament might help to sell the tract.

Thus it was pretty clearly as a protégé of Parliamentary Puritans among the City oligarchs that Middleton entered on his City employments. The majority of the Lord Mayors for whom he wrote pageants seem to have been strongly Puritan, and hence discreetly opposed on occasion to the policy of the Crown,[11] especially from 1618 onwards, when the pro-Spanish marriage negotiations were causing such active resentment in the City that eventually preachers who mentioned the matter in the pulpits were silenced and imprisoned. From time to time this influence is reflected in the pageants and speeches Middleton prepared for their ceremonial occasions.

---

[11] This impression is strongly confirmed by the Parliamentary speeches of the various Myddletons. (See Appendix A on Middleton's later patrons.)

III

The years of Middleton's association with the City were also, as it happens, a period of economic difficulty and, especially after 1620, of depression. The first ten years of the new reign had seen great commercial prosperity: but from 1615 onwards there was recurrent overproduction and unemployment in the clothing industry, and this worsened with the loss of European markets on the outbreak of the Thirty Years War in 1618. Throughout the 1620s the economy was stagnating, and starving people in the clothing counties were 'ready to mutiny for lack of work'. Even the biggest financiers and customs farmers felt the effect.[12] Thus Middleton was working for merchant princes, but for worried merchant princes,[13] caught between the discontent of the city poor on one side and the exactions and monopoly grants of a spendthrift court on the other.

In his mayoral show of 1616, Anthony Munday makes a central feature of the suppression of the Wat Tyler rebellion by Lord Mayor Walworth in Richard II's time. Walworth boasts:

> I made them [the rebels] stand,
> And in my sovereign's right, there I strook dead
> Their chiefest captain and commanding head.

This story had earlier been used by Nelson in the show of 1590. Walworth was particularly a hero of the Fishmongers' Company, and Middleton never wrote a pageant for them, which may be why he never shows virtue suppressing poor men in revolt. But he might anyway have found such a theme uncongenial. There is no attack on the rebellious poor anywhere in his work.

The Lord Mayor's pageant was essentially traditional in form, inheriting tableaux and even the actual stage property giants, 'green men' and floating islands from the midsummer shows of early Tudor times. In his first pageant, written for the inauguration of Sir Thomas Myddleton in 1613, Middleton departed from tradition by attempting much more in the way of sustained moral allegory than was usual (and more than would have been audible to anyone but the Lord Mayor and his immediate party). The diabolical figure of Error, in a chariot with his infernal ministers, offers to

---

[12] See Christopher Hill, *Reformation to Industrial Revolution*, p. 54.
[13] For example Sir Francis Jones, the customs farmer, whose mayoral pageant Middleton wrote in 1620, went bankrupt and absconded on the last night of his term, though believed a very rich man.

provide the Lord Mayor with slaves to tell him the going rate for bribes,

> The worth of every office to a hair,
> And who bids most, and how the markets are

and suggests that he should be able to make a good profit out of his year of office:

> For a need
> They'll bring thee in bribes for measure and light bread;
> Keep thine eye winking and thy hand wide ope,
> Then thou shalt know what wealth is, and the scope
> Of rich authority; ho, 'tis sweet and dear.
> Make use of time then, thou'st but one poor year. (vii, p. 242)

The temptations to corruption are, of course, resisted. Zeal and Truth drive Error away, and give better advice: and the City of London ('on her head a model of steeples and turrets; her habit crimson silk') recommends 'charity, which bounty must express/To scholars, soldiers, widows, fatherless'. The praise of City charity was traditional; but the explicit treatment of bribery and corruption was not. No doubt Middleton judged his audience rightly; for both the Puritan Sir Thomas and the City fathers continued to be his regular patrons. Indeed, the Lord Mayor was in far too big a way of business for 'bribes for measure and light bread' to be regarded as a very serious temptation. Weights and measures and quality of merchandise were a particular concern of Sir Thomas. He introduced a Parliamentary Bill for their better control, and in 1621, when over seventy years old, made 'a very religious speech and exhortation' to the whole assembly of the Grocers' company denouncing those who 'garbled' (adulterated) their wares. His pageant was evidently tailor-made to suit his personality and interests.

Another pageant, *The Triumphs of Honour and Industry*, written for the inauguration of the Puritan and Sabbatarian Lord Mayor Sir George Bowles[14] in 1617, though otherwise unremarkable, included (along with dancing Indians) greetings from a Spaniard, who spoke in Spanish. His part looks quite unremarkable in the

---

[14] Sir George Bowles, also of the Grocers, is reported when Lord Mayor to have stopped the royal retinue in their progress through the City during divine service on a Sunday to the astonishment of James I, who remarked that he had thought there was no king in England besides himself (*Some Account of the Worshipful Company of Grocers*, by Baron Heath (London, 1869), p. 261).

text, but according to report[15] he kissed his hand to the ladies and the Spanish ambassador, and behaved with a ridiculous affected gallantry, which delighted the crowds. This looks like a first sketch for the portrayal of Gondomar in *A Game at Chess*, and its popularity with the London audience may well have suggested the Black Knight character to Middleton. The show also included two ugly Spanish women, 'perfect hobgoblins', much to the annoyance of the Venetian reporter.

In the mounting tension between court and Commons in 1623, even the Lord Mayor's show expressed the class aspect of the conflict. The Lord Mayor inaugurated that year was Sir Martin Lumley, of the Drapers' Company, a rich merchant who had (like Quomodo in Middleton's *Michaelmas Term*) acquired lands in Essex and built a fine house there at Great Bardfield. Middleton goes out of his way to stress that Lumley's rise in the social scale is wholly justified. The central theme of the pageant (*The Triumphs of Integrity*) is that greatness derived from merit is far superior to greatness derived merely from high birth. The lesson is enforced through a procession of six mighty monarchs, among them Tamburlaine and Pertinax, who were 'originally sprung from shepherds and humble beginnings'. A solemn speech draws the moral:

> And 'tis the noblest splendour upon earth
> For man to add a glory to his birth,
> All his life's race with noble acts commix'd,
> Than to be nobly born, and there stand fix'd,
> As if 'twere competent virtue for whole life
> To be begot a lord: 'tis virtuous strife
> That makes the complete Christian, not high place,
> As true submission is the state of grace.
> The path to bliss lies in the humblest field.
> Who ever rose to heaven that never kneeled?
>
> . . .
>
> All this is instanced only to commend
> The low condition whence these kings descend.   (p. 387)

The comparison of the mighty Puritan draper, as a better Christian than many lords, to the mighty Tamburlaine, overthrower of monarchs, may seem absurd if acceptable flattery. It is noteworthy, however, that this Lord Mayor's son, another Martin Lumley,

---

[15] Report of Horatio Busoni, Chaplain to the Venetian Ambassador, *CSP Venetian*, 1617–19, xv.

became a Presbyterian member of the Long Parliament, on intimate terms with the noble Puritan Rich family, to whose Essex seat he succeeded in 1641, and thus had his small share in overcoming kings.[16]

For the time being, Lumley's pageant also reflects the moment of popular rejoicing and relief at the return of Prince Charles and Buckingham from Spain in 1623 without the dreaded Spanish Catholic bride. The traditional pageant device of a canopy with three crowns, a cloud and a sunbeam is reinterpreted by Middleton to fit this exultant mood:

> The cloud that swells beneath 'em[17] may imply
> Some envious mist cast forth by heresy,
> Which through his happy reign and heaven's blest will
> The sunbeams of the Gospel strikes through still;
> More to assure it to succeeding men,
> We have the crown of Britain's hope again,
> Illustrious Charles our prince, which all will say
> Adds the chief joy and honour to this day.   (p. 395)

Middleton's popularity with Puritan patrons reached its climax with the satirical play *A Game at Chess*, played at the Globe in August 1624 for nine highly profitable days, until the king heard of it and ordered it to be suppressed and the dramatist punished (see below, p. 151). Middleton went into hiding, and this may account for the fact that the 1624 Lord Mayor's pageant was written by John Webster, his only venture into this field.[18] Interestingly enough, this pageant makes a broad political reference, which would have been clear enough to the crowds, in presenting as one of its main tableaux a Monument of Gratitude, enthroning on a pedestal of gold

> Worthy Prince Henry, fame's best president,
> Called to a Higher Court of Parliament.

The Malone Society's editors comment:

When we find such remarkable prominence given to the figure of

---

[16] Marlowe's Tamburlaine probably owed his original popularity with the City audience to a similar view of him as a pattern for aspiring self-made men. Marlowe's patron was Walsingham, his company the Admiral's (whose popular repertory in the 1590s included much anti-Catholic satire and anti-Spanish history).

[17] The three golden crowns.

[18] Middleton was apparently on friendly terms with Webster, and wrote commendatory verses for the *Duchess of Malfi*, printed 1623.

the dead Prince Henry – a decade after his death. . .coupled with a most perfunctory reference to Prince Charles, the explanation may not only be that Henry had accepted the freedom of the company; for this pageant belongs to a time of strong Puritan feeling against Spain, against the proposed Catholic matches for Prince Charles, of the Puritan movement for armed intervention in the Palatinate, and when the legend of Prince Henry as the Protestant Hero and confirmed enemy of Spain was already being built up.[19]

It is uncertain whether Middleton was actually imprisoned for a time over *A Game at Chess.* At all events, after the plague had prevented any Lord Mayor's show in 1625, Middleton was again invited to design one in 1626 for the inauguration of Sir Cuthbert Hacket of the Drapers.[20] This, the last of Middleton's Mayoral pageants, suggests that the City fathers (and perhaps the dramatist) were anxiously trying to persuade Charles of their loyalty. There was need. Earlier that year the King's request for a loan of £100,000 had been turned down by a meeting of 300 wealthy citizens specially summoned to consider it; and the Court of Aldermen had then offered him only £20,000, to be repaid within a year on the security of the customs farmers. The City's failure to lend the full sum was probably due less to the royal dissolution of Parliament and the failure of the Cadiz expedition, though these were blamed by some contemporary observers, than to the lack of sufficient security (provided the next year by the transfer of Crown lands).[21]

The pageant is, indeed, full of the fine words that butter no parsnips – or not enough parsnips. For the first time in Middleton's pageants the theme of royalty is stressed throughout. The mayor is referred to consistently as 'the King's great substitute', and Government, mounted on the Chariot of Honour drawn by two golden-pelleted lions, declares that the City of London is the heart of the loyal nation:

> And as the heart, in its meridian seat,
> Is styled the fountain of the body's heat,
> The first thing receives life, the last that dies,

[19] *Malone Society Collections*, III (Oxford, 1954), p. xli.
[20] This was the company of which Middleton himself had become a freeman by redemption in 1626, probably with the aim of securing some assistance for his family after his death.
[21] Valerie Pearl, *London and the Outbreak of the Puritan Revolution*, p. 72.

These properties experience well applies
To this most loyal city, that hath been
In former ages, as in these times, seen
The fountain of affection, duty, zeal,
And taught all cities through the commonweal;
The first that receives quickening life and spirit
From the King's grace, which still she strives t'inherit,
And, like the heart, will be the last that dies
In any duty toward good supplies.
What can express affection's nobler fruit
Both to the King, and you his substitute?   (p. 408)

There was some criticism of the 'ill performance' of this pageant, and the one designed by Middleton and Christmas for the abortive Royal Entry was also attacked. The final payments made to Middleton and Christmas were delayed and made partly in kind, in the form of the pageant wagons themselves. It may be that the City was vexed because the king had cancelled the Royal Entry after so much money had been spent on it, and vented their anger on the designers; and this possibly accounts too for the more obsequious tone of the speeches.[22]

In any case, Middleton can hardly have been permanently in disgrace with his employers, for after his death in 1627 his widow Magdalen Middleton petitioned the City for money and received, not as a payment due her husband but as a gift, the sum of twenty nobles.[23] But it does seem that by this time there was beginning that change in the political make-up and personnel of the City government which transformed the Court of Aldermen from a body strongly influenced by Parliamentary Puritanism to become, after 1630, more or less submissive agents of the Crown's despotic rule.[24] A career like Middleton's would not have been possible in the next generation.

The effect on Middleton of his close professional and financial association with the City and its shows over the last fourteen years

[22] This may, however, have been shrewdly suiting the matter to the man. I have been unable to find that Hacket had any opposition or Puritan sympathies, as earlier mayors like Myddleton, Jones and Lumley had.
[23] Cited by Barker, in *Thomas Middleton*, p. 24. This presumably means that the City did not regard itself as owing Middleton any further payment for the 1626 pageants.
[24] See Valerie Pearl, *London and the Outbreak of the Puritan Revolution*, for a detailed and illuminating account of this change. Sir Thomas Myddleton died in 1630.

of his life must certainly have been to strengthen and deepen the City (and Puritan) political and social influences among which he had grown up, and to increase his sense of distance from the court. But to say he was 'bought over' is too simple. A man could be hired to produce *The Triumphs of Truth*, or to compile *The Marriage of the Old and New Testament*, but no one could have been 'bought over' to write the great tragedies of his final period – *The Changeling* and *Women Beware Women*.

9. Hard Times and 'Hengist, King of Kent'

The later years of Middleton's writing life were hard times in England. There was severe economic crisis, especially in the cloth trade. With the failure of the ill-conceived Cokayne project,[1] growing Dutch competition and the outbreak of war in Europe, cloth exports fell by half from 1615 to 1623; people in the clothing counties were starving and many London tradesmen and merchants were hard hit. A series of bad harvests in the early 1620s brought famine conditions over much of England and Scotland. In 1623 men on the Lincolnshire wolds were eating dog's flesh and old horsemeat, and people at Greystoke in Cumberland died 'for very want of food and maintenance to live'. The living standards of workmen in the towns and farm labourers in the country were declining all the time. Wages were frozen by law while prices continued to rise, and in the second decade of James' reign real wages for labourers reached perhaps the lowest level ever recorded.

Despite the savage penalties imposed on vagabonds, the landless and workless poor flocked to the towns, where many lived at a bare subsistence level. In bad years children died of hunger and cold in the streets of London; every few hundred yards there were whipping-posts for sturdy beggars. And meanwhile the prosperity and luxury of rich landlords and well-to-do gentry was advertised by the building of vast 'prodigy houses' of the nobility like Audley End and Hatfield, and innumerable manor-houses and great merchant-houses in the cities and suburbs. People were used to great differences of wealth and status, of course, but the total insecurity of peasantry and labouring poor, alongside the idleness and wealth of court favourites, office-holders and monopolists, represented a worsening

---

[1] The Myddleton family in Parliament were among the strongest opponents of the Cokayne project (a monopoly with royal backing for exporting cloth already dyed and finished). They were themselves associated with the older Merchant Adventurer monopoly, which was injured by the change.

situation which led to growing fear and repression by the authorities.[2]

Politically, too, these were years of growing tension, Crown and court reaching a crisis of unpopularity from around 1618 to 1624. The incurable extravagance of the court and the influence of corrupt vested interests, especially of Buckingham, last and most expensive of the King's favourites, doomed any attempt by ministers to make the monarchy solvent, and hence independent of Parliament. But the Commons would not vote taxes without discussing policy, above all the King's plans for a Spanish alliance and a Spanish Catholic marriage for his son, which he saw as a way out of the financial problems as well as a means towards peace in Europe. Moreover, Parliament's implacable hostility to Spain undoubtedly represented the feelings of most of the country, including the merchants and 'industrious people' in London, Kent and the South-East, and a large part of the audiences in the commercial theatres.

Conflicts as serious as these, however, could not be freely embodied in the drama because of the pressure of censorship and court control. Paradoxically, there was far less serious dramatisation of the relations between king and counsellors, court and people from 1615 onwards than there had been in the 1590s and early 1600s, when the issues were less acute. Shakespeare could afford to make fun of feudal honour and the pretensions of kings in *Henry IV*. His common soldiers, the night before Agincourt, could wish the heroic King Henry V were up to the neck in Thames, or could fight his battles on his own without their help – because the fundamental unity of Crown and country against foreign enemies could still be taken firmly for granted. Nothing like the broadly realistic treatment of popular rebellion in *Henry VI Part 2*, or the abuse of conscription by Falstaff, could well have been shown on the stage at the crisis of James' reign. The great Jacobean 'tragedies of state', in which Webster, Chapman, Jonson and Greville express the aristocratic aspect of the protest against court corruption and tyranny, belong to the first decade of James' reign, which was at least a more

---

[2] L. Salingar and his collaborators have noted a growing number of refusals by City authorities in the provinces in the 1620s to allow touring companies of actors to play at all – a trend which they ascribe to economic crisis and fear of unrest (*Les Comédiens et leur Publique en Angleterre, 1520–1640*), in J. Jacquot (ed.), *Dramaturgie et Société*, p. 571).

settled and prosperous time than the second.[3] In the worst famine years, indeed, touring companies in the provinces were more and more often denied the right to play at all, for fear of riots among the audience.[4]

Fletcher and Massinger, the most popular and fashionable dramatists at the Blackfriars in those years, adapted their style and themes to a time of danger and censorship. In 1619 they tried to catch popular interest, and directly to dramatise the religious wars in Europe and the supposed aggressive designs of Spain, in the topical tragedy *Sir John Van Olden Barnavelt*. The production, however, was held up by the censorship of the Bishop of London. The play was acted with his alterations, had a brief successful run (probably at the Globe to a popular audience), and was never revived, or even published, till the nineteenth century. After this experience, direct representation of modern history seems to have been felt to be too risky and increasingly unfashionable. Instead, the characteristic forms became either elegant and escapist court comedy (Fletcher, Davenant, Shirley) or fabulous tragi-comedy, in which a strong political situation involving royal power might be built up (as in *The Maid of Honour*, 1621, or *The Bondman*, 1623), but was then deliberately collapsed without the expected climax to allow a reassuringly happy ending. Massinger, in particular, seems torn between intense interest in political themes and fear of carrying them to a coherent conclusion, which would necessarily be tragic and have radical and disturbing implications.

II

Middleton's one historical-chronicle play, *The Mayor of Queenborough or Hengist, King of Kent*, bears all the marks of these crisis years. Probably staged around 1620,[5] it is one of his strangest works, at once powerful and inconsistent. Although it has become known (like *The Changeling*) by the title of its chief comic character, it is not really tragi-comedy, but rather tragical history, with a comic

[3] This genre has been brilliantly discussed by J. W. Lever in *The Tragedy of State* (London, 1971).
[4] Canterbury was one example: playing having once led to a riot, all plays by touring companies seem to have been banned by the magistrates in the 1620s.
[5] See R. C. Bald's critical edition (Amherst, Mass., 1938), which inclines to a date of 1619–20. Extracts from the play in the following pages are from this edition.

sub-plot parodying the serious events of the main story. Originally it seems to have had a good deal of topical reference which the audience could be expected to identify, as the prologue spoken by Raynulph the chronicler indicates:

> Fashions that are now called new
> Have been worn by more than you.
> Elder times have used the same,
> Though these new ones get the name.
> So in story what's now told
> That takes not part with days of old?

The subject, the invasion of Kent by the Saxons, is from ancient British history, and hence safer than something contemporary like *Barnavelt*. But although it would be excessive to try to find in the events of the main story, drawn as they are from the chronicles with melodramatic embellishments, a detailed political parallel with Jacobean times, there are points which must have given it topical audience appeal. Around 1620 anti-government circles were much preoccupied with Spanish plans to dominate Europe, and perhaps (as they believed) to conquer England by stealth or force. This probably influenced Middleton to revise older material on the heathen invasion of Kent.[6]

The play with its accompanying dumb-shows keeps in the main reasonably close to the chronicles. Yet given the mood of the time, and the interest in early history as a source of political wisdom, it does offer possible analogies with contemporary events for those who choose to draw them. The unworldly King Constantius, more interested in religion and study than in the daily business of government, could be seen in some aspects to resemble James I, yet in a sufficiently flattering sense to turn away wrath. The upstart noble Vortiger, who usurps first his power and then his throne, would give an outlet for resentment against over-mighty favourites; and in welcoming Hengist's aid against rebellion by the Commons, Vortiger is seen betraying Britain and its religion to a foreign invader, much as the Commons feared Buckingham with his Spanish and Catholic sympathies was about to do.

Moreover, always in the background of the play is the rumbling

---

[6] Behind this play may lie the lost plays of *Valteger* (1596) and *Hengist* (1597), referred to in Henslowe's records, as well as Foxe's *Acts and Monuments*. It may be relevant that the 1590s were also a time when a Spanish invasion was feared.

of discontent and mutiny among the poor, fallen on hard times
because of the glut in wool (explicitly mentioned) and the bad
harvests. The scene is nominally ancient Britain, but the economic
crisis, and the swarms of petitioners who besiege the King demanding redress of their grievances, are wholly Jacobean. The treatment
of such dangerously 'popular' themes in later Jacobean drama is
always limited by the demands of the censorship, and this is demonstrably true of *The Mayor of Queenborough*; but enough of it
remains to suggest a keen interest by the audience.

At the opening of the play the wicked noble Vortiger enters
carrying the crown, and bursts into an angry soliloquy, denouncing
the many-headed multitude whose election has barred him from
the throne:

> Will that wide-throated beast, the multitude,
> Never leave bellowing? Courtiers are ill
> Advised when they first make such monsters.
> How near was I to a sceptre and a crown!
> Fair power was even upon me; my desires
> Were casting glory, till this forked rabble,
> With their infectious acclamations,
> Poisoned my fortunes for Constantine's sons.
> Well, though I rise not King, I'll seek the means
> To grow as near to one as policy can,
> And choke their expectations.   (I.i.1)

When the saintly Constantius is unwillingly forced from his
monastery to be crowned, Vortiger volunteers to take all the tire-
some business of monarchy off his hands – much like the kind
favourites of the English Solomon:

> I see you are not made for noise and pains
> Clamours of suitors, injuries and redresses.
>   . . .
> To be oppressed is not required of you, my lord,
> But only to be King. The broken sleeps
> Let me take from you, sir: the toils and troubles,
> All that is burthenous in authority,
> Please you lay it on me, and what is glorious
> Receive't to your own brightness.   (I.i.141)

Constantius, however, is too conscientious to hand over power.
The ambitious Vortiger thereupon plans to 'vex authority from
him' by overwhelming him with the petty business he dislikes, and

sends all the discontented petitioners who throng the court – graziers, feltmongers, buttonmakers, whom he contemptuously terms 'the rank rout' – to afflict the king with their mercenary demands for trade protection and lower rents.

> *Buttonmaker.* Mine's a supplication for brass buttons, sir.
> *Feltmonger.* There's a great enormity in wool: I beseech your grace consider it.
> *Grazier.* Pastures rise twopence an acre – what will this world come to!...We are almost all undone, the country beggared.
> (I.ii.100)

The king, whose only interest is the spiritual life, gives them no satisfaction. ('We may all spend our mouths like a company of hounds in chase of a royal deer, and then go home and fall to cold mutton bones, when we have done.') All the same, the people have no use for tyrants, and when Vortiger gets the saintly king murdered and seizes his throne they rise in arms against the usurper, to his fury:

> *Vortiger.* Ulcers of realms! they hated him alive,
> > Grew weary of the minute of his reign
> > Compared with some king's time, and poisoned him
> > Often before he died, in their black wishes,
> > Called him an evil of their own electing.
> > And is their ignorant zeal so fiery now
> > When all their thanks are cold? (II.ii.11)

Vortiger is saved from deposition only by the timely invasion of Hengist the Saxon, who puts down the revolt for him, and in return is granted enough land to build a castle, whence he later wins the kingdom of Kent and challenges Vortiger for the rule of the whole country.

An analogy between Hengist's conquest and the dreaded Spanish takeover is deftly suggested in the scene of the Saxons' first victory, where there are two references comparing them to Romans. And it is stressed that by granting land to these 'misbelievers' Vortiger will be opening the door to paganism and civil strife:[7]

> > For you're strangers in religion chiefly –
> > Which is the greatest alienation can be,
> > And breeds most faction in the bloods of men. (II.iii.34)

---

[7] Middleton deliberately selects those versions of his story which bring out the differences in religion and the idea that in those times the will of the people, rather than primogeniture alone, determined who was to rule. This is pointed out by Bald in his Introduction to *Hengist, King of Kent*.

Throughout the play Hengist shows himself courteous to the commons and comics, pretending to have sympathy with their grievances, whereas Vortiger consistently insults and despises them.
Hated by the 'rank rout', Vortiger is left an easy prey to Hengist,
till he in turn is overthrown by the sons of Constantine, Aurelius
and Uther, the rightful heirs, with the support of the British lords
who rally against Vortiger as a traitor to religion:

1st Lord. When thou fled'st from heaven, we fled from thee.

(V.ii.72)

And Aurelius, burning the castle with Vortiger and his
wicked queen inside it, sees himself as the direct agent of divine
justice:

Aurelius.   Let wildfire ruin it,
          That his destruction may appear to him
          In the figure of heaven's wrath at the last day,
          The murderer of our brother!   (V.ii.2)

Finally Vortiger, at the point of death, acknowledges the justice
of his punishment:

Vortiger. Ambition, hell, my own undoing lust
          And all the brood of plagues, conspire against me.

(IV.iii.145)

Vortiger [to Roxena in the flames].
          Oh mystical harlot,
          Thou hast thy full due! Whom lust crowned queen before,
          Flames crown her now a most triumphant whore,
          And that end crowns them all.   [*Falls.*]

(V.ii.199)

The sexual side of the story, greatly enlarged by Middleton from
brief references in the chronicles, adds tension and sensation, and
may also carry a topical significance. Castiza in the play, developed
from a mere mention in the chronicle of the 'virtuous queen' put
away by Vortiger, is raped by her husband in disguise, then disgraced for it so that he can marry Hengist's daughter Roxena. And
Roxena herself becomes the 'mystical harlot', keeping Horsus as a
secret lover who attends on her till death, yet daring to affirm her
virginity on oath because 'they swear by that we worship not'.
Betrayal of religion through a disastrous marriage to a corrupt
woman thus becomes a central theme in the play, which it scarcely
is in the chronicles. It had, however, been strongly stressed by John
Foxe, who dealt with Vortiger in his *Acts and Monuments* as an

example of the disasters that follow when princes join marriage with infidels.

These added characters and scenes may be seen either as an element of sexual obsession never brought into unity with the rest of the play (as S. Schoenbaum argued in his pioneering chapter on *Hengist*)[8] or as 'emblematic' with an allegorical meaning, as Anthony Bromham has it in a more recent study.[9] Roxena consumed in flames in the final catastrophe can then image the Whore of Babylon, the Church of Rome itself, as seen by militant Protestants;[10] and Castiza can be the Church of England, reunited at the end to the rightful king.

This interpretation does make more coherent intellectual sense of the play as a whole (though not of all the sexually disturbing episodes in it). The sudden shift of conventions it involves, however – from passionate and powerful verse in the *Changeling* manner to flat emblem – remains awkward dramatically, given the violent human conviction of the Horsus–Roxena scenes. Moreover, topical allusions to such a dangerous matter as the Spanish marriage and its religious implications would need to remain sufficiently oblique to be denied if necessary, and with the long-standing ban on religious subjects in drama the point could scarcely be made very obvious in the staging. Open political-religious allegory, similar to that in *A Game at Chess* later, would clearly have been too risky for the players in 1620–3, when Puritan preachers were being silenced and imprisoned for commenting on the marriage plan. This may be why the 'emblematic' union of Aurelius with Castiza

8 *Middleton's Tragedies* (New York, 1955).
9 Here Bromham is developing and applying Glynne Wickham's view that, for early Stuart playwrights, 'the emblematic play was. . .a vehicle which because its form resembles that of a riddle, enables them to discuss religious, political and social issues notwithstanding the censorship. . .It often takes the form of a romance into which references to factual matters of a topical nature have been inserted. . .Interpretation of the emblem is thus a matter for the discerning spectator' (Wickham, 'Romance and Emblem: A Study in the Dramatic Structure of *The Winter's Tale*', in *Elizabethan Theatre*, iii (London, 1973)). I am indebted to Bromham's unpublished Ph.D. thesis, 'Rulers in the Plays of Thomas Middleton' (Univ. of London, 1978), for this reference and for much in the ensuing paragraph.
10 Dekker in *The Whore of Babylon* (1606) uses such an emblem: but the official and royal attitudes by 1620 were very different. The relation between certain Jacobean history plays and Foxe's *Acts and Monuments* is ably dealt with by Judith Doolin Spikes (without, however, mentioning *Hengist, King of Kent*) in 'The Jacobean History Play and the Myth of the Elect Nation', in *Renaissance Drama* (Evanston, 1977), pp. 117–48.

in the finale, which is found in the two extant MSS. of the play, was cut in the censored version on which the printed text is probably based, and most likely omitted in the original performance.[11]

III

The two MSS. of *Hengist* which have survived include much more *social* criticism than the text finally printed (probably from a censored acting version) in 1661, but how much of this was included when the play was staged we do not know. The problem was first noted by R. C. Bald, whose critical edition of 1938 lists all the passages of over two lines in the Lambarde MS. of the play (his basic text, belonging probably to the second quarter of the seventeenth century) which have been omitted from the printed Quarto. He believed that this MS. (like the Malone MS. of *A Game at Chess*) represented a copy meant for a reader, rather than a playhouse prompt copy, and that much of the original text may have been cut by the censor before stage performance, on account of 'the sensitiveness to anything that might be construed as criticism of the throne that was especially characteristic of the years of Charles I's despotism'. It is impossible to be sure which, if any, are the censor's own cuts, and which were made by the company or the author, perhaps in anticipation of censorship. However, the character of the cuts certainly indicates a political approach. What is particularly striking about these cut passages is their repeated insistence on the poverty of the common people, and the usurper's vulnerability to armed revolt by the commons.

The political moral of the whole is conventionally acceptable enough. Kings are strong and secure only when they attend to their subjects' grievances; but subjects should not rise in revolt, unless led by the magistrates and legitimate heirs. However, the Master of the Revels (or whoever else cut the play to make the shorter version) seems to have had a simple literal approach, rather like that of some of our modern would-be television censors. References to poverty, tyranny or armed rebellion were apparently felt to be dangerous, regardless of their dramatic context, and whether spoken by a good character or a villain.

Thus when Hengist first obtains the plot of ground to build his castle, his lieutenant Horsus reminds him that many rich men,

[11] See below for an account of the cuts and their political significance.

beginning with no more wealth than this, have founded dynasties,
>   And left their carcasses as much in monument
>   As would erect a college.   (II.iii.138)

Hengist elaborates the complaint about ostentatious funerals:[12]

>   There's the fruits
>   Of their religious shows too; to lie rotting
>   Under a million spent in gold and marble,
>   *When thousands left behind dies without shelter.*
>   *Having nor house nor food.*
> *Horsus. A precious charity!*   (II.iii.140)

The fashion for gorgeous four-poster marble tombs was at its
height in these difficult years. Immensely costly monuments like
those of the Cecils at Hatfield, the Russells at Chenies, the Earl of
Hertford at Salisbury must have made this reference telling enough.
It is not the traditional criticism of the rich man's luxury, but the
dangerous suggestion that the poor man's hardship is caused by it,
that the censor deletes.

Again, when Vortiger employs Horsus to get his virtuous queen
out of the way so that he can marry the wicked Roxena, Vortiger
reflects in soliloquy that his power should rightly be absolute,
beyond legal or moral restraints. His argument that kings ought to
be above the law is explicit in the MS., but cut in the published text.

> *Vortiger.*   After I was a King
>   I thought I never should have felt pain more;
>   That there had been a ceasing of all passions
>   And common stings which subjects use to feel,
>   That were created with a patience fit
>   For all extremities; but such as we
>   Know not the way to suffer, then to do't
>   How most preposterous 'tis. *What's all our greatness*
>   *If we that prescribe bounds to meaner men*
>   *May not pass these ourselves? Oh most ridiculous,*
>   *This makes the vulgar merry to endure,*
>   *Knowing our state is strict, and less secure.*   (III.i.98)

Once again the cut passage refers to the 'vulgar' waiting their time
to attack the 'less secure' state of the usurper.

A yet more curious example of the censor's sensitiveness is
the deletion of a metaphorical reference to vice in women as a

---

[12] The cuts in this and ensuing extracts are indicated by italic type, and are
to be found in Bald's edition of the play.

'potentate' on a triumphal progress, much like an expensive Stuart king:

> *Horsus.*   *The mischiefs*
> *That peoples a lost honour; oh they're infinite,*
> *For as at a small breach in town or castle*
> *When one has entrance, a whole army follows,*
> *In woman, so abusively once known,*
> *Thousands of sins has passage made with one:*
> *Vice comes with troops, and they that entertain*
> *A mighty potentate must receive his train.*   (IV.ii.272)

At the final exposure of Vortiger, Horsus declares in another deleted reference:

> *You have lost your thankfulness*
> *Which is the noblest part in king or subject.*   (V.ii.54)

To suggest that kings, like subjects, should be grateful for any help they got was seditious even in a villain's mouth – or so it seems.

The cumulative effect of the cuts (there are many more of them) is to reduce the impact of the play as history and as a comment on the ways of governors. Even uncut, it would still be melodramatic; but the expurgator's work here does make one realise the extraordinary difficulties that faced any dramatist setting out to use historical and chronicle material, however remote, in late Jacobean and Caroline times. It helps to explain why there is little later drama attempting a serious political treatment of English history such as Shakespeare made in the 1590s. A dramatist must either dilute and blur the issues of power, or he must eschew directly historical and political themes and limit himself to the tragedy of private life, where the Crown and court were less sensitive and the Jacobean–Caroline censorship, being political rather than moral, was less concerned to probe. With the single exception of *A Game at Chess*, this was the course followed by Middleton after *The Mayor of Queenborough*.

IV

The comic sub-plot, though critics have always found it incongruous, was apparently so popular with the original audiences that when the play was first printed (some forty years after the first performance), the Quarto was titled *The Mayor of Queenborough*.

after the chief comic character.[13] The connection of comic sub-plot with tragic main plot is tenuous, as often in the Jacobean drama, and it may have undergone changes by the actors, since seventeenth-century comics often improvised round their parts. It is clear, however, that the design was to parallel the tragic story of royal rivalry between Vortiger and Hengist, and the ultimate defeat of both by the true heir, with the farcical rivalry between the two plebeian candidates for Mayor of Queenborough, the unsuccessful 'rebellion' of the defeated candidate, and the final gulling of both by a troupe of strolling actors.

This kind of grotesque parody of serious events is what we find in the comic scenes of *Doctor Faustus*, often in Shakespeare (*Henry IV Part 1*, *King Lear*), and in Middleton's own *The Changeling*. But in *Hengist* the distance between the two plots has seemed too great and the connection too slight for the parody to be effective. Why, indeed, should a piece of pseudo-history of the saga type, set in the sixth century, have a sub-plot concerned with an obviously seventeenth-century election? And why was the scene set in Queenborough of all places?

A brief summary of the plot will suffice to indicate such connection as there is between the two stories. When Hengist first enters Britain he obtains from Vortiger a grant of as much land as a hide will compass. The hide is provided by one Simon, a tanner, who under Hengist's instructions cuts the hide up into thongs to take in a 'liberal circuit' on which he erects his castle (Thong or Tong castle near Queenborough). Simon thereby becomes a favourite with Hengist, now Earl of Kent, and when there is a dispute as to who shall be Mayor of Queenborough – the tanner or his rival Oliver the fustian-weaver – the townsmen wish to remit the decision to Hengist. He, however, throws it back to them to vote on, and after much bawdy cross-talk between the candidates they duly elect Simon. He comically presents the town's service to Hengist and Vortiger, but while Hengist receives it in a gracious and 'popular' manner, Vortiger (a right villain throughout) is contemptuous and rude:

> Forbear your tedious and ridiculous duties.
> I hate them as I do the rotten roots of you,
> You inconstant rabble. (IV.i.15)

[13] It appears under that title also in a list of plays protected for the Queen's Men in 1640.

Though both are usurpers, this behaviour tends to make the audience sympathetic with Hengist when he annexes another part of Vortiger's kingdom.

Later the unsuccessful candidate Oliver rebels against the Mayor, and is punished by having to watch a play performed by strolling players (a fearful torture, since he is a sectary). Meanwhile the actors use the play, which is about rogues and pickpockets, as a cover to steal the Mayor's purse and silver spoons – much to the delight of Oliver who thus gets some of his own back. As usual in Middleton, sectaries are guyed, but their persecutors are made to look foolish too.

It happens that there were disputed elections of considerable political importance at Queenborough and throughout Kent about this time, which may have given Middleton the idea. Queenborough in 1620 was a notorious 'rotten borough', a small decayed Kentish town depending on its oyster fisheries, which from earlier and more prosperous times had the right to elect a mayor and two members of Parliament. The elections were, however, customarily settled according to the wishes of the Constable or Captain of Queenborough Castle, a Crown appointment with some naval importance. Normally this meant that the Crown could expect to have a safe seat for its nominees here, as it could in the Cinque Ports near by, where the Lord Warden of the Cinque Ports by custom exercised a similar right of nomination.

In 1620, however, unease over the Spanish match and the King's pro-Spanish policy was intense among the opposition in Parliament and the 'country' peers – including a group within the Privy Council, headed by the Earls of Pembroke, Montgomery and Southampton.[14] Lord Zouche, Lord Warden of the Cinque Ports, was nervous about Spanish influence at court and refused to return the names sent him by the King. In the event Sandwich was represented by Sir Edwin Sandys, violently anti-Spanish and the most prominent opposition leader,[15] who defeated one of Zouche's 'moderate' candidates.[16]

[14] See Gardiner, *History of England*, iv–v; Willson, *King James VI and I*; Willson, *The Privy Councillors in Parliament* (Minneapolis, 1940); G. Aylmer, *The King's Servants* (London, 1974), all of which document this opposition in some detail.
[15] See Menna Prestwich, *Cranfield: Profits and Politics Under the Early Stuarts* (Oxford, 1966), pp. 289–90, and Willson, *Privy Councillors*, pp. 70–1, 79.
[16] Lord Zouche was later (1624) unwillingly pushed out of the Cinque Ports

At Queenborough the Constable of the Castle from 1616 on was Philip Herbert, Earl of Montgomery (subsequently 4th Earl of Pembroke). He was brother to the 3rd Earl of Pembroke (Lord Chamberlain and patron of the King's Men, for whom Middleton had been writing) and later the joint dedicatee of Shakespeare's First Folio. The Herberts were often in opposition to Crown policy at this time, especially over the Spanish match (though Pembroke was more strongly engaged than his brother), and their control over a number of Parliamentary seats, of which Queenborough was one, was an important factor in their political influence.

At the time when elections were pending for the 1621 Parliament, Montgomery duly wrote a letter 'from the Court at Theobalds' to the Mayor and Corporation of Queenborough, dated 6 November 1620. He reminded them that it had been the custom for the Captain of the Castle to nominate at least one of the MPs, and therefore requested them to choose 'my servant Palmer',[17] while approving their intention to elect 'my servant Frowd' (or Frend) to the other vacancy. However, it must have been confusing for the Mayor and Corporation to receive another letter, dated only three days later (9 November 1620), also from the court at Whitehall, and signed by the Duke of Lennox, which recommended them, if they chose any-one outside their own corporation, to elect Richard Hadsor, a lawyer and one of the royal commission investigating Irish affairs. Lennox was an old rival of the Herberts, and about to ally himself with a Howard heiress, the widowed Countess of Hertford. He represented the pro-Spanish policy, at this time the official policy of the Crown. Montgomery won and Palmer was returned (he later became Master of the Household to Charles I).

It may have been the intrusion of Lennox and his protégé that directly suggested the Hengist–Simon parallel to the dramatist. But the political parody probably had a wider general reference. In several Kentish towns, such as Sandwich and Canterbury, the 1621 elections turned into a three-way tussle between court magnates and their candidates, moderate Puritan gentry and magistrates, and

---

wardenship by Buckingham, who took over the job himself. Zouche received an annuity as compensation, but felt acutely aggrieved, according to his letters to his political ally the 3rd Earl of Pembroke.

[17] Roger Palmer, son of Sir Thomas Palmer, came of a Kentish family. His brother, Herbert Palmer, became a Puritan preacher and lecturer and was in conflict with Laud.

more radical sectaries.[18] Neither of Middleton's comic candidates, the roystering heathen-supported Simon (corresponding to the Spanish faction) nor the self-righteous 'town-born child' Oliver the sectary, could represent the 'moderates', and the gentry of Zouche's or Montgomery's faction could presumably laugh comfortably at both. However, local Parliamentarian and Puritan leaders were increasingly resentful of the whole practice of peers sending letters to influence elections, and a generation later Parliament was to forbid it.[19] All in all, the paralleling of low comedy and high politics, citizen factions and foreign invasions in *Hengist* seems to have been more like life than at first appears.

V

We do not know where or by whom *Hengist* was first performed. Although it was apparently acted by the King's Men at the Black-friars a number of times before 1640, there are signs that it was originally written for another company, perhaps Prince Charles'. Some early performances may well have been put on by a touring company to audiences in Kent, a county especially attractive to the players because it was near London, was densely populated, and owing to its importance for defence had relatively good roads. The King's Men, the King and Queen of Bohemia's company and Prince Charles' company are all known to have played at Dover in the years 1620–3, the most likely period for the first performance, and some at least of the plays were attended by the Lord Warden and his guests.[20] The addition of the comic sub-plot, with the knowledge

[18] 'In the early 1620s anyway, religious antipathy between moderate Puritans and separatists might well be a serious obstacle to the creation of a united front against the Government', says Peter Clark, discussing the Sandwich election in particular (*English Provincial Society* (Sussex, 1977), p. 332).

[19] On 18 Dec. 1641 Parliament sent Queenborough Corporation a copy of its general letter (preserved in the Queenborough Records in the Kent County Archives at Maidstone) declaring that it was an interference with liberty for peers to write to Boroughs seeking to influence Parliamentary elections, and asking that any such attempts should be reported to the Commons. Montgomery was the last holder of the office of Constable, and after him the post was abolished.

[20] The Dover town accounts list fourteen payments of gratuities to players from 1619–20 to 1623–4 – in contrast to Canterbury where the players are paid only to leave town without playing. An unusual Dover entry for 1623–4 records ten shillings given as a gratuity to the Lady Elizabeth's players 'having also His Majesty's licence, and the Master of the Revels' confirmation' (*Malone Collections,* IV (Oxford, 1965), pp. 51–2).

of local politics that it implies, suggests that Middleton had at least some kind of link with the county.

Certainly there is much in the play to appeal particularly to Kentish audiences. Many of the local gentry were keen antiquarians and would be interested in Kentish history as such.[21] Moreover, the fear of Spanish invasion there rose almost to panic in the early 1620s, Kent being the most vulnerable part of England and the haven of many religious refugee craftsmen from the Low Countries. Anti-Catholic analogies would be readily picked up in a county which had traditionally been a centre of Lollardism, of the Marian martyrs, and of Wyatt's rebellion against an earlier Spanish marriage (that of Queen Mary to Philip of Spain). Towns like Dover and Canterbury had above average numbers of militant Puritans and sectaries, possible models for Oliver.[22] The fight between court-sponsored nominees and local candidates would be of wide interest to townsmen, with contested elections throughout Kent in 1621 in which the Spanish policy was central. And the economic grievances of the 1620s, dramatised in the play, were especially severe in the cloth-exporting towns and among Kentish farmers.

Several of Middleton's known patrons (see pp. 258–83) had connections with Kent, notably Sir Thomas Myddleton, whose business interests linked him with the area.[23] Many of the Puritan court aristocracy and gentry, patrons of the drama, were also Kent county leaders or office-holders – the Sidneys, the Earl of Leicester, Lord Zouche, the Earl of Montgomery, the Walsingham family – all figures of the anti-Spanish or moderate Puritan trend, to whom *Hengist*, at least in its censored form, might well seem politically useful. But whether any of these actively patronised or encouraged

---

[21] Peter Clark in *English Provincial Society* (pp. 216–18) lists a number of these, including Sir Edward Dering, Sir Peter Manwood, Sir Roger Twysden and William Somner. I am much indebted to his general account of social and political tensions in Kent at this period, and to his personal help with some of the problems raised in this chapter.

[22] *Ibid.* pp. 177–8, 304–6, 322–5.

[23] Myddleton's 'dear master' Ferdinando Poyntz, the London and Antwerp merchant with whom he had been apprenticed, was also an engineer, and had carried out important harbour repair works at Dover in the 1590s before he was forced out of the job by the opposition of Lord Cobham and his associates. Both Poyntz and Myddleton owed the foundation of their fortunes to the patronage of Sir Francis Walsingham, also of a Kentish family. The Merchant Adventurers, in which concern Myddleton was prominent and which was hard hit by the Cokayne project, did much of its trade through the Kent ports.

it either in Kent or London we do not know. It may be only co-incidence that the Master of the Revels for a brief period from March 1622 to July 1623 happened to be another Kentish Puritan gentleman, Sir John Astley, known as a member of the 'German lobby', that is a strong supporter of the King and Queen of Bohemia and their cause.[24] All these connections may, however, have helped to make it possible for the play to be put on at all.

[24] Clark, *English Provincial Society*, p. 368. Astley was succeeded in 1623 by Sir Henry Herbert, of another 'opposition' family, who bought the office for £500 a year. Astley, who was officially appointed Master when Sir George Buck was declared mad, may have been exercising the duties even before 1622, and continued nominally as Master till his death (Bentley, *Jacobean and Caroline Stage*, vii, pp. 43–54).

10. *Political Satire: 'A Game at Chess'*

I

A Game at Chess, the anti-Spanish and anti-Catholic satirical play staged by the King's Men at the Globe in 1624, is unique not only in Middleton's work, but in the whole of early Stuart drama.[1] Nowhere else was the popular stage used for sophisticated critical satire on matters of intense political controversy. In ordinary times a piece like this could not have been shown at all: but then 1624 was no ordinary year. The play proved the greatest box-office success of the whole period, playing for an unprecedented run of nine days to packed houses before the King got to hear about it from the complaints of foreign ambassadors and had it closed down. Moreover it attracted an extraordinarily wide audience, including many whom we ordinarily think of as hostile on principle to the public theatres. 'There were more than three thousand persons there on the day that the audience was smallest', wrote the indignant Spanish Ambassador Coloma to the King. 'There was such merriment, hubbub and applause that even if I had been many leagues away it would not be possible for me not to have taken notice of it.'[2] And John Chamberlain wrote to Dudley Carleton that the play was

> frequented by all sorts of people old and young, rich and poor, masters and servants, papists and puritans, wise men etc., churchmen and statesmen.[3]

Among those who saw the play, he named Sir Henry Wotton, Sir Albert Morton, Sir Benjamin Rudyerd,[4] 'and a world beside', so

[1] In this chapter I am greatly indebted to the editions of R. C. Bald (1929) and J. W. Harper (1966). Important articles include J. R. Moore, 'The Contemporary Significance of Middleton's *Game at Chesse*', *Publ. Mod. Lang. Assoc.*, 1 (1935), pp. 761–8; and Edward M. Wilson and Olga Turner, 'The Spanish Protest Against *A Game at Chesse*', *Mod. Lang. Rev.*, xliv (1949), pp. 476–82.
[2] Cited by R. C. Bald, 'A New Manuscript of Middleton's *Game at Chesse*', *Mod. Lang. Rev.*, xxv (1930), pp. 474–8.
[3] Chamberlain to Carleton, 12 Aug. 1624; *Chamberlain Letters*, ed. McClure Thompson (London, 1966), p. 317.
[4] Rudyerd is quoted, in a speech in Parliament shortly after the failure of the Spanish match, as using the chess metaphor. 'It is true we have a hard

that evidently a number of distinguished people who normally patronised the fashionable private theatres north of the Thames took the trouble to cross the water to see it.

The immense commercial success of the play – which the actors must have foreseen to be willing to take the risk of putting it on – indicates that the audience would probably have enjoyed seeing much more critical, Parliamentary Puritan, anti-Catholic plays than it was normally allowed to do. It is the most striking reminder that the repertory of the early Stuart theatres as we know it is not a completely reliable index of the tastes of their audiences, or even of the attitudes of the dramatists themselves.

II

The main appeal of *A Game at Chess* was certainly to the city audience – to the merchants, shopkeepers, seamen and apprentices of London, who in general were strongly anti-Spanish and anti-Catholic. This was not merely a matter of anti-foreign prejudice. (There were few Spaniards living in London, and jealousy of foreigners taking custom and jobs was more likely to be directed at Huguenot or Dutch residents, as it had been in the riots of the 1590s.) But for nearly a hundred years Spain had been seen by those sections as the power trying to rule and dominate England – successfully thrown back in eighty-eight, foiled over the Gunpowder Plot, but always returning to the attack; and Catholicism had appeared as a foreign religion, the instrument of that would-be Spanish domination. Moreover the native secular opposition to monasticism and priestcraft, allied to the popular Lollard heresy, went back much further than that, and its strongest roots had always been among the lower classes and merchants in London and the south-east of England.[5]

However, interest in the subject went a good deal wider. Among the richest merchants there were many who were Puritan in sym-

---

after-game to play, but that should bind us now, as a spur, to quicken our industry and dispatch; and seeing the Prince hath made a posting journey into Spain for discovery, let us not be slow-paced in the remedies' (*Memoirs of Sir Benjamin Rudyerd*, ed. J. A. Manning (London, 1841)). Manning gives the date as March 1623, but references in the speech suggest it must be 1624.

[5] See Dickens, *The English Reformation*, pp. 48–50, 364 and *passim.*

pathy, who had made fortunes from trade and privateering at the expense of Spain in the West Indies and America, and who had close business connections with the Protestant Netherlands. They had never liked the peace with Spain; neither had a large section of the gentry.

The deep-rooted anti-Spanish and anti-Catholic feeling was roused to a new intensity after 1618, however, by the increasingly pro-Spanish policy of James I and the growing influence over him of the Spanish Ambassador Gondomar. The execution of Raleigh in 1619 at the direct instigation of Gondomar; James' failure to intervene on the Protestant side in Europe, and especially his refusal to give effective help to his son-in-law the Elector Palatine and his popular daughter Elizabeth, driven from their territories by the Catholic armies; above all, his project of pacifying Europe and solving his own financial problems by a Spanish alliance and a Spanish marriage for Prince Charles, which would certainly entail further concessions to Catholicism in England – all this roused popular feeling to fever heat.

Among ruling and court circles, from which the official patrons and censors of the drama were normally drawn, this indignation had in the early 1620s a number of sympathisers. The traditional fear of Spain and the Catholics was strong there too. Moreover many MPs and some peers (such as Brooke, Pembroke, and Saye and Sele) had developed interests in American expansion and colonisation which would be threatened by an alliance with Spain. A number of MPs thought a sea war against Spain in the West Indies, as well as providing opportunities for profit and trade advantage at Spanish expense, could divert the Emperor from his war against the Protestants in Germany.[6]

To James I, on the contrary, the Elector's actions in accepting the crown of Bohemia endangered the sacredness of monarchy and James' own position; it suggested that subjects might dispossess their kings. The King accused the Elector's envoy of coming to spread such ideas among the English people, 'that my subjects may drive me away, and place another in my room'. Both economic and political advantage made him obstinate in his pursuit of the Spanish match. This led to sharp clashes with the Parliament summoned in 1621, which demanded the right to debate foreign policy and

---

6   Russell, *Crisis of Parliaments*, p. 292.

expressed a deep anti-Spanish and anti-Catholic conviction which certainly represented majority opinion in the country.[7]

Accordingly James attempted to suppress criticism, especially of the marriage negotiations, by dissolving Parliament (16 January 1622), imposing silence on preachers (4 August 1622), and jailing men who opposed his policy or even discussed such matters in public. Outspoken clergymen like Everard and Ward, outspoken MPs like John Pym were imprisoned. Repression caused the popular spirit to 'burst out in irregular channels', and the Spanish ambassador's people were openly insulted in the streets. In one such incident in April 1621, reported by Gardiner,[8] a group of London apprentices who called out after Gondomar's litter 'There goes the devil in a dung-cart' came to blows with the ambassador's followers, and the unwilling Lord Mayor[9] was obliged by the Crown to sentence them to be whipped through the street. A crowd soon gathered round the cart, the youths were rescued, and the officials whose duty it was to carry out the sentence were driven away with blows. The Lord Mayor, appealed to by Gondomar, refused to take action, and Gondomar then appealed to James, who came down in person to the Guildhall. 'If such things were allowed, he said, he would place a garrison in the City and seize its charter.' The original sentence was carried out, and one of the apprentices died under the lash.

After the failure of the Spanish marriage project in 1623, when Prince Charles and Buckingham returned from their imprudent expedition to Spain without the Infanta, the citizens expressed their joy and relief with bonfires in the streets. The Strand was full of people shouting 'God bless the Prince of Wales' and holding up the royal carriage. And once again popular detestation of the Spaniards flared up in fighting with the staff of the Spanish Embassy – this time unpunished.[10] Through such events was the wide audience for *A Game at Chess* prepared!

By the middle of 1624 the immediate furore over the Spanish

[7] See Robin Clifton, 'The Fear of Popery', in C. Russell (ed.), *The Origins of the English Civil War* (London, 1973), pp. 144–67, and the editor's Introduction to the same volume.
[8] Gardiner, *History of England*, iv, pp. 118–19.
[9] The Lord Mayor at this time was Sir Francis Jones of the Haberdashers', the most Parliamentary Puritan of the City companies.
[10] The ambassador by this time was not Gondomar but Inojosa. See Gardiner, *History of England*, v, pp. 128–9, 203.

marriage had died down. But the fear of increasing Catholic influence at court, and a later Catholic takeover of the monarchy, was
by no means ended. Another 'lesser-evil' Catholic marriage for
Prince Charles was being planned. Moreover the rapidly growing
strength of the Arminian faction in the Church of England, which
was seen as half-way to Popery, alarmed the Puritan clergy and
their patrons, who rightly believed that the monarchy, and especially
Prince Charles, favoured the new doctrine and would appoint its
bishops accordingly.

Thus when *A Game at Chess* was conceived some time early in
1624, and finally staged in August of that year, it was not merely
flogging a dead horse, cashing in commercially on the mood of
bonfires and street parties that had followed the collapse of the
Spanish negotiations. The main political and religious issues between Crown and Parliament were still undecided, the tension once
again rising.

III

While its subject certainly makes it the least stageable of Middleton's plays now, *A Game at Chess* is much more than mere dramatised bigotry. Although it draws to some extent on scurrilous
popular pamphlets of the 'Secrets of the Nunnery' type, Middleton
makes only limited use of these;[11] and his major source is much
more sophisticated and original.

The centre of the dramatic effect was the impersonation of the
Spanish Ambassador Gondomar, who was 'counterfeited to the
life', the players having got hold of his cast-off suit, the litter in
which he was carried, and the special 'chair of ease' he sat in
because of a fistula. The idea of this impersonation, as well as many
details, are borrowed directly from the *Vox Populi* pamphlets of

---

[11] One such was *A Foot out of the Snare* (London, 1624; *S.T.C.* 11701), by
John Gee, Puritan divine and former Catholic, dedicated to Archbishop
Abbot with thanks for his conversion. Gee supplies a list of sins allegedly
regarded as venial by Catholic priests, which Middleton used, and some
brutal jeering at the Catholic martyrs, which the dramatist to his credit left
alone. Another was *Anatomy of the English Nunnery at Lisbon* (London,
1622; *S.T.C.* 21135), by Thomas Robinson (who claimed to have been a
mass-priest there), from which Middleton may have taken the Jesuits' use of
'obedience' to seduce a convert. Again, the tract is much more brutal than
the play; Robinson dedicated it to the mayor and aldermen of King's Lynn,
who had supported him as a student at Cambridge.

Thomas Scot, Puritan preacher and accomplished political satirist.

When the Spanish marriage negotiations and the popular opposition to the Crown were at their most intense in 1620, Scot wrote and published anonymously the first part of *Vox Populi*, which purported to be a record of Gondomar's report back to the Spanish government on his success in Britain in furthering the aim of a Spanish world monarchy. The publication was designed to coincide with Gondomar's arrival in England to begin his second embassy. The King was furious, and search was made for the author, whose identity was eventually given away by the printer; but Scot was forewarned of impending arrest, and escaped to Holland, where he lived under the protection of General Vere's soldiers, and secured the patronage of Prince Maurice of Nassau and the King and Queen of Bohemia, then exiles in the house of Sir Dudley Carleton, English Ambassador at The Hague.[12] At a time when comment on the Crown's Spanish policy was rigorously suppressed in England, Scot continued from 1621 to 1626 to write and publish a stream of pamphlets from the Netherlands attacking the Spanish match, urging full English intervention in the Palatinate and war with Spain; and these duly found their way on to the English market. In May 1624 appeared another instalment, *The Second Part of Vox Populi*, and this too was used by Middleton in the final version of his play.

The *Vox Populi* pamphlets are both witty and remarkably well informed politically. It seems clear that since there was no public reporting of Parliament, Scot must have had access to inside diplomatic and Parliamentary sources of information: and his fake report was so plausible that it was widely received as fact. He must also have enjoyed powerful protection, since the British authorities in the Netherlands knew what he was doing and seem to have made little attempt to interfere with him or to hand him over to the government at home. There are indications too that Archbishop

---

[12] *An Experimental Discovery of Spanish Practices* (1623; *S.T.C.* 22077) was dedicated by Scot to the King and Queen of Bohemia and Prince Maurice of Nassau. So was *The Second Part of Vox Populi* (Holland, 1624; *S.T.C.* 22102), in a preface which says he has 'had some dependence' on Prince Maurice and holds it his duty 'to repay some part of what I have gained under you, that is, observation'. He was appointed preacher to the English garrison at Utrecht, and was reported about to become household chaplain to the Queen of Bohemia when he was murdered there by a soldier in 1626 (Rev. Joseph Mead, letter dated London, 7 July 1626, Baker's MSS. xxxii.525).

Abbot, one of the anti-Spanish group in the Privy Council, used his influence to halt the proceedings against Scot in England.[13] The satirist must have had connections in London to get his subversive tracts exported and distributed – perhaps, like those of Samuel Hieron earlier, they were smuggled over in general cargoes by merchants trading with the Low Countries. We do not know how all this was organised: but it is suggestive that Middleton's earlier City patrons, the pious merchants Fishbourne and Browne, were importing copies of the Amsterdam Gazette (one of the early Dutch newsletters) which people like John Chamberlain wanting hot news of the wars in Europe were eager to get hold of.[14]

The idea of a stage play based on his tract may well have been suggested by Scot himself. For in *Vox Regis*, another pamphlet of 1624, he defends himself against the charge of having written *Vox Populi* 'not like a divine but like a fabulous poet', and argues that the stage too may be a valuable means of propaganda:

We see sometimes Kings are content in plays and masks to be admonished of divers things. . . .

And might I not borrow a Spanish name or two, as well as French or Italian, to grace this comedy with stately actors? Or must they only be reserved for kingly tragedies? Why not Gondomar as well as Hieronymo or Duke d'Alva? And why not Philip as well as Peter, or Alfonso, or Caesar? Or might I not make as bold with them, as they with our Black Prince, or Henry the Eighth, or Edward the Sixth, or Queen Elizabeth, or King James, or the King and Queen of Bohemia? If this be censurable for being a fiction, it is surely for lack of a fool, which, they say, comedies should not be without, and for a need, this witty objector may supply the place.[15]

If the Dutch and the Queen of Bohemia's circle were instrumental in getting Scot's pamphlets printed and distributed, it seems possible that the ultimate backing for *A Game at Chess* may also have come from them. But without powerful support in England, the nature

---

[13] On Thomas Scot's activities I have received invaluable help from Simon Adams, whose current research will throw much further light on his work.
[14] Chamberlain to Carleton, in a letter dated 26 Oct. 1616, asks Carleton to lend him his Gazettes, 'for I am disappointed of those I was wont to have, by the means of Ned Blount, from Fishbourne and Browne' (*Court and Times of James I*, ed. T. Birch (London, 1848), i, p. 434).
[15] *Vox Regis*, in volume of tracts by Thomas Scot, dated 1624 (*S.T.C.* 22102), pp. 34, 10.

of which will be considered later, it could never have been put on.

Apart from direct anti-Spanish and anti-Catholic attacks, Scot's pamphlets are interesting too for their radical Parliamentarian tone and their Puritan sympathies. The design of Spain, selected by the Pope 'to conquer and rule the nations with a rod of iron', is furthered, according to the Gondomar *persona* in the first part of *Vox Populi*, by alienating King and Parliament from one another.

A Parliament (quoth the Ambassador) nay, therein lies one of the chiefest services I have done, in working such a dislike between the King and the lower house...as that the King will never endure Parliament again, but rather suffer absolute want, than receive conditional relief from his subjects.[16]

The Catholics in the government, he says, put all the blame for difficulties in Parliament on the Puritans:

They use all their art and industry to withstand such a council, persuading the King he may rule by his absolute prerogative without a Parliament, and thus furnish himself by marrying with us, and other domestic projects without subsidies.

Again, Gondomar claims that James' aim of uniting the English and Scottish churches, which would be very bad for Spain, is being successfully frustrated by the Catholics and 'faint and irresolute' clergy and bishops, who 'stand stiff for all ceremonies, to be obtruded with a kind of absolute necessity upon them', thus making it impossible for the Scottish leaders to agree.

In the *Second Part of Vox Populi* (published May 1624, and hot from the press when Middleton used it), it is emphasised that the common people are the backbone of the anti-Spanish and anti-Catholic movement:

I must confess, quoth Gondomar, the common people of England bear generally an inbred spleen towards us, as it seemeth by many rude affronts, we were offered there by the baser sort, contrary to the will and pleasure of His Majesty of Great Britain.   (p. 12)

A coachfull of my gentlemen were by chance hard by the Savoy overthrown, but Lord what a shout was there among the multitude for joy...It is unpossible (quoth Gondomar) to charm the tongues of a multitude, besides they are people of the worser condition, for of the better sort we are respected with all observ-ance.   (p. 34)

[16] *Vox Populi*, in the same volume of tracts (*S.T.C.* 22102), p. 14.

Middleton does not pick up Scot's references to Parliament – that would certainly have been too dangerous. Indeed throughout *A Game At Chess* the king is represented as honourable and devoted to public duty, even when temporarily deceived. But the 'baser sort' and their fights with the Spanish ambassador's attendants are dramatised in the scene between Black Jesting Pawn (who 'prances after the Black Knight's litter') and White Pawn (III.i). White Pawn has the best of the insults and the punch-ups till another Black Pawn arrives, and the three go off still beating each other up. References to 'whipping' here would probably remind the audience that apprentices who insulted Gondomar's attendants were sentenced to be whipped. A similar brawl in the Strand on the return of Charles and Buckingham from Spain in 1623 had gone unpunished, however, the Commons rejecting the Crown's demand for action (it is to this incident that Gondomar directly refers in *The Second Part of Vox Populi*).

IV

Middleton's play was evidently written very quickly, and during the weeks while the players waited their opportunity to put it on it was apparently rewritten to make it still more topical. There was a dramatic precedent for the form Middleton gave to his journalistic material: an Elizabethan *Play of the Cards* caricaturing courtiers.[17] But *A Game at Chess* as we have it is unique in its style and structure, as in its boldness. The symbolic, stylised framework of the chess game has something in common with the allegorical city entertainments Middleton had been writing just before. It has some of the impact of ballet or fairy-story, with all the dramatic advantages of a conflict in which the issues are simplified to black and white, and interest can therefore centre on intrigue and exposure.[18] But this stylised form is mainly used as a setting for contrasting personalised caricatures (so personalised as to amount to mimicry

---

[17] Some courtiers wanted it banned, but the play was defended by Walsingham on the grounds that 'they that do that they should not, shall hear that they would not' (M. C. Bradbrook, *Rise of the Common Player* (London, 1962), p. 81).

[18] This still has its charms in an age of uncertain and shifting values: witness the immense popularity of J. R. Tolkien's *Lord of the Rings*, where the narrative is complex, but most of the characters comfortingly clear-cut on the side of good or evil.

rather than straight acting) of well-known public figures: in particular Gondomar (Black Knight); the turncoat De Dominis, Bishop
of Spalatro (Fat Bishop); and the Lord Treasurer, Cranfield (White
King's Pawn). We do not know how far the other leading roles
were mimicked in this way, but there is evidence that the King and
Queen, Prince Charles and Buckingham (White Knight and White
Duke) were presented not merely as stylised chessmen, but as
recognisable portraits of individuals.[19] The effect must have been
closer to modern TV satire than to 'straight' drama.[20]

Some of the subtler allegorical meanings critics have seen in the
play seem too strained to be convincing: notably the identification
of attempts to seduce the White Queen's Pawn with attacks on the
Palatinate. Allegory and symbolism had to be of a kind that could
be easily picked up in the theatre by a popular audience; and anything so complicated as this would simply be unintelligible in
dramatic terms. The main intention of the play is, on the face of it,
overwhelmingly clear. The seduction attempts represent Catholic
and Jesuit attempts to capture the individual soul, while the great
Spanish design of a 'universal monarchy' is the stake the arch-
schemer Gondomar plays for till he is defeated by the skill of
Charles and Buckingham.

The presentation of Gondomar certainly was not conventional-
ised, but mimicked and parodied with the use of his own possessions
as stage properties. In the lines his individual manner and seductive
charm are admirably caught – the energy, arrogance and sardonic
humour of the man. He thinks the ordinary rank-and-file of Jesuit
plotters inefficient and corrupt, by comparison with the 'pleasant
subtlety and bewitching courtship' by which he has endeared himself in England; and he sums up his plots in a splendid phrase
which must have gone home to the popular radical audience:

---

[19] Contemporary news-writers indicate that the King was angry because the
players presented not only Gondomar but 'someone else', i.e. himself, and
the assigned reason for suppressing the play was that it had brought modern
Christian kings upon the stage. The title-page of the first two quartos has
pictures which identify not only Gondomar and De Dominis, but the White
King (James), Black King (Philip IV), and a middle-aged White Queen
(Anne) 'with high forehead and prominently beaked nose, wearing...earlier
style of dress' (Moore, 'The Contemporary Significance of Middleton's
Game at Chess').

[20] On the dramatic technique of the play, see also Roussel Sargent's
valuable article, 'Theme and Structure in Middleton's *A Game at Chess*', x
Mod. Lang. Rev., lxvi, no. 4 (Oct. 1971), pp. 721–30.

> The court has held the city by the horns
> Whilst I have milked her.   (III.i.108)[21]

Gondomar had been on terms of close personal intimacy with James. However respectfully White King may have been played (and we do not know that he was), the Black Knight caricature was bound to be offensive in the extreme.

De Dominis, on the other hand, offered an opportunity too good to be missed for a kind of anti-clerical satire which, as we have seen, the dramatists dared not touch in the ordinary way. De Dominis was fair game, since he was only temporarily converted to an Anglican cleric, and had turned back to his Papist allegiance. The jokes against the Fat Bishop are strictly appropriate to De Dominis himself, who was greedy for more preferments in the English Church, reputedly a hard landlord ('I have racked/My tenants' purse-strings that they have twanged again') and a loose liver; but many of the audience probably enjoyed jokes against bishops anyway. Some of the wisecracks would have been equally suitable to certain *real* Anglican bishops, say to Milton's 'swan-eating old Bishop Mountaigne', whom (according to Peter Heylyn) Charles himself considered 'unactive and addicted to voluptuousness'. The Fat Bishop has little connection with the other plots, but the structure of the play could easily accommodate an extra caricature or two written in at the last moment. His greed and fatness is splendid stage stuff:

> *Fat Bishop's Pawn.*
> > I attend at your great holiness' service.
> *Fat Bishop.* For great I grant you, but for greatly holy
> > There the soil alters, fat cathedral bodies
> > Have very often but lean little souls. . .   (II.ii.1)

So is his ambition for more benefices; pluralism was one of the main Puritan grievances against the hierarchy.

> *Fat Bishop.* But where's my advancement all this while I ha'
> > gaped for't?
> > . . .
> > I am persuaded that this flesh would fill
> > The biggest chair ecclesiastical
> > If it were put to trial.
> > . . .
> > To be made master of an hospital

---

21 *A Game at Chess*, ed. J. W. Harper (London, 1966).

> Is but a kind of diseased bed-rid honour,
> Or dean of the poor alms Knights that wear badges.
> There's but two lazy beggarly preferments
> In the White Kingdom, and I have got 'em both;
> My spirit does begin to be crop-sick
> For want of other titles.   (III.i.6)

In the grand finale, all the Black side are kicked into the 'bag' – apparently the traditional 'hell-mouth' which was a stock stage property. The Black pieces fight and scuffle among themselves in the bag, and the Fat Bishop squashes all the others flat; his is the concluding line:

> Crowd in all you can,
> The Bishop will be still uppermost man,
> Maugre King, Queen or politician.   (V.iii.213)

It would be hard for the audience not to feel a more general application in that! The line of satire is one which extends back to Chaucer's Monk, who loved a fat swan best of any roast (that is, to the Lollards, whose ideas Chaucer so often embodies with sympathy), and forward to Milton and the Ranters. To underline the point, White Knight and White Duke are received on their visit to the Black House (V.i) with a dance around an altar, bearing tapers and surrounded by images, all of which is rejected by White Knight in an aside as 'a taste of the old vessel still, the erroneous relish' of Popery. Altars and images became one of the main points of dispute between the Laudians and the Puritans within the Church of England during the 1620s, and are often included in the subversive popular-theatre plays which got the actors into trouble in the later 1630s (see pp. 231–2 below).

The treacherous White King's pawn, who proves to be dressed in black underneath, is another last-minute adaptation. The lines particularly identifying him with Lionel Cranfield, Earl of Middlesex, the Lord Treasurer, were added in what seems to be the second draft. Cranfield had been impeached only in April 1624, officially for corruption, but partly no doubt for his opposition to Buckingham's new plans for an expensive war with Spain. Thus at his first entry he is hailed by Black Knight with the phrase *Curanda pecunia* ('money must be looked after'), which may indicate that he was made instantly recognisable as the Lord Treasurer. He promises Black Knight to block finance for defence against the Black House:

> There shall nothing happen,
> Believe it, to extenuate your cause
> Or to oppress her friends, but I will strive
> To cross it with my counsel, purse and power,
> Keep all supplies back, both in means and men,
> That may raise strength against you.   (I.i.318)

At the pawn's final exposure, White King denounces him as one whom he has raised (like Cranfield, who began as a city apprentice)

> From a condition next to popular labour,
> Took thee from all the dubitable hazards
> Of fortune, her most unsecure adventure,
> And grafted thee into a branch of honour.   (III.i.264)

The impersonation of Cranfield, if less broadly popular than those of Gondomar or De Dominis, would please those in the know who had engineered his impeachment – not only Buckingham and his clients, but Pembroke and his followers among MPs, and the City merchant interests who had come into conflict with Cranfield and the Crown nominees within the Virginia Company, such as the Myddletons, who were active in the impeachment debates.[22] This was thus another selling point for the play with City backers.

The exposure of people claiming to be White (or Protestant) as really Black (or Spanish Catholic) agents was, of course, good stage material, nothing being more effective in theatrical terms than a sudden unmasking. But the convention stood for something real: there were indeed a number of the King's officials who were either Catholics (often secretly) or in receipt of pensions from Spain.[23]

---

[22] Originally the traitor pawn may have been meant to resemble Sir Toby Matthew, son of the Archbishop of York who had turned jesuit: his hopes of a 'red hat' seem to survive from this first version. The second version, however, would be more widely topical, especially with a City audience.

[23] Spanish pensioners included the Earl of Dorset, and Lord Admiral Nottingham; the Earl of Somerset (who succeeded to the pension formerly paid to Robert Cecil as chief minister); the Duchess of Suffolk (wife of the Lord Treasurer) and the Howard family generally; Sir William Monson, Admiral of the Channel Fleet; Sir Thomas Lake, secretary to the King. The Spaniards also cultivated Queen Anne, and her confidante Mrs Drummond was a pensioner. Charles H. Carter, who gives these names (*Historical Journal*, vii (1964), pp. 189–208), thinks that the Spaniards did not get value for money, and that any pensioner (like Lake) who did stay pro-Spanish was following the lead of the Howards (the richer of whom didn't bother to collect) rather than that of Spain: but the concern of ordinary people is understandable. The proportion of peers who were Catholics was also very high – about a fifth at the outbreak of the Civil War (Stone, *Crisis of the Aristocracy*). These included many ministers - e.g. Windebank, Cottington

This lent some weight to the boast by the Black Queen's Pawn, a secular Jesuit, that the order has its agents everywhere, 'true labourers in the work/Of the universal monarchy' (I.i.50).

> Those are maintained in many courts and palaces,
> And are induced by noble personages
> Into great princes' services, and prove
> Some councillors of state, some secretaries,
> All serving in notes of intelligence.
>
> . . .
>
> So are designs
> Oft-times prevented, and important secrets
> Of state discovered, yet no author found.   (I.i.61)

Prince Charles and Buckingham (White Knight and White Duke) are shown as heroes; they enter the Black House (Spain) solely to unmask its plots, and not (as in life) to seek a bride. Indeed all reference to the Infanta and the Spanish marriage is discreetly suppressed. Instead, the heroes inveigle Gondomar into revealing his designs of conquest and his moral corruption, so that they can then expose him ('checkmate by discovery'). However, in the scene where they lead Black Knight on, the Duke's role is decidedly equivocal. While the dramatist is careful to include nothing that will raise a laugh or a jeer at the Prince's expense, he makes Buckingham accuse himself of faults well known to be his in reality[24] – gluttony, fatness and lechery, with more than a hint of homosexual lechery at that. Thus on his fatness and personal vanity:

> White Duke.   I fear fatness,
>   The fog of fatness, as I fear a dragon,
>   The comeliness I wish for that's as glorious. (V.iii.58)

On his lechery:

> White Duke.   But how shall I bestow the vice I bring, sirs?
>   You quite forget me, I shall be locked out
>   By your strict key of life.

and Portland – in Charles I's reign. 'The strength of Catholicism among such influential people – courtiers, aristocracy, gentry – was a principal reason why contemporaries feared it so deeply...Catholicism *was* a religion of the gentry' (Robin Clifton, 'Fear of Popery', in Russell (ed.), *Origins of the English Civil War*, p. 153).

[24] The Prince is also made to test Gondomar by accusing himself (much like Malcolm in *Macbeth*, IV.iii) of ambition and avarice, neither point being developed with much force. Since Middleton is known to have revised *Macbeth* for the King's Men, he was probably directly modelling his scene on that one.

Black Knight.   Is yours so foul, sir?
White Duke. Some that are pleased to make a wanton on't
Call it infirmity of blood, flesh-frailty,
But certain there's a worse name in your books
for't.
Black Knight. The trifle of all vices, the mere innocent,
The very novice of this house of clay: venery!
If I but hug thee hard I show the worst on't.

(V.iii.118)

The phrasing makes it clear that Gondomar was to suit the action
to the word, and hug White Duke hard to show how trifling a vice
his 'worse than flesh-frailty' was. True, after this bit of pantomime
had brought the house down, White Duke would be shown to have
accused himself falsely, thus helping to entrap Black Knight into
exposing his own wickedness. But by that time the audience would
have had its laugh at Buckingham's expense. And this is one of the
points that makes Buckingham seem an unlikely sponsor for the
play.

A Game at Chess appeals at several different levels, befitting the
audience which included both the 'popular' and 'select' public.
Some of the minor references might well be clear only to a few
with inside knowledge of court affairs. But the main targets of the
satire were such as would please the multitude – the readers of
Scot's tracts, the members of Puritan congregations, and the lower-
class anti-clericals. Not since Martin's time had there been such
lampooning of bishops and clerics for the delight of the lower
orders.

v

The crucial question remains: given the censorship, how was it
possible for the play to be put on at all? Although it could have
been staged only because of the exceptional divided-power situation
in 1624, when the heir to the throne and the favourite were pressing
for war with Spain against the policy of the old King, this does not
mean that the issues were then easy or safe to handle.

It has sometimes been suggested that the players felt secure
because they had the approval and sponsorship of the all-powerful
Buckingham. But this seems unlikely: for although one Catholic
marriage project for Prince Charles had been abandoned, another,

with the French princess Henrietta Maria, was now being energetic-
ally promoted by Buckingham himself, who was pressing the King
to make the concessions to English Catholics necessary to ensure it
– concessions which James had promised the Commons he would
never grant. (Buckingham was indeed out of town trying to persuade
James on this business while the play was running.) This, even apart
from internal evidence in the play itself, makes it very unlikely that
he was its political protector. For while Middleton's main butts
were the Spaniards and Gondomar, a great part of the effect is anti-
Papist rather than merely anti-Spanish, playing on the traditional
hostility of London people to Rome and all its works – and hence
hardly helpful to the Duke at that moment.

There was, on the other hand, much about the play that would
still be useful to Buckingham – the anti-Spanish satire and the jeers
at the Earl of Middlesex. This would probably be enough to ensure
Buckingham's neutrality – especially as he was out of London
during the run and could not see what the actors made of the
allusions to his character in the text – though hardly his enthusiastic
protection. The delay, after licensing, in putting on the play was
almost certainly due to the players' waiting for James' absence from
London; but they may have found Buckingham's absence con-
venient too.

Pembroke as Patron?

However, another great man is directly and certainly associated in
several ways with *A Game at Chess* – William Herbert, 3rd Earl of
Pembroke, the Lord Chamberlain and, after Buckingham, the most
powerful and influential of the peers. He had originally helped to
sponsor young George Villiers at court, to counter the influence of
Somerset and the Howards, but by this time was frequently in open
opposition to Buckingham, on the Catholic question and the French
marriage in particular. The evidence pointing to him as an important figure behind the play is varied and telling, if not conclusive.[25]

1. Pembroke, as Lord Chamberlain, was the senior official
responsible for the control of the drama. He was also the personal
patron of the King's Company, which staged it. We know that he
was personally acquainted with Burbage, and may well have had

[25] See Appendix A for further detailed evidence on Pembroke's Puritan
connections.

similar contacts with later leading actors and dramatists of the company.

2. The Master of the Revels, who was directly responsible for reading and licensing the play, was Sir Henry Herbert, a kinsman of Pembroke's, who had bought the reversion to that lucrative office under Pembroke and through his influence only a year before. Although called to account for licensing the play,[26] he seems never to have suffered for it.

3. After the Privy Council had summoned and punished the players, forbidding them to stage any plays 'till his Majesty's pleasure be further known', it was Pembroke who wrote to the President of the Council to inform him that James was now willing to end their punishment, 'in commiseration of those his poor servants',[27] and to permit them to act any other properly licensed play. Evidently he had interceded with the King on their behalf.

4. Thomas Scot, author of *Vox Populi*, was closely linked with opposition political circles abroad with which Pembroke sympathised and maintained discreet connections. The official proceedings against Scot, carried out by his bishop at the command of the Crown, seem to have been stopped in 1622 through the influence of the Calvinist Archbishop Abbot, Pembroke's close political ally.

Pembroke had, of course, a professional interest as Lord Chamberlain in the speedy restoration to favour of the King's Men, the best company of the time and the most valued royal entertainers.[28] Moreover he had intervened before to help playwrights in trouble with the law – notably Jonson, prosecuted for political references in *Sejanus* which were held to reflect on the monarchy, and imprisoned for jokes about James' sale of knighthoods and his Scottish courtiers in *Eastward Ho! A Game at Chess*, however, was a much more comprehensive political satire, and it seems possible that the lightness of the punishment here was related to the Lord Chamberlain's sympathy for the offence.

What we know of Pembroke's general political and religious

---

[26] Privy Council Register James I, vi, 425; printed in *A Game at Chess*, ed. R. C. Bald (Cambridge, 1929), p. 163.

[27] British Library Egerton MS. 2623, fo. 28, quoted in Bald, *ibid.* p. 164.

[28] The Lord Chamberlain's duties included the general supervision of court entertainment and of dramatic censorship. Although Pembroke held other offices, 'he would not have thought of trying to execute his principal post, first as Lord Chamberlain (1615–26) and then as Lord Steward (1626–30) except in person' (Aylmer, *The King's Servants*, p. 126).

attitudes confirms this. He is known to have been leader of the anti-Spanish group on the Privy Council, and widely regarded as 'head of the Puritans' (in the Venetian ambassador's phrase). His family had long and close associations with the militant Protestant cause in Europe, and with the House of Orange in particular, and he maintaned discreet contacts, through Ambassador Carleton, with the exiled Queen of Bohemia at The Hague. Moreover, he was a well-known friend and patron of Puritan writers and preachers like John Preston and Thomas Adams. In the last fifteen years of his life especially, he received dedications of a great number of Puritan and anti-Catholic sermons and tracts, appointed Puritans as his personal chaplains, and as Chancellor of Oxford used his influence to check the rise of Arminianism. He exercised great power in the Commons, where some thirty MPs were regarded as owing their seats to his patronage. (One of the best known, Sir Benjamin Rudyerd, is known to have attended the play.) Finally, his business connections in the Virginia Company and in mining aligned him with opposition merchants and colonisers, including some of Middleton's patrons among the City fathers.

The patronage of theatre and poets as an aid to the militant Protestant cause was, moreover, traditional in William Herbert's family circle. His great-uncle, the Earl of Leicester, had been a patron of Puritan preachers, and of Spenser, but also sponsored players (thereby scandalising the Presbyterian leader John Field, who though under Leicester's protection criticised him for it). His uncle, Sir Philip Sidney, friend of William the Silent and of the Huguenot leaders, a bold opponent of a Catholic marriage for Queen Elizabeth, was patron of Spenser and a famous defender of plays. Lady Pembroke, the Lord Chamberlain's mother, was patroness of Samuel Daniel, the manager under whom the Children of the Queen's Revels put on such risky plays in the first years of James' reign: and Daniel had himself been Pembroke's tutor. The polemical Puritan satirist George Wither repeatedly dedicated his most controversial poems to Pembroke; and Philip Massinger, son of the Pembrokes' former steward, had dedicated *The Bondman* to Philip Herbert as recently as 1623.

However, even if the Lord Chamberlain's protection was one of the factors encouraging the King's Men to put on the play, the fact is unlikely to have been at all widely known. Middleton himself may have known only that Sir Henry Herbert had somehow been squared, and that the players' friends at court would welcome a last-minute reference to the Middlesex affair. Pembroke was a canny political operator[29] – no one who was not could have managed to maintain a 'clandestine opposition' (as Aylmer calls it) within James' government for so long; and at times other opposition supporters thought him lukewarm and unreliable. Nevertheless, the discreet protection given by a group of the peers to Puritan preachers and writers was of great importance in strengthening that trend within the Church: and the long-standing commitment of the Herbert family to the moderate Parliamentary Puritan cause was finally evidenced when William Herbert's brother and successor, Philip, 4th Earl of Pembroke and Montgomery, became one of the leading peers on the Parliamentarian side in the 1640s.

VI

The backing of Middleton's City patrons for the production would seem likely, on the face of it, to have been more whole-hearted than that of the Lord Chamberlain. Certainly, although the dramatist was summoned before the Privy Council and had to go into hiding (he may even have been imprisoned for a short time), his City employers did not disown him. He continued in his post as chronologer; was employed to write another Lord Mayor's pageant in 1626; and was admitted to membership of the Drapers' Company by redemption in the same year. Moreover the City did, as we have seen, give some money to his widow. The recognition of Middleton's services was definite, if not handsome.

It seems likely also that during his period of concealment or imprisonment the dramatist got some help from Puritan businessmen. The Malone MS. of *A Game at Chess*, one of several copies made for readers while the play was banned from printing,[30] is dedicated with verses in the author's own hand as a New Year's gift to William Hammond, a rich Puritan member of the Haberdashers', who was apparently associated with Richard Fishbourne (in whose will he and his brother Edmond are named) and with the group that

[29] See R. E. Ruigh, *The Parliament of 1624* (Cambridge, Mass., 1971), p. 131.
[30] The scribe who made the copy, Ralph Crane, was also apparently a Puritan. He was himself the author of some religious verse, *The Works of Mercy* (1621; *S.T.C.* 5986). The unpublished MS. of *Barnavelt* is in his hand (F. P. Wilson, *Ralph Crane, Scrivener* (London, 1926)).

was buying up livings for godly preachers until halted by Laud.[31] No doubt some financial contribution (as commonly with dedications) was hoped for in return.

Sir Thomas Myddleton, the dramatist's first City patron, may also have been directly involved. He was an adventurer in the Virginia Company in 1623, when Nicholas Ferrar, son of Myddleton's partner of the same name, was active in the company and principal adviser to the opposition within it in resisting the threat to its patents. After the Company had lost its patent in 1623, Nicholas Ferrar the younger, elected MP in 1624, took a leading part in the impeachment of Cranfield, who had been foremost in the dissolution of the Virginia Company; Ferrar had also a long-standing association with the Queen of Bohemia, on whom he attended when she first left England in 1613. The attacks on Cranfield in the play would certainly have pleased the Myddletons and Ferrar, and may even have been included for that reason.[32]

VII

Patronage and protection, however, are something distinct from the social attitudes and ways of seeing embodied in a particular work of art. Middleton's great patrons had their own political and private reasons for appealing to the passions of the 'many-headed multitude' whom normally they were so careful to hold in check. But the play itself gives expression not to the cautious, tactically astute opposition of the grandees, nor to the stern Presbyterian discipline, but to the much more radical, sceptical, plebeian opposition of ordinary Londoners.

[31] William Hammond died intestate: some of his money apparently passed through his brother Edmond, also a Haberdasher, to the buying-up of impropriations and the appointment of godly preaching ministers, through a bequest to be administered by the Haberdashers' Company (Will of Edmond Hammond, probate granted 29 Apr. 1642; Pub. Rec. Office). Edmond Hammond's philanthropic bequests are commemorated on a memorial tablet in the church of All-Hallows-in-the-Wall, where he and his brother were buried and had long been parishioners.

[32] It is interesting that so many of Middleton's direct patrons had a connection with trade expansion or privateering in the Americas. Myddleton and the elder Ferrar had helped to finance Drake's and Raleigh's voyages, and had made a fortune from selling Drake's prizes. The pious Fishbourne was a privateer captain in his youth. And if Pembroke was of their number, he was deeply interested in establishing colonies first in Virginia and later (unsuccessfully) in Barbados. (See Appendix A.)

After Middleton's death he was referred to by the well-informed satirist William Hemminge as the Puritans' favourite dramatist (in contrast to Ben Jonson, whose caricatures of them were resented):

They quaked at Jonson as by him they pass
Because of Tribulation Wholesome and Ananias,
But Middleton they seemed much to adore
For's learned exercise 'gainst Gundomore.[33]

Middleton's open Parliamentary Puritan stand may account for the general absence of contemporary eulogy of him by actors or fellow dramatists; Jonson called him 'but a base fellow'. It is interesting that the main contrary instance, the poem of commendation by Nathanael Richards introducing the 1657 edition of *Women Beware Women*, is from another Parliamentary Puritan hand.[34]

The *Game at Chess* affair is important in refuting the idea that there was a total and insuperable hostility between the Parliamentary Puritan opposition and the theatres, and also in suggesting links between the dramatist himself and that opposition. But the play had no successors in its own genre. During the years which followed the balance of forces was never quite the same and the censor never relaxed so far again, perhaps because being summoned before the Privy Council for licensing this play gave him too much of a fright. It was not, indeed, the end of criticism of the Crown and opposition ideas in the drama, but no other play up to the Civil War presented them so boldly and unequivocally.

[33] 'Elegy on Randolph's Finger', 1630–2.
[34] Richards was the author of a book of Puritan and anti-Jesuit satires, and of an anti-tyrant play *Messalina*. He dedicated poems in 1641 to the City Parliamentary leader Alderman Thomas Soame, and his play in 1640 to Viscount Rochford, an opposition peer and former associate of Sir John Eliot.

II. *City Tragedy*

I

Middleton's two great tragedies, *The Changeling* (1621) and *Women Beware Women*, stand out sharply both from his earlier work and from other post-Shakespearean tragedy. What we have in these plays is not a complete turnabout, but rather a development of qualities and themes already traceable in Middleton's earlier comedies and tragi-comedies. All the same, there *is* a change, and a striking one, from the earlier work to *The Changeling*, which T. S. Eliot thought 'more than any other play except those of Shakespeare has a profound and permanent moral value and horror'.[1]

This change has been ascribed by some critics to Middleton's working for the King's Men after 1615, and thus coming under the influence, as adaptor and rewriter, of their Shakespearean repertory.[2] But this, though it may have contributed, cannot be a sufficient cause – Middleton's tragedies are very unlike Shakespeare's, and Fletcher managed to work for the King's Men, and as collaborator with Shakespeare himself, without any such radical deepening of moral awareness. The change must arise at least in part from the sharpening of social, political and religious conflicts in the 1620s, in which Middleton, unlike most other tragic dramatists of his time, was drawing closer to the Parliamentary Puritans in outlook and feeling. His associations with City Puritan groups were, as we have seen, increasingly close in these later years.

It is not oversimplifying, I think, to see in these last great plays – immeasurably his finest – something which we can fairly describe as 'city tragedy'. Of course, it is in no sense 'written to order', as *A Game at Chess* may quite possibly have been, and the actual

---

[1] David Holmes, in *The Art of Thomas Middleton*, makes a useful attempt to show a consistent line of social and moral criticism underlying Middleton's early comedies, and to refute the many critical attacks on him as merely cynical and amoral. But perhaps he proves too much, overdoing the morality and underplaying the bawdy: *A Chaste Maid* or *The Family of Love* are not as 'serious' in any sense as *The Changeling*.

[2] See David Frost, *The School of Shakespeare* (Cambridge, 1968), p. 52: 'For commercial reasons [Middleton] decided to compose "King's Men type" tragedy, which was primarily Shakespearean tragedy.'

behaviour of citizens is not idealised. But in its dramatisation of social mobility and ambition, its presentation of sex and marriage, its ethical and religious overtones, it is much closer to the concerns and values of a city and 'country' audience than to the diversions of a leisured and escapist court culture.

It may be significant here that the sources for these two plays are in the main popular Puritan compilations. Thus *The Changeling* is based on one of the most popular bourgeois works of the seventeenth century, *The Triumphs of God's Revenges Against the Crying and Execrable Sin of Murther.* Written by a pious merchant of Exeter, John Reynolds, it had run into thirteen editions by the beginning of the eighteenth century, and was coupled by the Puritan martyr Henry Burton with Foxe's *Book of Martyrs* and Dr Bearde's *Theatre of God's Judgments* as collections which would 'daunt the most professed Atheist, and reclaim the most incorrigible sinner'.[3] It is not known which of the many published accounts of the life of Bianca Capello served as the basis for *Women Beware Women*,[4] but a contributory source seems to have been an unpublished portion of Fynes Moryson's *Itinerary*: this publication was dedicated to the 3rd Earl of Pembroke, the most influential leader of the anti-Spanish group in the Privy Council.

It seems to me that what distinguishes Middleton's late tragedy most obviously from that of near-contemporaries – such as Webster, Ford, Massinger or Beaumont and Fletcher – is a combination of detached observation and moral consistency, which extends through the handling of situation, character and language alike. In contrast to these, or to the earlier work of Marlowe and Chapman, Middleton's strike a decidedly plebeian, citizen note, but without the touches of sentimentality and weakness of motivation which one finds even in the finest domestic dramas of Heywood (such as *A Woman Killed with Kindness* or *The English Traveller*).

Amidst growing tensions and conflicts within court and City, the aristocratic and intellectual side of the revolt against the corruption and oppression of Stuart absolutism expresses itself dramatically in the towering individual prepared at all costs, for good or ill, to vindicate his honour and his right to live out his life to the full – in the stoical defiance of Bussy, Vittoria, the Duchess of Malfi, Byron or

[3] Wright, *Middle-Class Culture in Elizabethan England*, p. 462.
[4] See Schoenbaum, *Middleton's Tragedies*, pp. 104–9, and the edition of the play by J. R. Mulryne (Manchester, 1975), pp. xxxviii–li.

Warbeck, as well as such heroes of the 'closet' drama as Greville's Mustapha.[5] This is indeed the mainstream of Jacobean tragedy.

The citizen element of the revolt is, however, different in its attitudes as in its way of life – serious, intensely and sometimes narrowly moral, stressing personal responsibility for sin, conscious of economic pressures and everyday tasks, and convinced by experience that idleness and immorality lead inevitably to disaster in this world as well as the next. It is this assured, strenuous and practical sensibility which characterises the later work of Middleton and his collaborator Rowley. His Beatrice and Bianca have nothing of the fascinating moral ambiguity of Webster's Vittoria or Ford's Giovanni and Annabella. The social pressures help to explain and motivate their actions without in the least excusing them. Webster's Vittoria seems to us a splendid creature, though fallen, her dignity greatest when she stands at bay, on trial or facing her murderers. This is not true of Middleton's Beatrice and Bianca, Livia and Isabella, in whom moral disintegration and deterioration is realistically dramatised – as indeed it is in Milton's Satan.[6] It is not surprising to find contemporary evidence (sometimes admiring, sometimes jeering)[7] that the later Middleton was the Puritans' favourite dramatist – once we realise that there could be such a creature, and that not all Puritans were implacable opponents of all plays. With more fashionable circles he was not particularly popular, and the only contemporary eulogy we know of is from a Parliamentary Puritan hand.

II

The realism of these late tragedies includes a very subtle and precise placing of the characters socially. This is in no sense mere local colour, detail for detail's sake – it is all relevant to the development of the protagonists and the central tragic theme.

In *The Changeling*, it is emphasised at the outset that Alonzo de

[5] See Lever's *The Tragedy of State* for an analysis of the social and political essence of these plays.
[6] The analogy is pointed out by Dame Helen Gardner in *A Reading of Paradise Lost* (Oxford, 1965).
[7] Admiring in the prefatory verses attached to *Women Beware Women* in 1657 by Nathanael Richards, himself a Puritan opposition writer around 1640; jeering in William Hemminge's 'Elegy on Randolph's Finger' or Ben Jonson's 'Speech According to Horace' (Underwoods, xliv), poking fun at Middleton's entertainment for the Bunhill shooting.

Piracquo is a brilliant match for Beatrice-Joanna; and this is the main basis of the marriage arranged for her by her father, Vermandero, Governor of the Castle. Thus Vermandero says of the bridegroom:

> The gentleman's complete,
> A courtier and a gallant, enriched
> With many fair and noble ornaments.
> I would not change him for a son-in-law
> For any he in Spain, the proudest he,
> And we have great ones, that you know.   (I.ii.215)

Alsemero, with whom Beatrice becomes infatuated at first sight, is not so great a catch, but nevertheless her social equal, son of a former officer friend of her father's. If Piracquo can be removed, Alsemero will be a socially acceptable husband for her. As for De Flores, a gentleman of her father's household, a mere 'follower', she regards him as so inferior socially that she can insult him as she pleases, and does not even notice that this repulsive-looking retainer nurses a deadly serious passion for her. It does not occur to her, spoiled and sheltered child of a noble family, that money may not be enough to pay him for killing Piracquo, or that he could aspire to seduce herself. When he reports the murder completed, she expects simply to pay him off and see the back of him.

Beatrice. Look you, sir, here's three thousand golden florins:
          I have not meanly thought upon thy want.
De Flores. What! salary? Now you move me.
Beatrice.   How, De Flores?
De Flores. Do you place me in the ranks of verminous fellows,
          To destroy things for wages? offer gold
          For the life-blood of man? is anything
          Valued too precious for my recompense?
Beatrice. I understand thee not.
De Flores.   I could have hired
          A journeyman in murder at this rate,
          And mine own conscience might have slept at ease,
          And have had the work brought home.   (III.iv.62)

Murder, to Beatrice, is a commodity, like anything else one buys: one pays someone to undergo not only the risk and the unpleasantness (as Piracquo's cut-off finger, brought as proof of the murder, rudely reminds her and us), but the guilt and conscience-pangs as well. The reference to 'journeyman' brings the point home sharply to the citizen audience. One may contrast the dead man's hand presented by Ferdinand to the heroine in *The Duchess of Malfi* – a more or less gratuitous piece of Grand-Guignol sensationalism, leading nowhere in particular in terms of plot or character – with the dead man's finger here, which forces Beatrice-Joanna to realise with visceral horror what she has done, and embodies in a single dreadful image the moral crux of the play.

Even after this, Beatrice tries still to play the fine lady, whose delicate ears must not be profaned by De Flores' coarse suggestions:

Beatrice.   I would not hear so much offence again
            For such another deed.

De Flores.   Soft, lady, soft,
            The last is not yet paid for.   (III.iv.105)

And when she does at last understand that he means to make her his mistress, she still clings desperately to the saving difference of rank:

Beatrice.   Think but upon the difference that creation
            Set 'twixt thy blood and mine, and keep thee
                there.

De Flores. Look but into your conscience, read me there;
            'Tis a true book, you'll find me there your equal.
            Pish! Fly not to your birth, but settle you
            In what the act has made you: you're no more
                now.
            You must forget your parentage to me:
            You are the deed's creature; by that name
            You lost your first condition, and I challenge you,
            As peace and innocency has turned you out,
            And made you one with me.   (III.iv.131)

By her involvement in the murder Beatrice has indeed made herself equal with De Flores. But she has learned nothing. The same moral blindness, the same conviction that her superior rank enables her to use inferior people simply as tools, again proves her undoing when she bribes her maid Diaphanta to take her place in the bridal bed and conceal her own loss of virginity. The 'bed-trick' was of course a commonplace of the drama, despite its inherent implausibility. Shakespeare uses it twice, in *All's Well* and *Measure for Measure*, with no attempt to handle it as anything more than a useful plot convention. But Middleton makes something deeply ironic out of it. For Diaphanta, though a servant, turns out, like De Flores, to be a human being with her own lusts and desires. We see Beatrice waiting in a terrified fury of impatience outside the bridal chamber, as the realisation grows that Diaphanta is *enjoying* herself instead of coming out punctually as instructed:

> One struck, and yet she lies by't! O my fears!
> This strumpet serves her own ends, 'tis apparent now,
> Devours the pleasure with a greedy appetite,
> And never minds my honour or my peace,
> Makes havoc of my right: but she pays dearly for't.   (V.i.1)

In a powerful television production,[8] Beatrice-Joanna was shown after the confrontation with De Flores as overwhelmed with guilty nightmares, projected on the screen as flashbacks to the murder itself. Immensely effective visually though this was, it perhaps diminished the real horror in the text – that Beatrice, despite her one glimpse of realisation after Piracquo's murder ('Bless me, what hast thou done?'), seems to have learned absolutely nothing morally from that experience. Terrified she is certainly, but of exposure. She still thinks she can hire servants to do the dirty work for her, and it is she, not De Flores, who first decides that Diaphanta must be killed as untrustworthy:

> No trusting of her life with such a secret
> That cannot rule her blood to keep her promise.   (V.i.6)

It is 'this whore', the servant whom she has induced to take her place, whom she furiously and vindictively blames – not herself. That she has no adequate moral sense of guilt for the murder, even on the brink of discovery, is shown when she confesses it to her husband Alsemero, expecting him to condone the killing because it was done for his sake.[9]

> Your love has made me
> A cruel murderess, a bloody one.
> I have kissed poison for it, stroked a serpent.
> That thing of hate, worthy in my esteem
> Of no better employment, and him most worthy
> To be so employed, I caused to murder
> The innocent Piracquo, having no
> Better means than that worst to assure
> Yourself to me.   (V.iii.65)

[8] By Anthony Page, shown 23 Jan. 1974 by BBC television.
[9] This scene is usually ascribed to Rowley: but this does not preclude consistency in the design and conception as a whole.

'Honour', in the sense of her worldly reputation for chastity, she understands and will kill for – ''Tis time to die when 'tis a shame to live' are her dying words. But she is not like Lady Macbeth or Macbeth himself, who feel the blood of their victims sticking on their hands. In a way her reaction is even more monstrous.

It is the cruellest irony of the play that inevitably Beatrice becomes more involved with her hated gangster-accomplice than with the husband for whose sake she has killed. When De Flores goes off to set fire to the house and murder Diaphanta, Beatrice expresses her commitment with horrid frankness (intensified by the secondary sexual meaning of 'serve'):

> His face loathes one,
> But look upon his care, who would not love
>   him?
> The east is not more beauteous than his service.   (V.i.69)

All the same, when their crimes are exposed, De Flores takes no chances that he will be left to torture and execution while she, as a great lady, gets off with lighter punishment; he stabs her and then himself. As in the crime, so in the punishment, her guilt is to make them equal.

Some critics have thought the virginity-trial scene ludicrous, unrealistic and a blemish on the play. Grotesque, in one sense, it certainly is, when Beatrice tries the effect of Alsemero's virginity-testing medicine on Diaphanta, so that she may copy the symptoms when she is tested herself. But the black humour is morally right. Such grotesque indignities are what the wicked bring upon themselves, rather than the lifetime of romantic love they hope for. The test is not really much more ludicrous than what may well have suggested it to Middleton's mind; the case of the notorious Countess of Essex, who was solemnly investigated and pronounced a virgin by a panel of discreet matrons – a marvel explained at the time by the news-writers on the supposition that another woman, veiled, had been substituted for the Countess. Such a scene could hardly be staged, but it is symbolised here; Diaphanta refers to the original pretty closely when Beatrice proposes the test to her:

> She will not search me, will she,
> Like the forewoman of a female jury?   (IV.i.101)

Indeed, after the Countess' remarriage to the Earl of Somerset had been permitted on the strength of the bogus test, she behaved very much like Beatrice-Joanna, in getting her husband's client

Overbury, who knew too much, murdered by accomplices in the Tower.[10] At her trial the Countess looked very attractive and shed tears. As has been noted, because of her rank and eminence she did not, though found guilty, suffer execution like the tool-villains she had hired, but was kept in the Tower with her husband for a time, and later allowed to retire into private life with him. Such protection by her rank may well seem normal to Beatrice. She does not really expect to have to suffer the full punishment for her crimes, and it is De Flores, not the law, who puts her to death in the end.

This is not to suggest that *The Changeling* as a whole derives directly from the Somerset case (though *The Witch*, much closer to it in time, may well (as we have seen) have been directly inspired by it). It is not so much a question of topical allusions, but rather of social patterns and sensibilities. Great people did not expect to be judged by the same standards as ordinary men and women. It is significant that peers could not normally be tried in the courts for anything but felony, and a good deal of private violence by them and their retainers was in practice tolerated. But this state of affairs was no longer taken for granted: a growing number of people believed the same moral and civil laws to be binding on all, regardless of rank and birth.

The 'tool-villain' seems to us one of the less satisfying conventional figures of the Elizabethan-Jacobean drama. The motives of Bosola, Flamineo, Pedringano are of peripheral interest only; in the last resort they kill because they are told to, and sudden conversion to compassion and remorse makes Bosola not so much sympathetic as unconvincing. It is De Flores who throws a hideously clear light on the assumptions underlying this role – that the gentry can always find some underling to commit their crimes for them. The new thing here is the enhanced awareness that people of inferior status are still people, with consciences and souls to be lost, and their superiors in crime are nothing more.

Again, Diaphanta, whose enjoyment of stolen sex costs her her life, is presented in a different way from the waiting women in Webster's tragedies. Zanche in *The White Devil* and Cariola in *The Duchess of Malfi* are merely less dignified low-life shadows of their mistresses. Indeed, Cariola's behaviour in the face of death is

---

[10] When the crime was eventually discovered, Somerset still hoped (vainly, as it turned out) that his influence and blackmailing hold on the King would be strong enough to prevent the principals from being tried.

deliberately made cowardly and degraded in order to highlight the aristocratic heroism of her mistress:

> I am Duchess of Malfi still.

For Webster, the distinctions of rank and birth are preserved even in the extremes of torment and death.[11] One is reminded of Sheridan's *Critic* burlesque of the whole 'degree' tradition in drama, in Mr Puff's splendid stage-direction: 'Enter the heroine stark mad in white satin, and her confidante stark mad in white linen'. It is a convention which Middleton's citizen realism firmly and decisively transcends.[12]

III

In the brilliant and terrifying tragedy of *Women Beware Women*, which on internal evidence seems to belong to roughly the same period as *The Changeling*, social status and social ambition are equally central to the action.[13]

Although concerned with the Duke of Florence and his mistress, this is not a 'tragedy of state' in the way that Chapman's and Webster's to some extent are: it is not about power in the wider sense. Indeed, it comes as a shock to realise that the Duke and Cardinal here are historically the same people as Duke Francisco and Cardinal Monticelso in *The White Devil*. There is nothing of the political intrigues and factions one finds in that play: the story is stripped down to its human and social essentials. The Duke is not shown primarily as ruler of his state, but merely as using his power to satisfy his personal lusts and pleasures – a grandee with a city mistress rather than God's deputy on earth, although, as the

---

[11] It is interesting that the comic-grotesque parody of *The Changeling*'s sub-plot is enacted not by lower-class characters but by madmen, whose antics suggest most effectively the unspoken and unspeakable desires of the 'serious' protagonists.

[12] Webster himself gives considerable evidence of 'opposition' feeling in other ways, of course. His plays can be seen, and almost certainly were seen, as a searing attack on the corruption of courts nearer home: and his Lord Mayor's pageant of 1624, with its apotheosis of Prince Henry, is as suggestive as any of Middleton's. But the viewpoint remains that of the angry and contemptuous gentry, rather than the citizen or plebeian one.

[13] The date of production has not been conclusively established; it was not published till 1657, and one at least of its recent editors (C. Barber, Fountainwell Drama Texts (Edinburgh, 1969) considers the question still 'wide open'. But most critics tend to date the play late (1623–7), on the grounds of its great power and maturity.

Cardinal points out to him, a great man who sins in public carries the additional guilt of setting a bad example to ordinary people (a rebuke which assumes that the same standards apply to both).

Some critics have seen in this play the terror of predestination and inexpiable sin; and this may well have been how it struck the Calvinist-minded in its first audience. But the most striking thing about *Women Beware Women* is the very consistent and comprehensible human and psychological motivation of the characters, given the social circumstances, a consistency uncommon in Jacobean drama.

Bianca, daughter of a noble family, has eloped with Leantio, who is far beneath her in birth and fortune. Because it is a runaway and imprudent match she has no dowry. As soon as the infatuated Leantio brings his bride home, his old mother (shown as naïve and credulous, but not as contemptible or absurd) sees at once the difficulties ahead:

Mother.   Such a creature,
            To draw her from her fortune, which, no doubt
            At the full time might have proved rich and noble;
            You know not what you've done; my life can give you
            But little helps, and my death lesser hopes;
            And hitherto your own means has but made shift
            To keep you single, and that hardly too:
            What ableness have you to do her right then,
            In maintenance fitting her birth and virtues?   (I.i.58)

Leantio, however, is arrogantly confident that by sexual prowess and male domination he can keep Bianca dutiful and obedient. For the moment she is physically infatuated with him, continually teasing him for kisses and embraces, and prepared to be pleased with her new life, however humble:

Bianca. Kind mother, there is nothing can be wanting
            To her that does enjoy all her desires:
            Heaven send a quiet peace with this man's love,
            And I'm as rich as virtue can be poor.
            Which were enough after the rate of mind
            To erect temples for content placed here.   (I.i.124)

However, Leantio is not a courtier or an Arcadian shepherd, but a mere factor employed by a rich merchant. Though sorely tempted by Bianca to neglect his work for lovemaking, he has to attend to business if he is to keep her in comfort. The clash between her aristocratic education, where love is a charming pastime for idle courtiers, and his strenuous mercenary city upbringing is beautifully dramatised in the scene where he parts from her to go on a five-day business trip (I.iii). The pleasure of sex in marriage, he says, is almost too much for his training in economy and hard work:

> For the time
> It spoils all thrift, and indeed lies abed
> T'invent all the new ways for great expenses.   (I.iii.10)

And when Bianca begs him to stay another night he almost relents:

> I've no power to go now, an I should be hanged.
> Farewell all business: I desire no more
> Than I see yonder: let the goods at quay
> Look to themselves: why should I toil my youth out?
> It is but begging two or three years sooner,
> And stay with her continually; is't a match?
> O, fie, what a religion have I leaped into!
> Get out again, for shame.   (I.iii.15)

But to sacrifice everything for love is for rich people, not for poor citizens who must get up early and keep regular working hours:

> Those that are wealthy, and have got enough
> 'Tis after sunset with 'em; they may rest,
> Grow fat with ease, banquet, and toy, and play,
> When such as I enter the heat o' the day,
> And I'll do't cheerfully.

So he braces himself:

> If I stay any longer, I shall turn
> An everlasting spendthrift: as you love
> To be maintained well, do not call me again,
> For then I shall not care which end goes foremost.
>   (I.iii.31)

And off he goes, leaving Bianca in tears of disappointment like a spoiled child, in the custody of her mother-in-law, who has been instructed to keep her safely locked up in the house like all the rest of her son's property:

> *Leantio.* The jewel is cased up from all men's eyes.
> Who could imagine now a gem were kept
> Of that great value under this plain roof? . . .
> Old mothers know the world: and such as these,
> When sons lock chests, are good to look to keys. (I.i.170)

It is no wonder that both women welcome the diversion of looking out of the window at the ageing Duke's procession. From this natural action all the rest flows: the great man sees Bianca, they are invited to dinner at the house of Livia, the good-natured Court procuress, and there Bianca is seduced and corrupted by the Duke.

The social setting in which all this happens is perfectly and economically realised. The mother, as the lines continually remind us, has been a working housewife, a suitable wife for someone in her son's social position. But Bianca, a lady born, cannot be expected to work, so the time hangs heavy on her hands. To be locked up, and taken out of her cupboard at the weekend as a recreation for the tired businessman, is no life for a beautiful young woman, used to expect leisure and luxury as a right.

Placed as she is socially, the old mother is honoured and flattered by an invitation to the great house of Lady Livia, which she can hardly refuse. For the same reason it is difficult for her to deny Livia's pressing invitations to stay all day: usually she has been asked only to the odd meal ('our Sunday-dinner and Thursday-supper woman'). This is why she has to confess that she has left Bianca alone at home (which Livia of course knows already), and allows her to be brought to the house and shown over the galleries and the 'naked pictures' inciting to erotic adventure.

Bianca's fall has sometimes been seen as evidence of the irremediably sinful nature of women. It has to be admitted, however, that she has at first little choice. Through the plotting of Livia and her accomplice Guardiano, she is deliberately confronted with the Duke in a lonely part of the house; and he is quite prepared to rape her if she will not take him willingly:

> *Duke.* I should be sorry the least force should
> lay
> An unkind touch upon thee. (II.ii.349)

To resist and appeal to his better feelings merely makes him more randy:

> Thou know'st the way to please me. I affect
> A passionate pleading 'bove an easy yielding,
> But never pitied any, they deserve none,
> That will not pity me. I can command,
> Think upon that. (II.ii.364)

Only after all these pressures have been exerted does he come to the mercenary temptation – wealth, honour:

> She that is fortunate in a duke's favour
> 'Lights on a tree that bears all women's wishes.
>   . . .
> And can you be so much your beauty's enemy
> To kiss away a month or two in wedlock,
> And weep whole years in wants for ever after?   (II.ii.375)

The seduction is inescapable. But so too is its effect on Bianca.
Treated as a chattel, as merchandise, as prey, she now regards herself as tainted goods ('mine honour's leprous'), and feels she may
as well sell to the highest bidder. From this time she is naturally
discontented with Leantio's humble status. The scene in which she
complains to her mother-in-law about the lack of modern fashionable furnishings in their home is masterly:

> This is the strangest house
> For all defects as ever gentlewoman
> Made shift withal to pass her love away in;
> Why is there not a cushion-cloth of drawn work,
> Or some fair cut-work pinned up in my bed-chamber,
> A silver and gilt casting-bottle hung by't?
> Nay, since I am content to be so kind to you,
> To spare you for a silver basin and ewer,
> Which one of my fashion looks for of duty,
> She's never offered under where she sleeps.

Mother. She talks of things here my whole state's not worth.
Bianca. Never a green silk quilt is there i' th' house, mother,
>   To cast upon my bed?
Mother.   No by troth is there,
>   Nor orange-tawny neither.
Biance.   Here's a house
>   For a young gentlewoman to be got with child in!
>   (III.i.16)

The mother's angry answer – still perfectly within her simple and
rather limited character – is in the true accent of the city craftsman
and the sense of dignity of the 'industrious sort':

> Yes, simple though you make it, there has been three
> Got in a year in't, since you move me to't,
> And all as sweet-faced children and as lovely
> As you'll be mother of: I will not spare you.
> What, cannot children be begot, think you,
> Without gilt casting-bottles? yes, and as sweet ones.

The miller's daughter brings forth as white boys
As she that bathes herself in milk and bean-flour!
'Tis an old saying, one may keep good cheer
In a mean house.   (III.i.31)

The appeal is directly to the feeling of a hardworking audience, against the useless luxury of court gentry – the contrast between those who must be served from silver plates, like Bianca, and those who eat from pewter. Leantio, coming home greedy with expectation of a sexually famished wife, is contemptuously thrown aside – demonstrations of conjugal affection are now as vulgar as pewter. As a last resort he tries desperately to shut her up in a dark cupboard, but too late – she defies him and they are sent for to the court, where the Duke flaunts his new mistress in her husband's face. The casual way he tosses Leantio a vacant office (Captain of the Fort) as a bribe for cuckolding him is an insult worthy of Buckingham himself:

Leantio.   a fine bit
To stay a cuckold's stomach: all preferment
That springs from sin and lust it shoots up quickly
As gardeners' crops do in the rottenest grounds.
                                                    (III.ii.46)

But like the low-born De Flores and Diaphanta in *The Changeling*, Leantio reacts not as a mere tool to be hired for money, but as a human being, if a shoddy one, with his own selfish interests to consider. Since he is not a gentleman and has never been trained as an officer, he realises at once that the job will not suit him. In any case, it pays less than his factorship. Instead, in his real grief at the loss of Bianca, he revenges himself by setting up as gigolo to the middle-aged widow Livia, who has fallen in love with his charms and offers him a gentleman's luxuries:

your page and footman,
Your racehorses, or any various pleasure
Exercised youth delights in.   (III.ii.371)

The climax to this Balzacian history of two souls damned by money and social climbing is reached when Bianca, now a great lady, receives Leantio tricked out in his new finery:

Bianca. You've an excellent suit there.
Leantio.   A chair of velvet.
Bianca. Is your cloak lined through, sir?
Leantio.   You're very stately here...

Bianca. I could ne'er see you in such good clothes
        In my time.
Leantio.   In your time?
Bianca.   Sure I think, sir,
        We both thrive best asunder.
Leantio. You're a whore.
Bianca. Fear nothing, sir.
Leantio. An impudent, spiteful strumpet.
Bianca. Oh, sir, you give me thanks for your captainship.
        I thought you had forgot all your good manners.
                                                    (IV.i.53)

What makes the presentation of social climbing here different in
tone – as it certainly is – from that in, say, Massinger's *City Madam*,
also concerned with citizens who succeed in adopting court fashion?
In Massinger the whole implication is that city women are sinful
and contemptible in aspiring to luxuries, such as silk gowns and
jewellery, to which only the aristocracy are entitled. A certain
standard is proper to ordinary citizens' wives, a rather higher one to
aldermen's ladies, and a much higher one still to the nobility.
Massinger is adopting what he thinks is the good old hierarchic
scheme of aristocratic values, as embodied for example in the
sumptuary laws. In Middleton, there is no suggestion that Livia,
being nobly born, is entitled to a life of luxury and idleness. On the
contrary, it corrupts her morally as surely as it does Bianca (who,
after all, originally comes of a noble family too).

The pride of such families in their birth and wealth is treated not
with respect but with sophisticated irony. Hippolito, himself guilty
of an incestuous affair with his niece Isabella, is sincerely shocked
when he hears of his sister Livia's liaison with the low-born Leantio.
Encouraged by the Duke's bait of a noble match for Livia, he proceeds to remedy the family dishonour by drawing Leantio (no
swordsman) into a duel and killing him. There is no suggestion of
any fine aristocratic values or moral outrage about Hippolito's
attitude – it is pure savage snobbery and personal greed. As he says
just before the duel:

        Put case one must be vicious, as I know myself
        Monstrously guilty, there's a blind time made for't,
        He might use only that – 'twere conscionable,
        Art, silence, closeness, subtlety and darkness
        Are fit for such a business; but there's no pity

To be bestowed on an apparent sinner,
An impudent daylight lecher.   (IV.ii.5)

Like Beatrice-Joanna, Hippolito will kill for 'honour' in the sense
of the public reputation of a lady and her family. Of honour as
personal integrity and honesty he has, quite genuinely, no conception.

The language and imagery of Middleton's late plays strongly
suggest the citizen atmosphere of the play. The language is plain
and spare, the imagery practical and homely, imagery of workshop
and counting-house, sewing and cooking.

> If lovers should mark everything a fault,
> Affection would be like an ill-set book,
> Whose faults might prove as big as half the volume.
>
> (*Changeling*, II.i.109)

> For if a woman
> Fly from one point, from him she makes a husband,
> She spreads and mounts then like arithmetic,
> One, ten, a hundred, a thousand, ten thousand.
>
> (*Changeling*, II.ii.60)

> I pray you do not teach her to rebel.
> . . .
> To rise with other women in commotion
> Against their husbands for six gowns a year.
> . . .
> She intends
> To take out other works in a new sampler.
>
> (*Women*, I.i.74)

> That pleasure should be so restrained and curbed
> After the course of a rich workmaster
> That never pays till Saturday night!   (*Women*, I.i.157)

> He has but a caterer's place on't, and provides
> All for another's table: yet how curious
> The ass is: like some nice professor on't,
> That buys up all the daintiest food in the markets,
> And seldom licks his lips after a taste on't.
>
> (*Women*, III.iii.39)

Food as a metaphor for sex is common and natural in the drama – Shakespeare in particular uses it frequently to evoke sexual hunger, satiety or perversion (Cressida gives the left-over 'orts and greasy scraps' of her love to Diomed, Hamlet's mother 'preys on garbage'). What is striking in Middleton's tragedies is not food-imagery as such, but reiterated metaphors from cooking and house-keeping. Troilus' 'concrete speech' is that of a young aristocrat, a consumer of feasts and fine wines:

> What will it be
> When that love's watery palates taste indeed
> Love's thrice repured nectar?

So too Cleopatra is an 'Egyptian dish', constantly associated in our minds with epicurean banquets. Antony feasts kings, has twelve wild boars roasted whole at a breakfast. But their tables are spread and cleared by servants: the principals are never associated with getting the meal ready. In *Women Beware Women*, Livia and Isabella are supposed to be court ladies, but their turn of speech often recalls the housewife. Livia says that since women are con-demned to make and serve up to husbands dishes they are not allowed to eat, such as obedience, they have a right to lick their fingers to taste them while cooking (I.ii). So Isabella leads Hippolito on:

> When we invite our best friends to a feast,
> 'Tis not all sweetmeats that we set before them;
> There's somewhat sharp and salt, both to whet appetite,
> And make 'em taste their wine well – so, methinks,
> After a friendly, sharp, and savoury chiding,
> A kiss tastes wondrous well, and full o' the grape.   (II.i.198)

And even more strikingly:

> She that comes once to be a housekeeper
> Must not look every day to fare well, sir,
> Like a young waiting-gentlewoman in service,
> For she feeds commonly as her lady does,
> No good bit passes her but she gets a taste on't;
> But when she comes to keep house for herself,
> She's glad of some choice cates then once a week,
> Or twice at most, and glad if she can get 'em.
> So must affection learn to fare with thankfulness.   (II.i.217)

IV

In his treatment of women, of sex and marriage, Middleton is very much a modern in his time. While most upper- and middle-class marriages in Tudor and Jacobean times were still business and property transactions arranged between parents, the idea of marriage as a freely chosen partnership based primarily on affection was becoming increasingly popular. The drama, with its insistence on love-matches, no doubt helped to encourage this idea, but could not move far ahead of audience opinion: it reflected as well as popularised a changing attitude among ordinary citizens. The old aristocracy might still take for granted dynastic alliances based on uniting two great estates or restoring a decayed landed family by marriage to a rich merchant's daughter. This was the background of the old Courtly Love tradition in literature, which assumed that true love would usually happen outside marriage. Wyatt's love-lyrics and Sidney's *Astrophel and Stella* came out of a still-living reality.[14] There are traces of it still in Chapman and Webster. But in humanist and especially in Puritan thought, increasing value was being attached to the wife as a helpmeet to her husband, a partner if not an equal in economic as well as family life. This implied at least a measure of personal choice before marriage, and rigorous chastity before and within it, with, as some of the most advanced thinkers believed, the possibility of divorce where love and companionship were lacking, and not only for adultery as canon law laid down. Milton's arguments in his divorce tracts about the nature of marriage as a personal relationship rather than a sacramental one were in the main tradition of Protestant thought from Luther onwards.

Like most shifts in ideas, this one had some practical basis too. In the towns, where the craftsman's or tradesman's household was the basic economic unit, the wife was no longer a mere drudge and

---

14 In the seventeenth century a typical case is that of William, 3rd Earl of Pembroke, patron of Shakespeare and later of Middleton, who was married to an heiress, but according to Clarendon 'paid much too dear for her fortune by taking her person into the bargain', and sought his satisfaction and companionship elsewhere. 'He was immoderately given up to women. But. . .he was not so much transported with beauty and outward allurements, as with those advantages of the mind as manifested an extraordinary wit and spirit and knowledge, and administered great pleasure in the conversation.' Love rather than lust, in fact. John Donne's marriage, made for love in defiance of worldly prudence, was described by the pious Walton as 'the most remarkable error of his life'.

beast of burden (as the peasant woman so often was), and it was
not yet a matter of pride for the middle-class husband in counting-
house or factory that his wife and daughter at home could live like
gentlewomen and did not have to work. The city woman at this
stage often played an active role in the business, as book-keeper or
saleswoman: her status in this role was higher, and to have an
intelligent, independent wife was a great help to getting on in trade.
Moreover, Puritanism itself was a household-based religion,
especially in early Stuart times, somewhat as the Jewish religion
still is; and this gave more importance and responsibility to the role
of wife and mother. It is no accident that women who could argue
about the Scriptures, even women preachers, are heard of frequently
among the Lollards of early Tudor times, as among the sects in the
seventeenth century.[15]

All this made the choice of a mate a sacred and even religious
duty to the serious Christian citizen. Since men were required to
love their wives, they must take care, the preachers taught, to marry
only such as they could love. 'Love is the marriage virtue, which
sings music to their whole life', said one Puritan manual: but love
must be based on choice; 'divers women have many virtues, and
yet do not fit with some men'.[16] So important was this choice that
many preachers thought the process known as falling in love, 'the
secret sympathy of hearts', should be regarded as the 'finger of
God',[17] 'a secret working', as Lucy Hutchinson describes it in her
own marriage.[18]

A difficult question was, therefore, what godly children should
do when parents unreasonably withheld consent, other than to 'pray
to God to melt the hard hearts of fathers', and implore the church
and the magistrates to intervene, since parents are 'no further made
the judges over the children, than as they can answer to God for

[15] See K. V. Thomas, *Women and the Civil War Sects, Past and Present*
no. 13 (Apr. 1958). See also Lucy Hutchinson's sketch of herself as a young
bluestocking, more interested in the Classics or writing poetry than in
clothes and fashion, in the *Memoirs of the Life of Colonel Hutchinson*.
According to her account, it was her intellect and education that first
attracted her husband to fall in love with her.
[16] Henry Smith, *Preparative to Marriage* (1593).
[17] Daniel Rogers, *Matrimonial Honour* (1642). Both quoted in W. and M.
Haller, 'The Puritan Art of Love', *Huntington Library Quarterly*, v, no. 2
(Jan. 1942), pp. 235–72.
[18] *Memoirs of the Life of Colonel Hutchinson*, ed. Rev. J. Hutchinson
(London, 1968), p. 49.

their carriage therein'.[19] To force children to marry against their will was increasingly seen as not only unwise but morally wrong.

Moreover, while Puritan teaching insisted most strongly on absolute chastity before and within marriage (and, in theory if not in fact, for men as well as women), yet to keep women secluded for fear of seduction was considered worthy only of Popish countries. Thus in the source for *The Changeling* the pious John Reynolds tells how Beatrice's husband

> curbs and restrains her of her liberty, and would hardly permit her to see, yea, far less to converse with any man; but this is not the way to teach a woman chastity; for if fair words, good example, and sweet admonitions cannot prevail, threatenings and imprisoning in a chamber will never, yea, the experience thereof is daily seen, both in England, France and Germany, where generally the women use (but not abuse) their liberties and freedom, granted them by their husbands, with much civility, affection and respect.[20]

It is in this setting that we must understand the sexual morality of Middleton's tragedies, which goes far deeper than the mere moralising condemnation of lust and adultery. In both of these plays, fathers or guardians assume the right to dispose of daughters and wards in arranged mercenary marriages, with tragic results. The girls, treated as chattels, lack the resources or the courage to win in open resistance, but try to satisfy their own desires by deceit or crime.

All this does not imply – as many critics seem to assume – a cynical view of love and marriage, or even necessarily of the predestined depravity of most human beings. Men and women are no doubt often weak and selfish, but they are also shown in these plays as living under terrible pressures which help to corrupt them.[21] They are the creatures of their environment as well as of original sin. And what makes it all the more terrifying is that the figures of family authority are not savage melodramatic villains like Webster's

---

[19] Daniel Rogers, *Matrimonial Honour.*
[20] The ideas in this passage are very close to what Middleton dramatises, not in *The Changeling* but in *Women Beware Women* – which may help to confirm that *Women* was not written earlier than 1621.
[21] As J. R. Mulryne puts it in his recent edition of *Women Beware Women* (London, 1975): 'Part of the originality of Middleton's works is that he appreciates, far more keenly than other dramatists of his day, the moral pressure exerted by a society's habit of mind' (p. lxvii).

Arragonian brothers in *The Duchess of Malfi*,[22] but respectable members of the governing classes. Vermandero in *The Changeling* is a decent, unimaginative military man, who dismisses his daughter's reluctance to marry the fiancé he has chosen for her as 'a toy'. The small-minded mercenary old men, Fabrizio and Guardiano, in *Women Beware Women* are simply putting through a business deal:

> *Guardiano.* He has been my ward now some fifteen year,
> And 'tis my purpose, as time calls upon me . . .
> To tender him a wife. Now, sir, this wife
> I'd fain elect out of a daughter of yours.
> You see my meaning 's fair: if now this daughter
> So tendered – let me come to your own phrase, sir –
> Should offer to refuse him, I were hanselled.   (I.ii.3)

The offer is tempting financially, and Fabrizio decides at once that Isabella must marry the half-witted ward:

> On with the mask! I'll hear no more: he's rich . . .
> Like him or like him not, wench, you shall have him
> And you shall love him.   (I.ii.84)

And the poor revolting half-wit is bullied too, with the threat of a heavy fine if he refuses.

> If you like the choice,
> Her father and her friends are i' the next room,
> And stay to see the contract ere they part . . .
> Like her, or like her not, there's but two ways,
> And one your body, th'other your purse pays.   (III.iii.10)

This disgusting system of wardship, under which wards were 'bought and sold like horses in Smithfield' (as the Duke of Newcastle put it), survived from feudal times simply because it was a source of profit to the king or to a courtier to whom he granted guardianship of the ward as a favour. But it was no longer taken for granted as right by a citizen audience in the 1620s, and in 1646 Parliament finally abolished it.

So, too, Bianca has been treated not only by her wealthy parents, but by Leantio, the husband she has eloped with, as a precious bit of property, to be locked up in his absence, with her mother-in-law as jailer:

---

[22] Though their harsh feudal pride is scarcely exaggerated by Webster. The efforts of some critics to make their view of the Duchess' remarriage to her steward the 'respectable' one seem absurd, in view of the tone of the play.

Leantio.   'Tis great policy
    To keep choice treasure in obscurest places:
    Should we show thieves our wealth, 'twould make them
        bolder.   (I.i.165)

And when he returns from his business trip, insufferably pleased
with himself and expecting her to be randier than he, the audience
cannot but feel he deserves to be cuckolded.

                    After a five days' fast
    She'll be so greedy now, and cling about me,
    I take care how I shall be rid of her.   (III.i.106)

This is not meant to be felt as any excuse for Bianca's behaviour:
but it must be noted too that corruption strikes down from above,
from the court, where a laxer view of marriage prevails.

The Duke's mixture of naked power, bribery and over-sweet
romantic rhetoric in his addresses to Bianca has the authentic ring
of the late-Jacobean court. One remembers the contemporary
amours of Buckingham, and the unfortunate partners married off,
by pressure and sometimes by main force, to his needier relatives.[23]
Such notorious scandals in the 1620s had made the Duke the best-
hated man among London citizens. They at least are very unlikely
to have taken the play as a fantasy picture of exaggerated Italianate
vice.

The changes Middleton made here in his probable source material
are interesting. In Malespini's *Ducento Novelle* (published 1609)
the Duke is a noble Renaissance lover, in the tradition of illicit
Courtly Love.[24] When he has Bianca at his mercy he does not
threaten or rape her, but persuades her with declarations of love, to
which at a later interview she yields. In Malespini the Duke, his
mistress and her husband live for a time in harmony, the husband
agreeing to allow the Duke secretly to bed with his wife from time
to time, and receiving advancement at court in return. It is the
husband's underbred arrogance and desire to reassert his virility by

---

[23] Thus Sir Edward Coke broke down the doors in his wife's house to get
at his daughter and carry her off to be married to a brother of the Duke's –
a marriage which predictably turned out badly. Sir Sebastian Harvey, a very
rich merchant and Lord Mayor, was under heavy pressure from the King in
person to marry his daughter to Buckingham's brother Kit Villiers, but
stuck manfully to his refusal, saying the girl was too young. G. P. Akrigg,
Jacobean Pageant (Cambridge, Mass., 1962), gives a variety of documented
examples of a similar kind.

[24] The point is made in Schoenbaum, *Middleton's Tragedies*, p. 111 – a book
to which I am much indebted.

a publicised liaison with a noble lady that primarily brings about his death, after he has ignored warnings from the Duke to be more discreet: and Bianca's marriage to the Duke follows. The Duke, in this version of the story, is certainly not guiltless (he is at least partly involved in the husband's murder), but he is discreet, gracious, a courtier and a gentleman: and the trouble with the husband is that he is a bank clerk, a bourgeois, with a middle-class notion of exclusive property in women, and unable to meet the demands of the aristocratic code of love-behaviour. In Middleton all this is transformed in the light of a consistent morality based on rigorous chastity in marriage – a citizen, middle-class or Calvinist view, as it has variously been described – for which there can be no gracious adulteries, and both Duke and factor are contemptible sinners.

It is odd that Middleton should ever have been represented as cynical for the view plainly embodied in the play, which, while its rigidity may seem unacceptable now,[25] is clearly not only more Christian but, in essence, more democratic than that in Malespini. A similar clash of codes, with a more cheerful outcome, is at the centre of *The Marriage of Figaro* a century and a half later. When Figaro bids defiance to his master the Count, who discreetly claims the feudal lord's right to seduce his bride before marriage, we can plainly hear in the confident jeering rhythms of the great aria 'Si vuol' ballare' the satirical music of the revolution to come.[26]

What is new in these plays is not so much the sexual situations as the ability of the women to reflect on them in general terms, and the natural way in which exploitation by men is shown as contributing to aggressiveness or deceit in women. The original audience was surely intended to sympathise up to a point, as a modern one would, with Isabella's resentment (spoken before she has been tricked into incest with Hippolito, when she is still idealistic):

> Marry a fool!
> Can there be greater misery to a woman

[25] Not that the Duke's attitude seems particularly acceptable either.
[26] Lucy Hutchinson, looking back after the failure of the Puritan revolution, describes James' Court around the era of *Women Beware Women*, with its 'fools and bawds, mimics and catamites'. 'Then began murder, incest, adultery, drunkenness, swearing, fornication, and all sort of ribaldry, to be no concealed but countenanced vices because they held such conformity with the court example' (*Memoirs of the Life of Colonel Hutchinson*, p. 62). Mrs Hutchinson wrote with passionate partisanship and from hearsay; but this was certainly how Puritan opinion saw the court of Buckingham's time.

That means to keep her days true to her husband,
And know no other man? So virtue wills it.
Why, how can I obey and honour him
But I must needs commit idolatry?

...

                   O the heartbreakings
Of miserable maids, where love's enforced!
The best condition is but bad enough;
When women have their choices, commonly
They do but buy their thraldoms, and bring great portions
To men to keep 'em in subjection.

...

Men buy their slaves, but women buy their masters;
Yet honesty and love makes all this happy,
And, next to angels, the most blessed estate.
That providence, that has made every poison
Good for some use, and sets four warring elements
At peace in man, can make a harmony
In things that are most strange to human reason.
O, but this marriage!   (I.ii.162)

The cynicism and good-natured immorality of Livia is shown as the natural product of a situation where women have no choice, yet are tied to lifelong obedience to their man – as in the speech already cited:

Fab.   Why, is not man
      Tied to the same observances, lady sister,
      And in one woman?
Livia.   Tis enough for him:
      Besides, he tastes of many sundry dishes
      That we poor wretches never lay our lips to,
      As obedience, forsooth, subjection, duty, and such
          kickshaws,
      All of our making, but served in to them;
      And if we lick a finger then sometimes,
      We're not to blame, your best cooks often use it.   (I.ii.37)

Even Bianca, by far the most repellent of the three women, can reflect on the over-repressive upbringing that has helped to make her what she is, the Duke's mistress.

      This was the farthest way to come to me,
      All would have judged that knew me born in Venice,

And there with many jealous eyes brought up,
That never thought they had me sure enough
But when they were upon me; yet my hap
To meet it here, so far off from my birthplace,
My friends, or kindred! 'tis not good, in sadness,
To keep a maid so strict in her young days;
Restraint breeds wandering thoughts, as many fasting days
A great desire to see flesh stirring again:
I'll ne'er use any girl of mine so strictly.   (IV.i.24)

This is not, of course, to imply that Livia or Bianca is expressing views of which Middleton approves – merely that in handling the issue dramatically he allows even wicked characters to make the most powerful case they can for their behaviour, and hence intensifies the reality of the conflict. This is indeed one of the qualities he shares with Shakespeare.

v

The conventional murder-in-a-masque ending to *Women Beware Women*, which is a traditional way of ending a murder play with divine justice meted out to all, has been criticised as being out of key with the naturalistic, almost Ibsen-like quality of the social and psychological tragedy up to this point. When Leantio and Bianca meet, each having been corrupted and gone to a new lover, 'they are in fact in hell, a naturalistic hell made out of their knowledge of what they have done to themselves and to each other. Here Middleton should have left them', according to G. A. Hibbard. It is a pity, he thinks, that in Act V the play becomes 'a melodramatic revenge play demonstrating the mentality – and incidentally, the fiendish ingenuity – of divine justice'. For similar reasons, the religious moral is a mistake. 'The intrusion of the Cardinal brings with it overtly religious ideas and motives alien to the whole tone and significance of the earlier part of the play.'

This seems to me a misunderstanding of Middleton's intention. Dramatically, one may well object to this particular murder-in-a-masque as almost impossible to stage in a tragic manner. *The Spanish Tragedy* and *The Revenger's Tragedy* both use this type of ending, but there the murders are simple stabbings, and hence actable. Here we have elaborate contraptions with poisonous darts, caltrops, cupids shooting with envenomed arrows, and conspirators falling through the wrong trap doors, while the Duke complains that something has gone wrong with the programme notes and dies still trying to understand the allegory. It seems at first sight like expecting a catharsis from the final sequence of the Marx Brothers' *Night at the Opera.*

Certainly Middleton and his audience were more used to this kind of allegorical pageant than we are (he wrote them regularly for city entertainments), and thus could better appreciate one in which all the effects went wrong as a weird means of mutual revenge and slaughter, and hence of divine vengeance. They would have appreciated the special irony of setting retribution in the midst of an expensive court entertainment, with Livia playing Juno Pronuba the marriage goddess. In many Jacobean masques courtiers notorious for their private lives spoke lofty lines in praise of chastity and wedded love; and Middleton had himself been commissioned to compose *The Masque of Cupid* for the Somerset marriage. But it must always have seemed grotesque as well as horrible, and was doubtless meant to do so. Bianca, Livia, Isabella and their men are not intended to achieve stoic dignity in the face of death, like Vittoria or Byron or the Duchess of Malfi; they are to be proved fools in the end. Still, for a modern audience it may be all too ingenious to be impressive.[27]

It is another matter, however, to argue that the 'overtly religious ideas' expressed by the Cardinal are an intrusion: they are a necessary part of the effect. If men and women were to avoid being swept along in the corruption and greed of the decaying court, it was usually by holding to a firm, even rigid religious and moral code: this was, historically, what helped to steel and give confidence to the opposition in country and city. One of the interesting points here is that Middleton, whom we know as an anti-Catholic satirist in *A Game at Chess,* here gives us a Cardinal quite different from the Machiavellian Monticelso in *The White Devil*[28] or the Arragonian in *The Duchess of Malfi,* or the pliable Friar and villainous Cardinal in Ford's *'Tis Pity She's a Whore* – a man who speaks much like the popular preachers of contemporary London, and who dares denounce the ruler to his face, as Cornelius Burges laid

[27] See the discussion of the masque in tragedy by Inga-Stina Ewbank, 'These Pretty Devices, a Study of Masques in Plays', in *A Book of Masques in Honour of Allardyce Nicoll* (Cambridge, 1970), pp. 437–47.
[28] Historically, of course, the same Cardinal as Middleton's.

down that a royal chaplain ought to do.[29] His words have a weight quite different from the conventional *sententiae* in Webster or in *The Revenger's Tragedy*:

> I know time spent in goodness is too tedious;
> This had not been a moment's space in lust now;
> How dare you venture on eternal pain
> That cannot bear a minute's reprehension?
> Methinks you should endure to hear that talked of
> Which you so strive to suffer.   (IV.i.230)

So, too, when Bianca dies, in her last words,

> Leantio, now I feel the breach of marriage
> At my heart-breaking.   (V.i.252)

she pays a kind of tribute to marriage as it ought to have been, which is essential to the final balance. For Middleton is not merely a cynic; he is a realist whose realism implies alternative standards to those he shows operating among the grandees and courtiers of his time.

As in Middleton's greater comedies – notably *A Chaste Maid in Cheapside* – the aristocratic social and economic code is shown here as utterly worm-eaten and corrupt. If there are no strongly drawn virtuous characters in the play, the old mother still comes nearest to expressing the sensibility of a city audience, in that comment:

> The miller's daughter brings forth as white boys
> As she that bathes herself in milk and bean-flour. (III.i.37)

This is recognisably the ethos of the Parliamentary Puritan opposition.[30] But there is no pretence that the citizen characters live up to it. As in the major comedies, idle aristocrats and mercenary citizens alike are treated with ruthless psychological realism.

Irving Ribner has argued that Middleton's tragedies are 'conditioned by a Calvinistic bias which leaves little room for the redemption of sinners'; and they have certainly a frightening consistency which is absent from the court tragi-comedy and

---

[29] *The Fire of the Sanctuary Newly Uncovered, or a Complete Tract of Zeal* (London, 1625; *S.T.C.* 4111), pp. 262–6.

[30] Bianca, who despises her shabby mother-in-law, describes her as a silly old woman, ready to be a bawd to her daughter-in-law for a few sweetmeats at a party. But the critics are wrong, I think, in taking this as conclusive evidence that we too are to despise the values to which she gives expression. She does not, of course, know of Livia's role as procuress to the Duke, though she is gullible and overimpressed by rank

tragedy of the 1620s and 1630s. But Ribner's view does not, it seems to me, fully render the strictly naturalistic psychology, the secular logic of cause and effect, sin and retribution which, for example, differentiate *The Changeling* from its popular pious source, in which divine intervention is much cruder and more external. One may see Beatrice and Bianca as predestined to their crimes. Yet the stress on individual conscience and the effect of wicked actions on character; the insistence that crime is a great leveller and that high rank in no sense palliates it; the concern for the dignity and responsibility of women, and the folly of mercenary 'made' marriages and of luxurious idleness – all these are aspects of a practical Puritan way of seeing, in which the doctrine of predestination is less important than the realities of everyday existence for the industrious sort.[31] It is a logical paradox, but a historical fact, that a belief in predestination went along with an acute sense of personal and public responsibility, a stress on individual conscience and achievement.[32] The ordinary parishioner, who was also the ordinary member of the audience at the public theatres, was probably more conscious of the *ethics* of the sermons – the industry, sobriety, restraint and prayer enjoined on the congregation – than of the controversies over covenant theology and the irrevocability of salvation or damnation.

[31] The aristocratic patrons of Puritan preachers and writers were often, of course, given to luxury and idle entertainments in their private lives. This was sometimes criticised by their protégés (see the letter of John Field to the Earl of Leicester cited on p. 266), more often perhaps tolerated because the patron's wealth and influence made him a valued political protector (see Thomas Adams' sermon cited on p. 281).

[32] See Christopher Hill, *Society and Puritanism in Pre-Revolutionary England*, *passim*, and the same author's 'Protestantism and the Rise of (London, 1974).

12. *Drama and Opposition, 1619–1640*

The twenty years before the Civil War are usually thought of as a time when the theatres were dominated by a courtly elegant Cavalier drama, or by light comedy foreshadowing that of the Restoration – the work, for example, of Beaumont and Fletcher, Shirley, Davenant and Brome. Much of what was shown, at court and in the indoor theatres especially, was indeed sophisticated entertainment for a leisured and fashionable public. Some of it was certainly escapist, unserious, sexually titillating. Yet to see, say, Beaumont and Fletcher as merely creating a fairy-tale world is too simple. They write for Jacobean courtiers and sophisticated men-about-town:[1] and as an acute critic puts it, 'their plays strike roots deep into a real world...Their "unreality" for us amounts to a criticism of much more than the two dramatists concerned. It is a judgment too of the habits of mind of an actual section of a historical society.'[2]

Nevertheless, the kind of criticism of Crown and court that did find dramatic expression in these years was potentially more serious and far-reaching than the 'first wave' of satirical attacks, mainly by the children's companies, in the opening years of James' reign. In the earlier period, plays in the private theatres had jeered at Scottish favourites, the sale of knighthoods, monopolies and even at the King's personal habits, 'so that it would make any afraid to hear them'. Later, especially after the outbreak of the Thirty Years War in 1618, companies at the public and popular theatres made a number of attempts to handle the central issues of policy and outlook in dispute between Crown and Parliament – a much more dangerous development.

Specifically, there were plays dealing with the Thirty Years War,

---

[1] Beaumont's father was a judge, Fletcher's a bishop, and they aspired, through the theatre, to consolidate a position as court gentry.

[2] John Danby, *Elizabethan and Jacobean Poets* (London, 1965), p. 161. The whole analysis of Beaumont and Fletcher here is profound, and the treatment of Great House patronage essential to understanding the literary scene in the early seventeenth century.

and enlisting popular support for the cause of the King and Queen of Bohemia against the policy of the Crown. There were plays about the killing of British merchants by the Dutch at Amboyna and the failure to exact reparations; about incompetent favourites disastrously appointed to high posts, particularly naval and military ones; about a king's right arbitrarily to tax his subjects; about undue reverence for rank; about Church courts used to enrich their officers; and about ceremonies and Popish practices within the Church.

Our impressions of this whole aspect of the drama – what we may term roughly the Parliamentary Puritan as distinct from the Cavalier trend – are restricted in several ways. For one thing, the most forthright plays, those which involve not merely glancing topical allusions but a whole alternative way of seeing the situation, seem (not unnaturally) to have been those of the popular theatres like the Red Bull and the Fortune, a great part of whose repertory has been lost.[3] The existence of many of the opposition and radical plays is known to us only through the records of censorship and prosecution (for example, the seditious play on the King's Scottish expedition of 1640, the 'book' of which was seized by the censor, and presumably destroyed). Few of them were revived or published after the Restoration, as so much of the court drama was.

A selection and sifting of a different kind took place in the nineteenth century, when our most popular editions were compiled. Nineteenth-century dramatic editors tended on the whole to be less interested in satire and chronicle than in the 'purer', more timeless imaginative forms of tragedy, comedy and tragi-comedy. The 'best plays of the old dramatists' were usually deemed to be those which concentrated on private human interest and characterisation, on sexual or sentimental themes, editors like Havelock Ellis having a particular interest in plays which treated the complex of sexual relationships with so much more frankness and variety than late-Victorian literature could do. Thus in the Mermaid series, enormously influential because for many years the only broad selection available to individual students, we find *The Guardian* but not *The Bondman* of Massinger; *Old Fortunatus* of Dekker, but not *If It Be*

---

[3] Among those surviving plays which appear to have been designed primarily for the popular open-air theatres (as distinct from those first played at fashionable houses like Blackfriars in the winter, and later outdoors in the summer) are such outstanding topical examples as *Sir John Van Olden Barnavelt*, *A Game at Chess*, *The Duchess of Suffolk* and *Albertus Wallenstein*.

Not a Good Play the Devil is In It or *The Wonder of a Kingdom*; and of Middleton *The Spanish Gipsy* but not *A Game at Chess*.

The taste which guided the selection is evident in the introductions, more frankly evaluative than such things usually are now. Thus Ernest Rhys, editor of the Dekker volume, loved the 'pure joy of life' in *Shoemaker's Holiday*, but found *If This Be Not a Good Play* 'an absurd semi-allegorical dramatic fantasy' (p. xxxvi), and *The Wonder of a Kingdom* 'a heartless production – more a cold study of motives and passions than a sympathetic recreation of them in forms of art' (p. xxxix). Havelock Ellis considered *Perkin Warbeck* 'the least interesting of his plays for those who care for the peculiar qualities which mark Ford's genius' (p. xii), though it 'ranks among our best historical dramas', and was included in his selection. Arthur Symons thought that 'Massinger, being no great spirit, winged, and having force to enter into the deep and secret places of the soul, found his place to be in a censorship of society, and was right in concerning himself with what he could do so well' (p. xxi). J. A. Symonds, in his introduction to A. W. Verity's selection from Heywood, thought it sad that *If You Know Not Me*, 'so interesting in its matter, should be almost valueless as a work of art'; none of Heywood's histories is in Verity's selection. Swinburne, in his introduction to the two Middleton volumes (1887), praised *A Game at Chess* as 'one of the most complete and exquisite works of artistic ingenuity and dexterity that ever excited or offended, enraptured or scandalised an audience of friends or enemies – the only work of English poetry which may properly be called Aristophanic': Havelock Ellis, the editor, did not however include it among his selected ten plays.

Even now, many of the plays discussed here have never been reprinted in a form students can buy. Some are available only in limited library editions seventy or eighty years old; most are expensive and out of print. Lecturers and critics naturally (and rightly) discuss those plays that students are likely to read or even to own; the rest are largely forgotten.[4] This is why, in this section, I quote at perhaps undue length from plays which, compared with Middleton's, may seem minor work. Some of them, nevertheless,

---

[4] The situation is gradually improving, thanks to series like the Regents Renaissance Drama and Revels texts. The Oxford World's Classics editions are also extending the recognised canon. Over much of the field, however, the Malone Society's excellent texts are still the only ones available.

retain the liveliness and boldness which gave them their original appeal to a wide audience.

Another reason why the notion of an 'opposition' drama seems strange is, of course, that where dramatists were writing largely for court circles they could hardly help being cautious and equivocal, perhaps half-hearted, in their handling of critical themes. 'Willing to wound and yet afraid to strike' they inevitably were, much of the time, and not only for reasons of censorship. Even to imagine a power beyond the king's remained difficult, almost unthinkable, right up to the Civil War. One need not assume, for example, that if Massinger so often appears to pull his punches, it is purely for reasons of censorship. How to modify the behaviour of kings, to redress grievances, to get some kind of consensus between Crown and Parliament *without* appealing to the unstable and ignorant multitude, and calling into action dangerous and subversive 'popular' forces – this was the problem of the Puritan lords and gentry as well as Presbyterian grandees and big businessmen throughout the period.[5] And lords and gentry were the main patrons and protectors of the drama. Few playwrights seem to have experienced the close citizen and Parliamentary Puritan connections and influences we have attempted to trace for Middleton.

II

Sir John Van Olden Barnavelt, attributed to Fletcher and Massinger, and played in 1619, is among the most noteworthy of the directly political plays. Like *A Game at Chess*, it relies on popular interest in anti-Spanish and anti-Catholic politics. The real Oldenbarnevelt, who had been on several Netherlands embassies to King James, had just been executed as a traitor. In the play he is represented (somewhat unjustly) as a proud and selfish old man, jealous of the governor (Stadtholder) and Calvinist general Prince Maurice of Nassau, leading his Arminian faction in armed revolt, and willing to accept Spanish help to further his own ambitions. He is defeated with the aid of the English garrisons in the Low Countries, and his conspiracy against the state is betrayed by his friend and confederate Leydenborch (whose imprisonment, along with his young

---

[5] See Christopher Hill, 'The Many-Headed Monster in Late Tudor and Early Stuart Political Thinking', in *Change and Continuity in Seventeenth-Century England.*

son, and suicide in prison is dramatised with much pathos, probably in Fletcher's part of the play). The tragedy builds up to the trial of Barnavelt, who refuses to admit treason but stands on his past services to his country, culminating in his beheading on stage. He dies, like Byron in Chapman's play, still unrepentant, with comic executioners (who recall the soldiers dicing round the cross in the old miracle plays) to provide a realistic humiliation and terror.

There is indeed some inconsistency in the portrayal of Barnavelt, who is unsympathetic most of the way through and becomes more attractive at the end. This may be due simply to the collaboration (Fletcher being much less critical politically than Massinger) or to some confusion of aim such as one often finds in Massinger's un-aided work, as if the playwright were alarmed halfway through by what he had done (a similar effect is observable in *The Bondman* and *The Maid of Honour*; see below, pp. 215–18). Dramatically, the effects tend to cancel each other out, so that the play as a whole lacks the concentrated power of some individual scenes.

The subject was, of course, highly topical, if delicate to handle. Although there was a ban on the representation of living monarchs on the stage, Prince Maurice of Nassau was not technically a sovereign but only a governor (an accusation that he aspired to monarchy was deleted by the censor before performance). Since James I had particularly disliked Barnavelt personally, and had entered into public theological controversy with him, the theme may have seemed to the players acceptable enough: a good Calvinist prince cutting off a bad rebel's head. But then Barnavelt, as well as a rebel, was an Arminian, and the Arminians were a growing power at court whose influence on royalty was much feared by the Puritan leaders. And worse, Barnavelt was shown as tolerating Papists and leaguing with Spain, just at the moment when the King's policy was veering in that direction and causing much popular antagonism. However careful the dramatists might be to show no disrespect to Prince Maurice or to the principle of sovereignty, they could hardly avoid giving offence.

The play was held up and censored on the intervention of the Bishop of London. After some delay its sponsors were apparently influential enough to get it staged nevertheless, and it played for some days to packed houses. But it was never revived, and remained unpublished – probably because of the fear of censorship – until Bullen found the MS. in the 1880s.

Modern commentators have suggested that the London audience would see an analogy between Barnavelt's execution and Raleigh's the year before;[6] but this seems unlikely. Barnavelt is not represented by the dramatists in a heroic light, and Raleigh was a popular hero just because (unlike Barnavelt in this play) he had never changed his policy but continued all his life to fight the Spaniards. The stage-Barnavelt's pleas for liberty and local autonomy sound more attractive to modern editors than they would to a Protestant city audience in the period of the Counter-Reformation, who would probably have heard them as menacing.[7]

The Duchess of Suffolk was staged for a popular audience at the Fortune in 1624, after being 'much reformed' by Sir Henry Herbert as 'full of dangerous matter'. Like Middleton's *Game at Chess*, it embodies to an exceptional degree the world-view, feelings and prejudices of ordinary London citizens, which gained unusually free expression that year.[8]

It is not hard to see why the 'matter' was thought dangerous. The story, set back in Queen Mary's time, concerns a royal and Puritan Duchess, forced to flee England by the persecuting Popish bishops, hounded with her family from place to place in Europe by the international bloodhounds of the Inquisition, and finally returning in triumph at the accession of the Protestant Elizabeth. The historical Duchess of Suffolk, after her Marian exile, had been a redoubtable patron of London Puritan preachers. But more important still, her sufferings as a refugee in Europe could be seen as a moving stage parallel with those of Queen Elizabeth of Bohemia, a Protestant heroine to the popular audience. In its characterisation and inci-

[6] See V. C. Gildersleeve, *Government Regulation of the Elizabethan Drama* (New York, 1908), p. 115; Bentley, *Jacobean and Caroline Stage*, iii, p. 417; and the edition of *The Tragedy of Sir John Van Olden Barnavelt* by W. P. Frijlinck (Amsterdam, 1922).

[7] In Thomas Scott's *Vox Populi* great prominence is given to Barnavelt as a direct agent of Spain, and the pamphlet concludes with general Spanish consternation at his exposure. On the other hand, Gondomar there regards it as his greatest triumph to have brought Raleigh to execution. This is probably how the patriotic London audience would have seen it too.

[8] Bentley notes (*Jacobean and Caroline Stage*, iii, p. 285) that in 1623–4 the Palsgrave's Men, who staged this play, brought an exceptionally large number of plays for licensing, their theatre and playbooks having been destroyed by fire in 1621. 'Most of the plays were probably poor things', he says, 'for of the fourteen plays licensed in this period of fifteen months, only *The Duchess of Suffolk* is now extant.' It seems possible however that some of them also contained risky political matter which prevented their wider distribution.

dents as well as its central theme, the play is the very model of a plebeian, lower-class way of seeing the contemporary crisis and is closely based on the historical account in Foxe's *Acts and Monuments*.[9]

The Duchess, though royal, immediately establishes herself in the affections of the popular audience. She is first seen dealing out alms to beggars, and, refusing aristocratic and royal suitors, bestows her hand on her honest steward, Bertie. The rejected noblemen call her 'madcap Duchess': she replies

His worth prevails, nor will I change my voice.

Edward VI is still on the throne; but on his death the Papist bishops Bonner and Gardner (presented as right villains) are released from prison and restored to power, where they immediately start to persecute:

Bonner. Where is my rival Ridley and the rest?
They now shall fire for this.

The bishops are determined to destroy the 'scornful Duchess' who has mocked them,

Thinking the sanctuary of her high birth
To privilege her fond presumption.

Dr Sandys, her chaplain, is forced to flee, and evades his pursuers in a splendidly natural scene. Two very realistic Kentish tilers, Hugh and Jenkin, are discovered starting work on a cold morning, with a tray of tiles and a ladder:

Tiler.   Stamp the frost out of thy feet into the mortar for me.
I'll catch me a heat or I'll beat it out at the stones.
[*Beats his fingers against his sides.*]
Jenkin. A good fire would do better with the fingers' ends.
Tiler.   But a pot of ale and a toast would do best of all
With a cold stomach. Over go to the *Cock*,
And see if he come o' the kind, if his ale will
Make a man crow. We'll leave our implements here.
They will not run away, and here's no great crowd
Of people in the town, but if they be stolen, we may find
'em.

They go off to the pub, and meantime Sandys, on the run, providentially finds their gear, climbs up the ladder and pretends to work.

---

[9] The British Library copy of the 1631 edition has no page numbers. Quotations are given in modernised spelling and punctuation from this copy (*S.T.C.* 7242).

When the pursuing soldiers ask if he has seen a man running away, he is able to misdirect them and so get clear, giving thanks to God. But the poor tiler, who admits to being 'the good Duchess of Suffolk's man', is arrested. Meanwhile the Duchess herself escapes from London on foot, carrying her child:[10]

> Still I look back, still start my tired feet,
> Which never till now measured London street.
>
> . . .
>
> Custom must steel thy youth with pinching want,
> That thy great birth in age may bear with scant.
> Sleep peaceably, sweet duck, and make no noise.

Reaching the coast at Leigh, they are hidden till they can take ship by a kindly merchant, who passes the Duchess off as his daughter. The good local constable takes his word for it and chats to the baby:

> Good Mistress White you're welcome to Leigh as I may say,
> We have an honest neighbour of your father.
> Is this your child? heaven bless the little mops,
> Alack, alack, it is as like the Grandsire
> As ever it may look, my pretty duck.

Meanwhile her faithful though rough-spoken servant, Fox, has induced Bishop Bonner, heading the hunt in person, to fall into a well, and the fugitives escape to Europe. After a brief brush with highwaymen, the Duchess, tired and hungry, goes into labour with her next child in a church porch, where her husband laments:

> Alas, alas, this is a homely place
> To bring a princess of such state to bed.
> A wide church porch is made her bedchamber
> And the cold stones her couch, here are no curtains
> But the bleak winds, cold clouds and storms of hail
> And they begirt her round. Heaven, for thy mercy,
> This poor distressed princess shield and save.

The sexton is about to rouse the town, but as if by miracle the good Erasmus, 'he that so highly loved Sir Thomas More',[11]

---

[10] This is poetic licence. The historical duchess departed in great state, accompanied by her major-domo, gentlewoman, joiner, brewer, kitchen-maid, laundress and fool, as well as her new husband. But many of the Marian exiles did go into poverty and hardship. (See Dickens, *The English Reformation*, p. 388.)

[11] More, though a Catholic martyr, remained a revered and popular figure among Londoners.

arrives in time to rescue them, speaking (of course) in Latin. While the Duchess is still lying-in the hunt catches up again; but she is hidden in a hearse with her baby, carried past the pursuers in a mock funeral procession, and once more escapes. The baby is his mother's greatest comfort:

> *Duchess.* We are not utterly devoid of friends.
> Behold, the young Lord Willoughby smiles on us
> And 'tis great help to have a Lord our friend.[12]

The dangers she has escaped are brought vividly before the audience with a cut-back to England, where Ridley, Latimer and Cranmer are sentenced to be burned. After further adventures, in which the Duchess defends her husband, sword in hand, she is finally saved from the wicked Duke of Brunswick by none other than the Palsgrave, who ignores the Pope's command to arrest her and takes her chaplain and servants into his employment. News of Queen Elizabeth's succession allows them to go home, where they are graciously received, and Sandys is made Archbishop of York.[13]

In the final scene outside the Marshalsea prison, when Bishop Bonner is being locked up again and good Grindal and the Protestant clergy let out, the Duchess is once again seen almsgiving for the poor prisoners. Like a sound Puritan benefactor, she is careful to distinguish between prisoners who are inside 'of policy', refusing to pay debts they can well afford to, who eat well in prison and have gardens and bowling alleys, and the really poor.

> One of you give amongst them forty angels,
> My troubles make me sensible of theirs.

The play concludes on a strong note of citizen patriotism:

> *Duchess.* Let's bend our pace towards famous London bridge.
> How pleasant is the prospect of the City,
> Now I have been five years a stranger here,
> Through the same to Whitehall to her grace
> That I may see my loving sovereign's face.

In the episodic style of popular theatre, this is a stirring adven-

---

[12] The historical Lord Willoughby became a noted commander against Spain in the Low Countries.

[13] Archbishop Sandys' son, Sir Edwin Sandys, was a leader of the Jacobean Parliamentary opposition, and had been arrested for his part in the 1621 session. He was also a leader of the anti-Crown group in the Virginia Company. The Palsgrave was the ancestor of the Elector Palatine, husband of James I's daughter Elizabeth and with her joint patron of the company staging the play.

ture piece, which was acted 'divers and sundry times with good applause'. The 'popular' moral points are strongly stressed throughout. The Duchess continually shows a judicious concern for the poor, and is not too proud to marry a social inferior, a servant, for love. All the servants indeed behave loyally and well; and support for 'the religion' is shown throughout as coming from workers, merchants, scholars, and the Palsgrave, rather than the gentry. The colloquial tenderness and fun with the babies would also appeal to the family sentiment of a city (as distinct from a court) audience. And the language, stumbling blank verse and all, is easy and conversational – much of it in a vernacular idiom which has endured till now (as when the tiler says his tools 'won't run away'). The whole thing represents an alternative, and perhaps a more direct way of dramatising strong nationalist and anti-Papist sentiment, rather than the subtle satirical one used in *A Game at Chess*. We do not know whether the play as we have it is before or after the censor's alterations (it was not printed until 1631). But it was certainly very sharp, not to say provocative politically, and, like Middleton's play, could perhaps have got past the censor only at that moment in history.

III

There was a definite attempt by City leaders to use the stage as a means of propaganda, when the East India Company[14] in 1625 commissioned a painting of the Amboyna massacre of 1623, where the Dutch East India Company's agents had tortured and killed a number of rival English merchants, 'and would have had it all acted in a play'; but the Privy Council was appealed to by the Dutch ministers in London, and stopped it for fear of disturbance on Shrove Tuesday,[15] the traditional day for apprentice rioting (which

[14] The Dutch East India Company was a monopoly, originally established by Oldenbarnavelt, and unpopular with the Amsterdam merchants whom it excluded from the trade, as well as with the British East India Company, its main rival. Similar sponsorship of both *Barnavelt* and this play is not excluded – certainly Oldenbarnavelt would have been very unpopular with the British East India Company, who had the sympathy of Prince Maurice. (See Carl J. Friedrich, *The Age of the Baroque* (New York, 1952), pp. 144–50.) Sir William Courteen, the merchant who was partner with the 3rd Earl of Pembroke in the Barbados venture in 1627, was one of those who incurred heavy financial losses as a result of the Amboyna disaster.
[15] *Calendar of State Papers Domestic, 1623–5*, p. 481, Locke to Carleton.

rather suggests that a public theatre performance, and not merely one for a privately invited audience, was intended). Apparently the play had actually been written, but because of the censorship it was never performed.[16] Important interests in the City were, of course, highly critical of the government for its failure to exact some reparation from the Dutch East India Company.

Further evidence of City and Puritan backing for plays in the early 1630s is provided by Walter Mountfort's *The Launching of the Mary or The Seaman's Honest Wife*, an awkwardly constructed little piece of much greater historical than theatrical interest. Mountfort was an official of the East India Company,[17] not a professional dramatist, and wrote the play on a voyage home from India in 1632.[18] In spite of its dramatic weakness, it was apparently acted, for the MS. which survives was cut by Sir Henry Herbert before licensing it in 1633 for stage performance – the cuts being, as usual, political ones. The performance may have been commissioned for an invited audience rather than one in the public theatre, perhaps a subsidised performance for the East India Company and their friends.

The action, such as it is, takes place during the building and launching of the company's good ship *Mary*, and consists of two separate parts, which alternate rather than connect. In one part, old Admiral Hobab, who fought the Armada, enquires about various charges of undermining the economy made against the East India Company, and is answered at great length by the governor and directors in blank-verse paraphrases of Thomas Mun's tract – *A Discourse of Trade from England unto the East Indies* (1621) – praising the company as a model employer and a pillar of the state. One extract will be enough to show the detail with which this material is included: it sounds less like drama than like an employer's case to a pay tribunal done into blank verse.

> Nor do our merchants trading into Spain,
> The Straits, to Venice, Lisbon or the like,
> Give entertainment unto novices
> Which have not some experience of the sea.
> But when all doors of charity are shut,

---

[16] *Ibid.* p. 485, Chamberlain to Carleton.
[17] He had carried letters from the directors to Ambassador Carleton and the Netherlands Company at The Hague in 1621–2.
[18] F. S. Boas, cited by Bentley, *Jacobean and Caroline Stage*, iv, p. 922–3.

> The East India gates stand open, open wide
> To entertain the needy and the poor
> With good accommodation. Two months' pay
> They have beforehand for to make provision,
> Needful provision, for so long a voyage,
> And two months' pay their wives are yearly paid
> The better to maintain their poor estate
> During the discontinuance of their husbands.
> If in the voyage he do chance to die
> The widow doth receive whate'er's found due,
> If not by will disposed otherwise,
> Which often happeneth to be such a sum
> As they together never saw the like.
> And when did any of these widows beg
> For maintenance in churches as some do?
> Blackwall proclaims their bounty: Limehouse
>   speaks
> (If not ingrate) their liberality.
> Ratcliffe cannot complain nor Wapping weep,
> Nor Shadwell cry against their niggardness.
> No, they do rather speak the contrary
> With acclamations to the highest heavens.　　　(l.1708)[19]

The other part of the play deals with the personal story of Dorotea Constance, chaste and industrious wife of a sailor in the company's service, whose long absence she laments:

> Oh, India, India, hadst thou ne'er been known,
> I should have had no cause to make this moan.　　(l.709)

Her virtue is assailed in turn by rich courtiers, land-captains and even a parson ('vicious vicar, painted priest'), but she resists them all and maintains herself by her needle. In contrast, her acquaintance among other seamen's wives, the wanton Tib Butt and Mall Spark, get easy money by going with men. Interestingly, she is taunted by them as a 'Puritan':

Dorotea [to Tib]. Immodest woman, are you not ashamed?
　　　　　Do you not blush to speak so filthily?
Tib Butt. Mary, come up, Mistress Puritan!...This young giglot is ever working, and yet she doth but live; and I never work, and yet live as well as she.　　　　　(l.939)

---

[19] *The Launching of the Mary*, ed. J. H. Walter, Malone Society (Oxford, 1933).

It is noteworthy, however, that this super-righteous 'Puritan' heroine goes to the theatre, and defends it as an honest and moral enjoyment:

> *Dorotea.* Am I suspected for incontinent
> Because sometimes to recreate myself
> I see a play? yea, such a one perhaps
> As makes me fear both shame and punishment?
> Do not good women thus? and more than thus
> Without suspicion?   (1.701)

Eventually she is rescued from poverty and plain sewing, through the good offices of the master of the *Mary* himself. Variety is afforded by the shipyard workers Trunnel, Oakum, Tallow, Tar and Sheathing Nail, good patriotic craftsmen fond of sitting down with a pot of ale to discuss the villainous Dutch and their massacre of English colonists at Amboyna. The censor cut all the inflammatory passages about Amboyna, as well as references to the state of the navy, anti-Catholic passages, and even the mildest of oaths (such as 'i' faith'), which somewhat diminishes the workshop realism. A typical deleted speech is the Admiral's:

> Myself have heard
> Of the unmatched, vile, miserable torture
> Those Dutch inflicted on some Englishmen
> At that Amboyna, and my soul hath yearned
> To hear their dire relation; but alas,
> My sorrow cannot help afflictions past.
> I cannot but admire how such a crew
> Of swinish beastly drunkards, baser than the sire
> Which first begot them (and he base enough)
> Durst spend their censure, or once dare to touch
> The honest subjects of a mighty monarch.   (1.116)

This kind of censorship is predictable. More surprising is the cutting of a later speech, on the face of it part of the routine praise of the East India Company's generosity and charities, and hence apparently innocuous:

> Are there not diverse children set a work
> To do some labour, such as may befit
> Their tender age and weak capacity?
> *Here may I (without boasting) intimate*
> *Repair of Churches, maintenance of scholars,*
> *Relief of [needy] preachers of the sacred word,*

And divers other acts of charity,
Which are by them religiously performed.   (l.1736)

It is hard to see why these harmless-looking lines should have been deleted, except that the whole subject of merchants subsidising poor preachers was a tricky one, just about at the time when the government was suppressing the Feoffees for Impropriations, for fear lest rich Puritan citizens should get too much power in the Church.

This play, however tedious as literature, does suggest that at least some City magnates continued to regard drama as a useful means of propaganda in their various disputes with the Crown.

IV

If one sees the Parliamentary Puritan movement in its true breadth and variety, Massinger's work is very evidently related to though scarcely part of it.[20] There is a sharply critical note in many of his plays, as far as the monarchy and its favourites and hangers-on are concerned. But it is the critical view taken not by the middling sort or the lower orders, but rather by the dissatisfied gentry and nobility: it represents as it were the aristocratic wing of the movement,[21] whereas Middleton sees as the 'industrious people' see. The wrongs Massinger dramatises are those done by kings to their nobility or to other princes, or the encroachment of greedy ambitious citizens on the dignity and privileges proper to rank and birth. His topical targets are court favourites, court monopolists, inefficient generals and admirals appointed because of the king's personal favour, greedy citizens and their families, and what he saw as a weak foreign policy. There are complaints of heavy taxes, too, and

20 This becomes clearer if one compares Massinger's work with that of Fletcher, which has been said by John Danby to supply 'the basis of what will later develop into the Cavalier mentality' (*Elizabethan and Jacobean Poets*, p. 161). S. R. Gardiner, in his celebrated article 'The Political Element in Massinger' (*Contemporary Review*, xxviii (Aug. 1876), pp. 495–507), dealt in detail with the historical correspondences between the plays and the policies of varying court factions at the time. He thought that Massinger's work in the 1630s (in particular *Believe as You List*) reflected an attachment to the Queen's faction against that of Lord Treasurer Weston, a faction which, though 'not one to which any Englishman can look back with satisfaction', may at least have seemed better than its rivals (p. 329).
21 See B. Manning, 'The Aristocracy and the Downfall of Charles I', in Manning (ed.), *Politics, Religion and the English Civil War* (London, 1973), and Stone, *Crisis of the Aristocracy*, chs. VIII, XIII.

the arbitrary levying of them – which seem to have become more outspoken in his later work, now lost. The hardships and sufferings of the poorer half of the nation scarcely appear. Massinger's kings, indeed, move like those of Beaumont and Fletcher in a closed circle of royalty and nobility, and the relations between them and the general run of their subjects scarcely figure in the plays.

Massinger's patrons were themselves aristocracy, notably Philip Herbert, Earl of Montgomery and from 1630 4th Earl of Pembroke (in whose family Arthur Massinger, the dramatist's father, had been steward and man of business),[22] and his son-in-law, the Earl of Caernarvon. It is not just a question of suiting the play to the patron, however. The probability is that Massinger, as son of a gentleman in the great household and business empire of the Herberts at Wilton, himself saw the world in terms of a noble order of patrons and aristocratic rulers, as he had experienced it in his youth. Gentry and aristocracy should remain as national rulers; upstarts, monopolists, favourites exploiting their physical charms to win wealth and power should be firmly put in their place. The virtues most admired in the plays are essentially the aristocratic ones – especially military courage and skill, gallantry, generosity, a keen sense of rank and birth and the responsibilities they entail.[23]

---

[22] Massinger appealed for financial help to William Herbert, 3rd Earl of Pembroke, but does not seem to have received any. He did, however, refer in the dedication to *The Bondman* (1624) and again in 1636 to having received some from his brother the 4th Earl of Pembroke. Aubrey says Pembroke paid Massinger a pension of £20 or £30 a year, which may well be true. (See T. A. Dunn, *Philip Massinger* (Edinburgh, 1957), pp. 21–4.)

[23] Lord Lovell's pride in his own rank in *A New Way to Pay Old Debts* has already been mentioned. A happy ending, in Massinger, requires not only pairing-off in marriage, but that each couple should be exactly matched in rank. Thus at the end of *The Guardian*, when the hero and heroine are to be united, Mirtilla the maidservant proposes to marry the young gallant Adorio:

Mirtilla.　　　　　I dare maintain my love
　　　　Is equal to my lady's.
Adorio.　　　　　　　But my mind
　　　　A pitch above yours: marry with a servant
　　　　Of no descent or fortune!
Severino.　　　　　　　You are deceived:
　　　　Howe'er she has been trained up as a servant,
　　　　She is the daughter of a noble captain,
　　　　Who in his voyage to the Persian gulf
　　　　Perished by shipwreck.
　　　　. . .
　　　　Now for her portion:

Honesty and thrift make little appearance, because the kind of
characters who work are not much in evidence. Essentially, it is a
nostalgic view.

The Bondman (licensed 1623, and dedicated to Montgomery) is a
fine example of these values embodied in tragi-comedy. Here the
city state of Syracuse is corrupted by favouritism and soft living; its
nobility indulge in luxury instead of training in arms, and object to
being taxed to pay for army and navy. The noble general Timoleon
denounces the senate house, where men rule who have no military
record but have risen from 'base arts and sordid thrift'.[24]

>   In this plenty
> And fat of peace, your young men ne'er were trained
> In martial discipline; and your ships unrigg'd
> Rot in the harbour, no defence prepared
> But thought unuseful; as if that the gods,
> Indulgent to your sloth, had granted you
> A perpetuity of pride and pleasure,
> No change feared or expected.   (I.iii.203)[25]

And he demands taxes to pay for war and defend liberty:

>   Do you prize your muck
> Above your liberties; and rather choose
> To be made bondmen than to part with that
> To which already you are slaves?   (I.iii.231)

When Timoleon leads the worthiest Syracusans to war against
Carthage, their slaves, left at home, revolt against their masters,
under the leadership of one Marullo, who marks them out a way to
liberty:

>   by strong hand to revenge
> Your stripes, your unregarded toil, the pride,
> The insolence of such as tread upon

>   So dear I hold the memory of my friend,
>   It shall rank with my daughter's.
> *Adorio.*   This made good
>   I will not be perverse.
> *Durazzo.*   With a kiss confirm it.   (V.iv.233)

At whatever cost in plausibility, the proprieties of status must be preserved.

[24] Gardiner, in 'The Political Element in Massinger', saw a reference here
to both Buckingham and Middlesex.

[25] *Plays and Poems of Philip Massinger*, ed. P. Edwards and C. Gibson
(Oxford, 1976), p. 325. Reference is made to this edition in the following
pages where Massinger's plays are mentioned.

> Your patient sufferings: fill your famished mouths
> With the fat and plenty of the land.   (II.iii.81)

The revolt is presented at this stage with what seems like a measure of sympathy, and some of Marullo's speeches, read out of the context of the play as a whole, have a startlingly revolutionary ring:

> Equal nature fashioned us
> All in one mould. The bear serves not the bear,
> Nor the wolf the wolf; 'twas odds of strength in tyrants
> That plucked the first link from the golden chain
> Wherewith the Thing of Things bound in the world.
> Why then, since we are taught, by their example,
> To love our liberty, if not command,
> Should the strong serve the weak, the fair deformed ones,
> Or such as know the cause of things, pay tribute
> To ignorant fools? All's but the outward gloss
> And politic form, that does distinguish us.   (II.iii.32)

For awhile the slaves are victorious, and their triumph is shown on stage – the great lady Corisca has to hold up her slave's train, and recognises that she is justly punished:

> I, that forgot
> I was made of flesh and blood, and thought the silk
> Spun by the diligent worms out of their entrails
> Too coarse to clothe me, and the softest down
> Too hard to sleep on; that disdained to look
> On virtue being in rags, that stopped my nose
> At those that did not use adulterate arts
> To better nature
> . . .
>   am made justly
> The scorn of my own bondwoman.   (III.iii.72)

However, as Marullo makes clear, the ideal is not really equality, but the acceptance by the natural rulers of their traditional responsibilities towards the ruled:

> Tyranny
> Drew us from our obedience. Happy those times
> When lords were styled fathers of families
> And not imperious masters.   (IV.ii.53)

This moral point having been made, the strong confrontation is deflated with startling suddenness. Marullo turns out after all to be a nobleman in disguise, seeking the hand of the princess (this of course accounts for the gallant powers of leadership he has shown in the revolt). The genuine slaves, far from sharing his noble ideals, are seeking the chance only to loot and rape and then become fat exploiting parasites themselves. They are easily cowed by the mere sight of a whip, without the need for bloodshed, when the army returns from war (though since the unworthy citizens have brought the revolt on themselves, the slaves are leniently dealt with). The point of view is very clearly that of the aristocracy and gentry who wish England to be great by an active anti-Spanish policy. And the very doubleness of vision is thoroughly contemporary – a burning anger at tyranny against nobility and gentry, coupled with an acute sense that the multitude must and should be kept down.[26]

Attacks on over-powerful effeminate favourites are common in Massinger's plays. The parallels with Buckingham, though not necessarily exclusively with him, would readily be drawn by the audience. The enemy's young Lord Admiral in *The Bondman* is

> a raw young fellow,
> One never trained in arms, but rather fashioned
> To tilt with ladies' lips than crack a lance.
>
> . . .
>
>   A steel helmet,
> Made horrid with a glorious plume, will crack
> His woman's neck.   (I.i.50)

Fulgentio in *The Maid of Honour* (1621) is the King of Sicily's 'state catamite', and 'trimmed up in a lady's dressing. . .might well pass for a woman'. He is 'a gentleman, yet no lord' (the gibe of the envious aristocrat rather than of the populace) and persuades the king against helping his natural allies abroad:[27]

[26] The Herbert family had considerable experience of peasant revolt. The 1st Earl of Pembroke, grandfather of William and Philip Herbert, had to put down a rising of levellers around Salisbury following the enclosure of Wilton Park in the 1540s; and enclosures made by the 3rd Earl of Pembroke in the Forest of Dean in 1612 led to riots among those of the poorer sort who lived by the spoil of woods (E. Kerridge, 'The Revolts in Wiltshire against Charles I', *Wiltshire Archaeological and Natural History Magazine*, 1958–9, pp. 64ff.).

[27] Gardiner ('The Political Element in Massinger', and also in *History of England, 1600–1642*, vii, pp. 200ff.) brings out the detailed parallels between the behaviour of Roberto, King of Sicily, here and that of James I in refusing effective aid for recovering the Palatinate. Gardiner assumes a date of 1631 for the play, when it could be seen as a warning to Charles I against repeating his father's mistakes. Modern scholars, however, favour an earlier

> His revenue lies
> In a narrow compass, the king's ear; and yields him
> Every hour a fruitful harvest.
>   . . .
> In the time of trussing a point, he can undo
> Or make a man: his play or recreation
> Is to raise this up, or pull down that; and though
> He never yet took orders, makes more bishops
> In Sicily, than the pope himself.   (I.i.25)

Yet these abuses are merely described, not dramatised; and it is noticeable that Massinger does not make the exposure and fall of such Buckingham-like counsellors into a gripping and terrifying dramatic confrontation, like the fall of Gaveston in *Edward II* or of Bushy, Bagot and Greene in *Richard II*. The favourites are discomfited, reproved, and either forgiven (like Sanazzaro in *The Great Duke of Florence*) or dismissed from the king's service and the play (like Fulgentio in Act III of *The Maid of Honour*), as if there were limits beyond which Massinger and perhaps his patrons, whose relations with Buckingham ranged from alliance to impeachment and back again, were not prepared to go.

Believe As You List, produced by the King's Men in 1631, is more consistent dramatically and more coherent politically than earlier plays like *The Maid of Honour* or *The Guardian*, where the topical references, though pointed, are incidental rather than central to the structure. It also gives us a fascinating glimpse of the Caroline censor at work.

The first draft was refused a licence by Sir Henry Herbert in January 1630, on the grounds that 'it did contain dangerous matter, as the deposing of Sebastian, King of Portugal by Philip the [Second] and there being a peace between the Kings of England and Spain'. The original King Sebastian was believed to have been killed in battle in 1578, and two years later Philip II of Spain annexed Portugal. Various pretenders arose, claiming to be Sebastian, and were supported by the discontented Portuguese; the most notable, backed for a time by the Republic of Venice, was executed by Philip III in 1602. There had been a topical English play by Dekker

---

date of writing, G. E. Bentley thinking 1621–2 the most likely (*Jacobean and Caroline Stage*, iv, pp. 797–8). This would make the allusions even more topical, and place this play among the group of unusually outspoken ones staged around the crisis of James' reign in 1619–24.

and Chettle (now lost) and pamphlets on the subject by Anthony Munday (1601),[28] appealing to general nationalist feeling against Spain, with whom England was then still at war.

However, by 1630 the subject had become dangerously topical in quite a different way. Sebastian, coming back to claim his usurped heritage, hounded from country to country and court to court by Spanish tyranny, with no ally brave enough to stand by him, offered all too direct and threatening a parallel with the exiled Frederick of Bohemia, still kept out of the Palatinate by Spain, with whom England had again declared peace in 1630. 'Such a play would clearly be intolerable to Charles', C. J. Sisson comments.

Massinger revised the play by substituting the story of Antiochus of Syria, set in Roman times, for that of Sebastian, and it was again submitted to Herbert, who licensed it unconditionally in May 1631.[29] The playwright made the alterations with minimum trouble to himself. The new proper names he chose for the revision were metrically equivalent to the censored ones, so that few lines needed rewriting: thus Spain became Rome, Sebastian became Antiochus, Venice became Carthage, Sebastian Nero became Demetrius Castor, and so on. But the similarity of the situation to that of Frederick still stands out clearly, as when Antiochus speaks of his lost territories:

> A tigress circled with her famished whelps
> Will sooner yield a lamb snatched from the flock
> To the dumb oratory of the ewe
> Than Rome restore one foot of earth that may
> Diminish her vast empire.   (I.i.86)

In one of the most powerful scenes, Prusias, King of Bithynia, who has promised to aid and shelter Antiochus, is persuaded by fear of Roman reprisals ignobly to give him up. Flaminius, the Roman ambassador, threatens him with brute force:

> You keep in pay, 'tis true, some peace-trained troops,
> Which awe your neighbours, but consider when
> Our eagles shall display their sail-stretched wings

---

[28] Munday had earlier been employed by Walsingham as an anti-Catholic propagandist. He collaborated with Middleton in a Lord Mayor's pageant, and was himself designer of several.

[29] The original MS., as revised by Massinger, was edited for the Malone Society by C. J. Sisson (Oxford, 1929), to whose edition and introduction my account here is much indebted.

Hovering o'er our legions, what defence
Can you expect from yours?   (III.iii.136)

The vacillating, unhappy behaviour of Prusias in this scene is indeed 'Charles all over', as Gardiner puts it.[30]

Believe As You List, unlike Massinger's other plays, maintains its tragic confrontation consistently to a stark ending, where Antiochus is left in captivity facing possible death. He is not, however, like the historical Sebastian, actually killed – the dramatist and his backers perhaps feeling that this would be depressing rather than encouraging to their cause. The manuscript contains a prologue in another hand, probably not by Massinger, which explicitly draws attention to the modern parallel in a mock-apology for the author:

> If you find what's Roman here,
> Grecian or Asiatic, draw too near
> A late and sad example, 'tis confest,
> He's but an English scholar at his best,
> A stranger to Cosmography, and may err
> In the country's name, the shape and character
> Of the persons he presents.

In his essay on 'The Political Element in Massinger' in 1876, S. R. Gardiner considered that these plays were written simply from 'the standpoint of the Herberts'.[31] A later critic has characterised Massinger as a 'king's man' who 'owed little political allegiance to the cause of the Herberts, or of anyone else for that matter', and merely criticised honestly what he saw.[32] There is no suggestion, however, that Massinger himself had any Puritan or Calvinist religious allegiance.[33] It is interesting, nevertheless, that several of his later plays touch on arbitrary taxation, one of the main grievances of the Parliamentary Puritan opposition. Thus in *The Emperor of the East* (1631), performed at both Globe and Black-

[30] 'The Political Element in Massinger', p. 324.
[31] *Ibid.* p. 316.   [32] Dunn, *Philip Massinger*, p. 174.
[33] Indeed it has been argued that he may have been a Catholic; but the external evidence for this seems tenuous in the extreme. The suggestion is based on certain allusions and episodes in the plays themselves. Thus *The Virgin Martyr* (Dekker and Massinger, printed 1622) is much in the style of the Catholic *tragedia sacra* of the Counter-Reformation period; *The Renegade* contains a portrait of an ideal Jesuit; Camiola, heroine of *The Maid of Honour*, retires to a nunnery at the end. The question remains open. (See Dunn, *ibid.* pp. 184–91; and L. G. Chubb, 'The Virgin Martyr and the Tragedia Sacra', in *Renaissance Drama*, vii (1964), pp. 103–26.) Henry Parker, Puritan lawyer, MP and Parliamentarian leader, wrote verses defending Massinger when attacked in 1633.

friars, the virtuous Pulcheria denounces court parasites who flatter the monarch into imposing unjust fines and levies:

> You roar out,
> All is the king's, his will's above the laws,
> And that fit tributes are too gentle yokes
> For his poor subjects; whispering in his ear
> If he would have their fear, no man should dare
> To bring a salad from his country garden
> Without the paying gabel: kill a hen
> Without excise. . .or, if the prince want
> A present sum, he may command a city
> Impossibilities, and for non-performance
> Compel it to submit to any fine
> His officers shall impose.   (I.ii.238)

The same point was apparently made with more damaging emphasis in *The King and the Subject* (1638), a lost play by Massinger of which we know only that it contained a tyrannous speech by a King of Spain, Don Pedro, who claimed the right to tax without control.

> Moneys? we'll raise supplies what way we please,
> And force you to subscribe to blanks, in which
> We'll mulct you as we shall think fit. The Caesars
> In Rome were wise, acknowledging no laws
> But what their swords did ratify.[34]

The MS. was read by King Charles himself, who agreed that it should be acted, but marked the passage 'This is too insolent, and to be changed',[35] as well he might do, at this period when the refusal to pay ship-money crystallised the main issue between Parliament and the King.

v

A more searing attack on the Buckingham type and his influence in military affairs was mounted by Arthur Wilson in *The Swisser*, acted at the Blackfriars in 1631.[36] We know exactly where Wilson

[34] The use of 'blank charters' to tax rich men without limit had been often referred to in earlier English history plays – notably in the anonymous *Woodstock* and Shakespeare's *Richard II* in the 1590s. Once again, it was the critical contemporary situation that made such a reference dangerous in 1638.

[35] *Dramatic Records of Sir Henry Herbert*, ed. Adams, p. 23.

[36] Wilson, *The Swisser*, ed. A. Feuillerat (Paris, 1904).

stood from his autobiography.[37] He was patronised by those notable
Parliamentary Puritan grandees the Earls of Essex and Warwick,
and lived on intimate terms with them; went with Essex on Vere's
expedition for the defence of the Palatinate (1620), and fought in
the Low Countries (1621–3) and on the Cadiz expedition (1625).
After a belated Oxford career, where he says he was 'accounted a
kind of Puritan among them', he entered Warwick's service, was
with him at the siege of Breda (1637), and subsequently helped to
hold Essex for the Parliament. On the situation which formed the
real-life background to *The Swisser* Wilson comments from personal
experience (p. 123):

> The attempt upon the isle of Cales [Cadiz] was foolish, managed
> by a Commander in Chief who could not make the best use of
> the fair advantages he found.[38]

Essex, he says, was sent by the King on the Cadiz expedition not
out of affection,

> but being a man beloved of the people, and the people not liking
> the Duke's exorbitant power in thrusting the king upon this war,
> which tended only to revenge his private injuries, which was so
> much against the Parliament and the people's mind.[39]

In *The Swisser*, the good general Arioldus lives out of favour on
his country estates, while the king's favourite, Timentes, effeminate
and incompetent, holds command and nearly loses the war. The
king's most faithful counsellor speaks boldly to his master:

> To tell ye, that you have destroyed the strength
> And safety of your kingdom, buried alive
> Those that knew how to act, more than to speak,
> Banished the prime of your nobility,
> Through discontents made 'em retire, and raised
> Such as dare only fight in words. How can
> Your armies thrive? The soldiers are grown heartless,
> And where there is a spirit, 'tis vented out

---

[37] Wilson, *Observations of God's Providence, in the tract of my Life*
(printed as an appendix to *The Constant Lady* (Oxford, 1814).
[38] Wilson, *ibid.* p. 123. Buckingham, himself generalissimo of the expedition,
appointed Sir Edward Cecil (later Viscount Wimbledon) as his deputy and
commander in the field, and it was he who was directly responsible for the
fiasco. See the account under Cecil in *D.N.B.*
[39] P. 123. One of the reports of the Thomas Scot murder in 1627 says that
the assassin was hired to kill him before he could publish his tract on the
Cadiz fiasco.

In such strange murmurings as might corrupt
The best obedience.   (I.i.150)

The day is saved by an outspoken mercenary officer and privileged 'railer', Andruchio the Swisser, who takes command efficiently in the field, and tells the king to his face the truth about his hangers-on:

The courtier at his cringe and smile, the statist
With an erect look and high language, never
Minding inferior things, the Judge with's Ha
Frighting the trembling prisoner, the critic
Shaking his empty noddle, and the gallant
With some quaint oath in's mouth.   (II.i.97)

The tone throughout is anti-court. At the climax, Andruchio threatens to kill the king, who has raped his daughter. The confrontation is presented in terms of a challenge to absolute power:

Andruchio. I must kill thee, king.
King. Thou dar'st not, slave.
Andruchio. I durst not, wert thou noble.
But since you have left that, I have left off
My loyalty. Prepare thyself to die.

Told that he has ravished the girl, the king cries:

Base peasant, wilt thou murder me for that?

Andruchio. For that? Is't not enough? Am I less sensible
Of injury by being poor? 'Tis means
And power that does revenge, not honour only.
She lives in cottages as well as courts,
And wants but only way t'affect her wishes,
Which I have found. Therefore as swift as thought
Call thy sins to account.
Yet I was honest while you had your virtue.
'Tis you have altered me. When kings do leave
Their goodness, they make every slave their master. (V.iii.15)

These are strong words, from a sympathetically presented subject to a king. As one might expect, however, the action from this point is transformed into play-acting, and the impending tragedy into a happy ending. After the audience has experienced the thrill of a threatened sacrilegious tyrannicide, the whole elaborate intrigue proves to have been a plot by good Count Aribert, disguised as Andruchio, to bring the king to his senses – no one ever *really* intended to kill him. No doubt the total effect was less alarming to

the censor, even for court production, because the play-king's main
offence was sexual licence, to which Charles I was not at all given.
He might thus be expected to

> compound for sins we are inclined to
> By damning those we have no mind to.

The action is not so different from Beaumont and Fletcher (say in
The Maid's Tragedy), but the tone of the verse and the moral comment is. It looks like a clear case of drama deliberately used by
Parliamentary Puritan interests, and in the military part of the
action the satirical criticism is pretty near the bone.[40] Indeed the
Essex circle seem to have spent much of their spare time in amateur
dramatic entertainments at their country houses, and it was apparently there that Wilson began to write plays. He says in his autobiography:

> The winters we spent in England [i.e. not campaigning in the
> Palatinate or the Low Countries]. Either at Drayton, my lord's
> grandmother's, Chartley, his own house; or some of his brother's,
> the Earl of Hertford's houses. . .Our public sports (and sometimes
> with great charge and expense) were masks or plays. Wherein I
> was a contriver both of words and matter. For as long as the good
> old Countess of Leicester lived (the grandmother to these noble
> families) her hospitable entertainment was garnished with such,
> then harmless, recreations.   p. 119

VI

Another sign of the times is the new angle given to a much-drama-
tised reign in Robert Davenport's *King John and Matilda*, written
and acted some time between 1628 and 1634. John Bale had written

---

[40] The cynical Cavalier attitude to the war in Europe, against which both
Massinger and Wilson are reacting, is well seen in the opening of Davenant's
The Wits (acted at Blackfriars 1634), where the gallant heroes throw up
their army careers to live by their wits at home:

> *Pert.* Faith, we have been to kill we know not whom
>   Nor why, led on to break a commandment
>   With the consent of custom and the laws. . .
> *Young Pallatine.* True, sage Pert.
>   What is't to thee whether one Don Diego,
>   A prince, or Hans von Holme, fritter-seller
>   Of Bombell, do conquer that parapet,
>   Redoubt or town, which thou ne'er saw'st before?
> *Pert.* Not a brass thimble to me.

From *Six Caroline Plays*, ed. Knowland, p. 352.

his famous Reformation *King Johan* a hundred years earlier, presenting John as a martyr poisoned for his noble resistance to the Pope. Shakespeare's *King John* (1596) showed a usurper and an inefficient king, who did not offer as much resistance to the Pope as he ought, but must nevertheless be supported by patriots against invasion and rebellion. Davenport, however, centres his play on the conflict between the lustful king and the honest barons. Unlike the earlier writers,[41] he makes the barons take their stand on Magna Carta (repeatedly appealed to by the Commons in defence of their rights in the early seventeenth century),[42] and denounce John for giving way to the Papal legate's demand for tribute, in defiance of their counsel. Fitzwater, the baron's leader, whose daughter Matilda John is out to seduce, tells the legate:

> Thus you may inform his Holiness:
> In a field called Running-mead 'twixt Staines and Windsor,
> After some bloody noses on both sides,
> I tell truth, I; there the king and barons
> Met for discussion of conceiv'd wrongs
> And indeed not misconceiv'd; our houses, honours,
> Our fathers' freedoms, the land's ancient liberties,
> Unjustly to increase some private coffers,
> Felt daily diminution; there to covenants drawn,
> Bearing the name and scuse of Magna Carta,
> Which many hundred years may be seen hereafter,
> King John subscribed, we swore him fealty.[43]

King John, like Charles in the 1630s, tries to ride roughshod over what he calls the 'unlawful liberties' extorted from him by the charter; but in the end the armed resistance of the barons, the fear of invasion and John's remorse for the martyrdom of the saintly Matilda restore him to a proper sense of his patriotic duties.[44]

---

[41] This includes Henry Chettle and Anthony Munday, authors of the two plays on *Robert Earl of Huntingdon* (printed 1601) which provide the main source for *King John and Matilda*.

[42] For example, in 1606–7, 1610, and especially by Sir Edward Coke in the 1620s. It had been appealed to by the Marian exiled clergy and many Puritan ministers much earlier, however. See Christopher Hill, *Intellectual Origins of the English Revolution*, p. 258 and *passim*.

[43] Davenport, *King John and Matilda* (II.iv), in W. A. Armstrong (ed.), *Elizabethan History Plays* (London, 1965), p. 377.

[44] Bruce, one of the baron leaders, at the end calls on the onlookers to:
> Look on the King's penitence,
> His promise for the Kingdom's peace.   (V.iii)

Fitzwater and Bruce in this play, unlike the barons in Shakespeare, never desert to the French, but they do take up arms against the king, and are left as moral victors at the end.[45]

The moral sympathies – city and country against court – are even more evident in Davenport's lively comedy, *A New Trick to Cheat the Devil*,[46] which reverses most of the social assumptions we take for granted in *A New Way to Pay Old Debts* or *The City Madam*. Young Slightall, gentleman son of an industrious father, is betrothed to Anne, a citizen's daughter; but her mother has higher ambitions for her, and induces her to throw him over for Lord Skales. Anne, at first seduced by dreams of grandeur, finds his lordship personally unattractive, and repents of her bargain; her father, Changeable, sides with her, and by a fantastic intrigue, in which he disguises himself as the devil, contrives to get her out of the hated marriage and reunited with her Slightall.

In this play the sharp 'levelling' note in the lines is fully borne out by the action. The value of a title is the main bait the mother holds out to the naïve girl:

Wife. How poor and slightly Mistress Slightall sounds.
Anne. Good troth, and so it doth.
Treatwell. But Donna Anna, Madona, Madam, Lady,
    What breadth those titles bear!
Anne.   And so they do!
Wife. Mistress! thou shalt have such to be thy servants,
    And curchy to thee when thou turn'st thy head,
    Bow at each nod, and make their farthingales,
    At every word thou speak'st, to kiss their heels.
        ... Where I was wont
    To call thee baggage, Nan, and paltry girl,
    I must not dare to speak to your honour
    Without a prologue of some half an hour long,
    Which must begin, an't please my ladyship.
    ...

But if John made any such promise, it has disappeared – possibly removed by the censor. The play was not printed till 1655.

[45] The edition of *King John and Matilda* printed in 1655 is dedicated by the printer, Andrew Pennycuicke (who says he acted Matilda in it) to Montague Bertie, Earl of Lindsey, Lord Willoughby of Eresby, and a direct descendant of Drue's Duchess of Suffolk.

[46] R. Davenport, *Works*, ed. A. H. Bullen (1882–9; repr. New York, 1964). The play was printed in 1639, but had been acted some time before that.

Anne. Here's gentry, and here's honour, mistress or madam,
   A single ambling nag, or a caroche
   With four, four great Dutch mares; a private gentlewoman
   Or a great Lady, my worship, or my honour:
   To be a wife to a squire of low degree
   Or a Lord Baron; Gentry will give place,
   And in a puff'd style his Lordship I'll embrace.

               (pp. 195–6)

Title and useless luxury are here firmly identified.

Slightall in his despair takes to drink and women, thereby getting into the usurer's clutches and piling up debts. His plainspoken servant Roger tries to deter him from these gentlemanly vices:

   How many months did your old father spend
   To purchase that you in few hours consume?

But Slightall angrily turns him away:

   Pox upon you, we shall have you turn Puritan,
   Leave big-mouthed oaths to swear by yea and nay:
   Th'art not for me.[47]   (pp. 205–6)

However, it is not moral argument that makes Anne change her mind, nor does she come to accept (like Meg Overreach or Gertrude Touchstone or the Frugal daughters) that city girls have no right to marry above their rank. She simply finds my lord disappointing as a man, and thus realises the emptiness of rank and title compared with human qualities and human affection. The episode is so striking, compared with what we think of as natural to the period, as to be worth quoting at length.

Anne. Troth, I felt no more honour from his lips
   Than from another man, nay, scarce so much,
   For Slightall kisses better.
Wife.   Minion, how?
Anne. I tell you as I find: his Lordship? Good now,
   Tell me, in what place of his body lies it,
   If in the face or foot, the crown or toe,
   The body, arm or leg, the back or bosom,
   Without him or within? I see no more
   In him than in another gentleman.
Wife. Part of it lies in what he left behind,

---

[47] Note that by the 1630s it was possible in the more plebeian plays for a good character to be described as a Puritan without his indignantly rebutting it – as Roger here, or Dorotea in *The Launching of the Mary*, above.

> Observance, state, retinue and attendance,
> Of which you must partake.
>
> *Anne.* Lord, who'd have thought it?
> Would he had sent that part of his lordship hither,
> And stayed himself behind: but where's his honour?
>
> *Wife.* Dost thou not see him there?
>
> *Anne.*   Him, but not it.
>
> *Wife.* How canst thou, fool? His nobility
> Lies in his blood.
>
> *Anne.*   'Tis that I fain would see.
>
> *Wife.* His blood?
>
> *Anne.*   Yes, if his lordship live in that.
> Would you match me to a thing invisible?
> Where I bestow myself I'll see and feel,
> And choose to my own liking.   (pp. 212–13)

What is fresh here is not just that Anne prefers her lover to a lord,
but that she can question and reject the value of nobility, blood and
birth as such. She argues the same case – human values and choice
in marriage – with great spirit to Lord Skales himself when she
refuses him:

> *Anne.* Till now I had thought your lords and noblemen
> Had been possessed of many worthier parts
> Where meaner men are scanted: but I find
> All's one, or little difference.
>
>   . . .
>
> Title, my lord, is a cold bedfellow,
> And many study style that marry cares.
> Can honour help in childbirth? or nobility
> Us privilege from throes?
>
> *Lord.*   Why, no such thing.
>
> *Anne.* What is this honour then?
>
> *Lord.*   Why, ceremony,
> The gift of princes, and the pride of States,
> Regard in the weal public, and employment,
> Respect and duty.
>
> *Wife.*   Which from his pre-eminence
> Must by mere consequence redound to you.
>
> *Anne.* You talk like an old woman, not like one
> That should make her first choice, as I must now.
> When I am grieved, can Honour cure my heart?

> If discontent, can my nobility
> Give ease unto my corsives? When your Lordship
> Is with your trulls and concubines abroad,
> Where is my loving husband then at home
> To keep me warm at midnight?

Lord.   I am he.

Anne. Sir, that's the thing I doubt.   (p. 215)

There is more than a slight echo of Falstaff here (as of Marlowe and Middleton elsewhere in the play). Anne, however, backs her rejection of Lord Skales and his presumed cavalier moral code with a direct appeal to religion against him:

> *Anne.*   But you more great,
> Under pretext of your nobility
> And countenance in Court, have from a husband
> Stolen a contracted and a married wife:
> For contract upon earth in heaven is marriage
> And celebrate by angels.   (p. 247)

The clash of world-views is finally resolved wholly in favour of the city values (and nobody so much as finds an alternative heiress for Lord Skales). The feeling throughout this play, light and popular though it is (and even more so in the fabliau under-plot), is something which in the 1630s context seems recognisably 'pre-revolutionary', though in a rather different sense from Prynne's *Histriomastix*. It is probably representative of a good deal of drama that has not survived, for it was apparently acted many times, and that implies an audience with a taste for such things. Among the lost plays are a number by Davenport himself, including *The Politic Queen* and *The Fatal Brothers* (1623), *Henry I* and *Henry II* (1624, both for the King's Company), and *The Pirate* (1626). If these had survived we might now see him as a major figure in this genre.[48]

VII

One of the most lurid political plays of the popular theatre was Henry Glapthorne's *Albertus Wallenstein*, first printed in 1639, after being acted by the King's Men, probably only at the Globe, at some time after 1634. Wallenstein was a natural tragedy-villain for

---

[48] Further evidence of Davenport's Puritan sympathies is contained in the poem, 'A Crown for a Conqueror' (collected by Bullen in his edition), a dialogue between the dying Saint and Christ.

the popular theatre, since he was one of the emperor's best-known mercenary generals, and commanded at the battle of Lutzen in 1632 where the Protestant hero Gustavus Adolphus fell. Wallenstein's changes of side for his own advantage ended in 1634 with his murder by some of his own mercenary Scottish and Irish officers, acting on the emperor's behalf. Glapthorne highlights this historical butchery by making Wallenstein a monster of cruelty to his (fictitious) son and daughter-in-law. The subject, though treated with gruesome poetic licence, was topical enough in itself to an audience still hotly committed to the Protestant side in Europe. But another kind of historical parallel is suggested by the Latin verses prefixed to the 1640 edition, exulting over the death of Wallenstein though careful not to approve of the emperor. These are the work of Alexander Gill the younger (son of Milton's headmaster at St Paul's), who had been in trouble with Star Chamber in 1628 for publicly drinking the health of Felton, assassin of Buckingham; and the final scene may well have recalled that event to some spectators. Leslie, leader of the assassins, speaks:

> *Leslie.* Yes, traitor-Duke, 'twas we who cut thy soul
> From thy weak twist of life, we who glory
> More in performing this brave act of justice
> Than had we gained the Empire thy ambition
> Aspired to; thy base treacheries to Caesar
> Are by us revenged.
> . . .
>
> *Wallenstein.* Receive my last breath in a curse: you have
> But played the hangman to perform heaven's justice.
> Forgive me heaven my past offence: I die
> Not for my ambition, but my cruelty.[49]

Glapthorne's father was bailiff to Lady Hatton, the formidable wife of Sir Edward Coke. The playwright seems to have had, or at least sought, Parliamentary Puritan patrons. His poems, published in 1643, include elegies on the 4th Earl of Bedford, and on Henry Earl of Manchester, 'both deceased during this present session of Parliament'; both are praised as moderate and pious men, and both were Parliamentarian opposition leaders on the eve of the Civil War. But like Marvell, he also had friends on the other side, and dedicated his poems (including *Whitehall*, a sorrowful lament

---

[49] *Plays and Poems of Henry Glapthorne*, ed. R. H. Shepherd, 2 vols. (London, 1874), ii, p. 80.

for the court) to 'my noble friend and gossip, Captain Richard Lovelace'; he died about the time they were published.

VIII

If there was an attempt by some opposition leaders to encourage use of the stage as a political medium, it seems likely that it was still continuing and indeed intensifying in the late 1630s. At a meeting of the Privy Council at which Charles I was present in 1637, Philip 4th Earl of Pembroke and Montgomery, who had succeeded his brother as Lord Chamberlain in 1626 and in the title in 1630, clashed sharply with Archbishop Laud over control of the drama. Pembroke wanted to allow the Blackfriars and other theatres to reopen, whereas Laud wished to keep them closed on the grounds that it was Lent and the plague was not yet over,

> concluding that if His Majesty did not command him to the contrary he would lay them [the players] by the heels if they played again. My Lord Chamberlain stood up and said that my Lord's Grace and he served one God and one King; that he hoped his Grace would not meddle with his place no more than he did in his; that the players were under his command. My Lord's Grace replied that what he had spoken in no way touched upon his place, etc., still concluding as he had done before, which he did with some solemnity reiterate once or twice. So the King put an end to the business by commanding my Lord Chamberlain that they should play no more.[50]

There seems to have been more to this quarrel than a demarcation dispute or a difference about Lent and infectious diseases. For the scrappy records available show a number of instances where, as tension grew between the prerogative government and the opposition in City, country and Parliament, the players put on plays that were boldly anti-ministerial, satirising Laud and his policies. Thus in 1634 Sir Henry Herbert had sent one Cromes, a pawnbroker in Long Lane, to prison 'for lending a church robe with the name of Jesus upon it to the players in Salisbury Court to present Flamen, a priest of the heathens'.

In the spring of 1639 the Red Bull–King's Company, playing at the Fortune, got into serious trouble and were fined £1,000 'for

[50] *Strafford Letters* II, 56, dated 23 March 1637, cited in Gildersleeve, *Government Regulation of the Elizabethan Drama*, p. 214.

setting up an altar, a bason and two candlesticks, and bowing down before it upon the stage, and though they allege it was an old play revived, and an altar to the heathen gods, yet it was apparent that this play was revived on purpose in contempt of the ceremonies of the Church'.[51] A Puritan news-book, *Vox Borealis*,[52] names the play as *The Cardinal's Conspiracy*, and describes how the pursuivants arrested the poor Cardinal and his consorts 'in the midst of all their mirth', and bore them away to the Court of High Commission, where 'they told the Archbishop that they took those examples of their altars, Images and the like, from heathen authors. This did somewhat assuage his anger, that they did not bring him upon the stage.' However, after a brief imprisonment, this Puritan source reports the players as 'falling to act *The Valiant Scot*, which they played five days with great applause, which vexed the Bishops worse than the other, insomuch as they were forbidden playing it any more, and some of them prohibited ever playing again'.[53]

A play called *The Whore New Vamped*, scandalously attacking the customs farmers and the King's supporters in the City, notably Alderman Abell, vintner and monopolist, was acted by the Red Bull players in September 1639, when the Attorney-General was ordered by the Privy Council to summons and punish the playwright, the players and whoever licensed it. Cain, the Red Bull's popular comic, called Alderman Abell 'a base, drunken, sottish knave', and another character boasted of having got 'a patent for 12d a piece upon every proctor or proctor's man that was not an arrant knave'.[54] The wine monopoly and the 'bawdy courts' were particularly unpopular with ordinary lower-class Londoners; so this was catering to the feelings of the 'many-headed multitude' with a vengeance.

On the very eve of the Civil War, in the spring of 1640, William Beeston, manager of the King's and Queen's Young Company at the Phoenix, produced a play commenting on current political

[51] Edmund Rossingham to Viscount Conway, 8 May 1639 (*C.S.P.D.*, 1639, pp. 140–1), cited in Bentley, *Jacobean and Caroline Stage*, i, p. 297.
[52] Published late 1640 or early 1641. This pamphlet has been convincingly attributed to Richard Overton, and is discussed below, p. 244. See Don M. Wolfe, 'Unsigned Pamphlets of Richard Overton', *Huntington Library Quarterly*, xxi, no. 2 (Feb. 1958).
[53] *The Valiant Scot* was the title of a real play, but probably here alludes to the defeat of the King's expedition by the Scottish Presbyterians in the Bishops' War.
[54] Bentley, *Jacobean and Caroline Stage*, i, p. 314.

affairs and not licensed by the Master of the Revels. Widespread opposition had been aroused by the King's military expedition to Scotland to suppress the revolt against the Prayer Book and the bishops that had just ended in failure. The play, Sir Henry Herbert says, 'had reference to the passages of the King's journey into the North, and was complained of by His Majesty to me with command to punish the offenders'.[55] The company was ordered on the Lord Chamberlain's warrant to stop acting as a punishment for playing when forbidden by the censor, but three days later Sir Henry Herbert 'at my Lord Chamberlain's entreaty' allowed them to act again after promises of good behaviour. Beeston himself was imprisoned in the Marshalsea on 4 May 1640 (we do not know for how long) and ousted from his manager's position; the courtier William Davenant was officially appointed by the Lord Chamberlain to take his place.

The Lord Chamberlain at this time was still the 4th Earl of Pembroke. Shortly afterwards, in 1641, he was dismissed from his office, ostensibly because of a brawl with the Earl of Arundel's son. Pembroke had himself been on the Scottish expedition in 1639 and strongly recommended peace. In 1640, as one of the commissioners appointed to negotiate with the Scots at Ripon, he had laid terms before Charles and recommended their acceptance: but instead the King directed Pembroke to return to London and raise £200,000 to meet the expenses of the expedition. In 1640 Pembroke used his influence to secure the return of many 'popular' MPs, and in 1641 voted for the impeachment of Strafford. The request of the Commons to the King to appoint him Lord Steward (December 1641) was refused.

There seems a distinct possibility that Pembroke may have indirectly patronised or sponsored a popular political play on the Scottish business, thinking he could get away with it as his predecessor perhaps did with *A Game at Chess* a generation earlier. But the conflicts now were much more serious; the power of the Crown, divided in 1624, was now embattled against him; and Sir Henry Herbert may have been unwilling this time to risk his lucrative office, even to oblige the head of the family.

The suggestion of a direct Pembroke interest is reinforced when we see that the company involved (the King's and Queen's Young Company or Beeston's Boys) first came in after the plague had

[55] *Dramatic Records of Sir Henry Herbert*, ed. Adams, p. 66.

closed the theatres in 1636–7 (at the exact time, that is, when Pembroke was quarrelling with Laud about reopening them). In 1639 they held the rights in much of Middleton and Massinger's work (including *The Changeling* and *A Fair Quarrel*) and in a number of the 'opposition' plays discussed here, including *The Bondman, The Maid of Honour, King John and Matilda* and *A New Trick to Cheat the Devil.*

Learned and scholarly drama which could also be interpreted as criticism of the government included Nathanael Richards' *Messalina* (1634–6) and Thomas May's *Julia Agrippina* (1638).[56] Both dramatists are reported, apart from the internal evidence of their plays, to have sympathised at some time or other with the Parliamentary opposition against the King.[57] A play called *Tyrannical Government Anatomised, or a Discourse concerning Evil Counsellors* was ordered by the House of Commons to be printed in January 1643. This is a translation of George Buchanan's *Baptistes Sive Calumnia*, a life of John the Baptist, originally a political allegory directed against Henry VIII's marriage to Ann Boleyn. 'By viewing Herod in a new light as Charles I, Herod's wife as Henrietta Maria, and John as themselves, the Parliamentarians must have considered the play remarkably apt', as A. L. Harbage comments.[58] The translation has been attributed, with a good deal of evidence, to Milton,[59] and indeed the verse sounds austerely Miltonic. The whole play, in structure and tone, bears a striking resemblance to *Samson Agonistes*, and is about the only English play which does. It is strictly classical in form, with its action reported by messengers and its moral chorus. A typical speech by the Queen, urging her husband Herod to strong action against the dangerous evangelist and agitator, begins to develop the characteristic Latinised phrasing, periods and inversions of the Miltonic style:

> Should you in such a tumult use no rigour,
> The wavering vulgar's fury being roused,
> The prince's laws, religion, power, contemned,
> Is to the base plebeians made a scorn.

[56] *Nero* (1624), perhaps the finest example of this type, sometimes attributed to May, is not known to have been performed in the theatre.
[57] Nathanael Richards has already been mentioned as the eulogist of Middleton. Tom May became the official historiographer of the Parliament.
[58] *Cavalier Drama* (New York, 1936; repr. 1964), p. 178.
[59] In the edition by J. T. Brown, printed in *George Buchanan: Glasgow Centenary Studies* (Glasgow, 1907), pp. 61–173.

What needs must be at length, feign to be done –
That the inconstant people are stirred up
To arms, that everywhere they all things burn
With woeful war, and villages left wasted,
Our virgins ravished, and our cities fired,
And with ambiguous fortune armies joined.   (p. 115)

Again, the Messenger's dignified requiem for John seems to foreshadow Manoah's austere epitaph for Samson.

Nuntius.   If death be
To be bewailed, let us bewail the dead,
Whose hopes do with their bodies lie interred,
Who do not think, their short sleep being done,
Their bones must rise again, and there remains
Another life: let wretched men bewail
Those that are dead, and only wretched lived.
None can be made by fortune miserable,
Though the like end of human life betide
The innocent and guilty, good and bad.
No man shall die ill, that hath lived well.   (p. 171)

Whether this is Milton's work or not, we know that at this time he
was seriously arguing for the use of the stage for propaganda to the
people. In *The Reason of Church Government* (1641) he suggests
that 'it were happy for the Commonwealth, if our magistrates
would take into their care. . .the managing of our public sports and
festival pastimes'. The people would thus profit from 'wise and art-
ful recreations'. 'Whether this may be not only in pulpits, but after
another persuasive method. . .in theatres, porches, or what other
place, or what may win most upon the people to receive at once
both recreation and instruction, let them in authority consult'.[60]

Things did not, in the end, go Milton's way. The stricter anti-
theatre Puritan leaders were strong enough in London to get playing banned under heavy penalties in 1642, although in practice
some performances continued throughout the interregnum in
private houses, and even at the Red Bull and Fortune, despite
periodic raids by the military. The ban was, no doubt, primarily an
anti-Royalist move, and has been so interpreted by most historians.
But it must be remembered that the Red Bull and Fortune audiences
were not the 'polite', whose theatres were the Blackfriars and the

[60] *Complete Prose Works of John Milton* (New Haven, 1953–), i, pp.
818–19.

Phoenix, but the mass of London citizens. The decision to suppress performances there too may have been aimed not only at players and dramatists – most of them Royalist, though not all[61] – but also at the danger of a new popular theatre emerging, appealing to the political and religious radicalism of the lower orders.

It may be significant that the ban was operated much more strictly against plays than against rope-dancers, acrobats and jugglers (who would seem, on the face of it, just as idle and corrupting). Apparently the censorship was, like that of the Stuarts, primarily a political one. Without it there might possibly have been a Leveller drama as well as Leveller tracts and oratory, for Leveller leaders such as Lilburne and Walwyn were less rigidly Sabbatarian than the new City authorities, rumoured to indulge in card-playing and drinking. Beyond them again lay the world of extreme beliefs, of Ranters and Libertarians, sexual liberation and communist social teaching, so strikingly revealed in A. L. Morton's *The World of the Ranters* and Christopher Hill's *The World Turned Upside Down*. That too would have had its influence on an uncensored popular drama. The fact that Sir William Davenant successfully persuaded the Cromwellian government to allow operas (on suitable themes, such as the anti-Spanish exploits of Sir Francis Drake) also suggests that it was particularly the popular plebeian theatre that was feared.

---

[61] One actor who fought on the Parliamentary side was Elliard (or Eylaerdt) Swanston. He had joined the King's Men some time before Dec. 1624, when he and others of the company signed a submission for playing *The Spanish Viceroy* without licence. He is said by Wright in *Historia Histrionica* to have professed himself a Presbyterian and taken up the trade of a jeweller. He specialised in villains, especially smooth ones, and may well have been the original Gondomar. Another Parliamentarian actor was John Harris (see below, pp. 252–5).

13. *From Popular Drama to Leveller Style: a Postscript*

What became of the literary traditions of 'opposition' drama after the closing of the London theatres? Clearly they did not continue either in the exiled Royalist theatre at Oxford or in the occasional surreptitious performances put on in the private houses of the nobility during the interregnum. The audiences and their interests were there too different: Fletcher, not Shakespeare, Jonson or Middleton, was the Cavaliers' favourite dramatist.

But while suppression of the public playhouses crushed the old drama out of existence, the printing presses in the 1640s worked with a freedom and range unknown before. Among the thousands of tracts and pamphlets issued in those years and preserved in the Thomason collection, above all in the radical news-sheets, manifestoes and pamphlets of the Leveller movement, the tradition of popular secular critical writing appears in a new and increasingly confident form. Leveller rhetoric intensifies the strengths of common speech. It is packed with proverbs and colloquial sayings, using concrete and sometimes coarse images from everyday plebeian life for vividness and wit. It is rhythmic, energetic and irreverent, as well as weighty and dignified when occasion requires.[1]

One of the main influences on Leveller style was of course the Bible – the only book many of the rank and file will have known well – and the plain preaching based on it. I want to suggest that

---

[1] There is no comprehensive modern edition of the writings of the Levellers in general or of Overton and Harris in particular. W. Haller (ed.), *Tracts on Liberty in the Puritan Revolution, 1638–1647*, 3 vols. (New York, 1934), contains in vols. ii and iii facsimile reproductions of pamphlets, including Overton's *The Arraignment of Mr Persecution*. W. Haller and G. Davies (eds.), *The Leveller Tracts 1647–1653* (New York, 1944), also contains writings by Overton, as does A. L. Morton, *Freedom in Arms* (London, 1975). For a more detailed literary critical analysis of Leveller writings, see Morton, 'The Leveller Style', in *The Matter of Britain* (London, 1966), pp. 73–82; the same author's Introduction to his selection of Leveller writings, *Freedom in Arms*; and Joseph Frank, *The Levellers* (Cambridge, Mass., 1955). For a more general account of the movement, see H. N. Brailsford, *The Levellers* (London, 1961); Christopher Hill, *The World Turned Upside Down*; G. E. Aylmer (ed.), *The Levellers in the English Revolution* (London, 1975); and Brian Manning, *The English People and the English Revolution* (London, 1976).

237

some of the most effective writers were also inspired by the other great source of instruction and culture that had been open to ordinary Londoners: the theatres and the published texts of their plays. This seems pretty clear from the evidence of style alone; but it can also be shown that some of these men had personal links with the theatre which must have helped to form them and their writings and to prepare their audience.[2] In this chapter I hope to make this clear, first for Richard Overton, whose connection with the drama has not previously been noticed; and then for John Harris, who is already well known to have been a professional actor before he became a news-writer with the Cromwellian army. The facts are interesting not only in themselves, but for the light they throw on the range of attitudes of dramatists and audiences in the 1630s, and the continuity they suggest between those audiences and the more radical, less Presbyterian elements among London Parliamentarians in the 1640s.

That Parliamentary Puritans of every shade on the eve of the Civil War had been united in hatred of the theatre is now seen to be a myth. Prynne, who really was a committed opponent of plays, was typical not so much of Parliamentary Puritanism as a whole, as of the most rigid and dogmatic Presbyterian section within it, with which both Cromwellian Independents and Levellers later came into political collision.[3] Certainly his views cannot be taken as representative of the Parliamentary Puritan outlook among the masses of ordinary Londoners in the 1630s. While at this date a considerable section of Puritan clergy (and of non-Puritan clergy for that matter)[4] and many Puritan lawyers, merchants and businessmen opposed the theatre as a moral snare and a waste of precious time, Parliamentary Puritan groups among the aristocracy included some of the best-known patrons of the drama, and among the more plebeian supporters of Parliament there must have been many, especially of the apprentices, who went to the popular playhouses. These last were the same kinds of people who thronged Palace Yard

[2] I have argued this case at greater length in an essay in M. Cornforth (ed.), *Rebels and their Causes* (London, 1978).

[3] He was fêted by the crowds, along with Burton and Bastwick, as a heroic martyr of Laudian repression rather than for his anti-theatre principles.

[4] Lancelot Andrewes did not approve of plays, though he did not make an issue of it at court, probably because for him loyalty to the monarchy seemed the more important issue; and Laud himself seems to have had no great liking for them.

to demand punishment for Strafford, who helped to fortify London against the King's armies, and who in the middle 1640s signed Lilburne's petitions and made up the Leveller rank and file.

When Parliament closed the theatres after the outbreak of war (September 1642), this did indeed gratify the anti-theatre lobby; but it was also an obvious security measure to prevent riotous assemblies and forestall possible Royalist propaganda by the court companies (and, for that matter, the dramatising of popular grievances). Entertainment was held to be unsuitable anyway in a time of civil war, which called rather for discipline and prayer. Those dependent on the theatres as actors, musicians, theatre staff and dramatists faced disaster, and some of the best regular playwrights, we are told a year or so later, were 'for mere necessity compelled to get a living by writing contemptible penny pamphlets'.[5]

Judging by the number of anti-Laudian, anti-Strafford satires in semi-dramatic form printed around 1642, some of these hard-up dramatists were aiming at a Parliamentary Puritan city audience rather than a Royalist one. These lively tracts return again and again to the same grievances already dramatised in the subversive plays against the bishops and their courts, against the persecution of Puritan ministers and the harrying of Puritan laymen, against rich churchmen greedy for tithes and monopolists who squeeze money out of the poor. What made them saleable was the variety of forms, incidents, satirical images and semi-dramatic burlesques through which the same argument was presented so as to seem new and entertaining. Among these pamphlets are a number attributed to the most humorous and inventive of later Leveller pamphleteers, Richard Overton.

The suggestion that Overton was at one time involved in the drama is supported by a good deal of varied evidence, none of it decisive in isolation but convincing if one looks at it as a whole. Little has hitherto been known about Overton's early life, but it has now been effectively shown that he was younger than earlier biographers supposed.[6] There is strong reason to believe that he

<hr>

[5] *The Actor's Remonstrance* (Jan. 1643–4), cited in Bentley, *Profession of Dramatist in Shakespeare's Time*, p. 134.
[6] E.g. J. Frank, *The Levellers*, pp. 39–40, and the article by C. H. Firth in *D.N.B.* The evidence has been studied in detail by Marie Gimmelfarb for her forthcoming book on Overton. I have benefited greatly from the facts she has made available to me and from discussing parts of this chapter with her.

was that Richard Overton who matriculated at Queens' College, Cambridge, in 1631.[7] His known work contains plenty of evidence that he was an educated man (if not necessarily university-educated), and Cambridge in the 1620s was a centre of Puritan scholarship and preaching. Nor was it only the gentry who went there. The town grammar schools, mostly non-fee-paying and often under strong Puritan influence, were sending boys in growing numbers in the early seventeenth century, boys who might come from families of farmers or small traders.[8] If we assume that Overton *cannot* have had such an education, we then have to explain how he came by the Latin quotations and other signs of learning in his work. It seems more likely on the face of it that he did.[9]

In the same year that he matriculated (1631–2) Overton acted in a Latin comedy called *Versipellis* ('The Turncoat'), the whole cast being Queens' men. One would dearly like to know more about this play. Unfortunately the text has disappeared; we know only that it was set at Antwerp, and that the author was probably Thomas Pestell (among whose papers it was found), who was a Leicestershire clergyman and chaplain to the Earl of Essex, and whose son, another Thomas Pestell, was one of the student actors.[10]

The elder Pestell was patronised by (and wrote flattering poems to or about) many of the Puritan peers who opposed the Laudian régime, notably Essex, Holland, Manchester, Warwick and Mandeville. He was summoned and fined by Laud's Court of High Commission in 1633 for scandalous behaviour, and especially for making insulting remarks and puns about Laud's Commissary Sir John Lambe:[11] so it seems not unlikely that *Versipellis* had a

---

[7] J. A. Venn, *Alumni Cantabrigienses*, iii, pt i, p. 289.

[8] This has been demonstrated in detail for Leicestershire schools by Joan Simon, 'Town Estates and Schools in the Sixteenth and Early Seventeenth Century', in B. Simon (ed.), *Education in Leicestershire, 1540–1940* (Leicester, 1968), pp. 3–26. Leicestershire was probably Overton's home county.

[9] My view on this is confirmed by that reached by a quite different route by Marie Gimmelfarb. She considers that he must have been about Lilburne's age (i.e. born 1610–15), and dates his Mennonite conversion and declaration of faith, written in Amsterdam, at around 1643.

[10] G. C. Moore Smith, *College Plays Performed in the University of Cambridge* (Cambridge, 1923), pp. 85, 109–10. The play manuscript was seen among Pestell's papers by J. Nichols, and described in his *History and Antiquities of the County of Leicester*, 4 vols. (in 8; East Ardsley, 1971), iii, p. 297.

[11] Lambe, along with Laud's other helpmate Dr Duck, is also a favourite target of jokes and puns in Overton's early pamphlets.

satirical, irreverent tone like that of many of Pestell's surviving poems.[12]

Cambridge in the 1630s was indeed a centre of religious conflict; for Laud was set on forcing the university, by tradition much more Puritan than Oxford, to conform to his rulings on doctrine, preaching and ceremonies. In 1636 he finally succeeded in establishing his own supremacy and right of visitation there, against strong opposition led by the Chancellor, Lord Holland.[13] The leaders of the Laudians in Cambridge were Matthew (afterwards Bishop) Wren and John (later Bishop) Cosin, both Masters of Peterhouse (next door to Overton's college of Queens'). Both figure much later in satirical pamphlets ascribed to Overton,[14] who seems to have kept an interest in Cambridge politics. His deep commitment to liberty of speech and discussion and religious toleration could well have been formed in the bigot-ridden university of that time.

The small world of college drama reflected these tensions. Though college plays were traditionally partly exercises in classical translation or imitation, partly slapstick, bawdy and schoolboy jokes, they might have topical local or social satire thrown in. The most gifted and popular Cambridge playwright of the time, Thomas Randolph, a young Fellow of Trinity somewhat over-inclined to drink and debt, was a protégé of Holland and patronised by the Puritan and anti-Laudian gentry.[15] His less gifted rival, Peter Hausted of Queens', after preaching over-zealously at the University Church against nonconformity, was dragged from the pulpit, arrested and mobbed by the Puritan townsfolk. Randolph's most popular play, *Aristippus*[16] (shown both at Cambridge and later in

12 See *The Poems of Thomas Pestell*, ed. Hannah Buchan (Oxford, 1940), which also reprints the full report of the 1633 case.

13 For the conflict in Cambridge see H. R. Trevor-Roper, *Archbishop Laud* (London, 1962), pp. 204–10.

14 E.g. *Copy of a Letter from John Lord Finch...to his Friend Dr Cozens* (1641); *Old News Newly Revived* (1641); *A Rent in the Lawn Sleeves* (1641); *Farewell Mitre* (1642).

15 His father was steward to Lord Zouche, an anti-Spanish peer since Elizabeth's time, part of whose estates lay in Northamptonshire and whom we have already met in connection with the background to Middleton's *Hengist, King of Kent*.

16 What G. E. Bentley calls the 'surprising' popularity of this play must have been largely due to the satirical jokes. In the British Library MS. (presumably the original acting version) a quack doctor advertises his skills, claiming that if it had not been treason he would have cured Gondomar of his fistula and England of a subsidy; these allusions are deleted in the printed copy. In the 1630 printed edition Prologue conjures up the spirit of

London), included anti-Spanish and pro-Parliament satirical references rather in the *Game at Chess* manner, which had to be cut out
when it was printed and several times reprinted from 1630 to 1635
(the year the author died).[17]

Randolph's general line is to balance mockery of 'Spanish'
Arminians and high-flyers with mockery of narrow Puritan sectaries.
This was about as far as one could hope to go with safety in the
1630s, and perhaps as far as he or his Puritan-Anglican court patrons
wanted to go. But it is noticeable, even so, that the anti-Puritan
satire in, say, *The Muses' Looking-Glass* is much less savage than
Jonson's in *The Alchemist*: Randolph's sectaries are good-natured
comics who can be won over to approve of plays with the right
moral.[18]

Randolph, perhaps through Holland's influence, apparently became regular dramatist at the Salisbury Court playhouse in London
around 1629–31, and had two plays produced there, though he was
back in Cambridge soon afterwards.[19] Overton is very likely to
have known him, since Thomas Pestell of Queens', his fellow-actor

Show, who is allowed to present the play only if he promises to keep off the
personal satire which has got him into trouble before. He swears to be
discreet:

> I will not touch such men as I know vicious,
> Much less the good: I will not dare to say
> That such a one paid for his fellowship
> And had no learning but in's purse: no officer
> Need fear the sling of my detraction.
> . . .
> You need not fear this show, you that are bad,
> It is no Parliament.
>
> (*Aristippus* (London, 1630; *S.T.C.* 20686), p. 3)

[17] Bentley, *Jacobean and Caroline Stage*, v, p. 972.

[18] Here the two godly playhouse hawkers who denounce plays change their
minds after seeing Randolph's edifying one:

> *Bird.* Hereafter I will visit comedies
> And see them oft: they are good exercises:
> I'll teach devotion now a milder temper;
> Not that it shall lose any of her heat
> Or purity, but henceforth shall be such
> As shall burn bright, although not blaze so much.
>
> (*Works of Randolph*, ed. W. C. Hazlitt (London, 1875)).

The sharp anti-Parliamentarian and anti-Puritan references in *Hey for
Honesty*, originally a play by Randolph, have been added much later by
one F.J., who revised the text long after the author's death, during or after
the Civil War.

[19] G. E. Bentley, 'Randolph's Praeludium and the Salisbury Court Theatre',
in J. MacManaway (ed.), *J. Quincy Adams Memorial Studies* (Washington,
D.C., 1948). See also Bentley, *Jacobean and Caroline Stage*, iv, pp. 966–7.

in *Versipellis*, must have been at least acquainted with Randolph.[20]

We do not know what Overton was doing in the later 1630s, before we hear of him late in 1640 as printer and pamphleteer, nor whether he ever had any links with the professional theatre, though Southwark, where he was living about that time, was one of the main centres of the popular theatre. All we can say is that he was connected with Cambridge dramatic circles, especially with anti-Laudian ones, and that some contemporary college playwrights certainly did become London theatre poets. Moreover, his pamphleteering activity begins around the time when the theatres were in difficulties and increases after they closed.[21] It would not be surprising, however, if Overton later kept quiet about any theatre link, since his opponents among the right-wing Parliamentarians would certainly have used it against him. John Harris was never allowed by the Royalist news-writers to forget that he had once been a 'player's boy'.

The news-book-cum-pamphlet *Vox Borealis*, probably the earliest of Overton's writings that we have, bears the mock imprint 'Printed by Margery Marprelate, in Thwackcoat Lane, at the sign of the Crabtree Cudgel: without any privilege of the Cater-Caps, the year coming on 1641'. Even more than the original Marprelate tracts of fifty years before, this one is full of theatre references. In form it is a colloquial dialogue, supposed to take place in the English camp at Berwick, between Jamie, a dialect-speaking Scotsman recently returned from London bringing the political news, and Willie, who has been with the English army during the disastrous Scottish expedition. They both hate the bishops; believe the English were defeated because the Scots had a good cause and they had not; and complain bitterly against the officers for their treatment of

---

[20] The Pestells at Packington in Leicestershire lived only a few miles from the Randolphs at Houghton. They had a common friend in James Duport, a common patron in Lord Holland. One Thomas Pestell (senior or junior) answered Randolph's mock-elegy on his own finger cut off in a brawl, with a 'Reply to Mr Randoll's verses on the loss of his finger'. Plays by Randolph and Pestell were probably both acted at Cambridge in the same season: then as now, drama enthusiasts in different colleges were likely to know one another. Overton may indeed have come from the same district: Marie Gimmelfarb traced Overtons living in Lea Grange Manor, near Twycross, and Pestell senior also held a living at Cole-Orton, otherwise known as Cold Overton, near Ashby de la Zouch (*Poems of Thomas Pestell*, ed. Buchan, p. xxxi).

[21] Marie Gimmelfarb thinks he may have been imprisoned for debt around 1642. If he was an actor or a playwright this would be very plausible.

private soldiers, and especially for discharging them to find their own way home, with 'but four or five shillings apiece to travel three hundred miles'.

Jamie's news from London includes a variety of detailed references to the censorship and suppression of political and anti-Laudian plays during the previous two years, showing both that the writer was closely acquainted with the London theatre world and that he was appealing to Parliamentarian readers who were at the same time sympathetic to plays. In particular, he tells how the players put on a play in which they bowed down to an altar, and then had to confront Laud personally in the Court of High Commission and argue that it was an altar to the heathen gods, and that they were not impersonating him or bringing contempt on the ceremonies of the Church. He refers also to the plays attacking proctors and wine monopolists, and to the boys' companies having been in trouble and some members imprisoned over a play having reference to the Scottish expedition itself.[22] We usually think of Laud now as the persecutor only of Puritan preachers and theologians, and especially of the theatre-hating Prynne. But he was also the terror of actors and dramatists who dared to criticise the prerogative government or the Church, and this may be one reason why he is a favourite personal target for Overton's satire in the early 1640s.

Two of the comic anti-Laud pamphlets of 1642 Overton actually signed. One was *Articles of High Treason Against Cheapside Cross* (1642), a dialogue between Mr Papist and Mr News, describing the pulling down of the 'popish' cross by 'the rabble rout', and concluding with the Cross's last will and testament:

Item, I bequeath the iron about me to make a clapper for his Holiness' passing bell. Item, I give and bequeath all the lead that is about me, to the hostile Catholics in Ireland, to make bullets to confound that cursed crew of heretics.

The will is signed (a zany Overtonian touch!):

The Cross + her mark.

The other signed pamphlet, *New Lambeth Fair* (1642), describes the selling-off of the bishops' now useless stock of accessories – lawn sleeves, robes, caps and beads – as fairings for children.

---

[22] All these were real plays, and did get the players into trouble with the censorship, as we know from other records (see pp. 231–3 above).

References to these two pamphlets in other contemporary tracts, repetition of particular devices, and stylistic echoes help to identify many other examples of Overton's work.[23]

The pamphlet which most strikingly shows the *dramatic* influence on Overton's writing is *Canterbury his Change of Diet* (1641), a six-page playlet satirising Laud (by this time a prisoner in the Tower), which refers in the text to 'Lambeth great Fair', and seems almost certain to be his.[24] The playlet is thus summarised on the title page:

1. Act. The Bishop of Canterbury having variety of dainties, is not satisfied till he be fed with tippets of men's ears.
2. Act. He hath his nose held to the grindstone.
3. Act. He is put into a bird-cage with the Confessor.
4. Act. The jester tells the King the story.

The humour is visual, slapstick and brutal, rather like that of *Ubu-Roi* (or of Marlowe's *Tamburlaine*). Thus in the first scene the Archbishop at table petulantly rejects a banquet of twenty-four dainty dishes, including cock and pheasant, quail and partridge. He demands something rare, such as a carbonadoed cheek.[25] And when the pious divine wants to ask a blessing on the meat, Laud roars 'ho, ho' (like the Devil in the old interludes), 'He knocking there enter divers Bishops with muskets on their necks, bandoliers and swords by their sides'. Doctor, divine and lawyer are pinioned by this grotesque guard, while Laud cuts off their ears 'to be dressed for his supper' and departs 'after a low curtsey' – a Mummers-play staging of the vicious martyrdom of Bastwick, Burton and Prynne.

The rest of the play is a fantasy of revenge. An honest carpenter, asked by Laud for the use of his grindstone to whet his knife, instead ties the Archbishop's nose to it; and when his 'Jesuit confessor' (who looks like Bishop Wren in the illustration) arrives to

---

[23] The pioneering work on these tracts was done by Don M. Wolfe twenty years ago in 'Unsigned Pamphlets of Richard Overton', *Huntington Library Quarterly*, xxi, no. 2 (Feb. 1958), pp. 167–201. Although I would dispute some of his attributions, I am heavily indebted to this article.

[24] It is convincingly identified, on this and other grounds, by Wolfe (*ibid.*). Wolfe had not noted the possibility that Overton was an actor or playwright and his attribution is not made with that in mind. The signed tract *New Lambeth Fair* (1642) incorporates large portions of the unsigned *Lambeth Fair* (1641), to which *Canterbury his Change of Diet* directly refers.

[25] Prynne had been branded 'S.L.' on the cheeks – Seditious Libeller.

poultice his wounds, Carpenter and Carpenter's Wife put both these 'cormorants' into a bird-cage ('They that have cut off ears at the first bout, God knows what they may cut off next'). A spirited woodcut shows the prisoners in the cage, 'and a fool standing by, and laughing at them, Ha, ha, ha, ha, who is the fool now?'[26] In the final act the jester (represented in the illustration with the traditional cap and bells) roars with laughter as he reports all this to the king.

> *Jester.* I waited long to hear them sing, at last they began to
>   chatter.
>
>   . . .
>
> *King.* What was the Song?
> *Jester.* One sung thus: I would I was at Court again for me.
>   Then the other answered: I would I was at Rome again
>   with thee.
> *King.* Well sirrah, you will never leave your flouts.
> *Jester.* If I should, my liege, I were no Jester.

The king fails to appreciate the joke; but though, like Lear, he reprimands the fool, calling him 'Sirrah', he does not threaten him with the whip.

The epilogue is a 'jig' – the traditional song-and-dance finale of so many Elizabethan plays – between a Parator (Apparitor, or summoner of the Ecclesiastical Court) and the fool, in which the Parator agrees, since his master is fallen and he can make no more profit, that in future 'we'll wear tippet fool-caps, and never undo men'. The *form* of the satire may have been suggested by the famous feast given by Laud for the King and Queen at Oxford in 1636, costing over £2,000 and followed by a play, Strode's *Floating Island*, parodying the mutilated Prynne in the play-hating Malevole. ('Locks which I have scorned/Must hide my ear-stumps.')[27]

Canterbury his Change of Diet is described by G. E. Bentley as a tract 'in the form of closet drama'. But the kind of play whose

---

[26] The immediate reference is to Archy Armstrong, official court jester to James I and Charles I, who had just been expelled from court by the Privy Council on Laud's instigation for gibing at him. ('Who's the fool now?' were among the 'scandalous words of a high nature' complained of.) When Laud was in the Tower, Archy, from retirement on his Cumberland estates, issued a volume of 'Archy's Dreams', which include a vision of Laud in hell, and other anti-prelatical fancies. Compared with Overton's semi-dramatic satires it is laboured and unimaginative. (See Enid Welsford, *The Fool, his Social and Literary History* (London, 1968), pp. 172–81.)

[27] Trevor-Roper, *Archbishop Laud*, pp. 291–2.

language and style it uses as model is utterly unlike the closet drama of Fulke Greville and other aristocratic writers. The idiom is obviously that of the live theatre with its sharply caricatured character types, its jigs, its snatches of folk-song, and its jesters who mix in serious matters and dare answer back to the king. Indeed it is not impossible that in these crisis years performances of this sort of show went on in private houses or barns. Whether this is so or not, the satire is obviously aimed to reach people who ordinarily go to plays, and by someone who knows the theatre well, if he has not actually been writing for it. Most of the funny parts would be unintelligible to an audience that was not familiar with acted plays, since they depend so much on visual effects and slapstick.

The Proctor and the Parator of May 1641, also ascribed by Wolfe to Overton, sounds very close to the actual play staged by the King's Company at the Red Bull in 1639, and suppressed by the Privy Council as

> a scandalous and libellous [play in which] they have audaciously reproached and in a libel personated not only some of the aldermen of the [City of London] and some other persons of quality, but also scandalised and libelled the whole profession of proctors belonging to the Court of Probate, and reflected upon the present Government.

Overton's dialogue, between Mr Sponge the Proctor and Mr Hunter the Parator, reveals an unholy conspiracy between them to search out offenders against the canon law and either fine them or get bribes from them to avoid prosecutions.[28]

> Country wenches would sell their petticoats rather to pay us than to endure a white sheet. . .[I] have gotten good booty from transgressors against holy-days, of chandlers, ale-houses, taverns, tobacco shops, butchers, comfit makers, gunsmiths, bakers, brokers, cooks, weavers and divers other malefactors against our terrible Canons and jurisdiction. . .I got no small trading by the Brownists, Anabaptists and Familists, who love a Barn better than a Church, and would come off roundly and secretly.

They do well out of 'lecturers, who would be silenced because they supplied their places too diligently: nay, I have got well too by some of their auditors for leaving their own parish churches and ministers,

---

[28] Mockery of the ecclesiastical courts and their venal officers and informers is a favourite theme in Middleton's early comedies too; see for example *The Family of Love* and *A Chaste Maid in Cheapside*.

and gadding after strangers'. 'Zealous honest ministers' who refuse
to wear surplices or christen children with the sign of the cross are
a steady source of profit. 'We do usually receive some bribe for a
New Year's gift, and the Judge he expects a good piece of plate for
his favour showed in ending causes according to the proctor's
desire.'

The broad popular alliance of godly ministers, sectarians, shopkeepers and ordinary sinners is thus evoked to rejoice at the downfall of Sponge and Hunter, who have fallen on evil times with the
decline of the Church courts and the endless profitable legal business
they involved. 'This certainty of the Triennial Parliament cuts our
combs for ever doing any great exploits for after times.'

A favourite device of Overton's, from these early tracts onwards, is
to write in the name either of real public figures (Laud, Lord Justice
Finch, Strafford, Attorney General Noy)[29] or of characters resembling morality-play figures or Jonsonian humours (Sir Simon Synod,
Gaffer Christian). Essentially this is a dramatic technique.

Thus *A Letter from John Lord Finch, late Lord Keeper, to his
Friend Dr Cozens, with a Commemoration of favours Dr Cozens
showed him in his Vice-Chancellorship* (1641) is written deadpan to
mimic the pompous tones of the judge himself. Finch, a Cambridge
man and the Star Chamber persecutor of Prynne, solemnly compli-
ments the high-flying Laudian Cosin for having set up altars,
crucifixes and holy pictures in Cambridge chapels, laments his
ejection from office, and congratulates himself on his own brilliance
in running away.

> Does the triple crown which you created in St Mary's illustrate
> still the vulgar speculation? Sir, if the tumultuary imprecations of
> the vulgar do oppose you, yet macerate not yourself.

In *Old News Newly Revived*, another 1641 pamphlet-dialogue
attributed to Overton, Finch is described on the run, in terms that
suggest a comic actor playing the part, 'a brother of the blade, with
a tilting feather, a flaunting periwig, buff doublet, scarlet hose, and
sword as broad as a lath, he looked as like a Dammee newly come
out of the North as could be imagined'.[30] Sir John Suckling too has

---

[29] Middleton's *Game at Chess*, where Gondomar and the Fat Bishop, De
Dominis, were impersonated on stage, showed how effective this could be.
[30] The lath dagger was the regular property of the Vice or comic devil in
the old morality plays.

fled, and 'the Blackfriars Actors have a foul loss of him. . .His coat of mail would not keep out their [the Scots] bullets, though it would Sir John Digby's rapier in the playhouse.'[31]

In *Canterbury's Dream* Laud tells how his slumbers in prison are broken by the apparition of Cardinal Wolsey, who compares their relative skill as extortioners; cites himself as an awful warning ('The ruin of us both was indeed in our times the joy and voice of the people'); and finally departs in a manner recalling Hamlet's father ('Much more I have to say, but this is the third summons of the cock, and to fill the number up, I must return unto the children of the night').

In *The Bishop's Potion*, a mock-dialogue between Laud and his doctor, the physician diagnoses 'certain raw crudities' lying on his patient's stomach. An emetic is prescribed and the Archbishop vomits up the symbols of all his transgressions, including the tobacco patent; the Book of Sports; a parchment with the Star Chamber Order against Prynne, Burton and Bastwick; a bundle of papers presenting livings to dumb-dog clergy and suspending preaching ministers; and finally, after a supreme convulsion, up comes the Mitre ('I had almost broken my lungs'). As a farcical image this harks right back to the 'Mar-Martin' plays of the 1590s (where the ape Martin was purged on stage), and indeed to Spenser. But the comic doctor with his grotesque cures goes back even earlier, to the Mummers' plays, and is a stock figure in college drama like Randolph's *Aristippus*. It is not exactly what one thinks of as Puritan in tone, but the symbolism is impeccable.

The most vivid example of this black humour at its cruellest is *A Description of the Passage of Thomas Lord Strafford over the River of Styx*, which again is full of theatre stuff.[32] Strafford is ferried across Styx by Charon, who complains that he's a very heavy ghost, having 'devoured three kingdoms'. Strafford is deposited on the opposite bank in the waiting arms of Attorney-General Noy, who has already devised a fine new money-raising project for the Hades régime. Charon, whose fare is only $\frac{1}{2}$d per ghost, is to be made to pay a penny a passenger 'as a gratification

[31] Sir John Suckling had already been a butt for Overton's satire in *Vox Borealis*.
[32] Wolfe's evidence for ascribing this to Overton is purely internal, based on content and word use. It could equally well – perhaps better – be ascribed to John Harris (see below, pp. 252–5), in whose writing Shakespearean echoes are common.

or ventage to great Pluto'. As Strafford describes to Noy the fall of himself and Laud, the style changes from burlesque to serious, and he speaks in straight and reasonably effective blank verse, using the traditional metaphor of shipwreck much as Clarence does in *Richard III*.

> And thus adventured while my bark touched heaven,
> Seas upon waves, and waves surmounting seas,
> They danced me down into a vast abyss
> Where I lay docked in quicksands to embrace
> A certain ruin.

He goes on to compare Laud's dejection in prison to that of Antony after Actium, in terms which suggest the writer may have known Shakespeare's play.[33]

> He like the Roman Antony, when he
> Tried his last fortunes in sad Actium's fight
> And left the grappling Eagles and his honour
> To fly in's beauteous Cleopatra's boat,
> And quite ashamed that anyone but he
> Should own that fame to conquer Antony,
> His heart quite broken, and his head bowed low,
> Whiles eightscore minutes wear in number out
> Their measured sands in the just glass of time,
> Durst not look up towards Heaven, nor tempt her eyes,
> Her eyes to him ten thousand thousand heavens
> More dear than thousand conquests;
> Just so his Grace, his faded head being laid
> On both his hands, his elbows on his knees,
> Will silent lean two or three hours together;
> And in that posture, sad he now must leave her,
> Stoops to his idol, greatness.

These early pamphlets show no interest in Laud's theology; there is nothing about Arminianism or predestination. The attack is on the riches of a Church which exploits the poor; the spending of ordinary people's money on 'trinkets' and frivolities of ceremony; the luxurious life-style of bishops, who live like lords and eat like gluttons; above all the persecution not only of Prynne, Burton and Bastwick but of all manner of ordinary men and women. It's the democratic aspect of the case that already interests Overton.

[33] Direct use of Plutarch would not have provided this image; neither would various Antony plays by the Countess of Pembroke and others.

Though he was not as yet in contact with Lilburne and Walwyn, the levelling note is already apparent.

Overton's known and much more famous pamphlets after 1645 are largely monologue or narrative rather than dramatic; but one of the best of all, *The Arraignment of Mr Persecution*, is in semi-dramatic form, and is believed to have served as the model for Bunyan when he wrote the trial of Faithful in *Pilgrim's Progress*. It is far more ambitious than the brief squibs of 1641–2, with a large cast of persecutors and tolerationists, judges and jurymen, powerfully suggesting the *mass* involvement at the peak of the Leveller movement. Moreover while the earlier pamphlets are bent on punishment for the persecutors, cruel in their exultation over the fallen, and crude in their anti-Popery, by 1645 the stress is on ending *all* persecution for religion, including that of Catholics, although the arch-persecutors (now personifications in the manner of the morality plays: Sir John Presbyter and Sir Simon Synod, rather than Laud and Strafford) are still consigned to everlasting flames, as responsible for most of the wars and civil wars in the world. This tract shows the growth in Overton's thought under the impact of Presbyterian and right-wing Parliamentarian persecution of sectaries like Lilburne, and his own involvement with the Leveller movement and with Anabaptism.

The success of Overton's dialogues and monologues also influenced other Leveller writers. Walwyn was already working closely with Overton in 1646 when he wrote *A Prediction of Master Edwards his Conversion and Recantation*, a mock-dramatic monologue supposed to be by the embittered Presbyterian author of *Gangraena*, and *A Parable or Consultation of Physicians upon Master Edwards*, a complete allegory in which the doctors Love, Justice, Patience and Truth operate to remove the abscess which has poisoned Edwards' brain.

All in all, Overton's writing is something new in English prose. Although many of his most successful pamphlets are presented as monologues by 'Martin Mar – Priest', I cannot agree with Joseph Frank that they are 'traditional and conformist' in style, merely repeating the achievements of Martin and anti-Martinists like Nashe fifty years before.[34] In spite of similarities, Overton is far more vivid, swift-moving and readable. He has more skill in sustained narrative and dramatisation, he is more consistently interesting and

[34] *The Levellers*, p. 259.

makes his meaning much clearer. It is here that the example of popular spoken drama must have been important.

A Leveller writer known to have been directly connected with the stage is John Harris, one-time professional actor. In 1634 he performed as a boy player in Norwich, probably on tour with the King's Revels,[35] the London company for whom Randolph had worked, which in that same year borrowed a church robe from a pawnbroker to present Flamen, a priest of the heathens – clearly a bit of deliberate anti-Laudian satire.[36] After the theatres closed he became a printer at Oxford.[37] He can be reckoned among the leading Levellers, and was a close associate of Lilburne, writing several pamphlets in his support under the anagram pseudonym of Sirrahniho. Harris was the craftsman on whom the Army Agitators relied to print their tracts and petitions during the revolt of 1647, and thereafter became for a time the army's official printer, marching with his press in the rear of headquarters. As well as editing other news-books, he set out late in 1648 to produce an uncensored Leveller newspaper, *Mercurius Militaris or the Army's Scout*, lively and humorous in style and full of dramatic allusions; it ran for five numbers before the censor's harassment forced him to stop printing it.

Harris is one of the most radical and sceptical of Leveller journalists, catching, as Brailsford says, 'the authentic tone of voice in which the agitators would address the New Model. Here are the clichés, the epigrams, the jokes which formed the common stock of their speeches.'[38] In *Mercurius Militaris* he mocks not only Parliament's proposed treaty with the King, but the institution of monarchy itself. Arguing that Parliament should get rid of the King altogether, he adapts Cassius' republican attack on Caesar, basing his rhetoric on Shakespeare's as naturally as on the soldiers' meetings.

[35] Bentley, *Jacobean and Caroline Stage*, ii, p. 462.
[36] *Dramatic Records of Sir Henry Herbert*, ed. Adams, p. 64. The broker spent the night in prison. 'The employment of such a robe for "a priest of the heathens" cannot have been innocent in intent' (Bentley, *Profession of Dramatist in Shakespeare's Time*, p. 179).
[37] H. N. Brailsford in *The Levellers* (London, 1976), pp. 410–12, gives a good summary of what is known about Harris, drawing attention to the Shakespearean echoes in his writing. Further detail is given in Joseph Frank, *The Beginnings of the English Newspaper* (Cambridge, Mass., 1961), pp. 165, 166, 192 and *passim*.
[38] Brailsford, *Levellers*, p. 411.

What doth Parliament but mock his sacred Majesty in proposing anything to him to be confirmed?...I wonder what strength it would add, or what goodness to the propositions if he should sign them: can a single man compel 300,000 men to observe them when they are laws? Or can he compel them to break them? What virtue unknown is in this name Carolus Rex? Why is this name adored more than another? Write that and Denzil Holles together, is not this as fair a name? Weigh them, is it not as heavy? Conjure with them, Denzil Holles will start a spirit as soon as the name Carolus Rex, and yet this mere puff of breath, this powerless name King Charles set so high in the vulgar hearts, that what would be vice in others his name like richest alchemy change to virtue and worthiness, and the subscribing this name to that which he can neither help nor hinder, must set him above his masters and conquerors, and permit him to bestride this narrow world like a colossus, when you victors must walk like petty slaves, and peep about under his huge legs to find yourselves dishonourable graves: *premoniti premuniti.*[39]

Harris' writings are full of these quick, easy references to the plays he must have known so well, and usually to Shakespeare – though Jonson comes in too. In the same *Mercurius*, he draws on Jonson's *Alchemist*, telling how Parliament has promised that the King may come to London in safety, freedom and honour:

This makes me think that the King is an Alchemist, and the Lords are his Mercury; they are his crude and his sublimate, his precipitations and his unctions; he can make them dance the philosophical circle four or five times in an hour, like an Ape through a hoop, or a dog in a wheel.   (p. 17)

And the servility Parliament may be expected to show to the returning King is described a few lines later in phrases that echo those of Kent about the sycophant Oswald (in *King Lear*, II.ii.76–80):

Most of the members, through fear or hopes, will become his apes, and shall laugh or weep, be hot or cold, change ever the garb, mode or habit as he varies.[40]

The connection with *Lear* is, I believe, not just a matter of

[39] *Mercurius Militaris*, no. 1, 10 Oct. 1648, p. 5 (B.L./E 467).
[40] *Mercurius Militaris*, no. 3, 24–31 Oct. 1648, p. 17. This does not, like the Julius Caesar extract, follow Shakespeare word for word; but the unusual use of 'garb' (see *Lear* II.ii.98) and 'vary' in this context makes it pretty certain that Harris had *King Lear* at the back of his mind.

phrasing, but of the whole line of thought. In the same issue of *Militaris* Harris is also writing:

> What work of the people does he for his wages? What good do they receive from him? He can neither make nor execute the laws, nor distribute any justice amongst them...But is it reason that a poor man shall be hanged for stealing 14d. and that a great man shall confess he sent his compeers to break houses, plunder and murder, and that thousands of families have been undone by them, and yet not so much as some reparations to be given them out of his lands.

Harris here may not be directly echoing *Lear* (IV.vi):

> Plate sin with gold,
> And the strong lance of justice hurtless breaks:
> Arm it in rags, a pigmy's straw does pierce it.

But when he is writing at high speed about the pretensions and folly of kings and the injustice of courts, at deeper levels Shakespeare works on his thinking, supplies language and precedents.

In *Militaris* No. 2 (10 Oct.–17 Oct. 1648) Harris notes that every tyrant and his sycophants are pretended worshippers of that demigod Authority (p. 12). Angelo in *Measure for Measure* seems an appropriate character for a journalist to have in mind when he is exposing the hypocrisy of the Scottish Jack Presbyters (as Harris is here). As usual, one Shakespearean reference triggers another: this time to *Henry VI Part 2*:

> He is the Lord's anointed...was anybody witness to his anointing? Or must we trust him upon his word only? If so, why might not Jack Cade be as well believed to have been Mortimer and rightful heir to the crown? Surely Jack Cade's tongue was never more double than his.   (p. 13)

Interestingly, Jack Cade comes in here not as a peasant revolutionary hero but (in Shakespeare's manner) as an impostor, a pretendking. On the next page Judge-Advocate Whalley is described as Falstaff describes the boozey Bardolph in *Henry IV Part 1* (III.iii):

> with his face like an ignis fatuus...the gentleman had been quenching the fire in his face, and the liquor proved too strong.
>   (p. 14)

Harris is not just sharing theatrical jokes with his readers. Few New Model soldiers in 1648 would have much experience of plays, as readers of Overton's pamphlets would in 1641–3. Simply, like the playwrights before him, Harris stole freely what served his purpose.

thereby enriching both style and ideas. What the dramatists, Shakespeare especially, provide is not of course any kind of programme or scheme of political thought, but images and phrases of great power and relevance.

Royalist court culture could not inherit the rich and complex traditions of the Jacobean theatre. For even though the players there required court patronage and lived under the threat of court censorship, their livelihood (at least in the public theatres) had depended on their appeal to a wider audience. It was indeed a well-known charge against the 'common player' that his need for approval by the multitude made him a subversive force. 'Howsoever he pretends to have a royal master or mistress, his wages and dependance prove him to be the servant of the people.'[41] In Elizabethan and Jacobean drama the common people do have a voice (even if what they say is not always enforced by the play as a whole), and often provide a sceptical commentary on the main heroic or royal action. One thinks of Henry V's soldiers before Agincourt, the gravediggers in *Hamlet*, the plebeian gibing of Lear's Fool, the outraged middle-class morality of Leantio's mother in *Women Beware Women*. In the courtly Cavalier plays of the 1630s this voice is silent, and the structural use of contrast has gone. It was something the Restoration did not restore.

Undoubtedly it was primarily the 'low' side of Shakespeare that led to his declining reputation in cultured court circles under Charles I. By the time the Beaumont and Fletcher Folio was published in 1647 (during a brief interval of the wars), Sir John Berkenhead, the leading Royalist news-book writer, in his commendatory verses could speak patronisingly of Shakespeare's outdated 'trunk-hose wit' as the result of writing too much for the mob, a style since surpassed by the more correct and elegant work of Fletcher; while William Cartwright dismissed Shakespeare as obscene and unfunny.[42] Moreover, while both Royalist and Puritan

---

[41] J. Cocke, *A Common Player*, 1615. Cited in Chambers, *Elizabethan Stage*, iv, p. 256.

[42] See the analysis of the Beaumont and Fletcher Folio verses and of Cavalier critical attitudes by P. W. Thomas, *Sir John Berkenhead* (Oxford, 1969), pp. 135ff. Among the many commendatory verses prefaced to the Beaumont and Fletcher Folio, the only Parliamentarian piece is by one John Harris, who describes himself as too unknown and unlearned to praise Fletcher effectively, and goes on to do so eloquently for another 126 lines. He does not mention Shakespeare, but works in eulogies of Essex (recently dead), Parliament and Queen Elizabeth.

pamphleteers were making use of playhouse allusions, it seems that the Parliamentarian writers did so more often, so that Berkenhead himself could jeer at a Puritan controversialist for closing the theatres, 'very wisely, lest men should track him, and find where he pilfers all his best similes'.[43]

The many-sided, dialectical embodiment of contradictory social forces and ideas that we find in the greatest early Stuart drama was no longer possible, given the deepening split in society, in audiences and within people's minds. This is already apparent in the plays of Middleton and Massinger in the 1620s. But something of the dramatists' intellectual energy passed to Milton, something of their vitality and ease in reaching a popular audience to the Leveller writers.

If we look back over the whole period of the Elizabethan and Jacobean drama, we must be impressed by the great influence of political censorship and control on what has (and has not) come down to us. Tudor and early Elizabethan drama was often political and didactic; much of it openly dramatised the economic grievances of the poor. A typical early play like Wager's *Enough is as Good as a Feast* (printed 1570), where the poor peasant hit by rack-renting and enclosure is a central figure, is so strongly social in its concerns as to emphasise by contrast how much social comment was restricted later, when state control was tightened up, the audience divided and the drama brought first under noble and then under royal monopoly control.[44] As soon as royal authority in the country began to be morally weakened and undermined, the levelling note and the popular anti-Papist tone reemerge – not of course in court drama, but wherever the playwrights dared to take some risk with a popular audience.

The final suppression of this drama coincides in time with the Cromwellians turning on their own left wing. And it is hardly surprising that after the Restoration the opposition plays were left

[43] John Berkenhead, *The Assembly Man*, written 1647. Cited in E. Sirluck, 'Shakespeare and Jonson among the pamphleteers of the First Civil war', *Modern Philology*, 53 (1955–6), pp. 38–99. Sirluck counts a large sample of theatrical allusions on the two sides and concludes that 'the Puritans used Shakespeare and Jonson approximately twice as often in political propaganda as the Royalists did'. He points out that earlier scholars have underestimated Shakespeare's reputation at this date because they failed to examine pamphlet literature.
[44] See David Bevington, *Tudor Drama and Politics* (Cambridge, Mass., 1968), for a full discussion of these themes in the period up to 1603.

in darkness. Attempts to revive the popular plebeian tradition at the Red Bull and elsewhere from 1659 onwards by Mohun, Rhodes, Jolly and others were finally brought to an end by the theatre-monopoly of the courtiers Davenant and Killigrew under Charles II.

Middleton's Parliamentary Puritan Patrons

It has become clear in the course of this study that Middleton's patrons, especially during the latter part of his career from 1615 onwards, had connections with the 'opposition' in court and Parliament. Moreover the thinking that underlies his later plays seems to have much in common with the views of the moderate Parliamentary Puritans. Similar inclinations towards 'country' against 'court' may be seen at the same period in the work of other writers, such as Michael Drayton and John Reynolds;[1] but Middleton is unusual in the closeness of his links with the City and with circles which must be considered as definitely Puritan. Some further information is assembled here about the social, economic and political connections of these patrons that presents a picture very different from the one usually presented of the social basis of art and drama at this time.

CITY PATRONS

Middleton's work directly for the City has already been described. It may, however, be useful to look more closely at the connections and life-style of those of his City patrons about whom we have information. These are:

1. Lord Mayors for whom Middleton wrote pageants
 Sir Thomas Myddleton
 Sir George Bowles (or Bolles)
 Sir Martin Lumley
 Sir Edward Barkham
 Sir Peter Proby
 Sir William Cokayne
 Sir Cuthbert Hacket

---

[1] See Richard F. Hardin, *Michael Drayton and the Passing of Elizabethan England* (Lawrence, Kansas, 1973), pp. 27–9, 83–92, 93–115, for an extremely valuable treatment of the ideology of opposition among the Jacobean country gentry, of which he sees Drayton as representative.

2. Businessmen to whom Middleton dedicated works
   Richard Fishbourne and John Browne
   William Hammond

The only one of these who was definitely a creature of the Crown was Cokayne, of the notorious Cokayne project. Sir Peter Proby, though a courtier when he became Lord Mayor, was a shrewd operator who, like Sir Thomas Myddleton, had been in Walsingham's employment (John Chamberlain calls him 'Secretary Walsingham's barber').

Most of them were entrepreneurs, the most active and thrusting businessmen of their time. Sir Thomas Myddleton had begun as an export merchant under Ferdinando Poyntz, and had been his factor in the Low Countries. As well as grocery and spices he was interested in sugar-refineries, and his brother Hugh in lead and copper-mining, clothworking and civil engineering. It was Hugh Myddleton who designed and carried through the New River project to supply London with water, despite technical difficulties and obstruction by landowners along the route. The dramatist Thomas Middleton's 'entertainment' for the opening of the New River commemorates this remarkable achievement. The water was supplied at a profit (the King and courtiers being large shareholders), but was made available freely to the poor in certain districts as a work of charity. Fishbourne and Browne, who traded with the Low Countries, apparently dealt not only in silks and clothing but in the 'corantoes' or news-books imported from Holland, which were the beginning of the modern newspaper.

A number of these men were not only merchants but moneylenders. In later life this seems to have been the main part of Sir Thomas Myddleton's business. Sir Francis Jones was another customs farmer who lent at interest (and eventually went bankrupt in the process). Richard Fishbourne's funeral elegy, by William Strode, refers to his 'religious usury' – laying up treasure in heaven by charitable gifts on earth – which suggests, if it does not prove, that he too was a moneylender.

The Myddletons were particularly interested in West Indian voyages, financing both Raleigh and Drake. Their kinsman William Myddleton was a noted seaman and privateer captain, who was present at the last battle of Grenville's *Revenge*. Richard Fishbourne in his youth was a privateer and captain of a privateering ship, the

Elizabeth Fishbourne, hence likely to favour a strong anti-Spanish policy. With other privateers he was on Drake's Cadiz expedition of 1587, which illustrates 'the fusion of private and national enterprise' in the sea-fighting against Spain. He took rich prizes in 1589, 1590 and 1591 (K. R. Andrews, *Elizabethan Privateering* (Cambridge, 1964), pp. 94, 113ff., 178, 255).

ACTIVE PURITANS

The Puritan sympathies of Myddleton and Lumley have already been mentioned. Sir Thomas contributed to 'wages' for a Dutch preacher, and financed the first Bible in Welsh jointly with Alderman Rowland Heylyn, a fellow Welshman and chairman of the Feoffees for Impropriations (who raised and managed a fund to buy up impropriations and install Puritan ministers, until Laud took alarm and suppressed the enterprise). Richard Fishbourne in his will endowed lectureships, one of which, at his native town of Huntingdon, was used to appoint a Puritan successor to Thomas Beard, the schoolmaster who greatly influenced Oliver Cromwell.[2] Another lectureship, at St Bartholomew's by the Exchange where Fishbourne lived, was held for many years by the Puritan leader John Downham. Part of William Hammond's fortune passed, through the will of his brother Edmond, to the Haberdashers, to be used to buy up impropriations and appoint godly ministers. Sir Martin Lumley in his will (1634) established a weekly lectureship at St Helen's, Bishopsgate. Such lectureships were indeed one of the most important means of challenging royal and Laudian policy in the Church and gaining a platform for the views of the 'middling sort'.

In 1622, when the famous Puritan lectures at St Antholin's were endangered by lack of money, the parishioners appealed to the Court of Aldermen for support. The committee of seven aldermen which recommended that the City should support them with £40 a year included Myddleton, Proby and Lumley; the Lord Mayor at the time, Sir Edward Barkham, was another for whom Middleton wrote a pageant. It was not until 1630, the year of Sir Thomas Myddleton's death, when the City government was increasingly under pressure from the Crown and becoming more subservient to

[2] Christopher Hill, *Society and Puritanism in Pre-Revolutionary England*, pp. 36, 93.

the King, that the Aldermen withdrew support from the St Antholin's lectures.[3]

The City government continually sought to impose stricter observance of the Sabbath, and in 1620 they approached the Bishop of London to enlist his cooperation in enforcing the Mayor's proclamation against Sabbath-breaking. On this issue they came into collision with Laud in the later 1620s.

Though they were Puritan in religion, we should not assume that these men were necessarily 'Puritanical' with the ascetic nineteenth-century connotations of the term. Their mansions at Chirk, Stansted Mountfichet, Great Bardfield and so on were as grand as those of the old county nobility, to equality with which they increasingly aspired. (Indeed Chirk had previously belonged to the Earl of Leicester.) A look at the Chirk Castle accounts, with their sack and venison suppers, is revealing. In 1612, for example, we find Sir Thomas Myddleton's steward debiting:[4]

3 yds of silver grogram to your doublet	£3. 6. 0
8 yds of crimson satin to make your hose	£6. 8. 0
3 ells of white taffeta sarsnet to draw out your hose	£1. 4. 0
5 dozen of gold buttons	£ 5.10
4 ells of rich black taffeta to make your cloak	£3.14. 0

In 1613 the accounts record two shillings given to three men for mowing the bowling alley, and fifteen shillings lost at bowls – so the future Parliamentarian general was obviously in the habit of playing and gambling on it. Expenditures on silk, satin and lace, carnation and pearl-coloured silk stockings, jewelled harnesses and saddles, fiddlers at Christmas and hunting-dogs, show how wrong it would be to think of these rich Puritans in terms of the hodden grey image. If they favoured austerity, it was principally for the poor.

We should not assume, either, that their attitudes to the stage were necessarily wholly negative. Sir Thomas Myddleton (senior), for one, was associated with the East India Company, which in 1623 commissioned a play on the Amboyna massacre, and who probably staged Mountfort's *Launching of the Mary* in 1632 (after Myddleton's death). Feeling against *Sabbath* playing was certainly very strong: we know from Richard Baxter how horrified he was,

---

[3] Dorothy Ann Williams, 'Puritanism in the City Government, 1610–1640', *Guildhall Miscellany*, no. 4 (Feb. 1955), pp. 5–8.
[4] From *Chirk Castle Accounts*, ed. W. Myddleton (St Albans, 1908), pp. 7ff.

as a young man staying with Sir Henry Herbert, to find the court on Sunday afternoons attending a play instead of a sermon. But this does not prove hostility to all drama, though William Hammond is the only one of this list to whom a stage play was actually dedicated.

While the bulk of these merchants' vast fortunes was left to their families, if they had any, they were often generous in charitable bequests, sometimes channelled through the livery companies. Most of them left considerable sums for the poor in hospitals and prisons, and in particular for setting up young men in trade or for apprenticing poor children. Such provisions are found in the wills of Sir Thomas Myddleton, his widow Anne, his brother Robert Myddleton, Sir Martin Lumley, Richard Fishbourne, John Browne and Edmond Hammond (brother of Middleton's patron William). If we think of the Puritan attitude to the poor as necessarily stern and impersonal, we shall be surprised to find Edmond Hammond, among his 150 charitable bequests (some very large), naming the individuals 'goodman Tooley, Capon, Brooke and Winkle' of his parish of All-Hallows-in-the-Wall, who are to receive £4 each. The testament of the old bachelor John Browne, who left a large part of his fortune by nuncupative will 'to pious uses', was contested not by some greedy Puritan usurer, but by his nephew Sir Thomas Gardiner, a Royalist who was later defeated as Recorder of London by the organised Parliamentarians.[5]

On occasion Middleton's patrons led the opposition to royal policy. The Parliamentary debates show the Myddleton brothers (at various times Hugh, Robert and Thomas were MPs between 1610 and 1630) opposing the Crown on many of its policies, especially taxes, grants of monopolies to 'new' upstarts like Cokayne, monopolies and impositions generally, and demanding the impeachment of Cranfield. Mr [Robert] Myddleton in April 1614 presented a bill against impositions and the exactions of the customs farmers, and roundly attacked the King's Speech from the class viewpoint that 'The heads of the matters of grace tend to the gentility, not to cities, boroughs, burgesses or merchants.'[6] He led the Commons attack on the Cokayne patent for dyeing and dressing cloth as 'a sepulchre – fair without, dead bones within', and wholly impracticable. If it

---

[5] A large part, however, was also left to his nephew and godson John Browne, and it may have been this that Gardiner was contesting.

[6] *House of Commons Journals*, i, p. 461.

went through he would have to turn off many of his workmen, of whom he and his partner employed over 3,000; and he complained that the Exchequer took £20,000 a year out of his and his partner's purse (20 May 1614).[7]

In 1614 Mr [Robert] Myddleton attacked corruption in the state, declaring that 'if it be considered what the merchant hath paid for impositions, if the King had received it, he should not need to require supply now', and warning of the 'danger lest the impositions, now covering the sea, should break over, and overflow the land'.[8] In 1623 Sir Thomas Myddleton was on the committee to enquire into who was responsible for advising the King on the new impositions on wines, sugars and grocery – which of course affected his own business. He seems to have been particularly active in the enquiries which led to the impeachment of Cranfield, Earl of Middlesex, the Lord Treasurer, and may well have entered Parliament on purpose to keep an eye on economic and trade policy.

In the next generation, their families largely took the side of Parliament. Sir Thomas Myddleton the younger, elder son of the Lord Mayor, who had been settled by his father at Chirk Castle in Denbigh, there to found a Presbyterian dynasty, became a Parliamentarian general, and the centre of what resistance there was to the King in North Wales.[9] 'It was probably in the family of Timothy Myddleton, the Lord Mayor's younger son, whom he had set up as an Essex squire, that John Jones of Maes y Garnedd learned the earnest Puritanism that made him a regicide, and the business experience he used in helping to govern Ireland for the Saints.'[10] Sir Martin Lumley, the younger son of the Lord Mayor for whom Middleton wrote a pageant, was a Presbyterian elder and sat in the Long Parliament as member for Essex, replacing Robert Lord Rich, with whose family the Lumleys were intimate. Sir John Wittewronghe, Sir Thomas Myddleton's stepson, was a Parliamentarian officer in Essex. Sir Hugh's son Henry, who held various court offices in the 1630s, was a Parliamentarian cavalry officer

[7] *Ibid.* p. 491.   [8] 18 Apr. 1614. *House of Commons Journals*, i, p. 467.
[9] A. H. Dodd, *Studies in Stuart Wales* (Cardiff, 1952), p. 47.
[10] *Ibid.* p. 47. In 1644 the parishioners of Stansted Mountfichet subscribed to enable Sir Thomas Myddleton 'to reduce North Wales to the obedience of Parliament'. The subscription list was headed by Timothy, who was Lord of the Manor (G. W. D. Winkley, *Short History of the Parish Church of St Mary, Stansted Mountfichet* (Ramsgate, n.d.)).

under Manchester. Sir Thomas Myddleton's daughter Mary married Sir John Maynard, a former courtier, later a Parliamentarian and Presbyterian MP in the Long Parliament, and subsequently a Royalist. He was one of the twelve sequestered MPs, and while in prison became associated with Lilburne, for whose release he later spoke in Parliament. Maynard's family continued to befriend Lilburne until the latter's death.

Thus Middleton's Puritan paymasters were typical of the rising business magnates of their time, however unlike the image we may have formed of such people. A great gulf, however, must have separated their attitudes and habits from those of the porters and seamen, brewers and craftsmen who stood in the yard of the Globe or Red Bull to watch the plays.

WILLIAM, 3RD EARL OF PEMBROKE, AS PATRON AND ASSOCIATE OF PURITANS

William Herbert, who succeeded his father as 3rd Earl of Pembroke in 1601, and became Lord Chamberlain in 1615, is described by Aubrey as 'the greatest Maecenas to learned men of any peer of his time: or since'. He is best known now as the patron of Shakespeare, Jonson, Chapman and many lesser poets, the joint dedicatee with his brother of the Shakespeare First Folio, the friend of John Donne. But it is less widely recognised that he was also a backstage leader of Parliamentary Puritanism, an important patron and protector of Puritan clergy and of Puritan and anti-Catholic writers. In view of the exceptional importance of the 'incomparable brethren' as patrons of the drama, it is important to know something of his connections and influence and the Puritans whom he patronised.[11]

Family associations

William Herbert's family were 'new' Henrician nobility created by the Tudors; they had a long association with the Reformers, and with patronage of Puritan writers and Puritan trends within the Church. His grandfather, Sir William Herbert, 1st Earl of Pembroke

[11] For dedications to Pembroke and others I have relied on the invaluable work by Franklin B. Williams, *Index of Dedications and Commendatory Verses in English Books before 1641* (London, 1962).

of the second creation (1501–70), married the sister of Catherine Parr, who became sixth Queen of Henry VIII, and was much favoured by the King. In the 1540s he received the rich estates of the dissolved abbey of Wilton, in Wiltshire, where he destroyed the monastic buildings and built the great family mansion (enclosing and depopulating to do so). He was executor of Henry VIII's will and councillor to Edward VI. He held Calvinist religious views, and his loyalty to Queen Mary and his military opposition to Wyatt's Protestant rebellion were always suspect.[12] On Queen Elizabeth's Council he advocated alliance with the Huguenots, and is said to have brought over persecuted Protestant weavers from the Low Countries, some of whom he settled at Wilton. Aubrey says he was regarded as 'an upstart, and much envied' by the Wiltshire gentry, and was illiterate though a brave soldier.[13]

The 2nd Earl, Henry Herbert, was an intimate of the Earl of Leicester, and married his niece, Mary Sidney, sister of Philip. Leicester, Sir Philip Sidney and the Countess of Pembroke were the most famous literary patrons of their time, and their help was particularly given to Puritan writers and preachers, in accordance with the anti-Spanish and anti-Catholic policies they favoured. Leicester's patronage has been studied in illuminating detail by Eleanor Rosenberg,[14] who suggested that to some extent this represented the deliberate effort of the Crown and the new aristocracy to control public opinion (particularly that of the London middle class) and the printing press. The universities, especially important since they trained the clergy, were controlled through their chancellors (for the greater part of the reign, Burghley at Cambridge and Leicester at Oxford); and companies of actors like Leicester's Men, sponsored by the great lords, were also subject to royal control and protection. The direction of Leicester's patronage was largely Puritan, in the Elizabethan sense of the term – surprising as this may sound. Miss Rosenberg comments, in words that are relevant for the 3rd Earl of Pembroke as well as his great-uncle:

It may be that our reluctance to recognise the elegant Leicester, Elizabeth's courtier, as a Puritan is the result of our long preoccupation with the Pilgrim Fathers – the psalm-singers and

---

[12] He originally joined Northumberland in proclaiming Lady Jane Grey as Queen, but changed his mind in time to avoid Northumberland's fate.
[13] *Aubrey's Brief Lives*, ed. O. Lawson Dick (London, 1962), p. 222.
[14] *Leicester, Patron of Letters* (New York, 1955).

rigid doctrinaires of the seventeenth century. In applying the term 'Puritan' to such men as Leicester, Warwick, Huntingdon, Bedford, the Sidneys and Walsingham, we must be careful to distinguish between Elizabethan Puritanism and the separatist Puritanism of the next century...The reformers and their noble patrons put loyalty to the crown before small matters of observance or doctrine, hoping always to purify the Church from within.[15]

The key-points of this 'broad, idealistic, humane' Puritan movement were, she thinks, an unsympathetic though tolerant view of hierarchy and surplice as vestiges of Papism; opposition to attempts by the bishops to enforce uniform religious practice; strong and intolerant anti-Catholicism; insistence on each man having the right to form his opinions by studying Scripture; and the demand for an educated and enlightened preaching clergy instead of 'blind mouths'. The movement 'was, for the time, democratic...it was not yet revolutionary' (p. 198).

Thus we find that Leicester, patron of the best-known actors of the time, Leicester's Men (who got the first royal patent in 1574), was also patron of the Puritan John Field, leader of the illegal Presbyterian classis movement. Field was imprisoned for his part in the First Admonition to Parliament, and several times suspended from preaching; in a letter of thanks to Leicester for intervening on his behalf he bitterly attacked his patron for supporting the players.[16] Another Puritan patronised by Leicester was Thomas Cartwright, who became Master of Lord Leicester's Hospital at Warwick; he advocated that bishops' revenues should be diverted for the use of the poor, the ministers and the universities.[17]

[15] *Ibid.* p. 197.
[16] Another interesting case of religious criticism of Leicester by a social inferior is in the correspondence between him and Thomas Wood (*Letters of Thomas Wood, Puritan, 1566–1577*, ed. P. Collinson (London, 1960). Wood, a Presbyterian country gentleman, criticised the Earl for not having done more to protect the conferences of preachers known as 'prophesyings'. Leicester defended himself by saying that he had preferred many preachers of the right sort and had always been for prophesyings, though some went too far and risked suppression. 'I will not excuse myself. I may fall many ways and have more witnesses thereof than many others who perhaps be no saints neither' (p. 14).
[17] This tends to refute the suggestion that the aristocracy patronised Puritan preachers for purely mercenary motives, hoping that they would be enriched by the lands and revenues of the bishops as they had already been by those of the monasteries (Rosenberg, *Leicester,* p. 198).

Sir Philip Sidney, Leicester's nephew and protégé and William Herbert's uncle, was not only politically but personally closely linked with the militant Protestant cause in Europe, and especially with William the Silent and the House of Orange. His personal friends included the Huguenot leaders Hubert Languet and Philippe Du Plessis Mornay (whose tract *A Work Concerning the Truth of the Christian Religion* Sidney partly translated); the scholar-printer Henri Estienne; the anti-Aristotelian logician and philosopher Peter Ramus, killed in the St Bartholomew's Day massacre; John Florio and Giordano Bruno. In England Sidney was patron of poets and scholars, notably Spenser (whose Puritan satires Middleton began by imitating), Richard Hakluyt and Abraham Fraunce. His death in battle in the Low Countries made him a symbolic Protestant hero long into the seventeenth century. Fulke Greville's biography of his friend, not published till 1652, typically makes Sidney's example a stick to beat Stuart policy in Europe.[18]

Lady Pembroke's household and circle at Wilton continued the same tradition, combining literary work and patronage of poets with a keen interest in Puritan theology and politics. Hugh Sanford, appointed tutor to the young William Herbert in 1586, was author of a Puritan tract, *De Descensu Domini Nostri Jesu Christi ad Inferos* (published at Amsterdam in 1611 after his death). Another of his tutors was the poet Samuel Daniel, who later dedicated his *Defence of Rhyme* to his former pupil the 3rd Earl of Pembroke. It was probably through Pembroke's influence at court that Daniel was appointed to his special position as manager and licenser to the Children of the Queen's Revels, Queen Anne's personal company (see above).

Financial interests

Pembroke was able to live 'about the Court before in it, and never by it' because he was immensely rich in his own right. 'As he spent and lived upon his own fortune, so he stood upon his own feet', says Clarendon. His pension as Lord Chamberlain was £3,600, which with 'diet' and minor perquisites added up to £4,862 a year; later as

---

18 For Sidney's connections and patronage, see John Buxton, *Sir Philip Sidney and the English Renaissance*, which also has valuable material on the Countess of Pembroke and the 3rd Earl of Pembroke as literary patrons. For Sidney as a propaganda-hero of the Protestant cause, see Roger Howell, *Sir Philip Sidney: The Shepherd Knight* (London, 1968).

Lord Steward he probably got something over £2,000 a year.[19] But his total income was enormously greater, of the order of £22,000 a year.[20]

His financial and business interests tended to bring the 3rd Earl into contact and sympathy with rising merchants, 'improving' land-owners and capitalist entrepreneurs, many of them with Puritan sympathies.[21] The family wealth was founded primarily on its Wiltshire lands, where the Herberts were improving landlords, and successfully increased their rental income to keep pace with the price rise. The estates lay in the clothing part of the county, the bulk of whose production was sent up to London to be either finished there or exported to the Continent, largely to Holland. The export trade was much more important to Wiltshire than the home market, and it was hard hit both by the Cokayne project of 1614[22] and later by the Thirty Years War, which produced heavy unemploy-ment.[23]

His Welsh estates may have been responsible for Pembroke's becoming an important shareholder and governor in the Society of London for Mineral and Battery Works (incorporated 1603–4) and the Mines Royal Society. Through these he was interested in the highly speculative mining and metallurgy business, and involved in the development of copper-smelting, iron, brass and wire-works in South Wales. The lead mines of Cardiganshire were first worked by men who farmed them from the Mines Royal Society: their royal monopoly gave them the right to erect a mint and impress labour. Sir Hugh Myddleton, goldsmith and brother of the Lord Mayor of London, paid £400 a year for the lease of his lead and silver mines in Cardiganshire, and was reputed by 1609 to be

[19] Aylmer, *The King's Servants*, pp. 205–6.

[20] *D.N.B.* gives this figure, adding that he died owing £18,000. The 4th Earl's income is estimated by recent research at £16,000 (J. P. Cooper, 'The Fortune of Thomas Wentworth, Earl of Strafford', *Economic History Review*, n.s., xi, no. 1 (Dec. 1958), pp. 227ff.).

[21] See the very long dedicatory epistle to Pembroke in Rowland Vaughan's *Most approved and long-experienced Waterworks* (London, 1610; *S.T.C.* 24603), which sets out Vaughan's achievements and projects in draining and irrigating land in Herefordshire and setting the poor to work in clothing factories; and asks the Earl's help and financial support in securing a godly, preaching minister, since the present 'counterfeit Puritan' does not preach.

[22] Opposition to this would bring the Herbert interests specifically into alliance with the MPs of the old Merchant Adventurers, including the Myddleton family, who bitterly attacked Cokayne in Parliament.

[23] *Victoria County History of Wiltshire* (Oxford, 1959), iv, pp. 151–5.

making £2,000 a year from his mining operations; most of these huge profits were sunk in providing a water supply for the City of London. In 1625 Myddleton was authorised to conscript labour anywhere in the United Kingdom to work his mines.[24] He was an MP and an associate of Raleigh.[25]

Pembroke was also deeply interested in exploration and colonisation, especially in the New World – a member of the King's Council for the Virginia Company in 1609, an incorporator of the North West Passage Company in 1612, of the East India Company in 1614, and of the Bermudas Company in 1615. In 1620 he patented 30,000 acres in Virginia, and undertook to send over emigrants and cattle.

In the crisis in the Virginia Company in 1623 Pembroke was allied with Nicholas Ferrar and Sir Edwin Sandys against the Earl of Middlesex and the Crown nominees, who finally got the company's charter withdrawn. (Pembroke helped to impeach Middlesex the next year.) Later he was associated (in 1627) with Sir William Courteen, a merchant with Dutch connections, in a venture to colonise Barbados: apparently Pembroke obtained the royal grant of a charter and Courteen put up most of the capital.[26] His consistent anti-Spanish attitude was no doubt partly connected with rivalry for trade and colonies in the Americas.[27]

Thus Pembroke was aligned, on economic as well as religious and political grounds, with the same groups who provided the City patronage for writers like Middleton, Dekker and Heywood. Powerful at court, his interests yet linked him more strongly with what was beginning to emerge as the Country Party in the House of Commons, in which his supporters and friends Sir Benjamin Rudyerd and Sir John Eliot played a leading role.[28] He had close

[24] D. J. Davies, *Economic History of South Wales prior to 1800* (Cardiff, 1933), p. 57.
[25] Valerie Pearl states he was a member of the little-known political and philosophical society called the Robin Hood Club, which met in a City tavern in 1613 (*London and the Outbreak of the Puritan Revolution*, p. 233).
[26] The venture proved a financial disaster because another courtier, Carlisle, obtained a rival grant of Barbados, which the courts upheld against Pembroke's.
[27] See Christopher Thompson, 'The Origins of the Politics of the Parliamentary Middle Group, 1625–1629', *Transactions of the Royal Historical Society*, 5th ser., xxii (1972), pp. 71–86.
[28] See S. L. Adams, 'Foreign Policy and the Parliaments of 1621 and 1624', in Kevin Sharpe (ed.), *Faction and Parliament* (Oxford, 1978).

links with the Dutch authorities, with Prince Maurice of Nassau, with the Ambassador to the Netherlands, Sir Dudley Carleton, and with the Queen of Bohemia, who held her exiled court at The Hague. In the Parliament of 1626 the Pembroke client MPs, led by Rudyerd, supported the waging of sea war against Spain in the West Indies by the big merchants as a profitable enterprise.[29]

Personality and politics

Pembroke as a personality is best known from Clarendon's account, which lays the emphasis (naturally enough) on the qualities which made him a great courtier and a respected if not loved counsellor to James I and Charles I. Unlike his brother, Philip 4th Earl of Pembroke, he did not live on into the Civil War period, and Clarendon is not obliged to qualify his praise by any political reservations, though he is extremely bitter about the 4th Earl, who became one of the most prominent Parliamentarian peers. So his attractive portrait of the 3rd Earl has come to stand for the ideal Shakespearean aristocrat, and Pembroke has sometimes, on the strength of this, been represented as firmly Royalist and Anglo-Catholic – from which it is inferred that, since he was Shakespeare's patron, the climate favourable to the greatest English drama was Anglo-Catholic, Royalist and anti-Puritan too.[30] This seems to me wholly misleading.

Pembroke in his later years was in fact closely associated with the Parliamentary Puritan opposition, and was important in it because of his privileged position and his great wealth, which gave him a measure of security and independence within the Buckingham-dominated power structure. According to Gerald Aylmer, 'the Herbert brothers continued to maintain a sort of clandestine opposi-

---

[29] See Thompson, 'Origins of the Politics of the Parliamentary Middle Group'.

[30] See P. Cruttwell, *The Shakespearean Moment* (New York, 1960), pp. 124–31, 250–2. In this interesting and provocative study Pembroke is specifically stated to have confined his favours to men 'whose opinions coincided with his (that is, Anglican and royalist)', and Cruttwell suggests that this fact may offer 'a clue to Shakespeare's opinions'. But I think he misreads Clarendon. If there is a clue here, it points rather to Parliamentary Puritan and latent anti-Royalist opinions like those of the 4th Earl. But the 'clue' is unsatisfactory anyway, for 1616, when Shakespeare died, was not 1624 or 1630, and Pembroke's opinions may well have shifted and sharpened a good deal in this period.

tion [to Buckingham] from within the government', even at a time when 'four other councillors were dismissed or suspended from the Board between 1624 and 1628'.[31]

In his youth Pembroke was a great patron of poets – William Browne, Joshua Sylvester, John Davies of Hereford, Joseph Hall and Francis Quarles. This aspect of his influence has been fully studied.[32] But he received few poetic dedications after 1615, when he became Lord Chamberlain, though a great many philosophical and theological works and sermons were dedicated to him. Certainly Pembroke at this time was becoming more involved in politics, and as Chancellor of Oxford he had many favours to confer on scholars. It is also possible that 'as he grew older he developed an increasingly profound religious feeling so that his attention turned more not only to statecraft and court politics but to theology and religion, and thus possibly away from poetry'.[33] It seems likely that the sharpening religious–political conflict and the rise of the Arminian faction led the Puritan-Anglican clergy to look to Pembroke as one of the most influential anti-Arminian lay leaders.[34]

Indeed Pembroke seems to have been widely considered as a likely patron of anti-Spanish and anti-Catholic writings of all kinds, judging from the number of books on these subjects dedicated to him. They included *The Triumphs of Nassau*, by Maurice Prince of Orange (translated by W. Shute), and J. D. Perrin's history of the Albigenses (translated by Sidney's friend and follower Sampson Lennard). There were works by Huguenot controversialists like Jean Hotman, Henri Estienne and Pierre du Moulin (chaplain to the brother of Philippe Du Plessis Mornay), an anti-Jesuit and anti-Catholic controversialist who 'ghosted' for James I, and clashed with Lancelot Andrewes when he opposed Arminianism and the divine right of bishops (in *De la vocation des pasteurs*). There was more polemic by Richard Sheldon, a converted Catholic who became a Protestant divine and royal chaplain, but was reprimanded and fell into royal disfavour for an anti-Catholic sermon at

[31] Aylmer, *The King's Servants*, p. 61.
[32] 'The Third Earl of Pembroke as a Patron of Poetry', by Dick Taylor, Jr, in *Tulane Studies in English*, 1955; and John Buxton, *Sir Philip Sidney and the English Renaissance*, 2nd edn (London, 1964).
[33] Taylor, Jr, 'The Third Earl of Pembroke', p. 67.
[34] Pembroke, as Chancellor of Oxford, congratulated the Vice-Chancellor on his efforts to prevent Arminianism from gaining a hold in the University (Russell, *Crisis of Parliaments*, p. 214).

Paul's Cross in 1622. Edward Chaloner, an Oxford divine whose Puritan *Six Sermons* were dedicated posthumously to Pembroke in 1629 (he died of plague in 1625), was brother to Sir Thomas Chaloner, who later signed the death warrant for Charles I. Daniel Featley, one-time tutor to Raleigh's son and domestic chaplain to Pembroke's friend, Archbishop Abbot, dedicated an anti-Catholic sermon to the 3rd Earl in 1630; he was strongly anti-Laudian in the 1630s, and gave evidence against Laud when he was charged with making 'superstitious alterations' in Lambeth chapel. (Later, in the 1640s, Featley defended bishops.) Other dedications include popular scurrilous anti-Catholic satires reviving memories of Gunpowder Plot and retelling monastic scandals, by George Jenney, J. Dawson, James Wadsworth and others. Perhaps the most striking of these is *Babel's Balm or The Honeycomb of Rome's Religion*, by George Goodwin, written in Latin and translated into English verse by John Vicars, a schoolmaster at Christ's Hospital, who was active in collecting money for the Feoffees for Impropriations and attended some of their meetings. Vicars' satire *Mischief's Mystery, or Treason's Masterpiece, The Powder Plot* (1617) was refused a licence in a later edition, the censor commenting: 'We are not so angry with the papists now as we were twenty years ago.' He was in contact with Bastwick and Lilburne over printing seditious books; in the 1640s he was a strong Presbyterian and bitterly denounced the Independents.

Finally in this genre, there are the much more lively Parliamentary Puritan verse satires of George Wither, which openly defend those now currently being abused as Puritans. At the same time Wither dissociates himself from those so-called Puritans whose religion consists only in denouncing harmless recreations; and he defends poetry and drama very much on the lines laid down by Sidney (whom he cites) in the *Apologie for Poetrie*, quoting Daniel, Drayton, Jonson and Chapman as good examples. 'The best e'er taught on earth, taught like a poet.' Wither was imprisoned in the Marshalsea for these satires in 1613: it was reported that Princess Elizabeth intervened to secure his release. Repeated addresses to Pembroke suggest that the original dedication was productive, or at least not repudiated.

Dedication of a book does not, of course, by itself prove that the man to whom it was dedicated knew the author or approved the contents, still less that he gave the financial help or preferment that was hoped for.[35] Nevertheless, those controversialists whom Pembroke definitely rewarded, and those with whom he is known to have been personally friendly, do seem as a rule to have had Puritan sympathies. One might suppose that as Chancellor of Oxford and a great man at court he would receive routine dedications of sermons and tracts indiscriminately from divines of every trend; in fact there are few which are not markedly anti-Arminian or Puritan in the broad sense.[36] A comparison with dedications to Buckingham (of which very few are Puritan, except in the years 1624–5, when he flirted with the Puritan leaders) shows the writers to have been surprisingly well informed about opinion at the top.

Connection with Puritan divines

It is significant that Pembroke was an intimate friend of John Preston, 'Prince Charles' Puritan chaplain',[37] the political preacher who in the critical years 1621–6 'governed the affairs of the Puritan faction'. Preston's contemporary biographer, T. Ball, tells us that 'the Earl of Pembroke and the Countess of Bedford had a great interest in him [Preston] and he in them'.[38] In 1621 Preston was made chaplain to Prince Charles at Buckingham's instance, and in 1622 Master of the Puritan Cambridge college of Emmanuel. As early as 1621 Preston, prompted by 'a very honourable member of the House of Lords', had written a paper opposing Prince Charles' Spanish marriage, which was 'copied out and spread among those of the Parliament they thought fit'.[39] From 1621 'Preston devoted himself to promoting the interest of Puritanism by political manoeuvre. He even used to insist that his pupils must be eldest sons, and so likely to be socially influential.'[40] Pembroke, with his great influence at court and in Parliament (he was reckoned to

[35] See H. S. Bennett, *English Books and Readers 1558–1603* (Cambridge, 1965), pp. 53–5; and *English Books and Readers, 1603–1640* (Cambridge, 1970), pp. 23–9.

[36] There are exceptions, such as Thomas Jackson and Joseph Hall.

[37] See Irvonwy Morgan, *Prince Charles' Puritan Chaplain* (London, 1957); and Christopher Hill, 'The Political Sermons of John Preston', in *Puritanism and Revolution*.

[38] T. Ball, *Life of the Renowned Dr Preston* (Oxford, 1885), p. 89.

[39] *Ibid.* p. 60.

[40] Christopher Hill, 'The Political Sermons of John Preston', p. 240; based on *The Diary of Sir Henry Slingsby*, ed. D. Parsons (1836), p. 318. For the practical influence of Puritan peers, see Lawrence Stone, *The Crisis of the Aristocracy* (Oxford, 1967), pp. 332–54.

control at least a dozen seats in the Commons in the 1620s),[41] was such a man as Preston could most effectively work with and through. In these years the state of 'the kingdom of grace abroad' – that is, the Protestant (or Calvinist) cause in international politics – was one of Preston's main concerns; he wished to see England actively participating in the struggle between Christ and Antichrist, light and darkness, Catholicism and Protestantism all over the world, and especially in Bohemia and Germany, the Netherlands and France.[42]

Samuel Hieron (1576–1617), a popular preacher and lecturer of Puritan sympathies, dedicated to Pembroke *Penance for Sin*, a volume of lectures on the Penitential Psalms, published in 1619. In the dedication he refers to Pembroke's having 'vouchsafed to admit me into your service' – possibly as a personal chaplain.[43] He is sure, he says, that his patron 'would not reject as rude such lectures, in which there was both a labour for such plainness as might best affect the conscience, and a purposed avoiding of that over-abundant artificialness, which might make them like those spiders' webs. . . which are said to be much in workmanship, but in profit nothing'. According to the author, Pembroke did read and approve the book before publication. Its tone is decidedly 'plain' and critical of rank and status:

> This is for all us who are called to Nathan's office, that we should put on Nathan's courage. . .God forbid the pulpit should be made a place of ranting, or a theatre for invectives. . .; yet far let it be from base flattery, and from daubing up the sins of greatness with untempered mortar. Let the King on the Throne hear of his failing, as well as the Maid at the Mill; the gentleman that sitteth in the Quire, as well as the poor that is ranged in the belfry. Let not our Sermons be as the Spider's web, through which do break the great flies, while only the lesser gnats are taken.[44]

---

[41] V. Rowe, 'The Influence of the Earls of Pembroke on Parliamentary Elections', *English Historical Review*, 50 (1935), p. 253.

[42] Christopher Hill, 'The Political Sermons of John Preston', p. 249.

[43] Hieron may have felt in need of this protection, for he is reported to have been the author of an earlier anonymous work, *A Defence of the Ministers' Reasons for Refusal of Subscription to the Book of Common Prayer* (1607), which was printed in Holland and sent over packed in the goods of a Plymouth merchant. Because of the censorship no bookseller dared sell it, and the whole edition was given away. (B. Brook, *Lives of the Puritans* (London, 1815), ii, pp. 270–3).

[44] S. Hieron, *Works* (London, 1620; *S.T.C.* 13380).

Another sermon by Hieron published in 1619, after the preacher's early death, on the text *Render Unto Caesar*, directly grasps the nettle of obedience to royal authority.

> Kings are bound to command in all things according to God. . . A man must be sure that in obeying Caesar he doth not disobey God. It may seem that by this there is some allowances of rebellion given to subjects in some case. For if it be lawful for them and their duty to withdraw and keep back their obedience, what is this but rebellion?   (p. 437)

The subject has no right, he says, to withhold taxes, or resist conscription or confiscation of goods, however tyrannical his king may be. Nevertheless:

> It is no sufficient reason for a subject to say universally, this I may do, this I must do, for my King commands me. . .In all these there must be a reference still to God, I must compare the laws of the King with the laws of God.   (p. 448)

The Sabbath and preaching are considered matters of principle; and there is a sharp attack on the policy embodied in the Book of Sports (1618) and Sabbath-breaking at court:

> They which make this day [the Sabbath] the day of their great feasts, of their revelling, fiddling, dancing, gaming, masking, rob God of his right, and for ought I know, thieves and robbers by the highway side may look to go to heaven as soon as he.
>   (p. 456)

It is significant to find Hieron fortified in his independence because 'in the doctrine of predestination, against all that flesh and blood doth oppose, Paul cites the authority of Scripture, by which to prove the authority of God to deal with his own creatures as he pleaseth'. In this light one realises how potentially subversive was the demand of men like Hieron for preaching ministers, against the peaceable and conforming 'dumb-dog' type who leaves his neighbours in peace:

> Alas (say they), poor man, he doth his best, and would you have more, he reads fair, and is of quiet behaviour, and careful to keep the goodwill of his neighbours, and to fit his public services to their contentment. Thus will they plead in behalf of such an one, that will yet cry loud against the painful teacher.[45]

Thomas Scot, B.D., Minister at St Clement's Ipswich, describes himself as Pembroke's personal chaplain, in dedicating an assize

---

[45] *A Bargain of Salt* (London, 1619), p. 474.

sermon, *Vox Dei*, to the Earl in 1623.[46] Judging by this sermon, much of which is devoted to attacking favourites and flatterers, and a later sermon of 1631, Scot too was strongly Sabbatarian and moderately Puritan in his outlook, which is not unlike Hieron's:

> So that the naming God's law before the King's is not bare compliment, and for manners sake only; but for the natural precedency thereof...Hence it is also that all good Kings and magistrates in scripture began their reign and government with doing something for God and religion, as is evident in Moses, Joshua, David, Solomon and the rest: and of famous memory was that of blessed Queen Elizabeth, who first bound up that tender babe the Church of England in the swathing band of reformation, before she provided anything for the establishment of her own throne.[47]

It is likely, though not certain, that this was the same Thomas Scot, B.D., one of the King's chaplains, who was in trouble about a sermon he preached before the King, published (with a dedication to Queen Anne) in 1616.[48] This sermon, on the text *Beware of Men*, as well as Catholics, particularly attacks flatterers and favourites

> that have your persons in admiration for lucre's sake...When they will they can both wink and weep with their eyes, as though they loved you and were your friends, but yet for all that, if you take not good heed, they will like serpents sting you without hissing.   (p. 23)

This is around the time of Somerset's fall, and the parallel is all too obvious:

> If the angels by plain force had not drawn Lot out of Sodom, he had perished in the sins of Sodom, as well as others that remained in it...You are no better than Lot was, nor wiser, than Lot was, nor loather to offend God, than Lot was. Presume not too much of your own strength, but remember you are man, and beware of your weakness.[49]

[46] *Vox Dei*, 'Injustice cast and condemned'. In a sermon preached 20 March 1622 (published 1623; *S.T.C.* 21873.5).

[47] *God and the King*, Assize sermon preached 1631 (published Cambridge, 1633; *S.T.C.* 21873), p. 9.

[48] This Thomas Scot of Ipswich cannot be the same as the author of *Vox Populi*, since he was still preaching five years after the satirist's murder. He may, however, have been a relative. Apparently Queen Anne as well as the preacher was in trouble about the sermon.

[49] *Christ's Politician and Solomon's Puritan*, 'Delivered in two sermons preached before the King's Majesty', 1616, pp. 23, 32. Queen Anne had

Another of Pembroke's chaplains was Robert Bruen, youngest brother of the well-known Cheshire squire John Bruen, a Puritan layman and patron of the Puritan preacher William Hinde, who commemorated him in a pious biography. It is noteworthy that Hinde held his living at Bunbury in Cheshire by the appointment of the Haberdashers' Company, under the Aldersey bequest in 1601; Bunbury was famous as an ideal Puritan parish of the sort the Feoffees for Impropriations through their operations hoped to multiply. Through Bruen there is thus a kind of link between the Pembroke circle and the groups of Puritan City merchants, especially the Haberdashers, who are known to have patronised Middleton.[50]

Lancashire merchants living in London are highly praised for setting up a fund to buy up impropriations in their native county, and contributing enough to maintain five or six preachers there, in a St Paul's Church sermon of 1628, dedicated to Pembroke by William Walker, B.D. This seems to be a direct eulogy of the activities of the Feoffees for Impropriations, at a time when the fear that this group of rich businessmen were increasing Puritan influence in the Church was already arousing concern and hostility from Laud and his supporters (who eventually suppressed them). The author expresses his confidence that Pembroke will give 'perfection and approbation' to this enterprise.[51] This again is a strongly anti-Catholic, anti-pluralist sermon.

Pembroke was also a patron of Cornelius Burges, who was appointed Chaplain-in-Ordinary to Charles I soon after his succession. In 1625 Burges published a tract, *The Fire of the Sanctuary newly uncovered, or a Complete Tract of Zeal*,[52] which he dedicated to Pembroke with gratitude for 'the honours you have done, and still do me', and a plea for 'protection to preserve this fire from Quench-coale'. Burges was later ejected for anti-Arminianism, and became one of the most prominent Presbyterian Parliamentarian

been associated, with Pembroke, in sponsoring young George Villiers as favourite, against Somerset.
[50] William Hammond, recipient of Middleton's dedication in the autograph copy of *A Game at Chess*, and his brother Edmond were both Haberdashers.
[51] On a less exalted level, Walker includes a joke against lay impropriators which might appeal to anti-Buckingham sentiment. 'As the clown said to the Bishop of Cullen praying in the Church like a Bishop, but as he was Duke going guarded like a tyrant, whither thinkest thou the Bishop shall go when the Duke shall be damned?' (p. 18; *S.T.C.* 24965).
[52] *S.T.C.* 4111.

divines in London in 1641–2, being then described as a leader of the City apprentices.

The *Tract of Zeal* is a discussion, largely political, and Calvinist in theology, of the duties and limitations of the zealously religious in rebuking sin.

> If any obstinate sinner should long to have these precepts of reproving and rebuking pulled out of the Bible as puritanical. . . for my part, let them; so he repeal the statutes that did first enact them. But until then, we that are God's ministers are bound to execute all laws within God's statute-book.   (p. 408)

More cautious than Hieron, Burges advises a minister threatened by authority not to resist but to fly; though when the servants of God are reproached and oppressed, 'such as by their place and greatness are able to give countenance to good men in good causes, should then hold it an honourable duty to show themselves' (p. 48). He is against 'democratic' running of the Church, or separation of Church and state authority, and denounces the 'Brownists, Anabaptists, Familists, and all the rabble of such schismatical sectaries (who may truly be termed Puritans)', whom he also calls 'mad Martin mar-prelates'.

On the other hand, the greater part of the tract discusses the duties of court preachers, who must not be discreetly silent like Ahab's chaplains, but must, if their calling requires it (i.e. if appointed by the authorities to preach to the King) tactfully show the King his faults without 'seditious rantings'. 'Must Ministers be meale-mouthed? No neither. . .If Princes grow sick of sin, they must abide a vomit.' But the rebuke must, if possible, be phrased so that only the royal sinner himself understands its application to him.

Pembroke's personal chaplain, Thomas Chaffinge, appears to have been at one stage a Puritan in the political as well as the doctrinal sense, as is evident from the remarkable funeral sermon he preached for his master in 1630, in which he warns of the coming danger of civil war between country and city, and of Spanish aggression and invasion, and rejoices that Pembroke's 'eyes shall not see, nor his ears hear that which shall wound his soul any more'.[53] His phrasing is strongly reminiscent of Preston's political sermons.

---

[53] *The Just Man's Memorial. Sermon preached at Baynard's Castle, 1630* (*S.T.C.* 4931). It appears that Chaffinge was embittered at his dismissal by

Another personal friend was Thomas Adams, 'the prose Shake-speare of the English pulpit' (as Southey called him), who was later in disfavour with Laud for too-outspoken preaching against Catholicism. He dedicated several books to Pembroke from 1615 onwards, including the folio of his collected sermons in 1629.

Pembroke's Puritan preachers and the stage

All these men were what we may call broadly Parliamentary Puritan sympathisers – in the sense that they were strongly anti-Catholic and anti-Spanish, opposed to what they saw as excessive ceremonial, strongly insistent on replacing 'dumb dogs' by godly preaching ministers, and critical within limits of aristocratic luxury and idle-ness. In doctrine they were anti-Arminian, insisting that grace came directly and irreversibly from God and not through the sacrament and the mediation of the priesthood.[54] Their style was the plain style of the popular preachers from Latimer onwards, rather than the flowing elaborate periods of John Donne or Lancelot Andrewes. But they were not separatists nor the 'Puritanical' kill-joys of later legend, nor do they seem to have been on principle hostile to the stage. They frequently draw metaphors from the theatre in their sermons, and some even suggest that the stage may be a useful means of influencing men's minds; and although they condemn those who waste their time at plays to the neglect of labour or study, it seems to be implied that this is a criticism of Sunday play-going or excessive playgoing, not of all plays as such. They speak of the theatre as part of their lives, and they expect it to be part of the life of their congregations. John Field had frankly rebuked his patron the Earl of Leicester for sponsoring players. I have, however, been unable to find that Preston, Adams, Bruen or Burges offered similar advice in the tracts and sermons they dedicated to Pembroke – perhaps because of the greatly increased status of the drama by their time. Thus John Preston in a sermon uses the stage as a metaphor for man's existence:

the 4th Earl, to whom he addresses some bold and cutting advice on how to carry on his brother's political work, without trusting in princes. He was at one time a preacher at the Temple, and seems to have modified his views by the 1640s.

[54] See Christopher Hill, *Puritanism and Revolution*, p. 243; Russell, *The Crisis of Parliaments*, pp. 210–18.

So doth the Lord, for this time the Battle is not to the strong, that is, men have not their reward here for the present time. Even as it is upon a Stage, both are let alone till they have acted their part, there is no alteration, but when they come off from the Stage, that is the time when the one is commended, and the other is discommended. So it is with the sons of God, and the sons of Man. God lets you both alone for the time, till you be gone off the Stage, that is the time you must look for the difference; there-fore. . .be not discouraged, because you have not much outward contentments, because you are not above, but below, for the present life, the time is not yet come.[55]

Thomas Adams, in a sermon dedicated to Pembroke, has a similar metaphor:

The earth is thy mother, that brought thee forth when thou wert not; a stage that carries thee while thou art; a tombe that receives thee when thou art not.[56]

In the same work (p. 95) he quotes the story of the virgin's choice of caskets, as used in *The Merchant of Venice*, as a metaphor for the soul's choice of good and evil; he also refers to the story of the Jew's pound of flesh, and may well have known the play. Another reference from the same work cites the drama:

Purpose without performance is like a cloud without rain, not unlike Hercules' Club in the tragedy, of a great bulk, but the stuffing is moss and rubbish.

In another sermon, addressed especially to 'gallants', Adams complains:

Are not the benches in taverns and theatres often well replenished, when these seats [in the church] are thin and almost empty? (p. 5)

But although he denounces young heirs who spend their time between the tavern, the brothel and the theatre, and 'cannot sit on their fathers' seats to do good in the Commonwealth' (p. 16), he goes on in the same sermon to use the stage metaphor again quite seriously:

I can show you many actors presenting themselves on the stage of this world; I see not Repentance play her part.

The preacher sees all the deadly sins on the stage of the world, but

---

[55] *The New Creature* (London, 1633; *S.T.C.* 20262), p. 42. I owe this refer-ence to Christopher Hill.

[56] *A Divine Herball* (1616), p. 7; in Adams, *Works* (1630; *S.T.C.* 105), p. 1018.

Among all those I see not Repentancy: Doth she stay till the last
Act? I fear the tragedy of many souls will be done first. (p. 22)

Adams argues that a young nobleman need not be criticised for
dressing richly or enjoying the usual pleasures ('Oh how comely
are good clothes to a good soul, when the grace within shall
beautify the attire without'); it is only 'profane roisterers' who are
denounced. So too in denouncing drunkenness, and wicked tavern-
keepers who encourage it,

I do not speak to annihilate the profession: they may be honest
men, and doubtless some are, which live in this rank; but if many
of them should not chop away a good conscience for money,
drunkenness should never be so welcome at their doors. (p. 54)

Thus to rebuke drunkenness was not to demand that all taverns
be closed; and by analogy it would seem that to criticise excessive
or Sabbath playgoing was not necessarily to argue against all plays.

Cornelius Burges, in his tract dedicated to Pembroke in 1625,
again compares the Church with the theatre:

Therefore from the beginning it pleased the Ministers that men's
sins should be laid open as upon a stage, the whole multitude of
the Church being witnesses of it.[57]

It was possible, then, to be what we should now think of as a
Puritan divine without sharing Prynne's attitude of root-and-branch
condemnation of the theatre, and even (like Thomas Scot the
satirist) to see its possibilities as a propaganda weapon, though
limited by the royal (and Royalist) censorship and control. Pembroke
was the most important of Puritan theatre patrons, but certainly
not the only one. (The Earls of Warwick and Essex are other
examples.)

In spite of Chaffinge's gloomy forebodings, the family tradition
of patronage was carried on by the 3rd Earl's brother, Philip
4th Earl of Pembroke and Montgomery, who succeeded on his
death in 1630. As well as a number of playwrights (Massinger,
D'Urfé, Habington), the editor of John Preston's posthumous sermons *The Saint's Qualification* (1633) dedicated them to Pembroke,
as did George Wither with a further book of poems (*Emblems
Ancient and Modern*, 1634–5). John Reynolds, who had been
imprisoned in 1624 for two years for his anti-Gondomar satires
Vox Coeli and *Votivae Angliae*, dedicated the later part of *Triumphs
of God's Revenges Against the Crying Sin of Murther* to the 4th Earl

57 *The Fire of the Sanctuary*, p. 456.

of Pembroke in 1634–5;[58] and the Puritan lecturer Shaw was protected against Bishop Neile by the fact that he was known to be
Pembroke's personal chaplain.[59]

The adherence of the 4th Earl to the Parliamentarian side in the
Civil War thus had behind it a long history in terms of economic
and religious alignment, rivalry for court office, and opposition to
the foreign policy of the Crown. A link between the attitudes taken
by the 3rd and 4th Earls is Michael Oldisworth, who was secretary
to both, an opposition MP and a close friend and associate of Sir
John Eliot. He married Susan Poyntz, a royal ward and great-niece
of Ferdinando Poyntz, with whom Sir Thomas Myddleton the elder
had been apprenticed and had business and friendly connections.

A note on sources used

Apart from the *D.N.B.* and sources cited in the notes, for information about Sir Thomas Myddleton and Sir Hugh Myddleton I
have consulted A. H. Dodd's article, 'Mr Myddleton the Merchant
of Tower Street', in S. Bindoff, J. Hurstfield and C. H. Williams
(eds.), *Elizabethan Government and Society* (London, 1961);
A. H. Dodd, *Studies in Stuart Wales* (Cardiff, 1952); *Chirk Castle
Accounts*, ed. W. Myddleton (St Albans, 1908); Samuel Smiles,
Lives of the Engineers (London, 1904). For information on Sir
Martin Lumley and Sir Thomas Myddleton the younger see
M. Keeler, *The Long Parliament* (Philadelphia, 1954).

On the St Antholin's lectures and the Puritan connections of the
City government in the 1620s, see D. A. Williams, 'Puritanism in
the City Government, 1610–1640', in *Guildhall Miscellany* (London),
i, no. 4 (Feb. 1955); and D. Williams Whitney, 'London Puritanism:
the Haberdashers' Company', *Church History*, xxxii, no. 3 (Sept.
1963).

[58] He had dedicated the third book of this work to the 3rd Earl in 1623.
John Reynolds seems always to have regarded Pembroke and Montgomery
as a likely patron, the MS. of his first (unpublished) poem containing a dedication to him probably about 1605. He was a merchant, who left Oxford
without a degree, but was tutor to Basil Fielding (son of the Earl of
Denbigh), who unlike his father became a Parliamentarian in the Civil War.
(See articles by J. H. Bryant, 'John Reynolds of Exeter and his Canon', in
Library, 3rd ser., xv (1960), pp. 105–17; xviii (1963), pp. 299–303. I am
indebted to Simon Adams for this reference.) The first book of *God's
Revenges* (1620–1) is the main source for *The Changeling*.
[59] Christopher Hill, *Society and Puritanism*, p. 108.

On Puritan influences in various City churches, see also Paul S. Seaver, *The Puritan Lectureships* (Stanford, 1970); and *The Vestry Minute Book of St Bartholomew by the Exchange, 1567–1676*, ed. E. Freshfield (London, 1890).

For bequests I have consulted the wills of Sir Thomas Myddleton, John Browne, Richard Fishbourne and Edmond Hammond in the Public Records Office, as well as information on those of Lady Anne Myddleton and Sir Martin Lumley in W. K. Jordan, *The Charities of London* (London, 1960).

For other information on City magnates I have used A. B. Beaven, *The Aldermen of the City of London* (London, 1913); Baron Heath, *Some Account of the Worshipful Company of Grocers* (London, 1869); R. G. Lang, 'London's Aldermen in Business 1600–1625', *Guildhall Miscellany*, xvii (Apr. 1971); J. Aubrey Rees, *The Worshipful Company of Grocers* (London, 1978); A. L. Johnson, *History of the Worshipful Company of Drapers of London* (Oxford, 1922); Menna Prestwich, *Cranfield: Profits and Politics Under the Early Stuarts* (Oxford, 1966); and Valerie Pearl, *London and the Outbreak of the Puritan Revolution* (Oxford, 1961).

A Note on Authorship

The canon of Middleton's plays has been the subject of a great deal of research and argument in recent years by some of the most eminent scholars in the field. The purpose of this note is not to contribute additional evidence, but to explain why, on the basis of the material research has made available, I have included or excluded particular plays in my treatment.

Some scholars have attributed *The Puritan* to Middleton, but it still seems to me unlikely to be substantially his.[1] The latest and most detailed argument for assigning it to him is put forward by David Lake in *The Canon of Middleton's Plays*.[2] But despite the great industry with which statistical material has been counted and analysed by computer, the result seems less than wholly convincing.

1. The title-page of the original Quarto, published by George Eld in 1607, describes *The Puritan* as 'Acted by the Children of Paul's. Written by W.S.' No evidence is produced by Dr Lake as to why this should be so if the play is really by Middleton. He admits this himself:

> Eld's attribution to 'W.S.' must remain a mystery; it does not seem likely that it was an attempt at fraud, in view of the other honest and correct attributions of Eld publications about this time. Possibly there was a 'WS' involved, who was 'revised out'. (p. 117n.)

As S. Schoenbaum has warned us, 'External evidence cannot be ignored, no matter how inconvenient such evidence may be for the theories of the investigator.'[3]

2. As Lake himself notes, the play as a whole is much cruder than other work of Middleton's at this time:

> The date of composition, 1606, implies that *The Puritan* is contemporary with *Trick* and *Mad World*...This synchronism

---

[1] The entry in the *Stationer's Register* (1653) of *The Puritan Maid, the Modest Wife and the Wanton Widow* must refer to a lost play: the title does not fit this one at all.

[2] Cambridge, 1975. Subsequent references to this work are given as page numbers.

[3] S. Schoenbaum, *Internal Evidence and Elizabethan Dramatic Authorship* (London, 1966), p. 162.

has deterred some critics, notably Barker, from accepting Middleton's authorship of what is admittedly a rather crude play. However, the argument from relative literary values is, as usual, a weak one. Since *The Puritan* was concocted to serve up 'merry jests' – i.e. broad farce – some crudity might perhaps be expected.
(p. 111)

Lake's own argument here seems to be that the play was crude because it was crude. It is indeed crude, not only compared with the contemporary *Trick* but with work accepted as earlier, *Phoenix* or *Michaelmas Term*: crude not only in feeling but in dramatic construction.

3. Lake allows that 'authorial attitudes' on religious, moral or political matters have sometimes been used as evidence of authorship, and that in some cases the argument may be plausible. 'For example, a clearly anti-Catholic play can hardly be attributed to a known Catholic.' On the other hand, arguments from Middleton's supposed morality or immorality are, as he says, matters of critical conjecture.
(p. 7–8)

If this play were Middleton's, however, it would be the only case in which he used the word 'Puritan' in the sense of the reforming party within the established Church, as distinct from separatists and sectaries; and he does not satirise such people elsewhere.[4] Moreover, it seems unlikely that if he were the author of this particularly notorious satire on moderate city Puritans ('Nicholas St Antlings' being an obvious hit at the congregation of St Antholin's), he would so soon have been employed by the Puritan Sir Thomas Myddleton (later patron of the St Antholin's lectures) to write the Lord Mayor's show in 1613, would have become a favoured employee of the City, or would have been described later by William Hemminge as the Puritans' favourite dramatist, while Jonson was regarded as their greatest enemy. The dramatist's attitude to Puritanism (indicated by the sense in which this 're-proachful name' is used), like the attitude to Catholicism, seems a mark of differentiation between writers as valid as many used by Lake.

4. The evidence from oaths, exclamations, placing of apostrophes, spellings and the like, impossible to examine in detail here, is often

---

[4] The reference to 'a tongue as loud as St Antling's bell' in *Roaring Girl* (1890 edn, p. 31) shows the phrase to be in common use, but does not constitute an exception.

tenuous, and in total far less convincing and decisive than the categorical conclusions drawn from it would suggest, both generally and for this particular play. ('We certainly can be confident that Middleton is the author of *The Puritan*' (p. 32).) A number of scholars have already pointed this out.[5] Leave aside examples of circular reasoning, numbers in many cases too small for statistical treatment, and omissions of evidence (for example, the operation of the censorship on oaths in the drama is incompletely and inconsistently taken into account). Even if one accepts all the 'markers' and 'pointers' at face value (which I do not think we ought to do), still in view of the 'W.S.' attribution, the crudity and the implied definition of 'Puritan', the facts would seem to suggest Middleton as reviser or copyist rather than author. He was working intensively for the Paul's Boys' Company at the time, and, as we know from the *Game at Chess* autograph copy, he wrote a good clear hand. He may well have been employed to prepare and revise playhouse copy for the press, especially during his earlier years in the theatre. The fact that many small 'Middletonisms' are *not* found in the printed text of *A Chaste Maid in Cheapside* (1630) is explained by Lake as an indication that the text was based on a scribal copy and the scribe must have 'revised them out'. It seems equally plausible that Middleton as scribe may have revised them in here.

Lake argues on the basis of similar tests that *The Family of Love* is not an unmodified play by Middleton. Here there is no title-page attribution to any author in the original printed text (1608). The play was first assigned to Middleton in Edward Archer's catalogue in 1656 (p. 29). By his usual statistical tests Lake diagnoses a collaboration between Middleton and Dekker, with extensive revisions by Lording Barry (who is not otherwise known as a Middleton collaborator). Again the evidence is somewhat tenuous, especially for Barry.

Unlike *The Puritan*, *The Family of Love* does not seem either too crude in workmanship for Middleton at this period or inconsistent with his attitudes. If there was collaboration, his exact share in it must remain uncertain; but there seems no reason to reject Archer's attribution altogether.

[5] See for example reviews by David Young in *Studies in English Literature*, xvi, no. 2 (Spring 1976), 343, and Catherine Belsey in *T.H.E.S.*, 10 Oct. 1975.

The Revenger's Tragedy, a more doubtful and complicated case, may also be briefly mentioned. The authorship, ascribed to Cyril Tourneur in Archer's catalogue of 1656, has been hotly disputed. For the last fifty years the main alternative proposed has been Middleton. It is impossible and unnecessary to summarise the whole controversy here: a note on the current position will have to suffice.

R. A. Foakes, after editing the play for the Revels series (1966), felt the evidence for Middleton was strong but not conclusive. 'In the end there remains conviction that *Revenger's Tragedy* differs from Middleton's known work in too many ways', and external evidence also tells against Middleton. 'All one can do is record the fact of uncertainty, but leaving the balance slightly tilted in Tourneur's favour – lacking a better candidate.' S. Schoenbaum, earlier a strong supporter of Middleton's authorship, by 1966 had come to think he had undervalued the counter-arguments based on external evidence: he would agree with Foakes, except for thinking the balance level rather than favouring Tourneur.[6]

Lake considers he has now settled the issue in favour of Middleton, largely on the basis of the spelling; but a close look at the tables makes this less convincing, and external and dramaturgic evidence the other way is largely ignored or dismissed. Part of the argument rests on single verbal parallels, but these do not amount to much when one considers Jacobean habits of plagiarism and legitimate borrowing: in many cases two or more dramatists may well have been using similar idiomatic phrases or sayings because they were in current use.[7] Many scholars have felt that *The Revenger's Tragedy* is very unlike the only undisputed work of Tourneur's we have (*The Atheist's Tragedy*), but that does not prove it to be Middleton's. 'The fact of uncertainty' still stands.

My own feeling that the play cannot confidently be taken as Middleton's is based on both dramatic and poetic style, as well as the external evidence; and these are not only general impressions.

---

[6] *Internal Evidence and Elizabethan Dramatic Authorship*, p. 257.
[7] For example, one of Lake's 'Middletonisms' is the joke about sons rejoicing at the death of fathers. This is used as an item of evidence that Middleton wrote *The Puritan*. By the same token, it might be construed as evidence that he also wrote *Hamlet* (see III.ii.129–33) and *King Lear* (I.ii.48–77), not to mention *Henry IV Part 2* (II.ii.1–39). The phrase 'son and heir', regarded in Lake's study as a 'Middletonism', is common in Shakespeare and is standard legal and conversational usage at the time.

For example, it would be too simple to think, like some earlier commentators, that one can deduce the writer's own background directly from the images he uses.[8] But the *kinds* of images may be at least as characteristic as the placing of apostrophes, and less liable to alteration in transmission. The author of *The Revenger's Tragedy*, for example, seems often to think in *coloured* images; some of the most famous and telling passages of the play are of this nature:

> Doth the silkworm expend her yellow labours
> For thee? (III.v.71)
> Fair meadows cut into green foreparts. (II.i.217)
> Strike thou my forehead into dauntless marble,
> Mine eyes to steady sapphires. (I.iii.8)
> Here's envy with a poor thin cover o'er't,
> Like scarlet laid in lawns. (II.iii.108)
> And ladies' cheeks were painted red with wine,
> Their tongues as short and nimble as their heels. (I.ii.180)
> Green-coloured maids would have turned red with shame.
> (IV.iv.66)

This kind of image is scarcely found at all in Middleton: his imagery is often visual, but black and white, gold and silver are the limits of colour in his tragedies. This is surely a very basic habit of the poetic imagination. I would certainly not suggest this *proves* that *The Revenger's Tragedy* is not by Middleton: there are other aspects of the imagery (especially in reference to tenants, landlords, rack-renting) which do resemble much in *Father Hubbard's Tales*, for instance. It merely reminds us that what comes out of the computer statistically depends on what evidence the researcher decides to feed into it, and this is something rather obvious which has not been fed in.

None of this is or can be conclusive – as Lake reminds us, Shakespeare wrote *Titus Andronicus* as well as *King Lear*. Given the carelessness of Jacobean playwrights about literary property, the transmission of texts through copying and recopying of torn prompt-books, the hasty collaborations and adaptations, certainty is unlikely to be reached. To quote Schoenbaum again:

> So far as the small particulars of style – individual words, phrases,
> lines – are concerned, the electronic computer may be expected

---

[8] Lake quotes (p. 9) attempts to do this for *Revenger's Tragedy* by Una Ellis-Fermor and Marco Mincoff.

to play an essential part, although we must discount some of the more fantastic claims made in their behalf. These devices, after all, are not mechanical brains with magical potencies but serviceable tools of human intelligence.[9]

[9] *Internal Evidence and Elizabethan Dramatic Authorship*, p. 198.

Index of names and plays